The John D. and Catherine T. MacArthur Foundation
Series on Mental Health and Development
Research Network on Transitions to Adulthood

On Your Own Without a Net

The Transition to Adulthood
for Vulnerable Populations

Edited by
D. Wayne Osgood, E. Michael Foster,
Constance Flanagan, and Gretchen R. Ruth

THE UNIVERSITY OF CHICAGO PRESS *Chicago and London*

D. Wayne Osgood is a professor of crime, law, justice, and sociology in the Department of Sociology at Pennsylvania State University. **E. Michael Foster** is a professor of maternal and child health in the School of Public Health at the University of North Carolina at Chapel Hill. **Constance Flanagan** is a professor in the Department of Agricultural and Extension Education at Pennsylvania State University. **Gretchen R. Ruth** is a research assistant at Chapin Hall Center for Children, University of Chicago.

The University of Chicago Press, Chicago 60637
The University of Chicago Press, Ltd., London
© 2005 by The University of Chicago
All rights reserved. Published 2005
Printed in the United States of America

14 13 12 11 10 09 08 07 06 05   1 2 3 4 5

ISBN: 0-226-63783-2   (cloth)

Library of Congress Cataloging-in-Publication Data
On your own without a net : the transition to adulthood for vulnerable populations / D. Wayne Osgood . . . [et al.], editors.
p. cm. — (The John D. and Catherine T. Macarthur Foundation Research Network on Transitions to Adulthood)
Includes bibliographical references and index.
ISBN 0-226-63783-2 (cloth : alk. paper)
1. Young adults—United States. 2. Youth with social disabilities—United States. I. Osgood, D. Wayne. II. John D. and Catherine T. Macarthur Foundation series on mental health and development. Research Network on Transitions to Adulthood and Public Policy.
HQ799.7.O5 2005
305.242′086′9′0973—DC22

2005004220

Contents

Foreword

MICHAEL S. WALD

There are currently twenty-four million twelve- to seventeen-year-olds in the United States. By the time they reach age twenty-five, the great majority of these youth will have made at least a minimally successful transition into early adulthood; they will have acquired the skills needed to connect with the labor force on a regular basis, and they will have established positive social support systems.

However, based on past trends, it is likely that at least a million and a half of these youth, from 5 to 7 percent, will reach age twenty-five without having successfully transitioned to independent adulthood. At an age when most young adults are benefiting from full-time work and close interpersonal relationships, these youth will not have connected to the labor force, and many will lack positive social support systems. About 60 percent will be men. Of these, over half will be in prison, while the remaining men will be mired in protracted spells of long-term unemployment. By age twenty-five, nearly all of these young women will have started families. Most of these young mothers, however, will face the daunting challenge of raising their children alone and with little income or with the help of their own impoverished families.

There are compelling reasons to decrease the number of youth who will not make a successful transition. Helping them become productive and emotionally stable would produce enormous social benefit. They now contribute little to the economy. Rather, as a group, they impose significant social costs, including criminal activity and the use of very expensive services. Most of the women face the challenge of raising children on their own; many have difficulty providing adequate care. Their children experience numerous problems and are at increased risk of placement in foster care.

The moral case for not abandoning these youth is equally compelling. Most were afforded little opportunity to succeed. The great majority grew up in very poor households. Many were abused or neglected by their families. They are the victims of failed schools, failed child welfare systems, and failed neighborhoods. Their poor outcomes are exactly what is predicted when children grow up under these circumstances. Moreover, while around 5 percent of the overall youth population does not make a minimally adequate transition, the proportion more than doubles for minority males, especially African-American males. Our society is unlikely to ever achieve racial equality if it abandons this group.

Over the past thirty years, there has been relatively little attention paid to this group by policy makers and researchers. The focus of both research and public policy has been primarily on younger children. Yet more than one in five adolescents will drop out of school, be incarcerated in the juvenile justice system, experience foster or residential placement, or become an unmarried parent. Many will experience several of these problems.

This book, a product of the John D. and Catherine T. MacArthur Foundation Research Network on Transitions to Adulthood, focuses on seven groups of youth who face especially great challenges in making a successful transition. Along with its companion volume (*On the Frontier of Adulthood: Theory, Research, and Public Policy*), it provides a comprehensive, in-depth examination of the processes involved in the transition from adolescence to young adulthood and the ways in which social programs and policies support or hinder successful transition. It is an enormously important volume.

The research reported in this volume makes clear that the adolescents within these groups face especially great challenges for making a successful transition. A significant proportion of these youth do not succeed. Unfortunately, all of the authors find that current policies often impede, rather than facilitate, the transition processes for these youth.

It is not surprising that the youth in these groups often fare poorly as young adults. As children and adolescents, they experienced learning problems, behavioral difficulties, and physical and mental illness. Many grew up in highly dysfunctional families. They all were identified as needing special services. However, due to major deficiencies in the quality and quantity of these services, and the depth of the problems facing these adolescents, many of these youth turn eighteen woefully unprepared to enter the labor force or to continue their education.

Their situation often worsens after they reach the legal age of adulthood. As the authors discuss, the process of transition from adolescence to adult independence has become longer and harder for all youth over the past fifty years. The increased importance, even necessity, of postsecondary education in order to earn an adequate income has lengthened the period of dependence. Those who do not go to college enter a highly unstable labor market. Most young adults experience detours on the road to economic independence, including periods of unemployment and periodic interruptions in their education. As a result, in our society, almost all youth require support until they have connected successfully with the labor force, which generally does not occur until their midtwenties.

Unfortunately, the majority of youth identified in this volume have extremely limited support systems, including family support, to help them through the difficult transition to adulthood. In fact, a constant finding of all of the authors is that public support is often cut off once these youth turn eighteen. Many lose access to special education, to health care, especially mental health services, to housing, and to protective services. These young adults are no longer required to attend school, and in some cases they may not be allowed to attend high school. Those who commit crimes have aged into a punitive adult criminal justice system. With the exception of those young adults who have aged out of foster care and are entitled to "independent living" services, there is no system responsible for helping young adults experiencing substantial difficulties. A variety of programs are available to some older youth, ranging from job training to various forms of adult education. However, these programs do not, for the most part, focus on the highest-risk youth. They generally serve youth who seek out training or education. The services they provide are critically important but not sufficient.

The lack of societal support for these most vulnerable youth stands in stark contrast to the extensive support provided to the best situated, most-likely-to-succeed young adults—the 25 to 30 percent of all youth who attend four-year colleges and obtain bachelor's degrees.

The great majority of these youth are embedded in networks—families, friends, and communities—that provide guidance, support, and help, both financial and otherwise, when they face the crises that are an inevitable part of the transition. The majority live in households with higher incomes. Beyond what their parents provide, society invests billions of dollars in these youth and provides them with an extensive support system. At college, they are provided room and board and health and mental health services; they have dorm counselors to guide them. They have the best-paid and most highly qualified teachers. There are career-counseling offices, and employers often come directly to campus to recruit. Youth and their families receive federally subsidized loans or benefit from highly subsidized tuition at public universities. They are among peers who encourage and facilitate their progress. While students attending two-year colleges have fewer support services, they too benefit from a system designed to aid their development and transition. Colleges also convey to their students a sense of being special, a message that is rarely, if ever, conveyed to vulnerable youth, who are ignored at best and demonized at worst.

As each of the authors shows, there is a compelling need to create a similar system of support and opportunity for those youth least likely to make a successful transition by age twenty-five and to attract youth to it. These youth need access to medical care, special educational services, economic support, and, in some cases, housing. These are often unavailable due to eligibility requirements or lack of resources. Moreover, access to needed services may require involvement with multiple agencies. Beyond individual services and programs, many need the continuing attention of a person dedicated to helping them overcome the many barriers they face in making a successful transition. Transition is a process, not an event. As Patience White and Leslie Gallay indicate in chapter 13, most of these youth need long-term sequential planning if they are to reach the goals of self-management and independence. Moreover, the youth must be fully involved in the decision-making process; many have little experience as independent decision makers.

Creating a comprehensive system is challenging. The population is diverse. Different youth face different barriers. There is variation in the nature and level of problems faced by women and men and by different ethnic groups. Young African-American and Native American males are at especially great risk. The fact that many of these youth are concentrated in a few highly disorganized urban neighborhoods, or live in rural areas with few services, exacerbates the problem of helping them.

Moreover, there is little in the way of research that can guide program planners. A continuing theme across the authors of this volume is the absence of longitudinal data. There is a pressing need to better understand the factors that serve as both incentives and barriers to these youth as they make decisions about whether to seek schooling, training, or work.

But this challenge is not insurmountable. It is feasible to fund the services that are needed. In fact, many dollars are already being spent on these youth, but mainly in ways that do not promote their ultimate connection; for example, in corrections and emergency health care. There also are individual programs that have been quite successful in reconnecting these youth.

The critical step is creating public will. Thus, the starting point for any reform is changing the public's awareness and image of the population. The public and policy makers at the local, state, and federal levels must conclude that society has an interest in helping, and an obligation to help, these youth through the transition to successful adulthood.

Each of the chapters in this volume offers important ideas on the steps that need to be taken to develop a comprehensive system. There are some promising developments as discussed in the chapters on foster youth (chapter 2), youth receiving special education services (chapters 8 and 9), and homeless youth (chapter 7). For example, federal law now requires that youth emancipating from foster care continue to receive services. Transition planning also is required for those receiving special education. However, as the authors point out, these systems are still drastically underfunded and the majority of youth are not being served.

The situation is far grimmer with respect to adolescents suffering from severe mental illness (chapters 10 and 11) and those in the justice systems (chapters 3 through 6); there is, of course, a great deal of overlap. There is little public support for helping these youth move towards successful lives. In fact, the justice systems even fail to prevent recidivism among the most troubled youth. It is essential to alter the goals of the juvenile justice system, so that helping these youth make a successful connection to education and/or the labor force becomes central. In addition, current laws dealing with young offenders, those eighteen to twenty-four, should be reconsidered. In the past, many states had young offender systems, recognizing that young adulthood is still a time of development and transition and therefore that efforts should be made at helping offenders succeed. There should be a return to young offender programs. A whole new system also is needed to meet the needs of those suffering from mental illness. As Lyons and Melton state, "Young people with mental health problems . . . move from one fragmented and disorganized patchwork of agencies and funding streams into another" (chapter 11).

Through the creation of the Research Network on Transitions to Adulthood, the MacArthur Foundation has provided a major stimulus for improving our knowledge of the critical period of early adulthood and the challenges various populations face in making a successful transition. This volume provides both a framework and specific information that should help policy development at the local, state, and national levels. Our country is now well on its way to developing a comprehensive system of services for children under age five. Hopefully, this volume, the ongoing activities of the network, and efforts by MacArthur and other foundations will start us on the way to developing a comprehensive system for older youth and young adults as well.

Acknowledgments

This volume was sponsored by the MacArthur Foundation Research Network on Transitions to Adulthood. The idea for this work came from the network as a whole, and the network provided the resources that made it possible. Thanks to that support, we recruited a top-flight group of chapter authors, and the authors and editors were able to meet twice to work together in developing the project. In the first meeting we discussed outlines for the chapters and made general plans for coordinating our coverage. The second meeting was devoted to discussing initial drafts of the chapters, with network members and chapter authors serving as discussants. These opportunities made it possible for all of us to build a coherent volume that we hope will set an agenda for policy and research addressing this critical period of life for youth who are at especially high risk for difficulties.

We owe a great debt of thanks to Frank Furstenburg, the director of the network, who has been steadfast in encouraging us, made sure we had the resources necessary for a first-rate effort, and helped us to hold high standards. We are also grateful to all of the network members for their assistance in planning the volume, for insights about the directions it should take, and for constructive critiques of chapters: Gordon Berlin, Mark Courtney, Sheldon Danziger, Vonnie McLoyd, Jean Rhodes, Ceci Rouse, Rubén Rumbaut, Rick Settersten, and Mary Waters. With her usual quiet efficiency and good cheer, network administrator Patricia Miller greatly eased our workload by handling complex meeting arrangements, organizing and sending mounds of material, processing the bills, and taking care of an endless list of other small matters. We also appreciate the support of our representatives from the MacArthur Foundation, Idy Gittelson and Connie Yowell.

We are also grateful to the William and Flora Hewlett Foundation for a grant to support the dissemination of this volume. Michael Wald, who was then with the foundation, took a special interest in our efforts as part of his concern with disconnected youth during the late teens and early twenties. This funding will increase the chances that these issues will come to the attention of people who can make a difference for future policy concerning these youth and that our efforts will contribute to a legacy of concern for struggles and needs of vulnerable youth as they try to make their ways into the world of adulthood.

We thank the authors of the volume's chapters for their fine efforts. All wholeheartedly responded to the call to join us in bringing systematic attention to the issues facing these special groups of young adults, and they maintained good humor as we imposed upon them several rounds of revisions.

Lee Carpenter gave us editorial assistance at a critical stage of our work, and Kim Zimmerman provided valuable secretarial support.

We thank our partners and families for their steadfast support of all of our efforts and for putting up with the long hours that this project required.

Finally, we dedicate this volume to the youth whose struggles and triumphs it describes. We hope that this volume calls attention to their needs and strengths and that it inspires policy makers to design policies that meet the former and build on the latter. We hope that a follow-up volume in a decade will be more substantial in terms of what we know about these youth and more hopeful in terms of how they are faring.

CHAPTER ONE

Introduction: Why Focus on the Transition to Adulthood for Vulnerable Populations?

D. WAYNE OSGOOD, E. MICHAEL FOSTER,
CONSTANCE FLANAGAN, AND GRETCHEN R. RUTH

The period from the end of high school through the twenties is enormously eventful and consequential. As individuals move from childhood to adulthood, they complete their educations, begin full-time employment, change residences, enter (and often exit) marriages and cohabitations, and become parents. In fact, all of these demographic changes are concentrated in this period far more than during any other time of life (Rindfuss 1991). As Arnett (2000) summarized, 95 percent of twelve- through seventeen-year-olds live with one or more parent, 98 percent are unmarried, less than 10 percent are parents themselves, and over 95 percent are students. By age thirty, 75 percent are married, 75 percent are parents, and less than 10 percent are enrolled in school. Young people must accomplish much during these ages, and for many this period is one of extended exploration as they try out alternative paths in all these domains before settling on long-term commitments (Arnett 2000).

What happens during the transition to adulthood also has great impact on young people's futures. For instance, youths who graduate from college during this period not only go on to jobs with higher pay and greater prestige (Chen and Kaplan 2003; Jencks et al. 1979; Kerckhoff, Raudenbush, and Glennie 2001), but they also participate more in political and civic affairs (Kingston et al. 2003; Milligan, Moretti, and Oreopoulos 2004). In contrast, those who experience problematic events during this age span, such as unsuccessful marriages, becoming a parent before marrying, or having difficulties with drugs or crime, in later years will have a more difficult time finding financial security, satisfying family relationships, and so forth (Cherlin 1992; McLanahan and Booth 1989; Newcomb and Bentler 1988).

The Research Network on Transitions to Adulthood sponsored and organized the present volume. This network, which is funded by the John D. and Catherine T. MacArthur Foundation and directed by Frank Furstenberg, was formed in recognition of the need for greater attention to this period of life by both researchers and policy makers. This is the second volume produced by the network, and it is a logical extension of the first, *On the Frontier of Adulthood: Theory, Research, and Public Policy* (Settersten, Furstenberg, and Rumbaut 2005). *On the Frontier of Adulthood* presents research by a large and varied group of scholars who address fundamental questions about the transition to adulthood using major national and international data sets. Their work documents many ways that this period of life has changed over the past century and notes how these changes present challenges to most youth and their families.

The research in *On the Frontier of Adulthood* concerns the broad, general population of youth in the United States (and some other industrialized countries as well). As the editors note (Furstenberg, Rumbaut, and Settersten 2005; Settersten 2005), if the transition to adulthood proves difficult for a large share of this general population, then there is great reason for concern about groups of youth who enter adulthood with special vulnerabilities. The present volume takes up this concern by focusing on several groups of young adults who have especially poor prospects as they make the transition.

The William T. Grant Foundation's well-known report, *The Forgotten Half: Non-College-Bound Youth in America* (William T. Grant Foundation Commission on Work, Family, and Citizenship 1988), highlighted the fact that some youth have far better prospects for successful and satisfying adult lives than others. In particular, the report focused on ways in which the odds are stacked against the large portion of young people who do not attend college. We take this theme one step further and concentrate on smaller populations of youths whose life circumstances present considerably greater challenges. An analogy might be that, if middle-class college-bound youth pass through the transition on relatively well-greased wheels, the transition is prone to be rough sledding for working-class non-college-bound youth, and it can be a minefield for the vulnerable populations.

The purposes of the present volume are (1) to identify the challenges facing those adolescents and young adults for whom the lengthening process of becoming an adult is likely most difficult and (2) to bring attention to policy issues concerning the transition to adulthood for these groups. These vulnerable youth often suffer from emotional and behavioral problems and have a history of problems in the school and the community. In addition, their families may be unable or unwilling to offer them the support that is so helpful to most other youth during this transition (Schoeni and Ross 2005). This support can include financial assistance needed to obtain the lengthy education required for professional occupations, child care when babies come sooner than steady incomes, and a place to stay when marriages fail or jobs are lost. But what about those in their twenties who have no family on which to call, whose pasts are so troubled that they have lost their family's goodwill, or whose families lack the resources to provide support? These questions are especially important for youth whose skills and abilities are so limited that they will always rely heavily on others.

This volume examines the transition to adulthood for seven populations that may be especially vulnerable during this period due to the special challenges that they face. Each of these populations is distinguished by its involvement in particular governmental programs:

- youth in the mental health system
- youth in the foster care system
- youth in the juvenile justice system
- youth reentering the community from the criminal justice system
- youth in special education
- youth with physical disabilities and chronic illness (those in the health care system)
- runaway and homeless youth (who are frequently involved in the juvenile court, foster care, and homeless shelter systems)

We chose these groups because they face exceptional challenges for making successful transitions into the major arenas of adulthood, such as employment, higher education, marriage, and parenthood. The greater challenges may stem from any or all of several sources. Some of the groups are hampered by limited abilities or skills, such as youth with physical disabilities and former special education students with learning disabilities. Others, such as young adults who spent their teen years in foster care and runaway and homeless youth, have been hindered by unreliable or nonexistent familial support. Tasks of the transition to adulthood, such as achieving financial and residential independence, are likely to be daunting for young people with physical disabilities, chronic physical illness, or mental illness. For others, such as the formerly incarcerated, involvement in government systems may have exacerbated their initial problems or have stigmatized them in a way that makes success less likely.

Though the causes and nature of their involvement may differ, all of these youth have depended on public systems in important ways and often for many years. That involvement poses new problems as they enter adulthood. Perhaps the most critical is the loss of support from systems that had provided benefits to them as children. In some instances, involvement in the system is phased out; in others, involvement ends abruptly. Some youth may transition into other, adult-oriented systems, such as vocational rehabilitation. In a few cases (such as youth who receive special education services; see chapters 8 and 9) programs are designed to smooth the transition to adulthood. From a public policy perspective these programs are noteworthy because they are among the few programs in the U.S. designed to improve the transition to adulthood per se.

These transitions generate a set of important and complex public policy issues. A major purpose of this volume is to consider the repercussions from ending this support at a time when other youth continue to receive so much assistance from their families.

THE CHALLENGE OF BECOMING AN ADULT IN THE UNITED STATES TODAY

Two themes from research on the transition to adulthood in the general population form the backdrop to our work on vulnerable populations. Strong support for both of these themes can be found in research presented in *On the Frontier of Adulthood* (Settersten, Furstenberg, and Rumbaut 2005), the earlier volume produced by the Research Network on Transitions to Adulthood, as well as in previous research on this period of life. The first theme is that the process of moving from adolescence to adulthood has become longer, more complex, and less orderly over the last fifty years. For these reasons, the transition to adulthood is now more challenging for all youth. The second theme is that a large share of youth in the general population draws heavily on the resources of their families as they make this transition. In this light it is especially problematic that governmental assistance for the vulnerable populations typically ends at the beginning of the transitional period.

The Lengthening Transition

At the start of the twenty-first century, making the transition to adulthood has become more difficult. Compared to the relatively orderly sequence that marked adult status for many (especially for middle-class whites) in the mid twentieth century (Modell, Furstenberg, and Hershberg 1976; Rindfuss 1991; Winsborough 1978), no modal pattern reflects the experiences of youth today. Rather, what constitutes a successful and complete transition is now less clear, and youth are less secure that decisions and investments made today will be the right choices for tomorrow.

From the early nineteenth century through the mid twentieth century, the transition to adulthood became progressively more standardized and orderly (Shanahan 2000). Improvements in health reduced the chances that the death of a parent would force teenagers into full-time work or care-taking (Uhlenberg 1974), and the advent of such institutions as foster care and welfare also made it less likely that adolescents would be forced into adult roles (Kohli 1986). Furthermore, with rising standards for universal education, the end of high school became the clear norm as the minimum age for home leaving, full-time employment, marriage, and parenthood (Hogan 1981).

By 1950, entry into adulthood had become an orderly and quick sequence of transitions, with completion of education and full-time employment (for males) followed by marriage and then parenthood. In the decade after the Second World War, the rapid expansion of the American economy, the array of benefits to veterans, and the growth of housing permitted or even promoted a rapid passage to adulthood (May 1990; Modell 1989). Favorable economic conditions and optimism about the future among people in their late teens and early twenties resulted in early family formation. By the time they reached their early twenties, close to half of American men were full-time workers, and women, full-time mothers.

The historical era of the "marriage rush" and "baby boom" lasted only a couple of decades. In the final third of the twentieth century, several trends led to increasing complexity and growing duration of the transition to adulthood. During the 1960s, rapid changes took place in both the labor market and in social attitudes about women's work and family roles. For example, by the mid-1970s, a high school education, which earlier in the century was uncommon, no longer sufficed to ensure a well-paying job, and many parents began to have difficulty supporting a family on a single wage (Furstenberg 2000; Sagawa 1998). Despite improving economic conditions in the 1980s and 1990s, the duration of the transitional period continued to increase, due at least in part to attitudinal changes of young people and to increasing educational expectations in the labor market (Fussell and Furstenberg 2005).

The lengthening of the transition to adulthood is especially evident in a growing period between leaving the home of one's parents and forming one's own family (Fussell and Furstenberg 2005). Unlike earlier times, most youth in the United States today move away from home by eighteen or nineteen, with only about 10 percent of men and 30 percent of women remaining there until marriage (Arnett 2000; Goldscheider and Goldscheider 1994). Meanwhile, from just 1970 to 1996, the median age of marriage increased from twenty-one to twenty-five for women and from twenty-three to twenty-seven for men (Arnett 2000).

Accompanying this change, there is no longer a clear standard or modal sequence among the major transitions to adult roles of ending education, marrying, entering the labor force, moving from home, and becoming a parent. Instead, their order varies enormously across individuals who face very different sets of opportunities and groups with different cultural practices (Mollenkopf, Kasinitz, and Waters 2005). In effect, the coupling between marriage, parenthood, and leaving the home of one's parents is now loose (Goldscheider and Goldscheider 1993). As the proportion of the population receiving higher education has grown from 14 percent in 1940 to 60 percent by the mid-1990s (Arnett 2000), youth commonly mix schooling with employment and/or parenthood (Shanahan 2000). Furthermore, women are delaying the birth of their first child, often until they reach their thirties (Rindfuss, Morgan, and Swicegood 1988; Rindfuss, Morgan, and Offutt 1996). Where the youth of the 1950s could follow a simple and short path from adolescence to adulthood, youth today must chart their own, and most of them will take much longer to do so.

Family Support during the Transition to Adulthood

Becoming an adult does not happen all at once, but rather it involves an extended period of semiautonomy during which youth move away from full dependence on their families (Arnett 2000; Goldscheider and Goldscheider 1999). Indeed, for this reason it is important to recognize the transition to adulthood as a special period in life when people face unique challenges. Although they leave behind the restrictions of childhood and adolescence, their financial resources are limited, as are the experiences and connections that would land them jobs with good pay. Thus, only gradually can they take on adult responsibilities. Typically, they remain at least partially dependent on others, especially their parents, for various kinds of assistance. For some, families provide partial support as they remain at home for a period after high school; for others parents pay a large share of college expenses. Furthermore, steps toward independence are often reversed. For instance, during their late teens and twenties, 40 percent of American youth move back to their parents' home at least once after leaving (Goldscheider and Goldscheider 1994).

Families provide assistance to their children during the transition to adulthood in many ways. Parents often continue to provide food and shelter; they may give their children money to assist with bills or major expenses like the down payment for a house; and they may help their children by giving their time for tasks such as child care. Families also may provide social or emotional support and the motivation crucial to achieving success during the transition. Attachment to parents, indicating positive parental support, is associated with higher academic achievement (Cutrona et al. 1994) and higher perceptions of scholastic competence during college (Fass and Tubman 2002). Parents can also be a key source of guidance for their young adult offspring, providing advice about topics such as careers, money management, housing, and health care. At the same time, the character of the parent-child relationship changes significantly during this period and one of the important tasks for young adults and their parents is to develop a more peerlike relationship.

During childhood and adolescence, governmental programs have played a major role in augmenting family resources for meeting the needs of the vulnerable populations, but those program services typically end early in the transition period. How problematic is this termination? It is useful to consider this in light of the amount of assistance that families provide to youth in the general population during the transition to adulthood.

In *On the Frontier of Adulthood*, Schoeni and Ross (2005) estimated the amount of money and time that parents provide to their children from age eighteen through thirty-four. They concluded that the average value of parental support (in 2001 dollars) across this age period was $2,200 annually, and the total across these years represents roughly one-third of the amount provided during the years of childhood. On top of this financial assistance, parents continue to give their children a great deal of their time. The average time assistance was 367 hours per year, which is roughly the hours of work in nine weeks of full-time employment. Schoeni and Ross also concluded that the amount of assistance has increased considerably over the last thirty years due to longer schooling, later age of marriage, and the increase in single parenting.

The amount of assistance that families provide during the transition clearly depends a great deal on the family's resources. For instance, youth receive less assistance if their families have less income, if the parents have less education, or if there are more siblings in the family (Amato and Booth 1997; Jayakody 1998; Steelman and Powell 1991). Schoeni and Ross calculated that the quarter of U.S. households with the highest incomes provide at least 70 percent more assistance to their children from age eighteen through thirty-four than do the quarter with the lowest incomes. Thus, assistance during this age period contributes to a dynamic of diverging pathways (Kerckhoff 1993) in which parents' educational and economic resources contribute to growing advantages for some youth over others. It seems likely that these vulnerable populations, who face a combination of larger challenges and reduced family support, will be at the greatest disadvantage in negotiating the transition to adulthood.

WHY THESE VULNERABLE POPULATIONS
DESERVE OUR ATTENTION

In this section we make the case for special attention to these particular vulnerable populations in terms of the greater challenges they face in making the transition to adulthood and in terms of the ending of their eligibility for governmental programs as they enter this critical age period.

Sources of Greater Challenge during the Transition to Adulthood

These vulnerable populations require our attention because they face great challenges in several areas during the transition to adulthood. First, some populations must accomplish additional tasks that most people in this age period do not face. For instance, runaway and homeless youth begin the transition in need of housing, rather than having the security of their family's home (see chapter 7). Youth with physical disabilities often need to arrange for medical services or devices to assist them with daily tasks (see chapters 12 and 13). Youth involved in the juvenile or adult justice systems often owe restitution in the form of money or labor, and their freedom may depend on following conditions of probation or parole that restrict their activities (see chapters 4 and 6). Such burdens may well reduce the chance of obtaining the additional education that would improve future job prospects or of finding an appealing partner and nurturing that relationship into a satisfying marriage.

Many of the vulnerable populations also confront greater challenges in the form of limitations on their skills, and these limitations may directly preclude their receiving opportunities available to others. For instance, reduced strength and range of movement (for youth with physical disabilities; see chapters 12 and 13) or learning disabilities and cognitive impairments (for youth in special education; see chapters 8 and 9) would rule out some appealing occupations. Indeed, members of many of these vulnerable populations have very limited skills at dealing with ordinary tasks of daily living for the transition to adulthood, such as managing money, obtaining housing, or even (for a substantial proportion of youth in special education) looking up telephone numbers (Foster and Gifford 2005).

Another type of limitation is learning disabilities, which are quite common not only among children and adolescents in special education (chapters 8 and 9), but in several of the other vulnerable populations as well. In the juvenile justice system (chapters 3 and 4), for example, 30 to 50 percent of all confined youth have identified learning disabilities (Foster and Gifford 2005). Other limitations include mental illness (for youth involved in the mental health system; see chapters 10 and 11) or behavioral difficulties (for youth involved in the justice system, chapters 3 through 6, and many runaway and homeless youth, chapter 7, or youth in foster care, chapter 2). Though these limitations would not preclude the physical and intellectual tasks required by a job, they could reduce the probability of successfully coping with requirements such as punctuality, reliability, and maintaining positive relationships with coworkers.

A third source of challenge for many of the vulnerable populations is the lack of family support. As we discussed above, youth in the general population typically receive a great deal of assistance from their families, and this support often appears critical for overcoming difficulties like becoming a single parent or losing a job. Furthermore, the greater financial resources of middle-class families allow them to continue to elevate their children's prospects of success above those of working-class and poor families. In contrast, youths in these vulnerable populations often come from families whose economic resources are limited. In other instances the quality of the relationships in their families is degraded, poor, or entirely absent. For example, children from poor, single-parent families are overrepresented among youth in the juvenile justice system, and delinquent youth are especially likely to have poor relationships with their parents or care givers (chapter 3). Similarly, children from poor, single-parent families are overrepresented in special education; 68 percent of those in special education come from families with incomes of less than $25,000 compared with only 40 percent of students in the general population (chapter 8). We should be especially concerned about those vulnerable populations that have no families to which they can turn, such as youth leaving foster care (chapter 2) and runaway and homeless youth (chapter 7).

We hasten to add that in many cases parents and extended family of vulnerable youth strive to be supportive, and thus it is often not a lack of motivation that hinders their support. As noted, for some families the financial burdens outweigh resources. Yet even committed families with good resources have a difficult task in helping young adults in these vulnerable populations succeed in confronting the challenges detailed in this volume.

The End of Eligibility for Governmental Programs

These specific vulnerable populations are of special interest, in part, because each is already the target of government policies and programs. For these youth, the transition to adulthood means the transition out of programs in which they have been involved, often for many years. In some instances, that involvement is phased out; in others, it ends abruptly.

For instance, children in foster care (chapter 2) are required to leave state care upon reaching a threshold age, which is between eighteen and twenty-one, depending on the state. Such policies reflect simplistic and outdated notions of childhood dependence and adult independence. Although independence may be a goal, it does not occur simply because one turns eighteen. In fact, late adolescence through early adulthood is a time for practicing independence by gradually assuming responsibility, with the guidance and support of adults. Many youth in foster care, like their age-mates who are not in the system, need the kinds of supports and guidance that families would provide. But when youth become too old, the state no longer provides supports for foster families. Thus, youth in this system may transition into other, adult-oriented systems, such as vocational rehabilitation.

Some systems do extend services into early adulthood and even accommodate the kinds of services they offer to the developmental needs of a specific population as it makes the transition to adulthood. For example, the federal law regulating special education (chapters 8 and 9), the Individuals with Disabilities Education Act (IDEA), mandates that public K–12 education systems develop a transition plan for each youth beginning at age fourteen. That plan stipulates that each child's individualized education plan include posttransition goals and a services plan for achieving these goals. These goals extend beyond education per se and include vocational training and life skills more generally.

For other groups, the age of majority signals a radical change in the character of treatment. Perhaps this is most obvious for those young people involved with the justice system (chapters 3 through 6). Without exception, youth are ineligible for the juvenile justice system for any offense committed after reaching the age of majority (eighteen in most states). At that point offenders are legally adults who are no longer dependent. Furthermore, our policies treat them as less malleable, assuming that they are unlikely to benefit from intervention and therefore less worthy of investments by the state. Accordingly, where the juvenile justice system is at least nominally oriented towards rehabilitation, the adult criminal justice system is explicitly punitive in orientation.

A common theme extending across all these groups, however, is that, because the individuals are no longer children, the state assumes less responsibility for them. During the transition to adulthood, the systems designed to address the needs of vulnerable groups during childhood either are no longer available, offer programs of greatly reduced scope, are complicated by new eligibility requirements, or are transformed to different missions. Even when service systems are available (as is the case for youth who were in special education or who have chronic illnesses), professionals are rarely trained to be attentive to the needs, competencies, and desires of young people at the brink of adulthood. Most professional training for service providers is specific to practice with children or with adults. Recently, there has come to be some specialized training for practice with adolescents, but there is virtually none for practice with young adults.

The present volume addresses the question of whether the programs during childhood and adolescence have been sufficient to prepare the vulnerable populations for successful transitions to adulthood. The growing duration and complexity of the transition to adulthood suggests that they are unlikely to be. If the transition to adulthood requires considerable family assistance for youth in the general population, then it is likely to be especially challenging for these vulnerable populations who have required additional assistance at earlier ages. After all, their involvement in governmental programs often has lasted over many years, and it is not obvious that their needs have been fully resolved. For instance, children in foster care remain in state care for nearly three years on average (33 months) (Foster and Gifford 2005). Similarly, many youth in all of the other vulnerable populations have had long involvements with those systems, and in some cases their families have been intimately involved with the system as well.

MORE THAN VULNERABILITY

Though this volume is devoted to groups identified by their vulnerabilities, those vulnerabilities do not tell the whole story. Finding strategies for improving chances for successful transitions to adulthood requires that we also attend to the potential for overcoming the challenges these vulnerabilities present. Accordingly, in this section we discuss the potential for positive developmental change during the transition to adulthood as well as two themes that will play a recurring role in our discussion of these groups and their experiences: resilience and social inclusion. These themes are important because they counter any sense that members of these groups are powerless victims or that the odds facing them are insurmountable.

Change and development during the transition to adulthood. Growth and development do not end when one becomes an adult, and each person's transition to adulthood is likely to be marked both by continuities with the past and by turning points that lead in new directions. Although the transition presents bigger hurdles for the vulnerable populations discussed in this volume, many will end up leading productive adult lives. In focusing on these groups we are not suggesting they are doomed to fail. In fact, with the right set of scaffolds from family, friends, service systems, and professionals who understand development during this phase of life, many will overcome these hurdles. The state has recognized the vulnerabilities of these populations at earlier points in their lives and has provided entitlements and programs to address their needs. It would be naïve to assume that further attention by policy makers would be pointless either because previous assistance has permanently resolved all difficulties or because the challenges are so great that their fate is sealed. Given the malleability of the young adult period and the potential for continued growth and development, extending systems of support during the transition should increase the likelihood that more members of these groups will lead productive adult lives.

The theme of resilience. The concept of resilience is especially valuable as part of a balanced view of the strengths and challenges facing the vulnerable populations in the transition to adulthood. The study of resilience seeks to understand how some individuals succeed in the face of difficult circumstances (Hauser 1999). A focus on resilience calls attention to strengths as well as deficits and to protective factors as well as risk factors. Protective factors can come from many sources, including individual attributes such as skills and personality traits, positive relationships with people who are supportive, and involvement in churches, clubs, and other community groups. Attention to resilience is a critical part of formulating effective social policy: we must understand the sources of successful transitions before we can design policies to enhance people's chances of success. Furthermore, resilience-based policies enable youth to take an active role in achieving success rather than merely "doing for" or "doing to" them. Accordingly, throughout this volume identifying protective factors and sources of resilience will be part and parcel of our consideration of the challenges facing these groups.

The theme of social inclusion. Where an understanding of resilience shapes the portrayal of vulnerable youth, a consideration of social inclusion emphasizes the importance of society's orientation to such groups. The theme of social inclusion rests on the principle that democratic societies are enriched by the full inclusion of their citizens in the ebb and flow of community affairs. Thus, the social inclusion paradigm focuses on eliminating policies and practices that alienate groups from their communities. Core themes of the social inclusion perspective include reciprocity (between states and citizens and between members of a local community); agency and rights of vulnerable groups; their power to negotiate as an interest group; and their sense of affection for and obligation to society. Social inclusion is a lens for viewing the unique ways that current policies and programs exclude particular groups of young adults. In terms of implications for policy, the social inclusion perspective pushes us to ask what policies would level the playing field and enable groups who are otherwise left out to participate fully as adult citizens.

CHAPTERS ON THE CHALLENGE
OF BECOMING AN ADULT

This volume includes chapters considering the challenge of the transition to adulthood for each of these seven vulnerable populations. Their purpose is to summarize what available research reveals about the transition for the members of the group, identifying areas where they are more and less successful, specifying which members of the population fare better and which worse in the transition, and examining the factors that produce those patterns. These chapters identify the issues that will be addressed in the remaining chapters, which concern the policy issues for the transition to adulthood in these same groups.

Here we briefly review some core topics that will be addressed in these chapters. Due to the limitations of available research, however, not every chapter will address each topic. Answering these questions requires long-term follow-up studies of groups that are often difficult to track, and relatively little funding has been available for this task.

Success at Entering Adult Roles

The transition to adulthood is often defined in terms of entering adult roles, such as becoming a parent and obtaining full-time employment, so these role changes will be a major focus of the chapters on challenges. Though this is far from the whole story, these roles loom large on the agenda of what must be accomplished between eighteen and thirty in order to set the stage for a satisfying adulthood.

Family roles. Many of the transitions into adult roles revolve around the family. A key transition in family roles is to leave the home of parents and guardians and establish one's own household. Doing so initially may involve moves to relatively transitory arrangements such as institutional housing (college dormitories or military barracks) and apartments with roommates. In the longer term, Americans generally expect to find more permanent living arrangements, as reflected in home ownership and long-term living partners. A second type of family transition involves stable romantic partnerships, including steady dating, cohabitation, and culminating, for most Americans, in marriage. Stability of and satisfaction with long-term romantic partnerships is another important aspect of adjustment during the transition to adulthood. The third principal role transition to adulthood in the domain of family is becoming a parent. Of course we are interested not only in whether members of the vulnerable populations become parents, but also in how well they fulfill that role.

Education and training. Though the end of schooling is a standard marker of movement toward adulthood, obviously it does not in itself indicate success. Rather, the more education or training youth acquire, the better their prospects in the world of employment as well as in other domains of life. We will be interested in the number of years of schooling, degrees earned (including high school, graduate equivalency, and college degrees), and other types of job preparation, such as occupational or vocational training.

Employment. Employment is a critical adult role, with entry to full-time employment as the usual marker. The nature and quality of employment has many dimensions. These includes hours of employment, earnings, and job stability as well as job satisfaction and occupational prestige.

Managing Adult Life

In addition to these transitions to adult roles, the chapters on the challenges of the transition will consider how the vulnerable populations fare in managing a variety of life tasks that are part of entering adulthood. One such task involves finding affordable *housing,* and thereby avoiding homelessness. This will be most problematic for youth who cannot fall back on their families for shelter. Maintaining one's *health* is another critical task. Most directly, doing so entails avoiding illness and injury. Thus, youth are more likely to enjoy good health if they avoid behaviors such as dangerous driving and high-risk sexual activities. Youth also are at risk, however, if they are not covered by health insurance. Obtaining that insurance can be especially problematic because so many youth in this age period have part-time or short-term employment.

For many youth in the vulnerable populations, the biggest challenges during the transition to adulthood come from avoiding problematic behavior. Getting in *trouble with the law* is a path that produces many life difficulties in the transition to adulthood, as is serious involvement in the use of *illegal drugs or alcohol.* Avoiding such problematic behaviors is an obvious issue for youth previously involved in the juvenile or criminal justice systems (chapters 3 through 6), but the issue is important for youth in many of the other groups as well. Youth leaving special education (chapters 8 and 9), for example, have high rates of arrest during early adulthood. Similarly, it is also important to maintain positive *mental health* during the transition to adulthood.

Race and Ethnicity

Many youth in the populations featured in this volume face additional challenges associated with other aspects of their lives. Of particular concern is the role that *race and ethnicity* play for the vulnerable populations. Youth from racial and ethnic minority groups are overrepresented in all of these groups, and being a racial or ethnic minority group member may add to an individual's disadvantage when making the transition to adulthood. Therefore, the issue of race and ethnicity and how this relates to the transition to adulthood will be addressed throughout the chapters on the challenges of the transition whenever useful research is available.

CHAPTERS ON POLICY FOR THE TRANSITION TO ADULTHOOD FOR VULNERABLE POPULATIONS

The second chapter in the pair addressing each vulnerable population will examine those policies and programs affecting the group. As Settersten (2005) notes in *On the Frontier of Adulthood,* there are many ways that public policies might be changed to enhance the prospects for the transition to adulthood for the general population of youth in the United States. No doubt many of these changes would be at least as beneficial to the vulnerable populations as to other youth. For instance, Settersten recommends that community colleges offer more useful courses of study and provide better student services. Doing so should increase the chances of success for those vulnerable youth who attempt to gain postsecondary education outside of four-year institutions. The policy chapters in the present volume will concentrate on issues that are specific to the vulnerable populations. In doing so, however, they often echo themes relevant to all youth, such as strengthening the institutions that serve this age group and enhancing the personal skills and resources of young people (Settersten 2005).

Each policy chapter will cover several basic themes: it will describe the programs, policies, and services affecting young people leaving each system; it will define and discuss program eligibility; it will outline the way in which services are delivered; and it will review existing evidence regarding the effectiveness of services offered. The goals of each policy chapter are to provide readers with a sense of the magnitude and adequacy of existing programs, to identify gaps in eligibility and service delivery, and to identify gaps in existing research.

Each policy chapter will begin by describing the programs and services available to young people making the transition to adulthood among special populations. This basic review will identify the key programs and the legislation that established and/or supports them. Each chapter will provide basic information on the size of those programs, in terms of both expenditures and number of participants. As the chapters will reveal, local, state, and federal policy makers all shape the various programs and services involved. In the case of special education, for example, transition services are mandated and partially funded by the federal government. Local school districts, however, are responsible for organizing and delivering the appropriate services. (For details, see chapter 9.) A key focus of the discussion, therefore, is on how responsibility for operating and financing each program is spread across the various levels of government. This variation is essential for understanding differences within and between states in program services and other characteristics. This variation is a key feature of these programs and is highlighted in the chapters themselves.

For several of the groups considered, recent years have seen dramatic changes in the programs and services affecting children and youth transitioning out of the service system. For example, as Courtney and Heuring discuss in chapter 2, the Foster Care Independence Act of 1999 dramatically increased funding for the independent living program, which offers services to young people leaving the foster care system. Each chapter will review recent policy changes and will consider the ways they have affected the size and nature of the programs involved.

A second focus of the policy chapters is program eligibility. Each will include a review of how children and youth enter the systems examined. Many children and youth encounter these systems, but not all are eligible for the transition services they provide. Some youth exit the systems before reaching the age at which services are available or are never involved to the degree required to receive transition services. In the case of juvenile justice, for example, many youth are handled informally by juvenile courts; they are returned to their families and/or receive punishments that do not involvement out-of-home placement. (For details, see chapter 4.) Understanding the process by which youth enter and exit (at younger ages) is essential to understanding the needs of young adults aging out these systems.

After reviewing how children and youth enter these systems, the chapters also will describe the program rules and features that affect eligibility for and receipt of transition services themselves. The discussion will highlight the key ages and transitions that end eligibility.

A third focus of each policy chapter involves service delivery. As the chapters will make apparent, the various programs offer an enormous array of services—educational opportunities, vocational training, counseling and support services, training in daily living skills, outreach services, family planning, and parenting classes, among others. A key topic addressed in these chapters is identifying the goals of these programs and the degree to which they match the needs of the youth involved (as identified in the first chapter in the pair). As with eligibility, each chapter also will consider the impact of recent legislation and policy initiatives on services provided.

The fourth focus of each policy chapter involves the effects of services and programs provided to youth transitioning to adulthood. Each chapter will review findings from available evidence and provide a sense of its quality. Each chapter will identify areas where existing research is inadequate for determining whether existing services are appropriate and efficacious. As discussed below, available research suffers from a variety of problems, such as samples that are small and unrepresentative and weak quasi-experimental designs that make it difficult to identify causal relationships between services and outcomes.

OUTLINE OF THE VOLUME

The chapters of this volume document the special challenges facing seven vulnerable populations during the transition to adulthood and articulate policy issues surrounding this transition. Chapters 2 through 13 concern the seven vulnerable populations discussed above. For five of the populations there is a pair of chapters, the first devoted to the challenges of becoming an adult for that group and the second to policy issues. For two of the groups, youth in foster care and homeless youth, these two topics are combined in a single chapter. Again, the purpose of the chapters on the challenges of becoming an adult is to summarize what we know about the transition for each group, to identify areas in the transition that are more and less problematic, and to explain why some members of the population fare worse than others in the transition. The second chapter in each pair examines those policies and programs affecting young people leaving the service systems that assisted them during childhood and adolescence. Each policy chapter provides a description of the programs and policies targeting the population of interest and addresses program eligibility, service delivery, and program effectiveness.

Summary of the Chapters

In chapter 2, Courtney and Heuring describe the challenges facing foster youth as they leave the protection of the child welfare system and examine current policies directed at helping these youth achieve independence. They start with a brief introduction to the child welfare system and describe the basic demographic characteristics of youth who age out of the foster care system. They then review the literature on how these former foster youth fare in young adulthood. Putting these findings in perspective, the authors explore how the background conditions of these youth and the experiences they have while they are in out-of-home care may contribute to the difficulties they face as they make the transition to adulthood. The chapter also provides a historical overview of policies intended to support foster youth in the transition to independent living and points out the limitations of current policies. The chapter concludes with a discussion of current policy issues. These revolve around the opportunities and challenges afforded by the Foster Care Independence Act of 1999 as well as gaps and problems yet unaddressed by policy makers. Some of these gaps, such as the poor integration of services, are addressed in the other chapters in the volume as well.

Chapter 3, by Chung, Little, and Steinberg, concerns the developmental needs of youth in the juvenile justice system and the ways that a successful transition to adulthood is compromised for this population. More than other chapters in the volume, this one focuses on the psychosocial capacities that develop during the adolescent years and lay the foundation for a successful transition to adulthood: in mastery and competence, in interpersonal relationships and social functioning, and in self-definition and self-governance, among others. Incarceration during the adolescent years arrests development in these areas in large part because it cuts youth off from the natural support systems and opportunities in the community that would scaffold their development. The policy shift in recent years towards punishment rather than rehabilitation has further reduced the likelihood that youth will exit the juvenile justice system psychologically mature and ready for a successful transition. Chung, Little, and Steinberg summarize the literature on turning points, which indicates that juvenile offenders who later make a successful transition to adulthood typically do so because they form intimate and committed relationships. Based on this knowledge about what works, they recommend that juvenile justice systems adopt practices that would enable young offenders to eventually commit to such relationships. In short, the system should adopt a more developmental approach to rehabilitation, one that would help offenders learn to make autonomous decisions, establish interpersonal relationships, and exercise self-governance.

Altschuler's chapter on policies affecting youth who have been involved in the juvenile justice system (chapter 4) begins by clarifying the several avenues by which youth arrested as juveniles can remain involved in the justice system during the transition to adulthood. He then considers the varying goals or philosophies that may guide the system and their consequences for the transition to adulthood. He concludes that it is much more difficult to promote resilience and social inclusion for these youth when priority is given to goals of deterrence and punishment, as has been the increasing emphasis of juvenile justice in recent years. Evidence indicates that several types of programs have promising results for juvenile offenders, both for incarcerated youth and for juvenile offenders in the community. Altschuler argues that continuity of care between these settings is critical to a successful transition to adulthood for youth who spend time in juvenile correctional institutions. He specifies five components of continuity of care: (1) continuity of control (i.e., a gradual reduction in restrictiveness), (2) continuity in the range of services, (3) continuity in service and program content, (4) continuity of social environment, and (5) continuity of attachments to responsible adults. Altschuler's chapter concludes with an analysis of the organizational issues that must be addressed to successful implement such a program.

In chapter 5, Uggen and Wakefield address the challenges of becoming an adult upon reentering the community from the criminal justice system. These authors argue that young people entering the criminal justice system fall behind their age cohort in standard markers of adulthood and are likely to reenter the community with the same deficits upon release. Uggen and Wakefield highlight the multitude of problems faced early on by this population, including the economic status of the family of origin, juvenile criminal history, substance abuse, health problems, and educational and occupational attainment. The authors conclude not only that this population starts off with deficits that will negatively affect a successful transition to adulthood, but that imprisonment further disrupts participation in adult roles, including those related to employment, family life, and civic engagement. The chapter proceeds to discuss how prisons fail to address such needs of inmates, which makes the transition to adulthood that much more difficult upon release. Uggen and Wakefield also review the challenges prisoners face when reentering the community and how these challenges delay a successful transition. With a focus on work, family, civic life, and stigma, the authors use a life course perspective to describe how early life disadvantages coupled with a punitive criminal sentence create great vulnerability for prisoners reentering the community and thereby severely impede the transition to adulthood. The chapter concludes by considering cross-national patterns in criminal punishment and age, race, and gender disparities in criminal sentencing that may further hinder transitions from prison to adulthood.

Chapter 6, by Travis and Visher, discusses policy issues concerning the transition to adulthood for young adults returning to the community from the criminal justice system. They explain that recent policy trends have exacerbated rather than eased the difficulties of this group as they return to the community. While incarceration rates have skyrocketed in recent decades, prison programs that might aid the transition have declined dramatically. There has also been an increase in "invisible punishments" that restrict former prisoners' opportunities, such as ineligibility for jobs and government programs. Travis and Visher review promising programs in the areas of employment, family, and health. They point out that currently few prisoners either work or receive job training while in prison, though there is good evidence that employment is associated with a successful reentry to the community. Family members are the most likely source of critical guidance and support after incarceration, but distant prisons, complex rules for visits, and expensive phone calls make it hard for prisoners to maintain family relationships. Travis and Visher point out that the high rates of infectious disease among prisoners mean that this population provides an important opportunity for reducing community-wide rates of illnesses such as HIV/AIDS, tuberculosis, and sexually transmitted diseases. In all of these areas they stress the need for coordination between correctional agencies and local community service providers.

In chapter 7, Hagan and McCarthy address both the challenges of the transition to adulthood and policy issues for homeless and runaway youth. The difficulties of these youth are often traceable to earlier life, with maltreatment by their families and early difficulties in school. Not surprisingly, they are considerably less likely to complete high school or have successful (and legal) employment. Their rates of early and risky sexual activity are high, and they spend their daily lives in dangerous settings. This chapter is unique in this volume for its attention to theoretical matters. Hagan and McCarthy develop an explanation of why some youth will succumb to a continued life on the street while others will find a path to long-term employment and a more conventional lifestyle. They see continued involvement in the street life as springing from a spiral of shame and defiance that results from a combination of early family maltreatment and negative interactions with law enforcement. Homeless youth experiencing this emotional reaction will find it especially difficult to endure the demands of the low-wage service jobs available to them. Hagan and McCarthy then turn to policy issues, discussing services for homeless and runaway youth, which typically are poorly funded and available for relatively few youth. The chapter ends with a comparison of the experiences of youth in two cities that take very different approaches to runaway and homeless youth. Hagan and McCarthy conclude that a heavy reliance on law enforcement rather than social welfare programs leads homeless youth into a subculture of street crime where conventional employment is uncommon and disdained.

Chapter 8, by Levine and Wagner, addresses the challenges during the transition to adulthood faced by youth who have been in special education. They begin the chapter with a description of the characteristics of youth who receive special education services. Focusing on students with learning disabilities, emotional disturbances, or mental retardation, the authors highlight challenges such youth face, particularly during their high school careers, and how this affects the transition period. They argue that high school experiences are crucial to success or failure in the transition, particularly because high school completion significantly affects trajectories during the postschool period. Specifically, the authors show that special education students have higher rates of course failure, grade retention, and absenteeism, while also being less likely to receive beneficial postsecondary education. The challenges youth receiving special education services face during the transition to adulthood are discussed in terms of themes of employment, independence, and social adjustment.

Levine and Wagner continue the discussion of youth who have been in special education and the transition to adulthood in chapter 9 by addressing the legislation and policy decisions aimed at this group. They describe how laws and regulations regarding education practices for youth with disabilities have evolved, including policies targeted at youth during high school as well as during the transition to adulthood. The chapter addresses the ways in which these policies affect opportunities for these youth to make a successful transition to adulthood. In particular, the authors discuss the lack of collaboration across and within agencies serving the population, and they argue that transition planning and postschool services and support are central to successful transitions. Levine and Wagner review strengths and weaknesses of existing policy and make recommendations for system reform.

In chapter 10, Gralinski-Bakker and colleagues use psychological and psychiatric perspectives to address the challenges faced by youth with serious mental disorders receiving residential mental health treatment. The authors begin with a review of the costs and prevalence of mental disorders during adolescence and the transition to adulthood. Because there is considerable continuity in mental disorders from adolescence through the transition to adulthood, Gralinski-Bakker and colleagues argue that this population is at great risk of failing to achieve success in the transition, in part because mental disorders during adolescence negatively affect normal development. For example, adolescence is a period when developing autonomy and interpersonal relationships are important for development, but achieving autonomy and developing positive relationships, particularly with family members or a caregiving adult, is very difficult for this population. In a review of the literature, including a twenty-five-year longitudinal study of inpatient psychiatric treatment by the authors, Gralinski-Bakker and colleagues discuss the poor outcomes displayed by many with mental disorders during the transition to adulthood, with a particular focus on difficulties faced in the community after receiving residential mental health care. For example, they note that this population has an especially difficult time finding employment due to both stigma and poor social skills stemming from difficulty regulating emotions and behaviors. The authors conclude with a discussion of resilience among this population, using clinical research interviews to describe adolescents' perspectives regarding their mental disorders and the impact of subsequent experiences on success during the transition to adulthood.

In chapter 11, Lyons and Melton contend that young adults with mental illnesses face a confusing patchwork of agencies and funding streams to obtain services. They note that even in childhood, eligibility for mental health services tends to flow through institutions such as schools or juvenile justice. In young adulthood not only are there fewer institutional connections through which mental health services could flow, but the door to service eligibility often closes. Even the diagnostic categories that make children eligible for services change as they approach adulthood. According to the authors, mental health policy should include universally available services that are responsive to transient problems often associated with the transition to adulthood. Policy also needs to include services targeted for specific populations with chronic mental health problems, and the authors make a detailed case for the need for differentiated services for different presenting problems. An effective system would also provide basic services needed by most young adults with mental health problems, including vocational and housing services and family support; it would focus on local community-based services; and it would be sensitive to issues of stigma associated with mental illness. Despite consensus about these core services, a focus on the individual and his/her problems is the more common approach. Lyons and Melton conclude their chapter with recommendations for how the mental health system could be truly responsive to individuals as they transition to adulthood.

Blum reviews what is known about adolescents with chronic physical disabilities as they make the transition to adulthood in chapter 12. Unlike prior generations, today over 90 percent of children born with disabling conditions survive to adulthood, making the transition to adulthood a new and uncertain experience. The end of formal education marks a great social disruption for adolescents with disabling conditions. Educational and employment opportunities and achievements are limited for this population. In addition, youth with chronic physical disabilities face challenges in forming relationships during the transition to adulthood, so social isolation is a major consequence of such a condition. The emotional well-being of such adolescents presents another challenge during the transition, as youth with chronic disabilities have an increased risk of developing psychological and behavioral problems. Such negative outcomes point to low levels of independence achieved by many young adults with disabilities. Blum argues that the level of independence a young adult with a disability achieves is key to success during the transition. Independence, in turn, is determined by factors involving the individual (such as gender and disclosure), his or her condition (such as degree of visibility and severity of condition), the family (such as life expectancy and genetic risks), and the environment in which they live (such as peers, health professionals, and community support). In conclusion, Blum notes that the problems faced by youth with disabilities largely reflect the social creation of disabilities rather than being a consequence of the inherent physical limitations of the disability itself.

Chapter 13, by White and Gallay, discusses policy issues concerning youth with special health care needs and disabilities (SHCN/D). For young adults with chronic illnesses or disabilities, monitoring and managing their health status is an everyday routine, making long-term planning for continuity of care a critical task for the transition to adulthood. Unfortunately, like other vulnerable populations, when youth with SHCN/D come of age they must deal with issues of access to and eligibility for the health care system. In addition, because their lives are so intimately tied to the public health care system, this group has to cope with an especially dense web of bureaucratic rules and regulations. Lack of access to health care is especially troubling insofar as health problems that may be routine for the average young adult often result in hospitalization for this population. Even when access to health care is available, young adults with SHCN/D face additional hurdles in getting developmentally appropriate treatment. Health care systems are organized to treat children or adults, but not those in transition to adulthood. Furthermore, the medical model is oriented towards curing disease, so people with disabilities are often treated as deficient. Instead of a medical model the authors recommend an interactional model that focuses on repairing relationships between individuals and institutions.

The volume concludes with chapter 14 by the editors, which offers some final thoughts on the transition to adulthood for these seven vulnerable populations. We begin by reviewing shared themes that emerge from the preceding chapters, including the overrepresentation of certain groups in these populations and the overlap among the vulnerable populations. Adolescents involved in one of these governmental programs, such as juvenile justice or foster care, are at high risk of being involved in others as well, such as special education or the mental health system. We continue with a discussion of the problematic outcomes during the transition to adulthood that are common among the populations. In general, outcomes for these populations are negative across many domains. The concluding chapter also discusses the need for additional research on the transition to adulthood for vulnerable populations and how programs and policies addressing these populations could be improved to facilitate the transition. The key policy issue throughout the volume is the need for greater investment in supporting the transition to adulthood for these groups. We draw on the theme of social inclusion as an overarching perspective on policy toward the vulnerable populations. This point of view emphasizes that negative outcomes for any one group have public costs for the larger society, and that an important policy goal for a democratic society is to provide opportunities that encourage full participation of all citizens.

In sum, the concluding chapter draws together the combined findings and implications of the preceding chapters. It calls for greater attention to the needs of these groups, in which society has already invested so heavily, during a problematic period of life in which most now receive little assistance.

REFERENCES

Amato, P. R., and A. Booth. 1997. *A generation at risk.* Cambridge: Harvard University Press.

Arnett, J. J. 2000. Emerging adulthood: A theory of development from the late teens through the twenties. *American Psychologist* 55: 469–480.

Chen, Z., and H. B. Kaplan. 2003. School failure in early adolescence and status attainment in middle adulthood: A longitudinal study. *Sociology of Education* 76: 110–127.

Cherlin, A. 1992. *Marriage, divorce, and remarriage.* Cambridge: Harvard University Press.

Cutrona, C. E., V. Cole, N. Colangelo, S. G. Assouline, and D. W. Russell. 1994. Perceived parental support and academic achievement: An attachment theory perspective. *Journal of Personality and Social Psychology* 66: 369–378.

Fass, M. E. and J. G. Tubman. 2002. The influence of parental and peer attachment on college students' academic achievement. *Psychology in the Schools* 39: 561–573.

Foster, E. M., and E. J. Gifford. 2005. Developmental and administrative transitions for special populations: Policies, outcomes, and research challenges. Pp. 501–533 in *On the frontier of adulthood: Theory, research, and public policy.* Edited by R. A. Settersten, Jr., F. F. Furstenberg, Jr., and R. G. Rumbaut. Chicago: University of Chicago Press.

Furstenberg, Frank F. 2000. The sociology of adolescence in the 1990s: A critical commentary. *Journal of Marriage and the Family* 62: 896–910.

Furstenberg, F. F. Jr., R. G. Rumbaut, and R. A. Settersten, Jr. 2005. On the frontier of adulthood: Emerging themes and new directions. Pp. 3–25 in *On the frontier of adulthood: Theory, research, and public policy.* Edited by R. A. Settersten, Jr., F. F. Furstenberg, Jr., and R. G. Rumbaut. Chicago: University of Chicago Press.

Fussell, E., and F. F. Furstenberg, Jr. 2005. Race, nativity, and gender differences in the timing of transitions to adulthood during the twentieth century. Pp. 29–75 in *On the frontier of adulthood: Theory, research, and public policy.* Edited by R. A. Settersten, Jr., F. F. Furstenberg, Jr., and R. G. Rumbaut. Chicago: University of Chicago Press.

Goldscheider, F. K., and C. Goldscheider. 1993. *Leaving home before marriage: Ethnicity, familism, and generational relationships.* Madison: University of Wisconsin Press.

Goldscheider, F. K., and C. Goldscheider. 1994. Leaving and returning home in 20th century America. *Population Bulletin* 48: 1–35.

Goldscheider, F. K., and C. Goldscheider. 1999. *The changing transition to adulthood: Leaving and returning home.* Thousand Oaks, CA: Sage Publications.

Hauser, S. T. 1999. Understanding resilient outcomes: Adolescent lives across time and generations. *Journal of Research on Adolescence* 9: 1–24.

Hogan, D. P. 1981. *Transitions and social change: The early lives of American men.* New York: Academic Press.

Jayakody, R. 1998. Race differences in intergenerational financial assistance: The needs of children and the resources of parents. *Journal of Family Issues* 19: 508–533.

Jencks, C. S., S. Bartlett, M. Corcoran, J. Crouse, D. Eaglesfield, G. Jackson, K. McClelland, P. Mueser, M. Olneck, J. Schwartz, S. Ward, and J. Williams. 1979. *Who gets ahead? The determinants of economic success.* New York: Basic Books.

Kerckhoff, A. C. 1993. *Diverging pathways: Social structure and career deflections.* New York: Cambridge University Press.

Kerckhoff, A. C., S. W. Raudenbush, and E. Glennie. 2001. Education, cognitive skill, and labor force outcomes. *Sociology of Education* 74: 1–24.

Kingston, P. W., R. Hubbard, B. Lapp, P. Schroeder, and J. Wilson. 2003. Why education matters. *Sociology of Education* 76: 53–70.

Kohli, M. 1986. The world we forgot: A historical review of the life course. Pp. 271–303 in *Later life.* Edited by V. W. Marshall. Beverly Hills: Sage.

McLanahan, S., and K. Booth. 1989. Mother-only families: Problems, prospects, and policies. *Journal of Marriage and Family* 51: 557–580.

May, E.T. 1990. *Homeward bound: American families in the Cold War era.* New York: Basic Books.

Milligan, K., E. Moretti, and P. Oreopoulos. 2004. Does education improve citizenship? Evidence from the United States and the United Kingdom. *Journal of Public Economics* 88: 1667–1695.

Modell, J. 1989. *Into one's own: From youth to adulthood in the United States, 1920–1975.* Berkeley: University of California Press.

Modell, J., F. F. Furstenberg, and T. Hershberg. 1976. Social change and transition to adulthood in historical perspective. *Journal of Family History* 1: 7–32.

Mollenkopf, J., P. Kasinitz, and M. Waters. 2005. The ever-winding path: Transitions to adulthood among native and immigrant young people in metropolitan New York. Pp. 454–497 in *On the frontier of adulthood: Theory, research, and public policy.* Edited by R. A. Settersten, Jr., F. F. Furstenberg, Jr., and R. G. Rumbaut. Chicago: University of Chicago Press.

Newcomb, M. D., and P. M. Bentler. 1988. *Consequences of adolescent drug use: Impact on the lives of young adults.* Newbury Park, CA: Sage.

Rindfuss, R. R. 1991. The young adult years: Diversity, structural change, and fertility. *Demography* 28: 493–512.

Rindfuss, R. R., S. P. Morgan, and K. Offutt. 1996. Education and the changing age pattern of American fertility. *Demography* 33: 277–290.

Rindfuss, R. R., S. P. Morgan, and G. Swicegood. 1988. *First births in America.* Berkeley: University of California Press.

Sagawa, S. 1998. Ten years of youth service to America. Pp. 137–158 in *The forgotten half revisited: American youth and young families, 1988–2008.* Edited by S. Halperin. Washington: American Youth Policy Forum.

Schoeni, R. F., and K. E. Ross. 2005. Material assistance received from families during the transition to adulthood. Pp. 396–416 in *On the frontier of adulthood: Theory, research, and public policy.* Edited by R. A. Settersten, Jr., F. F. Furstenberg, Jr., and R. G. Rumbaut. Chicago: University of Chicago Press.

Shanahan, M. J. 2000. Pathways to adulthood in changing societies: Variability and mechanisms in life course perspective. *Annual Review of Sociology* 26: 667–692.

Settersten, R. A., Jr. 2005. Social policy and the transition to adulthood. Pp. 534–560 in *On the frontier of adulthood: Theory, research, and public policy.* Edited by R. A. Settersten, Jr., F. F. Furstenberg, Jr., and R. G. Rumbaut. Chicago: University of Chicago Press.

Settersten, R. A., Jr., F. F. Furstenberg, Jr., and R. G. Rumbaut, eds. 2005. *On the frontier of adulthood: Theory, research, and public policy.* Chicago: University of Chicago Press.

Steelman, L.C. and B. Powell. 1991. Sponsoring the next generation: Parental willingness to pay for higher education. *American Journal of Sociology* 96: 1505–1529.

Uhlenberg, P. 1974. Cohort variations in family life cycle experiences of U.S. females. *Journal of Marriage and the Family* 36: 284–292.

Winsborough, H. 1978. Statistical histories of the life cycle of birth cohorts: The transition from school boy to adult male. Pp. 231–259 in *Social demography.* Edited by K. Traeber, L. L. Bumpass, and J. A. Sweet. New York: Academic Press.

William T. Grant Foundation Commission on Work, Family, and Citizenship. 1988. *The forgotten half: Non-college-bound youth in America.* Washington: William T. Grant Foundation.

CHAPTER TWO

The Transition to Adulthood for Youth "Aging Out" of the Foster Care System

MARK E. COURTNEY AND DARCY HUGHES HEURING

INTRODUCTION

Interest in the transition of foster children to adulthood is not new. Over eighty years ago, concerned about how the children they placed fared after being discharged to their own care, the State Charities Aid Association of New York commissioned Sophie Van Senden Theis (1924) to try to track down 910 of their former wards who, by that time, were adults. Working with a thoughtfully selected sample and achieving a more than respectable follow-up rate, Van Senden Theis provided a rich description of the post–foster care well-being of the association's former wards. Although some were doing well, many of the former foster children experienced problems that troubled the leaders of the State Charities Aid Association. Like similar reports produced in recent years, the New York study called for changes in the way the association cared for its wards and helped them after they left care.

To this day, youth who age out of the nation's foster care system are a population at high risk of having difficulty managing the transition from dependent adolescence to independent adulthood. They experience high rates of educational failure, unemployment, poverty, out-of-wedlock parenting, mental illness, housing instability, and victimization. They are less likely than other youth to be able to rely on the support of kin. The public policies and corresponding services intended to help them on their way are limited and fragmented. In short, the deck is stacked against them.

Yet these are, in a profound way, society's children. Government takes them away from the care of their parents under the presumption that government can and should do better. In fact, this act is at the core of the laws and policies that define the child welfare system. With the exception of incarcerated delinquents, foster youth are the only group of youth who are involuntarily separated from their families through government intervention with the sanction of the courts. Although the primary purpose of this separation is to protect youth from maltreatment by their caregivers, in removing them from their homes the state takes on all of the responsibilities associated with parenting youth, including those associated with preparing them for independence. To be sure, government takes on this task in the context of trying to reunify youth with their families of origin or, when this is not possible, trying to find them another permanent home through adoption. Nevertheless, each year government "emancipates" thousands of foster youth to "independent living," most of whom have barely reached the age of majority. Thus, at the end of the day it is government, acting as parent, that decides when foster youth are ready to be on their own.

This population is also important because it is the target of policy specifically directed at youth in transition. Since the 1980s, the federal government has provided funds for services intended to prepare foster youth to live independently when they reach the age of majority. Examination of the perceived need for such services and the adequacy of the policy response could help guide thinking about how to support *all* vulnerable youth during the transition to adulthood.

In this chapter, we describe the challenges facing foster youth as they leave the protection of the child welfare services system and examine current policies directed at helping them achieve independence. We start with a brief introduction to the child welfare system and the basic demographic characteristics of youth who age out of the foster care system. Then we review the literature on the young adult outcomes of former foster youth. Putting these findings in perspective, we explore how the background conditions of these youth and the experiences they have while they are in out-of-home care may contribute to the difficulties they face as they make the transition to adulthood. Finally, we provide a historical overview of policies intended to support foster youth in the transition to independent living and point out the limitations of current policies.

FOSTER YOUTH AND THE CHILD WELFARE SYSTEM

According to estimates from the federal Adoption and Foster Care Analysis and Reporting System (AFCARS), 542,000 children lived in out-of-home care on September 30, 2001, the most recent year for which national statistics are available (U.S. Department of Health and Human Services 2003). Of these children, 55 percent were black and/or Hispanic, 52 percent were male, and their median age was 10.6 years. Almost half (48 percent) of these children lived with nonrelative foster parents, 24 percent lived in relative or "kinship" foster care, 18 percent lived in group homes or other children's institutions, 4 percent in a preadoptive home, 3 percent were living at home during a trial home visit, 2 percent had run away from care but were still the legal responsibility of the child welfare agency, and 1 percent were living in supervised independent living settings (e.g., an apartment that is supervised by the child welfare agency). Although children living in kinship foster care remain in the day-to-day care of their extended families, the public child welfare agency has authority over these placements under the direction of the juvenile court and under the same laws used to supervise nonrelative foster care.

States operate their foster care programs under the legal framework provided by Title IV-E of the Social Security Act (42 U.S.C. 670). The juvenile or family court of the relevant jurisdiction supervises the care of children by state and local public child welfare agencies. Children enter out-of-home care[1] when a court determines that they should be removed from the home of their parents or another caregiver in order to protect them from abuse or neglect.[2] Child welfare agencies are required to make "reasonable efforts" to prevent placement of children in out-of-home care, usually in the form of social services for their families. When the child welfare agency and court deem these efforts unsuccessful and the child enters out-of-home care, the court must approve a "permanency plan" for the child according to timelines provided in federal law. Most commonly, the initial plan is for the child to return to the care of parents or other family members. Once again, the court generally requires the child welfare agency to make reasonable efforts to preserve the child's family of ori-

---

1. Although Title IV-E is referred to as the federal "foster care" program, this is somewhat misleading. In actuality, states claim federal funds for placement of children in a variety of forms of out-of-home care including foster family homes, kinship foster homes, group homes, and larger children's institutions. In this chapter we refer to the range of court-supervised living arrangements as "out-of-home care." States can claim IV-E reimbursement only for children who are eligible under the statute, which means that the child's parents would have been eligible for Aid to Families with Dependent Children (AFDC) at the time the child was removed from home and the child was placed in out-of-home care by court order. In other words, the federal government primarily supports foster care for children from *poor* families. About half of all children in foster care are not IV-E eligible, generally because their parents would not have been eligible for AFDC at the time the child was removed from home or because the child's placement was not eligible for reimbursement (e.g., the child was placed with a relative but the relative's home did not meet state foster care licensing standards).

2. A small proportion of children enter care through voluntary placement agreements reached between parents and child welfare agencies, but states can claim federal reimbursement for these arrangements for only 180 days. States usually obtain a protective order when a child placed under a voluntary agreement remains in care more than 180 days.

gin, in this case by providing services intended to help reunite the child with the family.[3] In many cases, however, children and youth cannot return to the care of their families. When this happens, the child welfare agency and the court attempt to find another permanent home for the child through adoption or legal guardianship.

The vast majority of children in out-of-home care will exit care to what are considered, in the parlance of the child welfare system, "permanent" placements. For example, of the estimated 263,000 children who left out-of-home care in the U.S. during FY 2001, 88 percent went to live with family, were adopted, or were placed in the home of a legal guardian (U.S. Department of Health and Human Services 2003). A few (3 percent) were transferred to another public agency such as a probation or mental health department and a few (2 percent) ran away and were discharged from care. Some 7 percent, or 19,008, remained in care until they were legally "emancipated," usually due to reaching the age of majority or upon graduation from high school. In practice, few states allow youth to remain in care much past their eighteenth birthday, though some will continue to make payments to an out-of-home care provider if the youth in their care is likely to obtain a high school diploma before their nineteenth birthday (Bussey et al. 2000). Illinois is the only jurisdiction to discharge a significant number of youth at twenty-one (Bussey et al. 2000).

A recent longitudinal study of the placement trajectories of older foster youth (i.e., those in a position to age out of the foster care system) puts their experience in out-of-home care into perspective. Wulczyn and Brunner Hislop (2001) analyzed placement histories and discharge outcomes of all youth in twelve states (n = 119,011) that were in out-of-home care on their sixteenth birthday. Three of their findings stand out. First, most of these youth had entered care since their fifteenth birthday and only 10 percent had entered care as preteens (i.e., twelve or younger). In other words, few youth who age out of care actually grow up in the foster care system. This should not be surprising given that the median age of children entering foster care is less than nine years and about half of all children leave care within one year of entry (U.S. Department of Health and Human Services 2003). Second, these older youth were less likely to be living with kin and much more likely to be living in congregate care (i.e., group homes or children's institutions) than the overall foster care population described above. For example, 42 percent were living in congregate care while only 12 percent were living in kinship foster care. Third, nearly half (47 percent)

---

3. The Adoption and Safe Families Act of 1997 allows courts to waive reasonable efforts requirements in some cases, such as when parents have previously been responsible for the death of another one of their children or the child being removed from home has been subjected to "chronic abuse."

of these youth were returned to their families at discharge from the child welfare system and more youth experienced other exits (21 percent, mainly transfers to other child-serving systems) or ran away from care (19 percent) than were emancipated (12 percent). In short, most older youth in out-of-home care enter care during their adolescence and relatively few remain in care until they officially age out. Moreover, many of these youth do not live in familylike settings while they are in care and relatively few live with kin.

These facts raise important issues when one examines the young adult outcomes of older youth leaving the foster care system and the policy framework established to help them during this transition. As we describe in more detail below, foster children in general face the disadvantages associated with coming from low-income families where they have been subjected to maltreatment. Youth who age out of care, by virtue of the fact that they generally enter care during adolescence, have often spent many years in these challenging circumstances prior to intervention by child protection authorities. Thus, the outcomes experienced by former foster youth during the transition to adulthood may be more a function of the problems that they brought with them to the child welfare system than what they experienced in out-of-home care. This raises an interesting question for policy makers: What responsibility should the child welfare system bear for preparing foster youth for independent living when the vast majority of them spend at most a year or two in the system, most either returning home or running away?

Support from family is recognized as an important contributor to successful adolescent transitions to adulthood (Furstenburg and Hughes 1995; Mortimer and Larson 2002). Yet placement in out-of-home care, by its very nature, threatens a youth's family relations and can therefore undermine family support. Even when a youth's parents are unlikely to be of much help during the transition or are a potential source of risk, members of the extended family may be available for support, but not if their relationship to the youth has been negatively affected by the youth's placement in out-of-home care. This potential disturbance in family relations may be particularly likely for youth who age out of foster care. Relatively few of them are placed with relatives, the placement setting that is arguably most likely to facilitate continuing relations with extended family. Moreover, a large percentage of these youth live in congregate care. Since congregate care facilities are generally staffed by relatively young shift workers who tend not to stay in their jobs very long, youth in congregate care may find it difficult to form the kind of lasting relationships with responsible adults that will help them move towards independence. Once again, the circumstances of youth who age out of care raise an important question for policy makers: How can child welfare policy help maintain supportive family relations for foster youth and build new relationships that can support youth during the transition to adulthood?

Current federal child welfare policy focuses on providing support for youth who age out of foster care, but as noted above this group represents a relatively small proportion of foster youth who leave the system near the age of majority. This raises important questions for policy makers. Should transitional services and supports be available only to youth who age out of foster care, or should all older youth leaving care receive such help, regardless of their discharge destination? Are the most needy former foster youth currently receiving services? For example, are runaway foster youth, the focus of recent media attention on "missing" foster children, really less in need or deserving of help than those who remain in care through emancipation (Anderson 2002; Kresnak 2002)? We will return to these questions after reviewing what is known about the well-being of former foster youth during their transition to adulthood and examining explanations for why the transition appears to be so difficult for them.

OUTCOMES FOR FORMER FOSTER YOUTH DURING THE TRANSITION TO ADULTHOOD

We reviewed research on adult outcomes of former foster youth to illustrate why this population should be a focus of attention for those interested in the transition to adulthood. We focused primarily on studies with samples that had aged out of care or who had at least left care in late adolescence. Restricting the research review to only those studies that examined foster youth that aged out of care would have left us with very little to review. Moreover, since we believe that policy should focus on a broader population than those who age out of care, we felt it appropriate to describe the outcomes of the larger group. We also sought studies that reported young adult outcomes (i.e., eighteen to twenty-four) as opposed to later adult outcomes, though a few of the retrospective studies included some subjects who were interviewed at an older age.

Although some studies compared outcomes for former foster youth to matched samples or national norms, this was rare. Fortunately, McDonald et al. (1996), in their review of research on the long-term consequences of foster care, used a variety of sources to compare reported outcomes from some studies to regional and national data sources for the appropriate period, most commonly the Statistical Abstract of the United States. These studies include those by Meier (1965), Robins (1966), Zimmerman (1982), Festinger (1983), Frost and Jurich (1983), and Jones and Moses (1984).

Readers are encouraged to refer to the appendix to this chapter for more detail on the studies we reviewed.

Several limitations of this research literature deserve attention. First, most of the studies are quite dated; significant changes took place over the past twenty-five years in the nature of the foster care population, including the foster care "baby boom" associated with the crack epidemic of the late 1980s and early 1990s and the rapid growth of kinship foster care (Wulczyn, Brunner Hislop, and Goerge 2000). Even fewer studies took place after states had begun to implement the 1985 federal law that provided funds for independent living services for foster youth. Thus, much of the available research may not accurately depict the characteristics of the population that is aging out of care today and the services and supports that are available to them. Second, many of the studies employ rather idiosyncratic samples that may not do a good job of describing the experiences of the general population of former foster youth. Third, most of the studies suffer from high rates of sample attrition since the researchers were often unable to locate many of the former foster youth after they left foster care. For example, the only national study of youth that aged out of foster care suffered a follow-up attrition rate of over 50 percent (Cook, Fleischman, and Grimes 1991).

Our review begins with a summary of research findings concerning several domains of outcomes experienced by former foster youth during the transition to adulthood: education, physical and mental health, substance abuse, criminal justice system involvement, family relations, employment and economic self-sufficiency, housing, and civic engagement. All of these outcomes are important indicators in their own right of the success, or lack thereof, of foster youth in managing the transition to adulthood. In addition, problems in any one of these domains can make success in another less likely. For example, educational deficits can lead to difficulties in maintaining employment that will provide for basic needs, which can then lead to housing instability. Indeed, making sense of the outcomes described below is complicated by the fact that research on this population has not examined the relationship between these outcomes, or the relationship between the outcomes and the experiences of foster youth before and during their stays in out-of-home care. Nevertheless, our review provides sobering evidence of just how difficult the transition to adulthood can be for former foster youth.

Education

Human capital is clearly important for success during the transition to adulthood, but studies of former foster youth find poor levels of educational attainment; the population fares poorly when compared to its peers. They have fewer years of education (Zimmerman 1982; Jones and Moses 1984). They are less likely to earn a high school diploma or GED (Zimmerman 1982; Festinger 1983; Frost and Jurich 1983; Jones and Moses 1984; Barth 1990; Cook, Fleischman, and Grimes 1991; Courtney et al. 2001). For example, Cook, Fleischman, and Grimes (1991) found that 66 percent of the eighteen-year-olds discharged from care in the U.S. between July 1, 1987, and June 30, 1988, had not graduated from high school. Only 54 percent of subjects had completed high school 2.5 to 4 years after they were discharged—low compared to the 78 percent of the eighteen- to twenty-one-year-olds in the general population. More recently, Courtney et al. (2001) found that 37 percent of their sample of former foster youth had not completed high school or obtained a GED within twelve to eighteen months of discharge from care (average age = 19.5 years).

Not surprisingly, given the low high school graduation rate of former foster youth, most studies find that they also have low rates of college attendance (Zimmerman 1982; Jones and Moses 1984; Barth 1990; Cook, Fleischman, and Grimes 1991; Courtney et al. 2001). For example, Jones and Moses (1984) found that only 7 percent of their sample of young adults who had spent at least a year in foster care had accumulated any college credit, though they were twenty years old on average at follow-up. Only 9 percent of the subjects in the study by Courtney et al. (2001) had taken any college courses in the twelve to eighteen months since they left care. In comparison, over one-quarter of the U.S. population between eighteen and twenty-four years old attended college during the period of the Jones and Moses (1984) study and between 35 and 37 percent of the population in this age range attended college during the late 1990s, when Courtney et al. (2001) conducted their study (U.S. Department of Commerce, Bureau of the Census 2002).

In summary, former foster youth must face the transition to independence with significant deficits in educational attainment, and they do not appear to make up for these deficits during the transition. These deficits put them at significant disadvantage in the labor market and likely contribute to some of the other negative outcomes they experience.

Physical and Mental Health

Former foster youth suffer from more mental health problems than the general population (Robins 1966; Festinger 1983; Jones and Moses 1984). Support for this conclusion comes from data on their use of mental health services and research assessments of their mental health. For example, after discharge from care, 47 percent of Festinger's (1983) sample of former New York foster youth, all of whom had spent at least five years in care, had sought help or advice from a mental health professional, a far higher rate than found in the general population. Jones and Moses (1984) reported that 3 percent of their subject population resided in residential or group care facilities after they left the foster care system, a much higher rate than the 0.3 percent of the general population (McDonald et al. 1996). Former foster youth suffer from higher levels of depression than the general population (Barth 1990; Cook 1992). Moreover, Courtney et al. (2001) had their subjects complete a standardized self-report mental health assessment, the Mental Health Inventory (Veit and Ware 1983), and found that the overall psychological health of the young adults in their sample was significantly worse than that of their peers of the same age and race.

Most research finds little difference between the physical health status of former foster youth and their peers, though this may be largely a function of a lack of attention to this outcome in research. Festinger (1983), Jones and Moses (1984), and Cook, Fleischman, and Grimes (1991) found no evidence of abnormal levels of physical health problems in the population they studied. In contrast, Zimmerman (1982) found that the young adults in her sample (nineteen to twenty-nine years old at follow-up), all of whom had spent at least a year in foster care in New Orleans, were more likely to report their health as "fair" or "poor" than the general population. In addition, among the former foster youth studied by Courtney et al. (2001), Caucasians reported poorer health on a standardized self-report health measure than the general population, whereas African-Americans in the sample reported health that was comparable to their peers. Although there is mixed evidence that former foster youth experience poor physical health, studies have found them to have difficultly obtaining affordable medical coverage, leading to untreated medical problems (Barth 1990; Courtney et al. 2001).

Simple summary measures of physical health may not do justice to the condition of former foster youth. For example, they face sexual and physical victimization that puts them at a particular disadvantage. In the Courtney et al. (2001) study, subjects were asked whether they had experienced any number of forms of physical victimization since they had left care. Some 25 percent of the male subjects and 15 percent of the female subjects reported that they had experienced some kind of serious physical victimization involving being "beat up," "choked, strangled, or smothered," "attacked with a weapon," or "tied up, held down, or blindfolded" against their will. Female subjects reported sexual victimization after their discharge from care. Of their female subjects, 11 percent reported having been sexually assaulted, 10 percent that they had been forced against their will to engage in oral or anal intercourse. Altogether, 13 percent of the females reported having been sexually assaulted and/or raped within twelve to eighteen months of discharge from care.

In summary, research is consistent in finding that former foster youth experience mental health problems during the transition to adulthood, but less consistent in finding other health problems; one recent study suggests that they experience serious physical and sexual victimization. The mental health problems experienced by this population are significant in their own right and raise concerns about the ability of these youth to achieve other important outcomes (e.g., maintain healthy relationships and obtain and maintain employment).

Substance Abuse

Studies report mixed findings with respect to the use and abuse of alcohol and illicit drugs by former foster youth. In a case control study, Robins (1966) compared male subjects who'd been diagnosed as alcoholics with those who had no clinical diagnoses. The alcoholics reported a higher rate of having lived in out-of-home care (76 percent) than those without clinical diagnoses (39 percent). One in eight (13 percent) of subjects in the Fanshel, Finch, and Grundy (1990) study of young adults (mean age of twenty-four at follow-up) that had been in private-agency foster care in Washington State reported extreme difficulty with drug abuse in their lives. About a third reported that drug use had been the source of problems in their lives at some point, a third had used cocaine, a third reported having used marijuana at least once or twice a week in the last year (18 percent used it every day), and about a fifth had used amphetamines during the last year. Barth (1990) found that 19 percent of his convenience sample of youth who had been "emancipated" from foster care in northern California (mean age of twenty-one at follow-up) reported drinking at least once a week while in care (comparable to high school students at the time) and that 17 percent had done so since leaving care. Since aging out of care, 56 percent of Barth's (1990) subjects had used street drugs. At the time of the study, 20 percent of the sample reported having used drugs in the last month. Of the youth who used street drugs while in care, only 25 percent reported using drugs more after care than while in care. In contrast to studies that suggest a high level of drug and alcohol use among former foster youth, the national study by Cook, Fleischman, and Grimes (1991) found that they used alcohol and other drugs at rates similar to or lower than those found in national surveys of young adults.

The research literature does not provide a very clear picture of the extent of substance use or abuse among former foster youth during the transition to adulthood. To some extent this reflects the fact that few studies have focused on this problem. In addition, youth who have serious substance abuse problems may end up moving from the child welfare system into the juvenile corrections system due to behavior associated with their substance abuse (e.g., drug dealing or theft directed at providing cash for drug purchases) before they have the opportunity to age out of foster care. At any rate, it is too early to tell how significant a problem substance abuse poses for former foster youth.

Involvement with the Criminal Justice System

Former foster youth have a higher rate of involvement with the criminal justice system than the general population (McCord, McCord, and Thurber 1960; Zimmerman 1982; Frost and Jurich 1983; Jones and Moses 1984; Fanshel, Finch, and Grundy 1990; Barth 1990; Courtney et al. 2001). Analyzing data from the Cambridge-Somerville Youth Study, McCord, McCord, and Thurber (1960) hypothesized that their subjects in foster homes would have a lower rate of adult deviance, but instead they found that the former foster youth were more likely than others to have had criminal records in adulthood (McCord, McCord, and Thurber 1960). Zimmerman (1982) found 28 percent of her male subjects and 6 percent of her female subjects from New Orleans had been convicted of crimes and served at least six months in prison, a much higher rate than the general population. Of Jones and Moses's (1984) subjects, 5 percent were in jail at the time of the study, an extremely high rate compared to the adult imprisonment rate of 1 percent in West Virginia in 1983 (McDonald et al. 1996). In the Fanshel, Finch, and Grundy (1990) study, 44 percent of the subjects had been picked up by police on charges at one time or another. Of the young adults in the study by Courtney et al. (2001), 18 percent reported having been arrested at least once in the twelve to eighteen months since leaving out-of-home care. The same number reported having been incarcerated—27 percent of the males and 10 percent of the females reported having been incarcerated after discharge.

The rates of criminal justice system involvement described above are cause for serious concern about the prospects of former foster youth during the transition to adulthood. Arrest and incarceration are troubling outcomes in their own right. In addition, a criminal record can limit the future employment and housing prospects of these youth. (For a more detailed discussion of challenges during the transition to adulthood faced by those involved in the criminal justice system, see chapter 5.) Finally, though the research does not provide conclusive evidence, some of the physical and sexual victimization experienced by these youth may be at least partly a function of their involvement in crime.

Family Formation

With respect to marriage, Meier (1965) and Cook (1992) found former foster youth were more likely to remain single than their peers. In contrast, Festinger (1983) found no difference between the marital status of her subjects and those of their peers in New York. Cook, Fleischman, and Grimes (1991) found the marriage rate of former foster youth to be similar to that of poor young adults, though much lower than that of all young adults in the comparable age range. Meier (1965) found a higher rate of marital separation and divorce among a sample of former Minnesota foster youth than that in the general population at that time, whereas Festinger (1983) found no difference. Cook (1992) found the former foster children represented in the National Survey of Families and Households to express less marital satisfaction than those in the overall national sample, whereas Festinger (1983) found no difference in marital satisfaction between her sample and national norms.

It should be noted that the mixed findings regarding marriage and marital satisfaction of former foster youth result from the findings of the study by Festinger (1983). All of the other studies with data on the subject suggest relatively poor outcomes for this population. Festinger chose to include only youth who had been in out-of-home care in New York City for at least five years. This characteristic of Festinger's study might explain why her findings are sometimes different from those of other studies with respect to a particular outcome. The study sample may not be very representative of youth who age out of care since most such youth enter care in late adolescence.

Studies have found that former foster youth have higher rates of out-of-wedlock parenting than their peers (Meier 1965; Festinger 1983; Cook, Fleischman, and Grimes 1991). For example, 31 percent of mothers in Festinger's (1983) sample were raising children on their own, and less than one-third of the parenting females in the study by Courtney et al. (2001) were married.

Several studies have also shown that former foster youth have children who struggle with health, education, and behavior problems (Zimmerman 1982) and who are involved in the child welfare system (Meier 1965; Jones and Moses 1984). In Zimmerman's (1982) study, 46 percent of the parents reported that their children had some sort of health, education, or behavioral problem. Of the former foster youth in Jones and Moses's (1984) study, 19 percent reported that they had a child in out-of-home care.

In summary, research findings are mixed regarding the success of former foster youth in forming their own families, though no studies show them to have better outcomes than their peers and most show less than desirable outcomes. Perhaps poor outcomes in this area should not be surprising given the generally troubled family histories of foster youth. Many of them have spent little or no time with good parental role models. In addition, the educational deficits, mental health problems, and criminal justice system involvement described above make many of these youth relatively undesirable potential marriage partners.

Employment and Economic Self-Sufficiency

Nearly all studies of former foster youth, and all of those we reviewed that were done in the past two decades, suggest that they face a very difficult time achieving financial independence. Availability of national and regional data makes it possible in many cases to compare this population to relevant samples and standards (e.g., the poverty level). For example, data from several studies show that former foster youth have a higher rate of dependency on public assistance than the general population (Pettiford 1981; Zimmerman 1982; Barth 1990; Jones and Moses 1984; Cook, Fleischman, and Grimes 1991; Courtney et al. 2001). Of the young adults in the national study by Cook, Fleischman, and Grimes (1991), 30 percent were receiving some form of public assistance. Nearly one-third (32 percent) of the participants in the Wisconsin study by Courtney et al. (2001) had received some form of public assistance since leaving care (40 percent of females and 23 percent of males). Females most commonly received Aid to Families with Dependent Children or Temporary Assistance to Needy Families (23 percent) or food stamps (20 percent), whereas males most often received Supplemental Security Income (12 percent).

Former foster youth have a higher unemployment rate than the general population (Zimmerman 1982; Jones and Moses 1984; Cook, Fleischman, and Grimes 1991; Goerge et al. 2002). They also have lower wages, which frequently leave them in poverty (Zimmerman 1982; Festinger 1983; Barth 1990; Cook, Fleischman, and Grimes 1991; Dworsky and Courtney 2000; Goerge et al. 2002). For example, two recent studies that used unemployment insurance claims data to examine the employment patterns and earnings of former foster youth found that their mean earnings were well below the federal poverty level for up to two years after leaving out-of-home care (Dworsky and Courtney 2000; Goerge et al. 2002).

Not surprisingly, many former foster youth experience financial trouble during the transition to independence. Of Barth's (1990) subjects, 53 percent reported that they had had serious money problems (not being able to buy food or pay bills) since leaving foster care, and one-third indicated that they had done something illegal to get money. Courtney et al. (2001) report that fewer than half (47 percent) of their study participants had $250 or more in savings when they left out-of-home care and 32 percent had money problems "most" or "all of the time" since leaving care.

In summary, the research consistently shows former foster youth fare poorly in terms of economic self-sufficiency outcomes during the transition to adulthood. They are less likely to be employed than their peers, more likely to rely on public assistance, and earn on average too little to escape poverty. No doubt the educational deficits of this group play a major role in their difficulty making headway in the labor market.

Housing and Homelessness

Information on the housing instability experienced by former foster youth comes from research on this population as well as research on homeless populations. Former foster youth have high rates of mobility and housing instability (Jones and Moses 1984; Fanshel, Finch, and Grundy 1990; Courtney et al. 2001). For example, 32 percent of the youth in the study by Cook, Fleischman, and Grimes (1991) had lived in six or more places in the two-and-one-half to four years since they had left care. Similarly, Courtney et al. (2001) found that 22 percent of the youth in their sample had lived in four or more places within twelve to eighteen months of exiting care.

Former foster youth also experience high rates of homelessness (Susser, Streuning, and Conover 1987; Sosin, Coulson, and Grossman 1988; Mangine et al. 1990; Sosin, Piliavin, and Westerfelt 1990; Susser et al. 1991; Cook, Fleischman, and Grimes 1991; Courtney et al. 2001). Most information on this problem comes from studies of adult homeless populations. Researchers have found former residents of out-of-home care to be represented at much higher rates across a variety of samples of street homeless populations, shelter residents, and psychiatric facilities that serve homeless populations than they are among the domiciled population (Susser, Streuning, and Conover 1987; Sosin, Coulson, and Grossman 1988; Mangine et al. 1990; Sosin, Piliavin, and Westerfelt 1990; Susser et al. 1991). Longitudinal studies of former foster youth also show this population to be at a heightened risk of homelessness. Cook, Fleischman, and Grimes (1991) report that 12 percent of the former out-of-home care residents in their national sample had sought housing assistance, 10 percent had used public shelters, and 25 percent had been without a place to live for at least one night since exiting the child welfare system. In the study by Courtney at al. (2001), 12 percent of the youth reported being homeless at least once since leaving out-of-home care. (For a discussion of the challenges faced by homeless youth, see chapter 7.)

In summary, former foster youth experience considerable housing instability including frequent periods of homelessness. Given the limited economic prospects of this group and the other problems described above (e.g., mental illness and corrections system involvement) it should not be surprising that many former foster youth have trouble staying put. However, poor housing stability among former foster youth may also be a function of their inability to rely upon extended family for housing assistance to the same degree as other young adults. Many foster youth lose their housing when they turn eighteen or graduate from high school. Courtney et al. (2001) asked youth about the circumstances under which they left the care of the child welfare system. Approximately 40 percent of their sample reported that they had to leave their last out-of-home care living arrangement because they were discharged from the child welfare system. Although many former foster youth are able to live with their families upon discharge from out-of-home care, they appear less able to rely on this housing resource than other youth. For example, one-third of the youth in the study by Cook, Fleischman, and Grimes (1991) were found to be living with extended family, compared to 53 percent of youth of a comparable age in the general population.

CIVIC ENGAGEMENT

Given the poor outcomes described above, it would be surprising if former foster youth were as civically engaged as their peers. Few studies of former foster youth have collected data on the civic involvement of this population, though some have reported on various measures of social isolation among this population, such as the lack of interaction with friends, neighbors, and coworkers. Most studies report relatively high rates of social isolation among former foster youth (Zimmerman 1982; Jones and Moses 1984; Cook 1992). Jones and Moses (1984) reported a very low rate of civic engagement for their subjects—only 30 percent of their subjects reported belonging to any organization, and three-quarters of those were religiously based. Cook (1992) found that former foster care children had fewer social involvements than nonfoster adults. In contrast, Festinger (1983) found that 45 percent of her subjects belonged to one or more community organizations, usually affiliated with a church, temple, or athletic group. In summary, the limited research on this topic indicates that former foster youth are not engaged in civic activities at levels that are supportive of healthy development. (For a similar argument made by Uggen and Wakefield concerning young adults in the criminal justice system, see chapter 5.)

Family Relations

One finding that is strikingly consistent across studies is the considerable ongoing contact former foster youth have with their families of origin after they leave out-of-home care (Harari 1980; Zimmerman 1982; Festinger 1983; Frost and Jurich 1983; Jones and Moses 1984; Barth 1990; Cook, Fleischman, and Grimes 1991; Courtney et al. 2001). The studies are not strictly comparable since they reported contact at different points in time after the youth have left care and measured contact using dissimilar metrics (i.e., weekly, monthly, annually). Nevertheless, taken together the studies suggest that former foster youth report that they are in contact with their mothers and to a somewhat lesser degree their fathers well into young adulthood. For example, at least monthly contact between former foster youth and their mothers ranged from one-third to one-half of respondents (Harari 1980; Zimmerman 1982; Festinger 1983; Courtney et al. 2001) with the same studies finding monthly contact with fathers to range from one-quarter to one-third of respondents. Those with siblings also maintain contact with their siblings over time. Courtney et al. (2001) found 88 percent of former foster youth with at least one sibling to have visited with a sibling at least once since discharge from out-of-home care.

This level of family contact is important since it suggests a possible source of natural support for former foster youth during the transition to adulthood. Indeed, most former foster youth who maintain contact with their family of origin report good relations with their kin. Festinger (1983) found that a majority of her New York respondents who were in contact with their biological families felt "very close" or "somewhat close" to their kin. Courtney et al. (2001), using the same survey questions as Festinger, found similarly high levels of expressed closeness between subjects and their mothers, siblings, and grandparents, but less favorable relations with their fathers. Studies also consistently show that a majority of former foster youth maintain ongoing contact with their former foster families, another potential source of support during the transition (Harari 1980; Festinger 1983; Jones and Moses 1984; Courtney et al. 2001).

Family relations are strong enough for many former foster youth that they go to live with kin after they leave care. Cook, Fleischman, and Grimes (1991) found that 54 percent of their respondents had lived in the home of a relative at some point after discharge from out-of-home care and one-third were living with a relative when interviewed 2.5 to 4 years after leaving care. Twelve to eighteen months after leaving care, nearly as many of the young adults in the study by Courtney et al. (2001) were living in the home of a relative (31 percent) as were living on their own (37 percent). As might be expected, however, given the troubled histories of most of these families, ongoing family relations were not without their problems. For example, Courtney et al. (2001) found that one-quarter of the young adults in their sample reported experiencing problems with their family most or all of the time. Barth (1990) found that 15 percent of his California subjects felt that they had no "psychological parent" or person to turn to for advice. Thus, while the family of origin remains a source of support for many former foster youth during the transition to adulthood, these youth are still less likely to be able to rely on this support than their peers, and they also must often weigh the benefits of ongoing family contact against the risks.

Summary

In summary, our review of the outcomes for former foster youth during their transition to adulthood is sobering to say the least. On average, they bring to the transition very limited human capital upon which to build a career or economic assets. They often suffer from mental health problems that can negatively affect other outcome domains, and these problems are less likely to be treated once they leave care. Although they were placed in out-of-home care due to abuse or neglect, not delinquency, they often become involved in crime and with the justice and corrections systems after aging out of foster care. Their employment prospects are bleak, and few of them escape poverty during the transition. Many former foster youth experience homelessness and housing instability after leaving care. Interestingly, in spite of court-ordered separation from their families, often for many years, most former foster youth can rely on their families to some extent during the transition to adulthood, though this is not always without risk.

A relatively recent study of youth who aged out of care in Wisconsin provides a perspective on how often former foster youth have difficulty managing the transition to adulthood. Courtney et al. (2001) found that 43 percent of the males in their sample and 32 percent of the females had experienced one or more of the following within twelve to eighteen months of leaving foster care: homelessness, incarceration, serious physical victimization, sexual assault, and rape. When the researchers included reliance on public assistance as an additional indicator of a difficult transition, the percentages rose to 56 percent of males and 54 percent of females.

One could come away from this review with the impression that placement in foster care is a ticket to a troubled transition to adulthood. However, it would be inaccurate to assume that poor outcomes are entirely the consequence of the time these youth spent in out-of-home care. Indeed, legal authorities removed them from the care of their families in the belief that this was necessary to protect them from harm. Youth leaving the care of the child welfare system have family histories, in addition to experiences in out-of-home care, that condition their ability to succeed in the transition to adulthood. A brief examination of how this history could contribute to poor outcomes in adulthood helps to frame our later discussion of policies intended to help foster youth achieve independence.

THE FAMILY HISTORIES OF FORMER
FOSTER YOUTH AND IMPLICATIONS
FOR THE TRANSITION TO ADULTHOOD

Children and youth enter out-of-home care because their safety is at risk. In 2000, an estimated 879,000 children were victims of abuse and neglect, 12.2 children per thousand, based on reports to child protective services agencies (U.S. Department of Health and Human Services, Administration on Children, Youth, and Families 2002). Of these victims, 62.8 percent suffered neglect,[4] 19.3 percent were physically abused, and 10.1 percent were sexually abused. Additional types of maltreatment were reported for 16.6 percent of victims. Approximately one-fifth of these reported maltreatment victims entered out-of-home care. The long-term consequences of child maltreatment for its victims are well-known and include problems in forming positive interpersonal relationships, physical and mental health problems, impaired cognitive development, reduced educational attainment, increased delinquency, and a greater likelihood to engage in risk behaviors (National Research Council, Panel on Research on Child Abuse and Neglect 1993). Thus, it is reasonable to expect that many older youth entering out-of-home care, in other words the group most likely to age out of care, bring with them extensive histories of trauma and neglect.

Furthermore, even the youngest children entering out-of-home care often suffer from significant disadvantages from the start. Problems such as lack of prenatal care, exposure to drugs and alcohol, malnutrition, abuse, neglect, and lack of health care grew at a rapid rate among children entering the foster care system during the late 1980s and early 1990s. For example, a study of foster children under thirty-six months old in California, New York, and Pennsylvania found that an estimated 58 percent had serious health-related problems in 1991, compared with 43 percent in 1986 (U.S. GAO 1994).

Although much time has passed since these developmentally challenged infants and young children entered out-of-home care, those left in care are now approaching the age of majority. To be sure, we have already noted that most youth who are emancipated from the child welfare system enter care during adolescence, not infancy. Nevertheless, it is precisely the foster care babies of the 1980s who exhibited serious health and behavioral problems who would have been least likely to be adopted and hence the most likely to remain in out-of-home care today. Thus, even those members of the aging-out cohorts of the

---

4. Most of this reported neglect consists of the parents' failure to adequately supervise a child or provide for a child's basic physical needs.

next few years who escaped long histories of parental maltreatment may still bring with them serious developmental deficits.

Finally, it is important to keep in mind that children and youth entering foster care nearly all come from poor families, with all of the disadvantages that entails (Courtney 1998). For example, a study sponsored by the United States Department of Health and Human Services, Office of the Assistant Secretary for Planning and Evaluation (2000) found that the vast majority of foster care entrants in three states studied came directly from families receiving welfare grants (85 percent in Illinois, 96 percent in California, and 90 percent in North Carolina). Not surprisingly, given the high level of poverty experienced by their families, the overwhelming majority of children and youth in out-of-home care come from single-parent families (Barth et al. 1994).

In summary, it is reasonable to assume that the vast majority of youth who age out of foster care entered the system with a variety of disadvantages that could continue to have consequences for them during the transition to adulthood.

THE OUT-OF-HOME CARE EXPERIENCE AND ITS IMPLICATIONS FOR THE TRANSITION TO ADULTHOOD

Out-of-home care should protect children from further maltreatment. Moreover, it should help them recover from the maltreatment they have already experienced and provide them with the kinds of age-appropriate and developmentally positive experiences all children need to become productive citizens. When out-of-home care accomplishes these goals, it improves the prospects of youth as they age out of care and experience the transition to independence. Yet research does not provide solid evidence that out-of-home care has a net positive or negative effect for children removed from their homes (McDonald et al. 1996). Given the troubled backgrounds from which children enter care, there is good reason to believe that many children are saved by the child welfare system. Nevertheless, research findings do suggest that certain aspects of the out-of-home care experience are less than ideal. When these conditions are present, out-of-home care may fail to ameliorate, or may even exacerbate, the problems that children bring with them into care and further compromise their transition to adulthood. As examples, we will describe three of these conditions: placement instability, poor attention to educational needs, and inadequate medical care.

For children in out-of-home care, more placements mean less stability. Much of the evidence suggests that fewer placements and a stable environment are associated with a higher degree of life satisfaction (Jones and Moses 1984), better physical functioning (Fanshel and Shinn 1978), higher educational achievement (Zimmerman 1982; Cook, Fleischman, and Grimes 1991), and improved adult functioning (Zimmerman 1982). Fewer placements have also been found to be associated with increased contact and an increased feeling of closeness with foster families after discharge from care (Festinger 1983), less criminal activity (Zimmerman 1982), increased life satisfaction (Jones and Moses 1984), and the ability to access health care and to avoid early parenthood (Cook, Fleischman, and Grimes 1991). English, Kouidou-Giles, and Plocke (1994) found the total number of a child's placements was a significant predictor of their readiness for independent living when they became older adolescents.

Yet children in out-of-home care often go through an alarming number of placements during their time in care. For the children in the Fanshel, Finch, and Grundy (1990) study of Casey Family Programs, their placement in a Casey home was, on average, the seventh living arrangement that they had experienced. The average time spent in the Casey Program, considered a long-term foster care program, was 3.5 years. The subjects averaged more than ten total living arrangements upon their exit from Casey care. Courtney and Barth (1996) found that, while the median number of placements for their sample of California foster youth was two, 17.4 percent of the youth experienced six or more placements before final discharge. Similarly, while 31.2 percent of the youths had only one spell in foster care, 5.2 percent went in and out of foster care four or more times. The youth who were in and out of care were more likely to experience poor discharge outcomes than those with fewer foster care spells.

Placement instability and the act of removing children from home itself may have other negative consequences during the transition to independence. Most youth rely heavily on their parents, siblings, and extended family for support during this period. Of course, it is not clear that these traditional sources of support are as beneficial for foster youth as they are for most youth. Nevertheless, the child welfare system may disrupt *positive* relationships between foster youth and members of their extended families, relationships that otherwise would have benefited these youth during the transition to adulthood. Of course, this common source of social support may be replaced or augmented when foster youth are adopted or otherwise able to form lasting relationships with foster caregivers. However, the frequency of placement moves experienced by many long-term residents of out-of-home care calls into question whether these new sources of support always outweigh the loss of family support occasioned by entry to out-of-home care.

Educational problems of youth in out-of-home care are a serious issue. Researchers commonly agree that among the challenges facing foster youth, low educational achievement has potentially dire consequences for quality of life in adulthood (Jackson 1994). Numerous studies have shown that foster care youth are at high risk of educational failure (Ayasse 1995; Cohen 1991; Altshuler 1997; Stein 1994; Jackson 1994). Evidence suggests that children enter out-of-home care behind in educational achievement and that they do not catch up while they are in care (Cook, Fleischman, and Grimes 1991; Fanshel, Finch, and Grundy 1990; Barth 1990; Festinger 1983). Children in out-of-home care perform at below-average levels in school (Allerhand, Weber, and Haug 1966; Fanshel and Shinn 1978; Fox and Acuri 1980; Zimmerman 1982). For example, Sawyer and Dubowitz (1994) found that a third of elementary-age foster children and two-thirds of high school–age foster youth had repeated at least one grade.

Educating foster youth can be extremely difficult, as multiple out-of-home care placements and frequent school changes cause many children to get lost in the educational system. Special needs of children often go unnoticed as they move from school to school, children suffer from a lack of consistent contact with teachers, school records are lost, and often teachers are unaware that a student is in out-of-home care. Studies have shown that guardians of foster children often do not monitor or assist with homework, do not consistently participate in school activities, and provide little financial assistance for education of foster youth (Blome 1997).

Finkelstein, Wamsley, and Miranda (2002) found that foster children face problems that other economically challenged children do not, problems that often affect their academic performance. They report concerns about maintaining ties with their biological parents and caring for siblings that often distract them from schoolwork. Mandated court appearances and doctors' appointments often cause them to miss school. Behavior problems prevent them from focusing in school, and they often avoid social interactions with their peers to keep their foster care status hidden. Alarmingly, this study found that the adults in these children's lives were generally unaware of the children's educational needs. Foster parents were most concerned with the children's behavior and rarely concerned about poor grades, nor did they regularly help with homework. Caseworkers were frequently unaware of the children's academic progress; school staff usually had no knowledge of a child's foster care background and how system demands might explain their academic difficulties. No one acknowledged primary responsibility for the educational needs of the foster children. In short, some evidence suggests that placement in out-of-home care may contribute to educational deficits that could make the transition to adulthood for former foster youth more difficult.

Children in foster care are at high risk of not receiving the medical care they need, which could contribute to continuing health problems during the transition to independence. Rosenbach, Lewis, and Quinn (2002) found that children in foster care had less continuous Medicaid coverage than children receiving SSI benefits or those in families receiving adoption assistance. United States General Accounting Office (1995) found that a significant proportion of young foster children did not receive critical health care services in the locations studied (Los Angeles County, New York City, and Philadelphia County). Despite state and agency regulations requiring comprehensive routine health care for the children, an estimated 12 percent of young foster children received no routine health care, 34 percent received no immunizations, and 32 percent had at least some identifiable unmet health need. Furthermore, an estimated 78 percent of foster children were at high risk for HIV due to parental drug use, yet only 9 percent had been tested for HIV. Without identification, HIV-infected children with mild or no symptoms cannot receive the early medical care known to be effective with young children.

The research literature cannot provide great clarity regarding the mechanisms that lead to the poor outcomes experienced by former foster youth during the transition to adulthood. Undoubtedly, the traumatic histories they bring with them into out-of-home care play a major role in limiting their prospects. In addition, in too many instances the child welfare system fails in its mission to do a better job raising these children than would have their parents. Our review of research on the young adult functioning of former foster youth leads us to the same conclusions as McDonald et al. (1996). They believed that their review of research on the long-term consequences of out-of-home care provided "convincing evidence that children in care are at high risk of 'rotten' outcomes as adults" (McDonald et al. 1996, 142). They went on to state:

> These outcomes are not simply a slightly diminished functioning or a failure to reach full potential, but may involve a failure to meet minimum levels of self-sufficiency (homelessness, welfare dependency, etc.) and acceptable behaviors (criminal activity, substance abuse, etc.). A problem of this magnitude deserves additional attention. (McDonald et al. 1996, 142)

Researchers who study former foster youth agree that life poses challenges that are more difficult for this group than for average youth and that not enough is done to prepare them for living on their own. Festinger (1983) found that 98 percent of her respondents discharged into their own care felt unprepared to be on their own. Courtney et al. (2001) found that about a quarter to a third of their subjects felt unprepared in several areas: 32 percent said that they did not feel prepared to obtain a job or manage money; 31 percent, to secure housing; 29 percent, to live on their own; 23 percent, to access health care. Few felt prepared for parenting. Barth's subjects "vehemently" called for "more preparation for independent living" (Barth 1990, 425).

We now turn to a description and critique of policies intended to help foster youth negotiate the transition to adulthood.

POLICY ISSUES

Since 1961, the federal government has reimbursed states for the costs of out-of-home care provided to poor children removed from home by court order.[5] Nevertheless, until recently, states that wished to provide housing to foster youth over the age of majority had to do so using state funds, since federal foster care funding could not be used for this purpose. Moreover, though in principle states could always use federal Child Welfare Services (Title IV-B of the Social Security Act) and Social Services Block Grant (Title XX) funding to support social services to help foster youth prepare for the transition to independent living, other priorities nearly always came first.

In the 1980s, child welfare advocates began to push for dedicated funding to help foster youth prepare for adulthood. Their advocacy efforts were based on anecdotal evidence from out-of-home care providers concerned about the plight of youth aging out of care and a few early studies of the population (Meier 1965; Zimmerman 1982; Festinger 1983). In 1985, the Independent Living Initiative (Public Law 99-272) provided federal funds to states under Title IV of the Social Security Act to help adolescents develop skills needed for independent living. Funding for the Independent Living Program (ILP) was reauthorized indefinitely in 1993 (Public Law 103-66) allowing states to engage in longer-term planning of their programs. The ILP gave states great flexibility in the kinds of services they could provide to Title IV-E–eligible youth who were at least sixteen and no more than twenty-one years old. Basic services outlined in the law included outreach programs to attract eligible youth, training in daily living skills, education and employment assistance, counseling, case management, and written transitional independent living plans. ILP funds could not, however, be used for room and board. The federal government required very little reporting from states about the ILP beyond creation of state ILP plans and had "no established method to review the states' progress in help-

5. Although states provide out-of-home care to nonpoor children, they can claim federal reimbursement only for boarding payments made on behalf of children whose parents were eligible for Aid to Families with Dependent Children (AFDC) at the time of removal from home. This eligibility requirement remains in effect even though AFDC was replaced by Temporary Assistance to Needy Families (TANF) in 1996.

ing youths in the transition from foster care" (U.S. GAO 1999, 3). The General Accounting Office found that at least 42,680 youths in forty states (only about 60 percent of all eligible youth) received some type of independent living service in 1998 (U.S. GAO 1999).

Most recently, the Foster Care Independence Act (FCIA) of 1999 (Public Law 106-169) amended Title IV-E to give states more funding and greater flexibility in providing support for youths making the transition to independent living. The FCIA doubles federal independent living services funding to $140 million per year, allows states to use up to 30 percent of these funds for room and board, enables states to assist eighteen- to twenty-one-year-olds who have left foster care, and permits states to extend Medicaid eligibility to former foster children up to age twenty-one. An amendment to the law allows Congress to appropriate $60 million per year for education and training vouchers of up to $5,000 per year for youth up to twenty-three years old; Congress allocated $42 million to the program in FY 2003.

State performance is a much higher priority under the FCIA than under earlier iterations of federal policy in this area. The Department of Health and Human Services (HHS) is required to develop a set of outcome measures to assess state performance in managing independent living programs, and states will be required to collect data on these outcomes. In addition, the FCIA requires that 1.5 percent of funding under the statute be set aside for rigorous evaluations of promising independent living programs (i.e., using random-assignment evaluation designs whenever possible). The program created by the FCIA is named the Chafee Foster Care Independence Program (the Chafee Program) after the late Senator John Chafee, a legislative advocate for foster youth.

Before providing a critique of current policy, a brief description of what the Chafee Program actually funds is in order. The term "independent living services" describes a wide range of approaches to meeting the needs of youth who child welfare authorities expect to age out of foster care or have already done so. Unfortunately, no neat categorization adequately captures the range of these services, and there are no reliable national data on their scope. In general, public and private agencies delivering these services tend to provide multiple services, serve broad and sometimes ill-defined populations, and may focus on multiple outcomes. One typology of independent living services categorizes them into life skills training, mentoring programs, transitional housing, health and behavioral health services, educational services, and employment services.[6]

Although these categories largely capture the range of independent living

6. The description of independent living services provided here is a summary of material in Courtney and Terao (2002).

services, they can obscure certain common elements of the programs that deliver such services. For example, many programs provide some form of case management. Similarly, many programs employ a youth development philosophy. This philosophy emphasizes opportunities for youth to contribute to their community, increase their personal confidence, and provide guidance to other youth. Categorization of services can also give the false impression that programs specialize in providing a specific category of services. In fact, a survey of programs by Sheehy et al. (2001) found that few programs that focus on preparing foster youth for adulthood provide only one service and that many provide a wide range of services. Thus, it is important to keep in mind that independent living services are generally delivered in the context of more comprehensive social service programs.

In addition, categorization of services does not provide complete information about state and local *policies* intended to support independent living. For example, as noted above, some jurisdictions allow youth to remain in foster care longer than others. Some states have waived tuition for foster youth who attend state colleges or universities. Similarly, at least one state (Illinois) has created a wage subsidy for youth under twenty-one who have aged out of foster care. Such policies might ultimately have more influence than independent living services on outcomes for former foster youth during the transition to adulthood. Nevertheless, states spend much of their funding from the FCIA on services, which therefore warrant attention.

Approaches used to teach foster youth and former foster youth life skills range from didactic classroom-based courses to programs that more directly involve youth in practicing tasks that they will be required to master in order to survive on their own. Social workers, foster parents, independent living program staff, other foster youth, or some combination of the above may teach life skills. This service is probably the most common element of independent living programs.

Mentoring services attempt to connect youth to formal and informal institutions and build their social capital through relationships. Most programs try to help establish connections between youth and caring adults, but some peer mentorship programs also exist. Some programs rely on volunteer mentors while others recruit and pay adults to provide mentoring.

Housing is one of the most important service areas in that youth are responsible for obtaining their own housing once they transition out of state care. Some of the biggest problems associated with housing are landlords unwilling to rent apartments to youth and unavailability of suitable housing. The FCIA has assisted with this challenge by extending funding for room and board through age twenty-one, though that level of funding is inadequate. Foster youth and former foster youth use a wide range of housing services (Kroner 1999). The services vary in terms of the amount of time youth can receive help, the ownership of the housing (i.e., a private landlord, private social service agency, or a public entity), and the level of supervision the youth receive.

The Chafee Program extends eligibility for state-financed health care through age twenty-one, at state discretion. Services provided in this area include those intended to prepare youth to manage their own medical needs and connect youth with appropriate health/mental health resources in their own communities. In addition, some programs provide services, particularly behavioral health services, directly to youth.

Some independent living services focus on improving the human capital of foster youth and former foster youth. Programs that focus on educational outcomes provide services that assist youth with accessing necessary educational resources, increase their literacy, help them select a career field or sectors of interest, connect them with educational/vocational programs, or provide an educational/vocational program.

A youth's success in obtaining and maintaining self- or family-supporting employment after leaving care may be significantly related to the quality of employment training and experience gained while in care. Programs offer a variety of employment-related services including providing youth opportunities for career exploration, helping youth develop educational and career plans, providing career-related work experience, connecting youth with career role models, and building partnerships with local educational institutions, industries, and employment programs.

Our description of the range of services funded by the Chafee Program should not lead the reader to believe that these services are available to all foster youth and former foster youth. On the contrary, the best U.S. government estimates suggest that two-fifths of eligible foster youth do not receive independent living services (U.S. GAO 1999). Even of those who do receive services, it is likely that very few receive the range of services described above, though available research suggests that many need all of them. Moreover, service availability varies widely among states and even among counties within states (Sheehy et al. 2001).

Opportunities Stemming from the Foster Care Independence Act

The FCIA is a considerable improvement over the former ILP. It represents a doubling of federal funding for independent living services and does not require states to increase their level of support in order to access these additional dollars. In percentage terms, this is the largest increase ever made in a major federal child welfare funding stream. Like the ILP, FCIA funding is an entitlement and therefore does not require an annual congressional appropriation. The influx of funds has led to a new round of program development and experimentation around the country.

Allowing states to spend some of the new funds on housing for youth between eighteen and twenty-one is a major improvement over the previous law. Almost all advocates for foster youth and independent living service providers believe that housing support is essential for helping many youth achieve independence. They point out that it can be difficult to engage youth in other supports, such as employment and education programs, when they do not have stable housing. Similarly, the educational deficits of these youth make the availability of education and training vouchers helpful.

Another significant policy shift is the provision of federal reimbursement for the costs of Medicaid coverage for former foster youth between the ages of eighteen and twenty-one. Prior to this change in federal policy, former foster youth could receive Medicaid only if they were eligible for other reasons (e.g., poor young women with children), meaning that few were eligible. As the literature review above points out, former foster youth have a variety of continuing mental and physical health needs. Their traumatic backgrounds make it especially important that they have consistent access to mental health services, but research suggests discontinuities in their mental health care. For example, Courtney et al. (2001) found that former foster youth were less than half as likely to use mental health services after discharge from out-of-home care as they were while they were in care, despite the fact that they exhibited no improvement over time in their relatively poor mental health status.

The new focus on outcomes monitoring and program evaluation is a welcome feature of the FCIA. As U.S. GAO (1999) pointed out, few states had made any effort to assess the adult functioning of their former wards in the policy context of the old ILP; the most notable exception is the follow-up study by the state of Wisconsin (Courtney et al. 2001). The FCIA is the first federal child welfare legislation that specifies measures of well-being for states to monitor. Moreover, the allocation of funds that must be used to rigorously evaluate independent living services provides hope that the field may be guided in the future by more than "practice wisdom" alone.

Challenges Facing the New Policy Regime

In spite of the improvements in policy represented by the FCIA, there remain many gaps in support for former foster youth, both because of the limitations of the law itself and because of how it is likely to be implemented by states and localities. Although $140 million represents a significant increase in funding for independent living services, this is still a small amount when compared to the size of the eligible population. Putting aside the fact that the FCIA allows states to use Chafee Program funds to provide services to youth under the age of sixteen, as of September 2001 there were 100,056 youth sixteen or over in out-of-home care (U.S. Department of Health and Human Services 2003). Thus, approximately $1,400 were available per year per eligible youth, hardly enough to provide the array of services envisioned in the legislation. Moreover, this estimate of the eligible population only includes those youth living in out-of-home care. In other words, it leaves out those youth over eighteen who have aged out or otherwise left care.

If approximately 20,000 youth per year age out of care, and therefore about 60,000 youth are eligible for housing assistance during any given year, then if states spent the maximum of 30 percent of Chafee Program funds on transitional housing (i.e., $42 million) they would have $700 per person to spend. Clearly, this would not go far in the urban areas where the vast majority of former foster youth live. Even if only one quarter of former foster youth needed housing assistance, this would leave only about $2,800 per person. Of course, these calculations rely on the unrealistic assumption that there is no cost of administering Chafee Program funds and that every dollar would go directly to the youth themselves.

At least the basic funding for the FCIA is an entitlement for the time being. Although the law currently includes a mechanism for funding educational and training vouchers for foster youth, this benefit is limited by the willingness of Congress to allocate the necessary funds. Given the federal budget outlook for the next several years it appears unlikely that Congress will fully fund these vouchers. Ultimately, success of the FCIA in achieving its stated goals will require significantly more funding than provided in current law.

Actual implementation of the FCIA is likely to fall far short of the hopes of advocates for several additional reasons. First, only a few states have chosen to extend Medicaid eligibility to former foster youth (Eilertson 2002). This ensures that many foster youth will still experience potentially harmful discontinuities in their health and mental health care when they leave the child welfare system. This is a shortsighted state-level policy. For example, a number of states have begun to use Medicaid to fund community-based alternatives to expensive institutional care for emotionally disturbed adolescents in out-of-home care, but they do not always provide the same range of services to adults. States that extend Medicaid eligibility to former foster youth can maintain youth in such "wrap-around" service programs while sharing the cost with the federal government instead of cutting off services when youth reach eighteen and running the risk that the youth will suffer unnecessarily and need hospitalization solely at state expense.

Second, poor integration and coordination of independent living services for foster youth with the efforts of other public institutions continues to plague this field of social services provision. To be sure, former foster youth are eligible for whatever services exist in a given community for poor young adults who face challenges making the transition to adulthood (e.g., vocational rehabilitation services for persons with disabilities). However, in many jurisdictions, child welfare agencies attempt to reinvent the wheel by providing services that are not within their realm of expertise. For example, many public agencies either provide directly or fund through private contracts employment services for foster youth instead of working with existing workforce development agencies that have seasoned staff and longstanding relationships with local employers. Similarly, the influx of funding for transitional housing has led some public child welfare agencies to attempt to develop new housing programs on their own or with traditional residential care providers instead of working with existing providers of services to runaway and homeless youth. Ironically, because few child welfare agencies have historically had funding for transitional housing, runaway and homeless youth service providers pioneered the creation of transitional housing programs that served foster youth among other at-risk youth populations.

Compounding the fact that child welfare agencies have limited experience providing support for education, employment, and transitional housing is the fact that the institutions traditionally charged with these roles are not always eager to be of assistance to youth transitioning out of foster care. Ensuring that foster youth have at their disposal the range of services that will maximize their potential for success will require more coordination of services than currently takes place. This is particularly true in rural areas, where child welfare agencies seldom operate on the scale necessary to support a wide range of independent living services.

A third challenge to the effective implementation of the FCIA is the poor knowledge base supporting independent living services. Program managers want to know what works in helping foster youth successfully transition to adulthood, but answers are hard to come by. Although the field of youth services has developed a set of general youth development principles in recent years, remarkably little empirical evidence exists to support particular independent living services. A recent review of research on the effectiveness of independent living services for foster youth came to the following conclusions:

Because of the paucity of studies that evaluate the effectiveness of independent living programs and the numerous methodological limitations of those that do exist, no definitive statement can be made about program effectiveness. Even less is known about the effectiveness of independent living programs with respect to specific populations. Only a focused and sustained program of rigorous evaluation research will remedy this situation. This research will need to involve experimental designs, larger samples than have been employed in the past, and better measurement of both the interventions and outcomes of interest. (Courtney and Bost 2002, 24)

Perhaps the most important limitation of current policy is its target population. As we noted at the beginning of this chapter, few youth actually age out of the child welfare system, yet this population is the primary focus of federal legislation. We believe that this is a problematic policy. A better approach would be to extend eligibility for services provided by the Chafee Program to a much broader group, perhaps all foster youth who spent time in out-of-home care after the age of sixteen. Consideration of the size and unique needs of the broader population of foster youth approaching adulthood helps illustrate the unintended consequences of current policy.

Many foster youth, even those who have been in out-of-home care for some time, are discharged from care to a member of their family of origin, usually a parent. This group dwarfs in size the group that ages out of care. Independent living service providers seldom reach out to these youth, even those that received independent living services while they were in care, assuming that the task of helping them manage the transition to adulthood has passed back to the family. Moreover, few service providers receive funds to serve these youth since they are not eligible for services funded through the FCIA. Yet at some point, generally not too long before sending them back home, society forcibly separated these same families from their children. Research suggests that many of these familial relationships are tenuous at best and that many of these youth will find themselves in need of another place to live and other adults to rely on for advice before long. Sadly, practice and policy surrounding independent living services for foster youth still pays too little attention to the importance, whether positive or negative, of the families of these youth.

The failure to take account of family dynamics in designing policy in this area has yet another unfortunate consequence. In recent years, states have begun to have some success in creating new permanent families for older youth though adoption and subsidized guardianship. Foster parents are most commonly the adults who adopt or accept legal guardianship of these youth. Anecdotal evidence suggests that some legal advocates for children are advising foster parents against becoming adoptive parents or taking on legal guardianship of foster youth, lest the youth lose eligibility for independent living services such as housing subsidies and educational scholarships provided by state and local jurisdictions (Mark Testa, personal communication, May 14, 2002). For a number of years, adoption advocates have raised concerns about the ways that a focus on provision of independent living services can skew child welfare practice away from trying to find permanent homes for foster youth. Current federal law renders ineligible for independent living services youth who exit care to adoption or subsidized guardianship. If this provision of the FCIA actually reduces the likelihood that foster parents will take on legal responsibility for the youth in their care, this would be a most unwanted outcome.

Lastly, what of the children who run away from out-of-home care in the year or so before reaching the age of majority? These youth may be the most at-risk of poor adult outcomes, and there are more of them than there are youth who age out of care. To be sure, this group can be very difficult to engage in services. Yet, as recent media reports point out, too often child welfare agencies make little or no effort to reconnect with these youth after they vote with their feet and leave out-of-home care (Anderson 2002; Kresnak 2002). This group may be the best source of information about what is missing from current efforts to engage foster youth in preparing for independence. At any rate, failure of the architects of independent living programs to try to reengage runaway foster youth and of policies to target their needs indicates a reluctance to serve the most needy foster youth.

One would be hard pressed to find an adolescent population in more need of help during the transition to independence than those approaching adulthood in the child welfare system. These youth are the victims of their own kin. Too often, when the state has stepped in to be their parent it has failed to do justice to this solemn responsibility. The current federal policy framework is not ideal. The resources devoted to helping this population are still inadequate. Still, there may now be enough support in place to allow some jurisdictions to set an example for others by finally treating these youth as if they truly were *our* children. Such examples might help build the political will necessary to make needed changes in federal policy.

APPENDIX

STUDIES OF POSTDISCHARGE OUTCOMES

Citation	Study type	Sample	Data sources	Data studied	Attrition rate
Van Senden Theis 1924	Retrospective without a comparison group	n = 797 adults, ages 18–40, who had been in foster care with the New York State Charities Aid Association between 1898 and 1922. Of these, 562 remained in out-of-home care until adulthood, while 235 were adopted by foster parents.	Observation, interviews, agency records	Self-support, education, criminality	Not reported
McCord, McCord, and Thurber 1960	Prospective with a comparison group	n = 38 adults in their early 30s, 19 of whom had been in out-of-home care. Subjects were involved in the Cambridge-Somerville Youth Study, a delinquency study of 255 urban boys from lower-class families between 1937 and 1945, when the children were 9–17 years of age.	Direct observations made during the subjects' childhoods, records of adult deviant behavior	Criminality, alcoholism, mental health	21%
Meier 1965	Retrospective without a comparison group	n = 66 young adults who had been in foster care in Minnesota for at least five years and had not been returned home, and who had been discharged between July 1, 1948, and December 31, 1949.	Interviews, questionnaires	Homemaking, living arrangements, employment and economic circumstances, health, marriage, parenting, social relationships, sense of well-being and social effectiveness	20%

Study	Design	Sample	Data source	Outcome measures	Percentage
Allerhand, Weber, and Haug 1966	Retrospective without a comparison group	n = 50 boys who had been discharged from a residential treatment center for emotionally disturbed chidren. Subjects were located two years after discharge, at the average age of 18.	Agency records, interviews	Adaptation (behavior, role-fulfillment and role consistency) and adaptability (intrapsychic balance)	4%
Robins 1966	Retrospective with a comparison group	n = 524 child guidance clinic patients, 16 percent of whom had lived in foster homes and 16 percent in orphanages for at least six months	Interviews	School problems and achievement, marital history, adult relationships, military service, job history, history of arrests and imprisonments, financial dependency, geographic moves, history of deviant behavior, physical and psychiatric diseases, alcohol and drug use, intellectual level, cooperativeness, willingness to talk, frankness, and mood	21%
Harari 1980	Retrospective without a comparison group	n = 34 adults ages 17–23 who had exited from foster family care as adolescents	Questionnaire, interviews	Interpersonal affect and self-esteem scales from the Jackson Personality Inventory	60%
Pettiford 1981	Retrospective with a comparison group	n = 614 former foster youth	Listing of all youth discharged from foster care, public assistance rolls	Dependency on public assistance	56%

Citation	Study type	Sample	Data sources	Data studied	Attrition rate
Zimmerman 1982	Retrospective without a comparison group (limited normative data)	n = 61 young adults, ages 19–29, who were in foster care in New Orleans between 1951 and 1969 for at least 12 months and had not been adopted.	Interviews	Housing status, educational attainment, employment history, income, social support, life satisfaction, family life and relationships, physical and mental health, views regarding foster care experience	64%
Festinger 1983	Retrospective without a comparison group (normative data provided)	n = 277 young adults, ages 22–25, who had been in New York's foster care system for at least five years.	Interviews, questionnaires	Education, employment, welfare dependence, marriage, partnership, children, social support, community participation, health, substance abuse, trouble with the law, and perceptions of well-being	54%
Frost and Jurich 1983	Retrospective without a comparison group	n = 96 previous residents of a long-term residential care center for abused and neglected children ages 6–18. All subjects had been in care at least six months.	Subjects' case files, questionnaires, interviews	Educational attainment, employment history and financial stability, relationship formation, criminal behavior, contact with welfare offices, hobbies and other activities, opinion of the care they received	46%

Study	Design	Sample	Data source	Outcomes measured	
Jones and Moses 1984	Retrospective without a comparison group (limited normative data)	n = 38 adults who had been in foster care in West Virginia for at least one year	Interviews	Education, employment, welfare dependence, living arrangements, health, family and social relationships, criminal justice involvement, and experiences in out-of-home care	48%
Fanshel, Finch, and Grundy 1990	Retrospective without a comparison group	n = 106 adults in their 20s and 30s who had been placed in Casey Family foster homes between 1966 and 1984 for a mean of 4.7 years.	Agency records, interviews	Housing, income, education, employment, marriage, parenting, crime, emotional health, social support, and substance abuse	41%
Barth 1990	Retrospective without a comparison group	n = 55 young adults, ages 17–26, who had been emancipated from foster care between the ages of 16 and 19.5.	Interviews	Housing, income, employment, education, criminal activity, contact with foster and/or birth families, physical and mental health, access to health care, substance abuse, satisfaction with foster care and preparation for independent living	25%

Citation	Study type	Sample	Data sources	Data studied	Attrition rate
Cook, Fleischman, and Grimes 1991	Retrospective without a comparison group	n = 810 former foster youth in seven states and the District of Columbia, ages 18–23, with a median time in care of 2.5 years	Interviews	Employment, education, income sources, housing, parenthood, social support, health care, and drug and alcohol use	51%
Cook 1992	Retrospective with a comparison group	n = 107 noninstitutionalized former foster children over age 19 with an average age of 37 and an average length in placement of 7 years	1988 National Survey of Families and Households	Life happiness, self-esteem, depression, marital happiness, parental relations, social isolation	34% overall (not reported for foster care group)
English, Kouidou-Giles, and Plocke 1994	Retrospective with a comparison group	n = 431 youth age 16 or older in Washington State in 1990. Subjects were in foster care for over six months.	Case files, caregiver interviews, youth telephone interviews	Placement history, assessment of independent living skills (education, employment, housing, ability to manage money)	14%
Dworsky and Courtney 2000	Retrospective without a comparison group	n = 6,274 former foster youth who were at least 17 years old when they were discharged from Wisconsin's out-of-home care system.	Unemployment insurance files, Client Assistance for Reemployment and Economic Support (CARES)	Employment, earnings, public assistance	Not applicable

Courtney et al. 2001	Prospective without a comparison group	Wave 1: n = 141 foster youth, ages 17–18; wave 2: n = 113 members of the wave 1 group. Interviews were conducted 12–18 months after youth were discharged from foster care.	Interviews	Wave 1: Demographic characteristics, family background, history of maltreatment and reasons for placement, receipt of mental health or other social services, current health and mental health status, education, employment, delinquency, social support, foster care experiences and preparation for independent living; wave 2: living arrangements, income, employment, receipt of public assistance, education, health care needs, mental health, social support, trouble with the law, traumatic events such as physical or sexual assaults, and preparation for independent living	Wave 1: 5%; wave 2: 20%
Goerge et al. 2002	Retrospective with a comparison group	n = 4,213 foster youth who aged out of care in California, Illinois, and South Carolina	Unemployment insurance files, AFDC/TANF files	Employment and earnings	Not applicable

REFERENCES

Allerhand, M. E., R. E. Weber, and M. Haug. 1966. *Adaptation and adaptability: The Bellefaire follow-up study.* New York: Child Welfare League of America.

Altshuler, S. J. 1997. Foster children at school: Success or failure? *Adoption and Fostering* 14: 38–49.

Anderson, T. 2002. 500 foster kids missing. *Los Angeles Daily News,* October 1. Retrieved on October 27, 2002, from http://www.dailynews.com/Stories/0,1413,200_percent257E20954_percent257E896518,00.html.

Ayasse, R. H. 1995. Addressing the needs of foster children: The foster youth services program. *Social Work in Education* 17: 207–216.

Barth, R. 1990. On their own: The experiences of youth after foster care. *Child and Adolescent Social Work* 7: 419–440.

Barth, R., M. E. Courtney, J. D. Berrick, and V. Albert. 1994. *From child abuse to permanency planning: Child welfare services pathways and placements.* New York: Aldine de Gruyter.

Blome, W. W. 1997. What happens to foster kids: Educational experiences of a random sample of foster care youth and a matched group of non-foster care youth. *Child and Adolescent Social Work* 14: 41–53.

Bussey, M., L. Feagans, L. Arnold, F. Wulczyn, K. Brunner, R. Nixon, P. DiLorenzo, P. J. Pecora, S. A. Weiss, and A. Winterfeld. 2000. *Transition for foster care: A state-by-state data base analysis.* Seattle: Casey Family Programs.

Cohen, D. L. 1991. Foster youths said to get little help with educational deficits. *Education Week on the Web,* June 12, http//www.edweek.org/ew/vol-10.

Cook, R., E. Fleischman, and V. Grimes. 1991. *A national evaluation of Title IV-E foster care independent living programs for youth in foster care: Phase 2, Final Report Volume 1.* Rockville, MD: Westat.

Cook, S. K. 1992. *Long term consequences of foster care for adult well-being* (Ph.D. dissertation, University of Nebraska, Lincoln).

Courtney, M. E. 1998. The costs of child protection: Implications for welfare reform? *Future of Children* 8: 88–103.

Courtney, M. E., and R. P. Barth. 1996. Pathways of older adolescents out of foster care: Implications for independent living services. *Social Work* 41: 75–83.

Courtney, M. E., and N. Bost. 2002. *Review of literature on the effectiveness of independent living services.* Chicago: Chapin Hall Center for Children at the University of Chicago.

Courtney, M. E., I. Piliavin, A. Grogan-Kaylor, and A. Nesmith. 2001. Foster youth transitions to adulthood: A longitudinal view of youth leaving care. *Child Welfare* 6: 685–717.

Courtney, M. E., and S. Terao. 2002. *Classification of independent living services* (unpublished report). Chapin Hall Center for Children at the University of Chicago.

Dworsky, A., and M. E. Courtney. 2000. *Self-sufficiency of former foster youth in Wisconsin: Analysis of unemployment insurance wage data and public assistance data.* Madison, WI: IRP, found at http://aspe.os.dhhs.gov/hsp/fosteryouthW100/.

Eilertson, C. 2002. *Independent living for foster youth.* Washington: National Conference of State Legislatures.

English, D., K. Kouidou-Giles, and M. Plocke. 1994. Readiness for independence: A study of youth in foster care. *Children and Youth Services Review* 16: 147–159.

Fanshel, D., S. J. Finch, and J. F. Grundy. 1990. *Foster children in life course perspective.* New York: Columbia University.

Fanshel, D., and E. B. Shinn. 1978. *Children in foster care: A longitudinal investigation.* New York: Columbia University Press.

Festinger, T. 1983. *No one ever asked us: A postscript to foster care.* New York: Columbia University Press.

Finkelstein, M., M. Wamsley, and D. Miranda. 2002. *What keeps children in foster care from succeeding in school? Views of early adolescents and the adults in their lives.* New York: Vera Institute of Justice.

Fox, M., and K. Arcuri. 1980. Cognitive and academic functioning in foster children. *Child Welfare* 59: 491–496.

Frost, S., and A. P. Jurich. 1983. *Follow-up study of children residing in the Villages* (unpublished report). The Villages, Topeka, KS.

Furstenburg, F. F. and M. E. Hughes. 1995. Social capital and successful development among at-risk youth. *Journal of Marriage and Family* 57: 580–592.

Goerge, R., L. Bilaver, B. Joo Lee, B. Needell, A. Brookhart, and W. Jackman. 2002. *Employment outcomes for youth aging out of foster care.* Chicago: Chapin Hall Center for Children at the University of Chicago, found at http://aspe.os.dhhs.gov/hsp/fostercare-agingout02/

Harari, T. 1980. *Teenagers exiting from family foster care: A retrospective look.* (Ph.D. dissertation, University of California, Berkeley).

Jackson, S. 1994. Educating children in residential care and foster care. *Oxford Review of Education* 20: 267–279.

Jones, M. A., and B. Moses. 1984. *West Virginia's former foster children: Their experiences in care and their lives as young adults.* New York: Child Welfare League of America.

Kresnak, J. 2002. Photos of missing foster kids could go on state website. *Detroit Free Press,* September 13. Retrieved on October 27, 2002, from http://nl3.newsbank.com/nl-search/we/Archives?p_action=list&p_topdoc=11&p_maxdocs=210.

Kroner, M. J. 1999. *Housing options for independent living programs.* Washington: Child Welfare League of America.

Mangine, S., D. Royse, V. Wiehe, and M. Nietzel. 1990. Homelessness among adults raised as foster children: A survey of drop-in center users. *Psychological Reports* 67: 739–745.

McCord, J., W. McCord, and E. Thurber. 1960. The effects of foster home placement in the prevention of adult antisocial behavior. *Social Service Review* 34: 415–419.

McDonald, T. P., R. I. Allen, A. Westerfelt, and I. Piliavin. 1996. *Assessing the long-term effects of foster care: A research synthesis.* Washington: Child Welfare League of America.

Meier, E. G. 1965. Current circumstances of former foster children. *Child Welfare* 44: 196–206.

Mortimer, J. T., and R. W. Larson. 2002. Macrostructural trends and the reshaping of adolescence. Pp. 1–17 in *Changing adolescent experience: Societal trends and the transition to adulthood.* Edited by J. W. Mortimer and R. W. Larson. Cambridge: Cambridge University Press.

National Research Council, Panel on Research on Child Abuse and Neglect 1993. *Understanding child abuse and neglect.* Washington: National Academies Press.

Pettiford, P. 1981. *Foster care and welfare dependency: A research note.* New York: Human Resources Administration, Office of Policy and Program Development.

Robins, L. N. 1966. *Deviant children grown up: A sociological and psychiatric study of sociopathic personality.* Baltimore: Williams and Wilkins.

Rosenbach, M., K. Lewis, and B. Quinn. 2000. *Health care conditions, utilization, and expenditures of children in foster care.* Washington: Office of the Assistant Secretary for Planning and Evaluation, U.S. Department of Health and Human Services.

Sawyer, R. J., and H. Dubowitz. 1994. School performance of children in kinship care. *Child and Neglect* 18: 587–897.

Sheehy, A., E. Oldham, M. Zanghi, D. Ansell, P. Correia, and R. Copeland. 2001. *Promising practices: Supporting transition of youth served by the foster care system.* Portland, ME: Edmund S. Muskie Institute of Public Affairs.

Sosin, M., P. Coulson, and S. Grossman. 1988. *Homelessness in Chicago: Poverty and pathology, social institutions, and social change.* Chicago: University of Chicago, School of Social Service Administration.

Sosin, M., I. Piliavin, and H. Westerfelt. 1990. Toward a longitudinal analysis of homelessness. *Journal of Social Issues* 46: 157–174.

Stein, M. 1994. Leaving care: Education and career trajectories. *Oxford Review of Education* 29(3): 349–360.

Susser, E., E. L. Streuning, and S. Conover. 1987. Childhood experiences of homeless men. *American Journal of Psychiatry* 144: 1599–1601.

Susser, E., S. Lin, S. Conover, and E. Streuning. 1991. Childhood antecedents of homelessness in psychiatric patients. *American Journal of Psychiatry* 148: 1026–1030.

U.S. Department of Commerce, Bureau of the Census. 2002. *Current Population Survey* (unpublished data). Retrieved on January 30, 2003, from http://nces.ed.gov/programs/digest/d02/tables/dt186.asp.

U.S. Department of Health and Human Services, Administration for Children and Families, Administration on Children, Youth and Families, Children's Bureau. 2003. *The AFCARS report: Preliminary FY 2001 estimates as of March 2003.* Retrieved on February 6, 2004, from http://www.acf.hhs.gov/programs/cb/publications/afcars/report8.htm

U.S. Department of Health and Human Services, Administration on Children, Youth and Families. 2002. *Child maltreatment 2000.* Washington: U.S. Government Printing Office.

U.S. Department of Health and Human Services, Office of the Assistant Secretary for Planning and Evaluation. 2000. *Dynamics of children's movement among the AFDC, Medicaid, and foster care programs prior to welfare reform: 1995–1996.* Washington: U.S. Government Printing Office.

United States General Accounting Office. 1994. *Foster care: Parental drug abuse has alarming impact on young children.* Report no. GAO/HEHS-94-89. Washington: U.S. General Accounting Office.

United States General Accounting Office. 1995. *Foster care: Health needs of many young children are unknown and unmet.* Report no. GAO/HEHS-95-114. Washington: U.S. General Accounting Office.

United States General Accounting Office. 1999. *Foster care: Effectiveness of independent living services unknown.* Report no. GAO/HEHS-00-13. Washington: U.S. General Accounting Office.

Van Senden Theis, S. 1924. *How foster children turn out: A study and critical analysis of 910 children who were placed in foster homes by the State Charities Aid Association and who are now eighteen years of age or over.* New York: State Charities Aid Association.

Veit, C. T., and J. E. Ware, Jr. 1983. The structure of psychological distress and well-being in general populations. *Journal of Consulting and Clinical Psychology* 51: 730–742.

Wulczyn, F., and K. Brunner Hislop. 2001. *Children in substitute care at age 16: Selected findings from the Multistate Data Archive.* Chicago: Chapin Hall Center for Children at the University of Chicago.

Wulczyn, F., K. Brunner Hislop, and R. Goerge. 2000. An update from the Multistate Foster Care Data Archive: 1983–1997. Chicago: Chapin Hall Center for Children at the University of Chicago.

Zimmerman, R. B. 1982. Foster care in retrospect. New Orleans: School of Social Work, Tulane University.

CHAPTER THREE

The Transition to Adulthood for Adolescents in the Juvenile Justice System: A Developmental Perspective

HE LEN CHUNG, MICHELLE LITTLE, AND LAURENCE STEINBERG

The authors acknowledge the support of the John D. and Catherine T. MacArthur Foundation.

INTERVIEWER: *What do you want to be doing in five years, when you're twenty-two?*

SUBJECT: *I don't really know. I want to try and finish school in here [residential facility] before I leave so I can work for my old boss when I get out. The problem is that I don't know if he'll take me back after this. I heard that he hired someone else right after I got arrested. Someone in here told me that the program's good at hooking kids up with jobs when they leave, so I'm hoping that this will happen.*

Interview with an incarcerated juvenile offender

INTRODUCTION

Historically, professionals advertised two dismal findings about juvenile delinquency—that nothing works (i.e., youthful offenders cannot be rehabilitated) (e.g., Martinson 1974) and that there are no success stories (i.e., delinquents are destined for failure) (e.g., Farrington et al. 1988). According to forecasts, delinquents would exhibit poor adult outcomes (e.g., unemployment, welfare dependence, mental health problems), drain millions of dollars from social services agencies, and then pass their legacy of problems to the next generation of teenagers. Indeed, it is well-established that young offenders demonstrate a poor ability to adjust between the ages of eighteen and twenty-five—precisely during the years when most people gain the level of education and training needed for their future achievements (William T. Grant Foundation Commission on Work, Family and Citizenship 1988).

Today, professionals can advertise several encouraging findings—that juvenile offenders are not all destined for failure, that cost-effective treatments can work, and that success stories among ex-offenders do in fact exist (see Loeber and Farrington 1998). In particular, researchers have found that *successful* adults with prior involvement in the juvenile justice system often experience *turning points* in early adulthood that enable them to direct their lives in a positive direction (Laub, Nagin, and Sampson 1998).

Despite recent encouraging findings, young offenders continue to face significant challenges during their transition to adulthood. Practitioners and policy makers are just starting to understand the processes by which court-involved youth achieve healthy adult outcomes. This chapter tries to shed light on three important questions about the transition to adulthood for teenagers involved with the juvenile justice system: (1) what types of challenges do these youth face during the transition?; (2) why do certain individuals achieve positive turning points in early adulthood while others do not?; and (3) how can the juvenile justice system provide opportunities that support youths' achievement of healthy turning points and positive adult outcomes? Framing our discussion is the very important and difficult mission of the juvenile justice system—to deter crime while balancing the interests of public safety and the rehabilitation of individual adolescents. We draw specific attention to the very existence of a juvenile court and why its separation from the criminal system is so critical: adolescents have significant developmental needs that should be managed differently from the needs of adults. Because Altschuler (chapter 4) focuses on general juvenile justice system policy and programs that facilitate or hinder individuals' transition to adulthood, we discuss general principles of developmentally appropriate justice system responses to delinquent youth.

Our discussion is divided into three major parts. First, we describe the population of youths involved with the juvenile justice system and the problems that they are known to have during the transition to adulthood. We focus on domains such as education, employment, and family life and explain how court-involved adolescents show discouraging outcomes even when compared to other *vulnerable* populations. Second, we outline the capacities that youths need to achieve in order to become healthy and productive adults. We focus on the importance of psychosocial development during the transition to adulthood and highlight the role of context in facilitating the achievement of healthy outcomes. Third, we discuss the value of promoting positive development among young offenders and discuss obstacles faced by the juvenile court in trying to realize this goal. We pay particular attention to the plight of incarcerated adolescents and describe three challenges that practitioners and policy makers need to address if they want to help court-involved youth make a successful transition to adulthood.

ADOLESCENT OFFENDERS: SUPER-PREDATORS OR TROUBLED TEENS?

The U.S. juvenile justice system processes over 2.5 million juvenile arrests annually and makes decisions about nearly 5,000 delinquency cases every day. The system impacts the lives of some 8–10 percent of all American youths between the ages of ten and seventeen, a figure that has almost quadrupled within the last few decades (Puzzanchera et al. forthcoming). (See chapter 6 for Travis and Visher's discussion of policies associated with these trends.) In particular, court involvement disproportionately affects ethnic minority youth, especially African-American males. For example, while black youth make up about 15 percent of the general juvenile population, they account for about 30 percent of juvenile arrests and 45 percent of adolescents in residential placement. In contrast, while Caucasian and Hispanic teenagers account for about 80 percent of the general youth population, they account for about 65 percent of juvenile arrests and 40 percent of adolescents in residential facilities (Sickmund forthcoming). The overrepresentation of ethnic minority teenagers at the deep end of court involvement is evidenced not only by their confinement rates in juvenile facilities, but also by the disproportionate rates of their prosecution as adults (67 percent of juvenile defendants in adult court are black, and 60 percent of juveniles sent to adult prison are black; Bureau of Justice Statistics 1998).

Usually, the public perception of delinquency highlights the criminal and sometimes callous side of adolescent offenders—that they account for one in every five arrests in the United States and cause substantial economic, physical, and emotional hardships for their victims, the families of their victims (as well as their own families), and the larger community. The most damaging depictions of juvenile delinquents as *super-predators* or psychopaths-in-training arrived in the mid-1990s, following a period when youth violence in this country was at its highest in contemporary times. Such images caused citizens to fear for their safety and policy makers to get tough on crime, the idea being that punitive responses (e.g., incarceration, adult prosecutions) would keep dangerous youths off of the streets, prevent them from reoffending, and ultimately preserve public safety (Feld 1998).

The current reality is that the United States is not under attack by juvenile super-predators and that the rate of youth violence has been steadily decreasing since its peak in 1994 (Snyder forthcoming). All the while, there is cause for concern about a depiction of adolescent offenders that is usually not advertised to the public. It is the portrait of youths whose lives are marked by the accumulation of disadvantage and whose considerable problems are likely to continue into adulthood if left untreated (e.g., Sampson and Laub 1997). The image highlights the troubled and neglected aspects of these young offenders' lives—that they often struggle with multiple problems at home, school, and in their communities even before their first contact with the court, and that they often lack the individual, family, or neighborhood resources to improve their situations.

It is well-established, for example, that most juvenile offenders evince some combination of problems that are likely to compromise positive youth development: poor school performance (e.g., truancy, low grades), mental health problems (e.g., substance abuse, depression), unstable and unsupportive family relationships, poverty- and crime-ridden communities, delinquent peer influences, and the absence of positive role models (Hawkins et al. 1998). It is also well established that these problems can create significant developmental challenges during the transition to adulthood, precisely when young offenders are learning to take on mature roles and responsibilities in society (Moffitt et al. 2002).

LINK BETWEEN COURT INVOLVEMENT AND ADULT OUTCOMES FOR YOUNG OFFENDERS

In the companion chapter, Altschuler notes that the juvenile justice system plays a vital role during the transition to adulthood for two related reasons: (1) correctional experiences can impact individual development during the adolescent years; and (2) in many states, adolescent offenders can and do remain under juvenile correctional authority into their adult years. Two particular judicial decisions have a significant impact on the nature of youths' involvement with the justice system during the adolescent and early adult years: whether a case is handled by the juvenile court or transferred to the adult criminal system, and the type of sentence or disposition adolescents are required to complete. In chapter 4 Altschuler discusses how juveniles are transferred to the adult court, and in chapter 5 Uggen and Wakefield describe the challenges that individuals face as members of the criminal justice system. The juvenile court generally makes decisions about where a youth is processed and how he or she is sentenced based on factors related to amenability to treatment, the adolescent's potential threat to the safety of others, and the need for mental health services. Typical factors considered in these decisions include the youth's age, current offense, past delinquent history, family situation, and psychological history. Ultimately, these decisions dictate major outcomes for young offenders in terms of where they live, the requirements of their court participation, the types of services that they receive, and the people with whom they interact.

Of the near 1.7 million delinquency cases processed by the juvenile court in 1999, about 57 percent were handled formally through petitions via the juvenile court system. Of these petitioned cases, about 7,000 (1 percent) were transferred to the adult criminal court and almost 650,000 (66 percent) resulted in youths being judged delinquent for their crimes by the juvenile justice system. Among those found delinquent, about 400,000 (62 percent) were placed on probation, 160,000 (24 percent) were ordered to some type of residential placement (e.g., juvenile correctional facility, residential treatment center, group home), and 63,000 (10 percent) were given other court sanctions such as paying fines or restitution (OJJDP Statistical Briefing Book 2002). While the provision of services for adolescent offenders is not well-documented, it is safe to assume that most delinquent youth experience a combination of sanctions throughout their involvement with the juvenile court (e.g., placement in a residential facility followed by probation upon release, probation in the community along with payment of fines). It is also safe to assume that court requirements follow many individuals into their adult years. In 1997, for example, almost 15,000 of the residents in juvenile residential facilities were between the ages of eighteen and twenty years old (Sickmund 2000).

Considering that many young offenders can and do remain under juvenile correctional authority into adulthood, surprisingly few studies have examined the impact of juvenile court decisions on the adult outcomes of young offenders. What professionals do know is that delinquent youth, as a group, typically show poor adjustment and lag behind their peers on traditional markers of adult success. For example, adolescent offenders are notorious for experiencing educational failure and having problems securing later employment. According to one study, only 12 percent of formerly incarcerated youth (74 percent less than the national average) received their high school diploma or General Equivalency Degree (GED) as young adults (Habermann and Quinn 1986; National Center for Education Statistics 2001). This finding has significant implications because educational attainment is so strongly linked to both employment and earnings. It is estimated, for example, that only 11 percent of high school dropouts have jobs that pay over $300 per week, and that over their working lives, high school dropouts will earn about $212,000 less than people who have a diploma or GED and $812,000 less than those with a four-year college degree (Rentner, Jennings, and Halperin 1994). Not surprisingly, in light of their educational deficiencies, incarcerated adolescents have trouble finding employment as adults, and their contact with the justice system has lasting adverse effects on their legal earnings (Fagan and Freeman 1999; Freeman 1992;

Wolfgang, Thornberry, and Figlio 1987). Studies show that delinquent youth are at least seven times more likely than their nondelinquent counterparts to show a history of adult unemployment and welfare dependence (Sampson and Laub 1990), and that men without prior arrest records earn 15 percent more annually than men with at least one conviction in their past (Grogger 1995).

The problems that juvenile offenders have as adults extend beyond the domains of education and employment and into spheres like criminal behavior, psychological health, and interpersonal relationships. More specifically, almost half of incarcerated juvenile offenders end up returning to the justice system after they are released (Bullis et al. 2002); the ones who do not return (as well as the ones who do) often experience serious adjustment problems such as interpersonal troubles and mental health disorders, particularly substance dependence (Moffitt et al. 2002). Within the population of juvenile offenders, those who report relatively higher rates of delinquent behavior are especially at risk for poor adult outcomes; they are five times more likely to be arrested between the ages of seventeen and twenty-five, nearly seven times more likely to be arrested later in adulthood, three to five times more likely to be divorced (if they were ever married), and more likely to father multiple unexpected, and often unwanted, children (Moffitt et al. 2002; Sampson and Laub 1990).

Juvenile offenders show worrisome adult outcomes even when compared to other *vulnerable* groups, including other populations whose transitional difficulties are discussed in this volume. The most discouraging comparisons are in the domains of educational attainment and employment, where in a recent study of teenagers "on the outs"—a term used by young offenders to describe their transition from residential facilities back to the community—only about 30 percent of young adults were engaged in either school or work twelve months after their release (Bullis et al. 2002). Bullis and his colleagues contrasted this statistic with engagement levels of 65 percent for adolescents exiting programs for emotional disturbances and 75 percent for those leaving special education programs. The authors did not speculate about why juvenile justice youth show especially poor engagement rates compared to other groups, but did note that individuals with special education disabilities fared worse than their peers without disabilities.

IMPORTANCE OF PSYCHOLOGICAL DEVELOPMENT FOR MAKING A SUCCESSFUL TRANSITION TO ADULTHOOD

In recent years, many professionals have turned their attention to the so-called resilient adolescent offenders, those who show successful adult outcomes such as desistance from criminal activity, movement away from a deviant lifestyle, and the development of productive patterns of activity in family and work roles (Sampson and Laub 1993). While researchers are not clear about how many delinquent youth fall into this category, studies have found that some ex-offenders experience *turning points* during late adolescence and early adulthood that help them to move in a positive direction after their experiences with the justice system. For these resilient individuals, the most important factor for the achievement of turning points is the development of supportive relationships with peers or adults, such as a girlfriend or boyfriend in the neighborhood or a concerned counselor in a treatment facility. The supportive social bonds that develop in these relationships are thought to serve as a form of social capital because the relationships can provide young offenders with valuable resources as they strive to take on adult roles and responsibilities—emotional resources such as encouragement, educational resources such as information about getting into college, or occupational resources such as job advice (see also Hagan 1993). It is believed that these resources and related opportunities help to facilitate the transition to adulthood because they gradually pull young offenders out of a criminal lifestyle (especially criminal social networks) and get them involved with and invested in healthy activities such as employment, school, or parenthood (Laub, Nagin, and Sampson 1998).

For teenagers involved with the juvenile justice system, access to resources and opportunities are likely dictated (for better or worse) by their experiences with the court. When asked about taking on adult roles and responsibilities, Sean, a nineteen-year-old participant in an ongoing longitudinal study of juvenile offenders (Mulvey, Cauffman, and Steinberg 2003), described his situation as an "uphill battle":

SEAN: I want to finish high school but by the time I got home [after being locked up for 10 months], I couldn't get re-enrolled. I'm thinking of not going back and just working full-time. Luckily, my P.O.'s been real helpful and found a place where I can work even if I don't get my degree or GED.

INTERVIEWER: Are you worried at all about the future?

SEAN: The main thing is that I'm not sure I'm any good at living on my own, you know, doing adult stuff. I've been in and out of different placements for so long, and I'm not sure I'll know what I'm doing out there, if I'll make good decisions.

While Sean identified his probation officer (P.O.) as an important resource for finding a job, he directed attention to a concern about not being *ready*, or in some way prepared, to take on the responsibilities likely to accompany his transition to adulthood. Indeed, in their seminal studies of delinquent youth, Glueck and Glueck (1974) found that it was not the achievement of any particular age or event, but rather the achievement of "adequate maturation" that helped individuals change their deviant ways and adopt adultlike responsibilities. To date, juvenile justice practitioners and policy makers have devoted little attention to understanding this process of maturation, perhaps because it is assumed that young offenders will naturally achieve *adequate* levels of maturity as they get older and enter the adult world (see Moffitt 1993). What is sorely missing from our understanding of delinquent youths' transition to adulthood is a focus on psychological development, specifically a focus on how young offenders develop a level of maturity that helps them to become healthy and productive adult members of society.

In this chapter, we discuss the maturation process in terms of psychosocial capacities that help adolescents make a successful transition to adulthood. We consider these capacities to be a specific and under-studied component of human capital, "psychosocial capital," if you will, because they provide resources for individuals to create and take advantage of positive life experiences. If we want to improve adult outcomes for delinquent youth, we need to understand not only what characterizes successful ex-offenders with respect to their roles and activities (e.g., employment, freedom from drugs) or in terms of the social bonds that help them to desist from delinquent activity (e.g., having a supportive relationship with a P.O.), but also the factors that underlie these outcomes (National Research Council 1993). In other words, we need to understand the processes that help young offenders *become* healthy and productive adults.

To understand the impact of court involvement on the transition to adulthood for young offenders, we take a close look at what it takes to become a successful adult in U.S. society and the experiences of adolescents involved with the juvenile justice system. Three principles serve to guide our discussion: (1) important psychosocial capacities develop during late adolescence that permit the successful transition into adult roles and responsibilities; (2) the development of psychosocial capacities is greatly influenced by the context in which it takes place (e.g., family, peer group, school, and, for many delinquent youth, correctional facilities); and (3) by facilitating the psychosocial development of young offenders, juvenile justice practitioners and policy makers can improve the odds that delinquent youth will experience positive turning point opportunities and go on to become successful adults.

WHAT IT TAKES TO BECOME A SUCCESSFUL ADULT

Making the successful transition from the dependency of adolescence to the self-sufficiency of adulthood is a process that requires the coordination of many skills. These capacities are epitomized in a concept called psychosocial maturity (e.g., Greenberger 1984) and require development across three important domains: mastery and competence, interpersonal relationships and social functioning, and self-definition and self-governance (see Steinberg 2002). In order to achieve sufficient psychosocial maturity, and along with it the capacities to function as independent and productive adults, individuals in contemporary industrialized society need to complete a series of developmental tasks in each of these three areas. A healthy transition to adulthood is optimally supported when these tasks are completed between the ages of sixteen and twenty-four, a transitional period that spans the years of late adolescence and early adulthood. It is important to first describe these developmental tasks in some detail in order to ask whether and in what ways experiences within the juvenile justice system can facilitate or hinder successful psychosocial development.

With regard to *mastery and competence,* by the end of the transitional period mature individuals are expected to have developed the knowledge and skills necessary to understand, participate in, and enjoy society's activities of production, leisure, and culture. They are expected to have achieved levels of education and vocational training so that they can learn to function as productive members of society. With regard to *interpersonal relationships and social functioning,* by the end of the transition mature individuals are expected to have the social skills necessary to interact appropriately with others and be able to establish and maintain intimate relationships that are satisfying to themselves and their partners. They are expected to function cooperatively and collaboratively in groups and to feel, as well as to exercise, responsibility toward the larger community in which they live. With regard to *self-definition and self-governance,* by the time they enter their midtwenties, mature individuals are expected to have developed a positive sense of their own worth as individuals and the capacity to behave responsibly and morally in the absence of externally imposed supervision. They are expected to be independent and know how to set and achieve personal goals that are meaningful to them (see, e.g., Greenberger and Sorensen 1974). Although it is not expected that these tasks will be completed by the end of adolescence, it is expected that individuals will make significant headway in each of the three domains before they move into their early adult years (Erikson 1980).

In general, researchers have found that people who show high versus low levels of psychosocial maturity (e.g., can relate well to others, are able to secure or keep a job, can successfully manage their day-to-day lives without an adult to oversee their actions, etc.) make more socially responsible decisions and show healthier outcomes as young adults (Greenberger 1982; Steinberg and Cauffman 1996). It is reasonable to assume that psychosocially mature individuals are successful during the transition precisely because they are prepared to handle the roles and responsibilities that accompany adulthood—roles and responsibilities that, in contemporary society, require interpersonal skills, instrumental competence, and responsible autonomy. In particular, mature individuals have presumably established personal goals for themselves, as well as developed the abilities to create opportunities that are consistent with these goals (e.g., because they are competent enough to get the job that they want) and profit from the experiences (e.g., because they are responsible enough to maintain the job). In these ways, psychosocially mature individuals are able to manage their environment in such a way that that they can create and capitalize on positive experiences.

It is well-established that successful completion of the developmental tasks of late adolescence and early adulthood reflects interactions between individuals and their social environments (Bronfenbrenner 1979). To date, the contexts that have received the most research attention are the family and peer group. A large body of research suggests that caring, committed, and supportive parents or guardians play a significant role in facilitating individuals' healthy psychosocial development (for a review, see Collins and Laursen 2004). Specifically, such adults who actively advocate for adolescents (e.g., introduce them to potential employers, present them with job opportunities) improve the chances that they will be invested in and prepared to take on adult roles and responsibilities (Furstenberg et al. 1999). The peer group context also has a significant impact on the transition to adulthood because the social support found in peer groups can not only accentuate the beneficial impact of a supportive home environment but also compensate for family relationships that are not sufficiently supportive (for a review, see Brown 2004). In particular, peer support can be important for leading adolescents toward adult-approved activities and deterring them from antisocial behavior.

Outside of the family and peer settings, characteristics of the broader community context like the school, workplace, and neighborhood environment can have significant impacts on youths' psychosocial development and, ultimately, their successful transition into adult roles and responsibilities (see Graber, Brooks-Gunn, and Petersen 1996). In general, while fostering academic skills, the school setting can give youth opportunities to forge relationships with positive role models (e.g., teachers), interact with prosocial peers, and experiment with extracurricular activities (Eccles and Templeton 2002). The work setting, while providing vocational skills, can provide youth with opportunities to establish a path to financial independence, learn about expectations that society has for adults, and experience the positive consequences of exercising responsible behavior (e.g., getting a raise for successful job performance) (Greenberger and Steinberg 1981). The neighborhood setting, while offering job opportunities, can also provide adolescents with access to resources such as youth groups in which adolescents can develop social competence, prosocial peer networks, and values about civic commitment (for a review, see Leventhal and Brooks-Gunn 2004). Indeed, research has shown that participation in structured and goal-oriented extracurricular activities, work experiences, and community programs is related to positive adolescent outcomes such as low levels of problem behaviors, high degrees of academic success, and high levels of psychosocial maturity (National Research Council and Institute of Medicine 2002).

Ideally, during late adolescence and early adulthood, individuals get to live and participate in social settings that help them to carve out their personal identities, decide what values and activities are important to them, and develop the interpersonal, educational, and occupational skills needed to achieve their goals as adults. Contexts like the family, peer group, school, and workplace serve as important learning environments because they provide individuals with opportunities and resources that prepare them to take on mature roles and responsibilities. Making a successful transition to adulthood is a process that, under the best of circumstances, is promoted by the support and protection of adults, a sense of purposefulness about the future, and the freedom to explore possible life directions in the realms of family, education, work, love, and friendship (Arnett 2000; Steinberg 2002).

THE REHABILITATIVE NEEDS OF ADOLESCENTS AND YOUNG ADULTS INVOLVED WITH THE JUVENILE JUSTICE SYSTEM

Considering the poor adult outcomes that are typical for adolescents involved with the juvenile justice system, it is reasonable to assume that many delinquent youth are psychosocially ill-prepared to make a successful transition to adulthood. This is not to say that the juvenile justice system causes poor adult outcomes or that the system should be solely responsible for improving them; however, an important mission of juvenile justice is indeed to provide treatment and rehabilitative services to young offenders (see Tolan and Gorman-Smith 1997). As discussed in the companion chapter by Altschuler (chapter 4), the contemporary juvenile court has moved away from a rehabilitative focus and made increasing commitments to ideals that mirror the more punitive, deterrence-oriented adult criminal justice system. The shift toward a "get tough" mode of juvenile justice is particularly evident in statistics showing how adolescents have been processed by the juvenile court in recent years—for example, adolescents are now being detained and incarcerated for less serious crimes, and juveniles are being transferred to the adult criminal court at younger ages (Sickmund forthcoming).

To better understand the link between juvenile justice decisions and the adult outcomes of young offenders, three issues are important to consider: (1) how juvenile justice programming influences individuals' ability to complete developmental tasks of late adolescence and early adulthood; (2) whether young offenders possess risk factors that can interfere with psychosocial development during the transition to adulthood; and (3) whether justice system responses expose individuals to harmful experiences that compromise their chances of becoming successful adults. We discuss each of these issues, while Altschuler (chapter 4) describes promising programs that demonstrate positive outcomes for young offenders.

Impact of Juvenile Justice Programming on Achievement of Psychosocial Maturity

Of the possible court sanctions (e.g., probation, restitution, community-based mental health services), incarceration may have the greatest impact on young offenders' ability to achieve psychosocial maturity. While periodic monitoring by probation officers and community programs can alter individuals' usual routines, incarceration leads to major adjustments in the relationships and activities that youths experience in their everyday environments (e.g., leaving family and friends, withdrawing from school, quitting a job in the neighborhood). In relocating to a residential placement, adolescents and young adults must live and participate in new learning environments and prepare for adult roles and responsibilities using resources that may be unfamiliar to them (e.g., finding support from a residential counselor instead of an adult in their neighborhood). As discussed by Altschuler, incarcerated youth also face significant challenges when they leave residential facilities and return to their communities because they are likely to experience some discontinuity of care between the institutional and noninstitutional settings.

In some cases, the services that individuals receive while incarcerated help them to achieve feelings of mastery, interpersonal competence, and self-governance. Tony, for example, an eighteen-year-old participant in an ongoing longitudinal study of juvenile offenders (Mulvey, Cauffman, and Steinberg 2003) described his placement as "just what was needed" to get his life on the right track. During a follow-up interview, Tony reported that after he completed his ten months at a residential facility, he chose to stay at the program to get his high school diploma. Tony stated that he was better off remaining in placement until graduation, rather than going home without a degree in hand. For Tony, going home meant returning to a dangerous neighborhood with too many distractions to focus on his schoolwork. He reported feeling ill-prepared to fight the street pressure of his old friends and stay focused enough to finish school and get a job. Tony stated that the facility was helping him to grow up and that the staff members were working to set up job contacts for him in his old neighborhood. He reported feeling more confident in his ability to be responsible, keep a job, surround himself with good people, and move his life in a positive direction.

During the interview, Tony reported feeling particularly prepared for employment because of completing what he considered to be valuable auto repair classes at the residential facility. Indeed, research suggests that correctional programming, which includes educational and vocational training components, contributes to positive adult adjustment among formerly incarcerated youth (e.g., lower rates of recidivism, higher rates of employment) (Lipsey and Wilson 1998). However, to the extent that some young offenders show poor adult outcomes for reasons other than educational deficiencies or a lack of job skills, training programs likely make a limited impact on young offenders' adjustment to adulthood. These programs may contribute to positive outcomes, for example, by helping youths master certain job skills or find employment, but the programs are not designed to *train* youths to be more psychosocially mature. Thus, an adolescent may learn the skills needed to fix a car while incarcerated, but he may return to the community and show that he lacks the responsibility to report to work on time or the interpersonal skills to get along with his coworkers and employer. As noted earlier, the achievement of psychosocial maturity is facilitated over time in an environment that promotes autonomy, self-direction, and social competence. Thus, it is through a better understanding of the social environments in which young offenders live and participate that practitioners and policy makers are likely to best prepare delinquent youth for the roles and responsibilities that accompany adulthood. We now briefly describe the impact of involvement with the juvenile justice system on young offenders' interactions within the family, peer group, and community contexts.

Research suggests that youths' involvement with the juvenile justice system can have a direct impact on the quality of relationships with their parents. Studies show that the stigma associated with formal legal sanctions (e.g., probation, incarceration) can initiate problems between youths and their parents, and, unfortunately, further deteriorate what is sometimes an already troubled relationship. Specifically, juvenile arrests can engender adults' shame and embarrassment about their own parenting skills and cause parents to react negatively towards their adolescents (e.g., become less trusting, more hostile, more controlling) (Ambert 1997; Conger and Simons 1997; Patterson, Reid, and Dishion 1992). A recent longitudinal study found that the negative impact of delinquency on parenting was fully explained by youths' experience of legal sanctions (Li 1999; Stewart et al. 2002), and that these sanctions predicted negative adult outcomes for young offenders (e.g., reconviction, poor achievement, unemployment).

One of the consequences of poor parent-adolescent relationships is that individuals may lose the support of their parents precisely during the time when parental support and advocacy can facilitate the transition to adulthood. The parent-adolescent relationship may be especially strained for incarcerated youth, as adolescents and their families face physical separation for long periods of time. Juvenile justice programming that works to preserve and improve the support of parents and other caring adults is likely to give young offenders the best chances of becoming healthy and productive adults. Indeed, autobiographical stories of ex-offenders suggest that the presence of adult role models, and in particular the development of relationships with supportive correctional professionals (e.g., counselors, staff members), is extremely important for helping them to desist from crime and get involved with healthy adult activities (Hughes 1998). As noted earlier, the active support of parents and other caring adults significantly improves the chances that youths will be invested in and prepared to take on mature roles and responsibilities.

Mounting evidence suggests that satisfying interpersonal relationships with peers are important for helping young offenders make a healthy adjustment to adulthood. Not surprisingly, maintaining interpersonal relationships can be especially difficult for adolescents who are ordered to residential placement. Relocations to facilities inevitably cause disruptions in peer relationships that for some young offenders may be the primary source of positive support. Unfortunately, incarcerated adolescents have little opportunity to forge alternative prosocial relationships while away from home; because their social interactions are under close scrutiny and their peers are typically other delinquent youth, incarcerated offenders usually have limited opportunities to socialize with and benefit from interactions with positive peers.

In addition to being cut off from important sources of healthy social development, incarcerated adolescents are likely exposed to the negative effects of associating with deviant peers. Several longitudinal studies have revealed that peer group interventions, a format that inherently aggregates adolescents with histories of antisocial behavior, actually result in increases of problem behavior (e.g., drug use, crime conviction) (Dishion, McCord, and Poulin 1999). This negative effect is related to the amount of time deviant peers spend together and the degree of social dysfunction and deviance among youths. The results of experimental studies suggest that the negative effects of this "deviancy training" persist over time, with perhaps worse outcomes seen in settings where especially deviant and dysfunctional youth are aggregated and segregated from less antisocial adolescents.

While providing incarcerated youth with adequate peer support is a tremendous challenge, it is a goal that can have positive effects on youths' psychosocial development and their outcomes as adults. Under the best of circumstances, young offenders gain access to on-site activities that promote cooperative effort, commitment, and sportsmanship among residents. In this way, although adolescents may not establish significant relationships with prosocial peers while detained, they have the opportunity to participate in activities that can foster interpersonal competence and social functioning. Ideally, young offenders exit the system having acquired values of cooperation and commitment among peers that they can apply to their relationships in the community as young adults. The positive influence of peer support on adult outcomes is especially true for romantic relationships, where quality marital bonds show a gradual and cumulative impact on young offenders' desistance from crime (Laub, Nagin, and Sampson 1998).

While a youth's arrest often signifies serious problems to friends, family, and neighbors, the social stigma and rejection associated with court involvement is especially salient for incarcerated youth, who are essentially cut off from their usual community activities and social networks (Moffitt 1993). Unfortunately, early criminal labeling can create serious obstacles for young offenders as they search for jobs, especially in businesses that focus on direct customer contact or relations (e.g., trade occupations, child care). Because employers sometimes resist hiring youths who are (or have been) involved with the juvenile justice system, the stigma of court involvement can have a lasting negative impact on individuals' ability to get a job and become financially stable as adults (Task Force on Employment and Training for Court-Involved Youth 2000). (See Lyons and Melton's discussion of stigma as an impediment for youth with mental health problems in chapter 11).

Not surprisingly, early criminal labeling has a psychological impact on young offenders' views of themselves. In looking at adolescent self-conceptions, Oyserman and Markus (1990) found indirect support for the link between criminal labeling and youths' orientation to the future. While nondelinquent youths reported a balance between fears and expectations for themselves, delinquent youths reported many more doubts than expectations. The long-term developmental impact of labeling can be tremendous, as youth may lose a sense of purposefulness about their future prospects and respond by withdrawing from conventional activities and seeking support and esteem from deviant peers and social networks (Hagan 1993). This process of social exclusion also takes place at a formal level, as correctional policies across America have made it exceedingly difficult for young offenders to participate in activities like qualifying for housing assistance or voting in elections (Travis, Solomon, and Waul 2001; see also Uggen and Wakefield, chapter 5).

As discussed in the previous section, youths' participation in healthy activities in the larger community (e.g., workplace, neighborhood) can have a beneficial impact on their psychosocial development during adolescence and early adulthood. Indeed, young offenders who receive mental health services in the community often report that their relationships with adult community members (e.g., neighbors, employers) help them to engage in positive activities like school or work, develop healthy goals and values, and gain skills that will help them to adjust to adult roles and responsibilities (see Huey and Henggeler 2001). In chapter 4, Altschuler notes that incarcerated adolescents face significant challenges as they return to their communities, as they are likely to experience some discontinuity of care (e.g., cessation of drug treatment once they leave correctional facilities). Thus, juvenile justice programming that strives to facilitate this transition can improve the chances that youth will maintain any gains made while incarcerated and go on to show healthy and productive adult outcomes in the community (e.g., Altschuler 1984).

Risk Factors That Interfere with Psychosocial Development

The second important issue that confronts juvenile justice practitioners and policy makers is a concern that has beset the system for many years—treating tremendous levels of unmet mental health needs within the young offender population. Although estimates vary, most studies indicate that mental disturbance among court-involved youth is three times as high as in the general adolescent population (Grisso 2004). According to such reports, more than 670,000 adolescents who are processed in the juvenile justice system each year would meet diagnostic criteria for one or more alcohol, drug, and/or mental disorder, as would nearly two-thirds of male and three-quarters of female detainees (Teplin 2002). In light of such statistics, many professionals argue that the juvenile justice system has become a de facto mental health service agency for disadvantaged, minority youth (Knitzer 1996).

Careful examination of the mental health needs of young offenders reflects complex and often severe emotional, behavioral, and learning problems. While it is not clear what percentage of delinquent youth possess learning disorders, incarcerated adolescents demonstrate significant academic deficits (e.g., reading, math, written and oral language), and perform well below others their age regardless of their intellectual abilities (Foley 2001). Rates of disruptive behavioral disorders are very high among young offenders (greater than 40 percent), a finding that is the same for both males and females in this population. Interestingly, the rates of affective disorders (e.g., depression, anxiety) are also considerably higher than the rates found in the general population (at least 25 percent among female detainees and nearly 20 percent among male detainees) (Teplin 2002). The mental health disorder that co-occurs most frequently by far with serious delinquency and likely causes the most significant problems for young offenders is substance use. Between 50 and 75 percent of incarcerated youth with mental health problems also experience troubles with drug dependence, a problem that is strongly linked to severe adjustment difficulties during adulthood (Cocozza 1997; Otto et al. 1992).

As other authors in this volume describe, untreated psychological and educational problems during adolescence can result in serious and costly psychiatric morbidity by adulthood (see Gralinski-Bakker, Hauser, Billings, and Allen, chapter 10, on challenges for youth in the mental health system, and Levine and Wagner, chapter 8, on challenges for youth involved with special education). With respect to adolescents involved with the juvenile justice system, one study found that young offenders with educational disabilities are less likely than their counterparts without such vulnerabilities to receive their high school diplomas and almost three times as likely to get rearrested and return to the juvenile justice system after their release from residential placement (Bullis et al. 2002; Foley 2001). Not surprisingly, young offenders with mental health needs are at particular risk of having trouble preparing for and adjusting to the demands of adult roles and responsibilities—things like graduating from high school, securing a job, and developing meaningful interpersonal relationships (Moffitt et al. 2002). Unfortunately, the juvenile justice system as it is currently designed is neither equipped nor philosophically driven to effectively address such psychological vulnerabilities among incarcerated youth (Cocozza and Skowyra 2000; Hecker and Steinberg 2002; Soler 2002).

Harmful Experiences that Compromise the Successful Transition to Adulthood

An issue of particular concern for incarcerated youth is that of protection from hazardous living conditions in residential placement (Snyder and Sickmund 1995). In a recent study, the Office of Juvenile Justice and Delinquency Prevention (OJJDP) found that 62 percent of all delinquent males reside in overcrowded facilities, and that overcrowding can strain available service resources within settings as well as foster tensions between and among staff members and residents (OJJDP Statistical Briefing Book 2002). Other studies have suggested that such tensions encourage harsh styles of control, including the use of restraints and isolation for managing misbehavior among residents (e.g., Parent et al. 1994). Specifically, some evaluations have reported that staff members use physical punishment and humiliation to punish adolescents and even fail to prevent fights, rapes, and other acts of violence between young inmates (Bartollas, Miller, and Dinitz 1976). The toll of hazardous living conditions is reflected in data indicating that during a one-month period residential programs across the United States witnessed 2000 physical injuries and 970 attempted suicides among young residents (Snyder, Sickmund, and Poe-Yamagata 1996).

Protection becomes an ever greater issue when adolescents are placed in facilities that house adult criminals alongside juvenile offenders. By one estimate at the end of 1997, 15,620 youths under the age of nineteen were serving time in adult correctional facilities, 1,484 of whom were under the age of sixteen (American Correctional Association 1998). The placement of juveniles in adult prisons not only puts youth into close contact with adults who have long antisocial histories, but also increases the chances that juveniles will experience or be exposed to incidents of violence. Studies show that adolescents in adult facilities, compared to youths in juvenile institutions, are twice as likely to be beaten by staff, one-and-a-half times as likely to be attacked with a weapon, five times as likely to be sexually assaulted, and almost eight times as likely to commit suicide (Forst, Fagan, and Vivona 1989).

While the link between court involvement and individuals' exposure to harm is not entirely clear, it is well-established that both the experience and observation of aggression and violence can disrupt normative psychosocial development, as well as cause or exacerbate psychological problems (Sampson and Lauritsen 1994). In one study of adolescent offenders, researchers found that exposure to violence was linked to higher levels of criminal offending, and sexual abuse was linked with psychiatric comorbidity (Brown et al. 1999). The fact that juveniles in adult prisons experience or are exposed to increased levels of violence is particularly worrisome, as few adult correctional agencies offer mental health services or even provide training to staff members, that target the needs of adolescents and young adults (Fagan and Zimring 2000).

CONCLUSIONS

Discussions of juvenile justice policy and practice seldom consider the psychosocial needs of late adolescents and young adults, focusing instead on the primary goal of deterring offenders from future criminal behavior and secondarily on facilitating the educational and occupational success of youths who are exiting from the justice system. As a consequence, current justice systems tend to emphasize punishment, which presumably promotes desistance, and academic or vocational training, which presumably facilitate future success in school and work. While punishment and training are important components of the justice system's response to juvenile offending, they alone are unlikely to significantly improve the poor adult outcomes that are typical for delinquent youth. In order to make a successful transition into adult roles and responsibilities, individuals need to enter adulthood with sufficient psychosocial maturity to make autonomous decisions, establish satisfying interpersonal relationships, maintain gainful employment, and exercise self-governance.

The considerable problems faced by young offenders after they exit the juvenile justice system suggest that they lack foundational psychosocial capacities that facilitate a smooth transition into adult roles. Put most bluntly, however, the context of juvenile justice intervention is one that is more likely to arrest individuals' development than promote it. The deficiency inherent in an overly punitive approach to juvenile justice (e.g., transferring juveniles to adult court at young ages) is that it generally fails to address the underlying psychosocial capacities that young offenders need to develop if they are to demonstrate responsible adult outcomes.

Our analysis suggests that we need to reexamine the goals and methods of the juvenile justice system from a developmental perspective if we are to understand how to facilitate the successful transition of juvenile offenders into healthy adult roles and responsibilities. Such a perspective identifies the specific psychosocial tasks of late adolescence and asks how their negotiation is facilitated by the context in which young people come of age. As we have suggested, the necessary conditions for successful psychosocial development in late adolescence and early adulthood include the presence of supportive adults as well as opportunities to develop responsible autonomy, acquire important competencies, and establish satisfying relationships with peers.

Facilitating the achievement of psychosocial maturity requires practitioners and policy makers not only to address factors that promote it (e.g., contextual factors like the support of caring adults or peers), but also factors that may hinder it (e.g., substance dependence, social stigma attached to arrest and incarceration). It may be unrealistic to think that a justice system, which must honor its responsibility to adequately punish youths for their crimes, can replicate the conditions known to facilitate healthy development among nonoffenders. It is not unrealistic, however, to expect that the system will honor its responsibility to not impede young offenders' development such that it compromises their chances of becoming healthy and productive members of society.

REFERENCES

Ambert, A. 1997. *Parents, children, and adolescents: Interactive relationships and development in context.* New York: Haworth.

American Correctional Association. 1998. *1998 Directory of juvenile and adult correctional department, institutions, agencies, and paroling authorities.* Lanham, MD: American Correctional Association.

Altschuler, D. M. 1984. Community reintegration in juvenile offender programming. Pp. 365–376 in *Violent juvenile offenders: An anthology.* Edited by R. Mathias, P. DeMuro, and R. Allinson. San Francisco: National Council on Crime and Delinquency.

Arnett, J. 2000. Emerging adulthood. *American Psychologist* 55: 469–480.

Bartollas, C., S. J. Miller, and S. Dinitz. 1976. *Juvenile victimization: The institutional paradox.* New York: Wiley.

Bronfenbrenner, U. 1979. *The ecology of human development: Experiments by nature and design.* Cambridge: Harvard University Press.

Brown, B. 2004. Adolescents' relationships with peers. Pp. 363–394 in *Handbook of adolescent psychology.* Edited by R. Lerner and L. Steinberg. New York: Wiley.

Brown, T. L., S. W. Henggeler, M. J. Brondino, and S. G. Pickrel. 1999. Trauma exposure, protective factors, and mental health functioning of substance-abusing and dependent juvenile offenders. *Journal of Emotional and Behavioral Disorders* 7(2): 94–102.

Bullis, M., P. Yovanoff, G. Mueller, and E. Havel. 2002. Life on the outs: Examination of the facility-to-community transition of incarcerated youth. *Exceptional Children* 69: 7–22.

Bureau of Justice Statistics. 1998. *Juvenile felony defendants in criminal court.* Washington: Bureau of Justice Statistics, Office of Justice Programs, U.S. Department of Justice.

Cocozza, J. 1997. Identifying the needs of juveniles with co-occurring disorders. *Corrections Today* 59: 7.

Cocozza, J. J., and K. Skowyra. 2000. Youth with mental health disorders: Issues and emerging responses. *Juvenile Justice* 7: 4–13.

Collins, W. A., and B. Laursen. 2004. Parent-adolescent relationships and influence. Pp. 331–361 in *Handbook of adolescent psychology.* Edited by R. Lerner and L. Steinberg. New York: Wiley.

Conger, R. D., and R. L. Simons. 1997. Life course contingencies in the development of antisocial behavior: A matching law approach. Pp. 55–100 in *Developmental theories of crime and delinquency.* Edited by T. P. Thornberry. New Brunswick, NJ: Transaction Books.

Dishion, T. J., J. McCord, and F. Poulin. 1999. When interventions harm: Peer groups and problem behavior. *American Psychologist* 54: 755–764.

Eccles, J., and J. Templeton. 2002. Extracurricular and other after-school activities for youth. *Review of Education* 26: 113–180.

Erikson, E. H. [1959] 1980. *Identity and the life cycle.* New York: Norton.

Fagan, J. F., and R. B. Freeman. 1999. Crime and work. Pp. 225–290 in *Crime and justice: A review of research.* Edited by M. Tonry. Chicago: University of Chicago Press.

Fagan, J. F., and F. Zimring, eds. 2000. *The changing borders of juvenile justice.* Chicago: University of Chicago Press.

Farrington, D., B. Gallagher, L. Morley, R. J. St. Ledger, and D. West. 1988. Are there any successful men from criminogenic backgrounds? *Psychiatry* 51: 116–130.

Feld, B. C. 1998. Juvenile and criminal justice systems' responses to youth violence. Pp. 189–263 in *Youth violence.* Edited by M. Tonry and M. H. Moore. Chicago: University of Chicago Press.

Foley, R. 2001. Academic characteristics of incarcerated youth and correctional education programs: A literature review. *Journal of Emotional and Behavioral Disorders* 9: 248–259.

Forst, M., J. Fagan, and T. S. Vivona. 1989. Youth in prisons and training schools: Perceptions and consequences of the treatment-custody dichotomy. *Juvenile Family Court Journal* 40: 1–14.

Freeman, R. 1992. Crime and economic status of disadvantaged young men. Pp. 112–152 in *Urban labor markets and job opportunities.* Edited by G. Peterson and W. Vroman. Washington: Urban Institute Press.

Furstenberg, F. F., G. H. Elder, T. Cook, J. Eccles, and A. Sameroff. 1999. *Managing to make it: Urban families and adolescent success.* Chicago: University of Chicago Press.

Glueck, S., and E. Glueck. 1974. *Delinquents and nondelinquents in perspective.* Cambridge: Harvard University Press.

Graber, J. A., J. Brooks-Gunn, and A. C. Petersen, eds. 1996. *Transitions through adolescence: Interpersonal domains and context.* Mahwah, NJ: Lawrence Erlbaum.

Greenberger, E. 1982. Education and the acquisition of psychosocial maturity. Pp. 155–189 in *The development of social maturity.* Edited by D. McClelland. New York: Irvington.

Greenberger, E. 1984. Defining psychosocial maturity in adolescence. *Advances in Child Behavioral Analysis and Therapy* 3: 1–37.

Greenberger, E., and A. Sorensen. 1974. Toward a concept of psychosocial maturity. *Journal of Youth and Adolescence* 3: 329–358.

Greenberger, E., and L. Steinberg. 1981. The workplace as a context for the socialization of youth. *Journal of Youth and Adolescence* 10: 185–210.

Grisso, T. 2004. *Double jeopardy: Adolescent offenders with mental disorders.* Chicago: University of Chicago Press.

Grogger, J. 1995. The effects of arrest on the employment and earnings of young men. *Quarterly Journal of Economics* 110: 51–72.

Habermann, M., and L. Quinn. 1986. The high school re-entry myth: A follow-up study of juveniles released from two correctional high schools in Wisconsin. *Journal of Correctional Education* 37: 114–117.

Hagan, J. 1993. The social embeddedness of crime and unemployment. *Criminology* 31: 465–491.

Hawkins, J. D., T. Herrenkohl, D. P. Farrington, D. Brewer, R. F. Catalano, and T. W. Harachi. 1998. A review of predictors of youth violence. Pp. 106–146 in *Serious and violent juvenile offenders: Risk factors and successful interventions.* Edited by R. Loeber and D. P. Farrington. Thousand Oaks, CA: Sage.

Hecker, T., and L. Steinberg. 2002. Psychological evaluation at juvenile court disposition. *Professional Psychology: Research and Practice* 33: 300–306.

Huey, S. J., Jr., and S. W. Henggeler. 2001. Effective community-based interventions for antisocial and delinquent adolescents. Pp. 301–322 in *Handbook of psychological services for children and adolescents.* Edited by J. N. Hughes and A. M. La Greca. New York: Oxford University Press.

Hughes, M. 1998. Turning points in the lives of young inner-city men foregoing destructive criminal behaviors: A qualitative study. *Social Work Research* 22: 143–151.

Knitzer, J. 1996. Children's mental health: Changing paradigms and policies. Pp. 207–232 in *Chil-

dren, families, and government: Preparing for the twenty-first century. Edited by F. Zigler, S. L. Kagan, and N. W. Hall. New York: Cambridge University Press.

Laub, J. H., D. S. Nagin, and R. J. Sampson. 1998. Trajectories of change in criminal offending: Good marriages and the desistance process. *American Sociological Review* 63: 225–238.

Leventhal, T., and J. Brooks-Gunn. 2004. Diversity in developmental trajectories across adolescence: Neighborhood influences. Pp. 451–486 in *Handbook of adolescent psychology.* Edited by R. Lerner and L. Steinberg. New York: Wiley.

Li, Spencer De. 1999. Legal sanctions and youths' status achievement: A longitudinal study. *Justice Quarterly* 16: 377–402.

Lipsey, M. W., and D. B. Wilson. 1998. Effective intervention for serious juvenile offenders: A synthesis of research. Pp. 313–345 in *Serious and violent juvenile offenders: Risk factors and successful interventions.* Edited by R. Loeber and D. P. Farrington. Thousand Oaks, CA: Sage.

Loeber, R., and D. P. Farrington, eds. 1998. *Serious and violent juvenile offenders: Risk factors and successful interventions.* Thousand Oaks, CA: Sage.

Martinson, R. 1974. What works?: Questions and answers about prison reform. *Public Interest* 35: 22–54.

Moffitt, T. E. 1993. Adolescence-limited and life-course-persistent antisocial behavior: A developmental taxonomy. *Psychological Review* 100: 674–701.

Moffitt, T. E., A. Caspi, H. Harrington, and B. J. Milne. 2002. Males on the life-course-persistent and adolescence-limited antisocial pathways: Follow-up at age 26 years. *Development and Psychopathology* 14: 179–207.

Mulvey, E., E. Cauffman, and L. Steinberg. 2003. Pathways to desistance. Unpublished grant proposal. Law and Psychiatry Program, University of Pittsburgh School of Medicine.

National Center for Education Statistics. 2001. *Dropout rates in the United States: 2000.* Washington: U.S. Department of Education.

National Research Council. 1993. *Losing generations: Adolescents in high risk settings.* Washington: National Academy Press.

National Research Council and Institute of Medicine. 2002. *Community programs to promote youth development.* Edited by J. Eccles and J. Gootman. Washington: National Academy Press.

OJJDP Statistical Briefing Book. 2002. http://ojjdp.ncjrs.org/ojstatbb/asp/JCSCF_Display.asp ?ID=qa220&year=1999&group=1&type=1.

Otto, R. K., J. J. Greenstein, M. K. Johnson, and R. M. Friedman. 1992. Prevalence of mental disorders among youth in the juvenile justice system. Pp. 7–48 in *Responding to the mental health needs of youths in the juvenile justice system.* Edited by J. J. Cocozza. Seattle: National Coalition for the Mentally Ill in the Criminal Justice System.

Oyserman, D., and H. R. Markus. 1990. Possible selves and delinquency. *Journal of Personality and Social Psychology* 59: 112–125.

Parent, D. G., V. Lieter, S. Kennedy, L. Livens, D. Wentworth, and S. Wilcox. 1994. *Conditions of confinement: Juvenile detention and corrections facilities.* Washington: Office of Juvenile Justice and Delinquency Prevention, Office of Justice Programs, U.S. Department of Justice.

Patterson, G. R., J. B. Reid, and T. J. Dishion. 1992. *Antisocial boys.* Eugene, OR: Castalia.

Puzzanchera, C., A. Stahl, T. Finnegan, H. Snyder, R. Poole, and N. Tierney. Forthcoming. *Juvenile court statistics, 1999.* Washington: Office of Juvenile Justice and Delinquency Prevention, Office of Justice Programs, U.S. Department of Justice.

Rentner, D., J. Jennings, and S. Halperin. 1994. *A young person's guide to earning and learning.* Washington: Center on Education Policy and American Youth Policy Forum, data from Bureau of Census, Education Attainment in the United States.

Sampson, R. J., and J. H. Laub. 1990. Crime and deviance over the life course: The salience of adult social bonds. *American Sociological Review* 55: 609–627.

Sampson, R. J., and J. H. Laub. 1993. *Crime in the making: Pathways and turning points through life.* Cambridge: Harvard University Press.

Sampson, R. J., and J. H. Laub. 1997. A life-course theory of cumulative disadvantage and the stability of delinquency. Pp. 133–162 in *Developmental theories of crime and delinquency.* Edited by T. P. Thornberry. New Brunswick, NJ: Transaction Books.

Sampson, R. J., and J. L. Lauritsen. 1994. Violent victimization and offending: Individual-, situational-, and community-level risk factors. Pp. 1–14 in *Understanding and preventing violence,* vol. 3: *Social influences.* Edited by A. J. Reiss, Jr. Washington: National Academy Press.

Sampson, R. J., J. D. Morenoff, and F. Earls. 1999. Beyond social capital: Spatial dynamics of collective efficacy for children. *American Sociological Review* 64: 633–660.

Sickmund, M. 2000. *Census of juveniles in residential placement 1997.* Pittsburgh: National Center for Juvenile Justice.

Sickmund, M. Forthcoming. *Juveniles in corrections.* Washington: Office of Juvenile Justice and Delinquency Prevention, Office of Justice Programs, U.S. Department of Justice.

Snyder, H. N. Forthcoming. *Juvenile arrests 2000.* Washington: Office of Juvenile Justice and Delinquency Prevention, Office of Justice Programs, U.S. Department of Justice.

Snyder, H. N., and M. Sickmund. 1995. *Juvenile offenders and victims: A national report.* Washington: Office of Juvenile Justice and Delinquency Prevention, Office of Justice Programs, U.S. Department of Justice.

Snyder, H. N., M. Sickmund, and E. Poe-Yamagata. 1996. *Juvenile offenders and victims: 1996 update on violence.* Washington: Office of Juvenile Justice and Delinquency Prevention, National Center for Juvenile Justice.

Soler, M. 2002. Health issues for adolescents in the justice system. *Journal of Adolescent Health* 31 (supp. 16): 321–333.

Steinberg, L. 2002. Psychosocial development in late adolescence: Suggestions for a research agenda. Unpublished manuscript.

Steinberg, L., and E. Cauffman. 1996. Maturity of judgment in adolescence: Psychosocial factors in adolescent decision-making. *Law and Human Behavior* 20: 249–272.

Stewart, E. A., R. L. Simons, R. D. Conger, and L. V. Scaramella. 2002. Beyond the interactional relationship between delinquency and parenting practices: The contribution of legal sanctions. *Journal of Research in Crime and Delinquency* 39: 36–59.

Task Force on Employment and Training for Court-Involved Youth. 2000. *Employment and training for court-involved youth.* Washington: U.S. Department of Justice, Office of Justice Programs, Office of Juvenile Justice and Delinquency Prevention.

Teplin, L. 2002. Psychiatric disorders in youth in juvenile detention. *Archives of General Psychiatry* 59: 1133–1143.

Todis, B., M. Bullis, R. D'Ambrosio, R. Schultz, and M. Waintrup. 2001. Overcoming the odds: Qualitative examination of resilience among adolescents with antisocial behaviors. *Exceptional Children* 68: 119–139.

Tolan, P. H., and D. Gorman-Smith. 1997. Treatment of juvenile delinquency: Between punishment and therapy. Pp. 405–415 in *Handbook of antisocial behavior.* Edited by D. M. Stoff, J. Breiling, and J. D. Maser. New York: Wiley.

Travis, J., A. L. Solomon, and M. Waul 2001. *From prison to home: The dimensions and consequences of prisoner reentry.* Washington: Urban Institute.

William T. Grant Foundation Commission on Work, Family and Citizenship. 1988. *The forgotten half: Non-college-bound youth in America.* Washington: William T. Grant Foundation.

Wolfgang, M. E., T. P. Thornberry, and R. M. Figlio. 1987. *From boy to man, from delinquency to crime.* Chicago: University of Chicago Press.

CHAPTER FOUR

Policy and Program Perspectives on the Transition to Adulthood for Adolescents in the Juvenile Justice System

DAVID M. ALTSCHULER

I am grateful to Rachel Brash, who provided valuable research assistance, suggestions, and editing.

INTRODUCTION

As Chung, Little, and Steinberg make clear in chapter 3, young people caught up in the juvenile justice system face a transition to adulthood that is fraught with challenges. For instance, a large proportion of juveniles at the point of arrest (more than half in numerous cities) test positive for illegal drugs (National Institute of Justice 2000), and by some estimates approximately one out of every five juveniles arrested has a serious mental health problem (Cocozza and Skowyra 2000; Mears 2001). The rates are likely higher among incarcerated youth.

A substantial number of youth become involved in the juvenile justice system. In 2000, the number of delinquency cases receiving either formal or informal probation totaled 658,771 (Stahl, Finnegan, and Kang 2002). Based on a one-day count in 1999, another 108,931 juvenile offenders were being held in public and private residential custody facilities (Sickmund and Wan 2001). At midyear 2002, an estimated 7,248 youths under the age of eighteen were being held in adult jails and an estimated 3,055 were being held in adult prisons (Harrison and Karberg 2003). While the nearly 800,000 young people involved in juvenile and adult corrections constitute a relatively small proportion of the approximately seventy-one million persons below age eighteen in America, they clearly represent a human capital resource that on public policy, economic, social, and humanitarian grounds cannot be ignored.

This chapter examines the consequences of varying correctional goals, philosophies, and practices on the transition to adulthood for adolescents and teenagers in the juvenile justice system. It explores the two major themes highlighted in this volume, building and maintaining resilience and promoting social inclusion. While the companion chapter (chapter 3) in this volume by Chung, Little, and Steinberg discusses the general principles of developmentally appropriate responses to juvenile offenders, the focus here is policy and program efforts that facilitate as well as hinder the successful transition to adulthood.

Juvenile justice policy affects this transition in three ways. First, young people who reach the "age of majority" remain under juvenile correctional authority (sometimes for years) in many states if they commit a crime before reaching the state's age of majority. In such instances, these young offenders are in juvenile correction programs during some or all of their transition to adulthood. Second, some adolescents are released from correctional authority before reaching the age of majority. For these young people, the transition to adulthood may be influenced by their experiences while under the control of correctional authorities. Those experiences and the policies that shape them may enhance or impede the success of the later transition. Third, justice policies in some states cause adolescents to be transferred or waived directly into criminal court and, if convicted, into adult corrections. As a result, these young people spend some or all of the transition to adulthood under adult correctional authority.

This chapter's principal concern is with promising and innovative ways to promote and enhance the transition to adulthood. When adolescents are released from correctional authority before reaching the age of majority, one concern focuses on the best way to set the stage for the impending transition to adulthood. When adolescents enter their transition to adulthood while under juvenile correctional authority, the concern should be on preparing for law-abiding community living and establishing the needed requisite skills. When adolescents spend their transition years under the authority of the criminal justice system, the policy issues raised by Travis and Visher (chapter 6) are relevant, and many of the themes they discuss are applicable to juvenile justice as well.

THE PHILOSOPHY AND MISSION OF CORRECTIONS

Whether a youth is under the auspices of the juvenile or of the criminal justice system, key issues surround the overall orientation, philosophy, and mission of corrections. These broader considerations are critical because correctional goals associated with deterrence and punishment can actually impede other correctional goals, such as rehabilitation and prosocial reintegration into the community. Building and maintaining resilience, as well as promoting social inclusion, can be much more difficult to achieve when deterrence and punishment goals overshadow services and practices associated with rehabilitation and reintegration goals.

The broad mission of correctional sanctioning encompasses deterrence, punishment, and the provision of various services and treatment. Over the years, however, the corrections policy pendulum has swung between a "get tough" mode and a rehabilitative focus (Bernard 1992). Over the past two decades the former has been ascendant (National Research Council and Institute of Medicine 2001). This mode involves a greater use of incarceration, longer terms of imprisonment and correctional supervision, handling more juveniles in the criminal justice (i.e., adult courts and corrections) system, and reshaping the juvenile justice system in the image of the more punitive, deterrence-oriented criminal justice system. Similarly, the move to handle juvenile offenders in the criminal justice system is driven primarily by a desire for more deterrence, punishment, and incarceration.

Historically, while a strain of punishment and deterrence was always evident, juvenile justice has focused primarily on the offender, treatment, and rehabilitation services. However, because of concern about deprivation of liberty and a lack of rehabilitative treatment in some juvenile facilities and institutions, courts began to address rights of due process and equal protection under the law in the 1960s.

Some critics have characterized the juvenile justice system as being insufficiently punitive for certain types of juvenile offenders and too time-limited in its jurisdiction (DiIulio 1995; Feld 1997). Others have criticized the criminal justice system for being insufficiently rehabilitative and potentially detrimental to public safety in the long run (Zimring 1978, 2000). In light of these criticisms, how can deterrence and punishment coexist with treatment and rehabilitation services in either the juvenile or the criminal justice system, and what impact will the combination have on the transition to adulthood?

The debate over the last decade about deterrence and rehabilitation suggests to some critics that the two may be largely irreconcilable (see, for example, Bazemore and Umbreit 1995). Advocates of deterrence or zero-tolerance policies often view "doing time" or being appropriately punished as justice precisely because the sanction is harsh, demanding, depriving, and properly retributive. These advocates regard other purposes, such as rehabilitation or restoration, as undermining the intent of the punishment and see such efforts as coddling offenders. Punishment or retributive justice refers mainly to sanctioning as a punishment that is deserved, quite apart from whether it results in deterrence.

Meanwhile, supporters of rehabilitation and treatment fear deterrence or zero-tolerance may cause offenders to emerge from the correctional system embittered, disadvantaged, or vengeful. If so, new barriers to making a successful transition to adulthood can emerge. These barriers include closing off employment opportunities, limiting eligibility for entry into training or educational programs, and even creating difficulties in developing a positive peer group and stable prosocial personal relationships. Some authors have taken a conceptual middle ground, supporting a balanced approach that may include community justice or restorative justice principles (see, for example, Altschuler 2001; Bazemore and Griffiths 1997; Bazemore and Umbreit 1995). Even with a balanced approach, however, how well can punishment and rehabilitation coexist?

The recent emphasis on retribution has been reflected in changes both in law and in funding at the federal, state, and local levels. As a result, corrections has experienced a shift of support away from such areas as drug treatment, education, vocational training, job placement, housing assistance, and mental health services. Family involvement and attention to living arrangements following release have long been an Achilles' heel of corrections, where efforts and expertise have paled in comparison to the demonstrated need. Consequently, developing resilience and gaining acceptance in legitimate prosocial circles can be quite difficult to achieve.

Juvenile Justice and Transition to Adulthood

The transition to adulthood for young people from age eighteen into the mid-twenties cannot be separated from what happens earlier in life. As noted by Chung, Little, and Steinberg (chapter 3), specific risk and protective factors both directly and indirectly impact how young offenders will fare during and after their transition into adulthood. As demonstrated in other chapters in this volume, other vulnerable youth, or for that matter all young people, may also find this to be true. One notable difference, however, is that the experience of corrections, either positively or negatively, is another crucial avenue of influence. Hundreds of thousands of young people under age eighteen are at stake.

If the juvenile corrections system is of vital concern for the transition to adulthood because it sets the stage at an earlier formative developmental period, it is of more direct concern because young people eighteen and older can and do remain under juvenile correctional authority in many states. This can happen in several ways. Despite the fact that original juvenile court jurisdiction in delinquency matters includes offenses committed by individuals up to age seventeen (in thirty-seven states and the District of Columbia), many states retain juvenile court jurisdiction for dispositions resulting from these offenses until an individual reaches the age of twenty (thirty-two states and the District of Columbia). From 1992 to 1997, seventeen states extended the age limit for juvenile delinquency disposition (Snyder and Sickmund 1999). In California, Oregon, and Wisconsin, juveniles can remain in the system through age twenty-four, while in Colorado, Connecticut, Hawaii, and New Mexico, juvenile court jurisdiction may be retained even longer (National Research Council and Institute of Medicine 2001). Thus, growing numbers remain in the juvenile justice system well into the transition to adulthood.

Criminal Justice and Transition to Adulthood

As noted above, adolescent offenders may be handled by criminal courts and adult corrections. Adolescent offenders may even begin serving a sentence in a juvenile facility and then be transferred to an adult prison when they reach the age of majority. All states have established mechanisms that allow juvenile cases to be prosecuted in criminal court. The three major mechanisms—judicial waiver, statutory exclusion, and concurrent jurisdiction—differ according to who makes the decision to transfer, or waive, the case. (For a discussion of issues confronting young offenders exiting adult corrections, see Travis and Visher [chapter 6].)

The most common mechanism, the judicial waiver, allows juvenile court judges, at the request of the prosecutor, to waive juvenile court cases to criminal court based on the defendant's past juvenile record and failure to respond to past interventions (Snyder and Sickmund 1999). In 1999, only Massachusetts, Nebraska, New Mexico, and New York did not have a judicial waiver provision (Griffin 2000). Most state statutes limit judicial waivers by age and offense criteria and by the "amenability" of juveniles to treatment. States do vary in the discretion they give the judge.

States are increasingly using a second transfer mechanism—statutory exclusion provisions. These laws exclude certain young offenders from juvenile court based on their age or the type of offense committed. In 1999, twenty-nine states had such provisions (Griffin 2000) for acts such as capital offenses, other murders, or violent offenses. States also have begun excluding a broader range of felonies. The third transfer mechanism, concurrent jurisdiction, permits prosecutors to decide whether to file a case in juvenile or criminal court (Snyder and Sickmund 1999). State appellate courts have ruled that prosecutor discretion is an "executive function," similar to routine charging decisions in criminal cases and therefore not subject to judicial review and due process standards.

In addition to the three transfer mechanisms, juvenile court judges in some states may impose adult correctional sentences on young offenders that extend the term of commitment beyond the upper age of juvenile jurisdiction. The several variations of such "blended sentences" involve incarceration in the juvenile or adult correctional system, or both.

CONSEQUENCES FOR THE TRANSITION TO ADULTHOOD

The vast majority of all incarcerated offenders, juvenile and adult, eventually will reenter the community. When they do, they likely will face difficulty remaining crime free and functioning productively. What is specifically required for these individuals to successfully reenter the community, and what might pose barriers? The keys to success are being literate, holding a legitimate job, and maintaining stable and positive personal relationships, all of which are dimensions of a successful transition to adulthood. Various policies make it hard, if not impossible, for people who have been involved in the justice system to obtain employment, qualify for housing assistance, receive vocational training, and even vote (Travis, Solomon, and Waul 2001). Based purely on deterrence and punishment, these policies discourage social inclusion and impede an ex-offender's ability to build and maintain resilience. By contrast, if deterrence and punishment goals can be balanced by services and treatment, individuals may more easily transition into adulthood and society. As discussed above, the juvenile justice system's traditional orientation is more compatible with policies and procedures associated with making a successful transition to adulthood than is the criminal justice system. Yet much of that emphasis has been lost in the current get-tough reforms across the nation.

While it is one thing to argue that deterrence need not be an aim of incarceration, it is of course quite another matter if incarceration contributes to reoffending. Some research suggests that time spent in prison or jail actually *increases* some individuals' risk of reoffending; this work underscores the danger of largely unchecked deterrence and punishment strategies (see, for example, Byrne and Kelly 1989; Shannon et al. 1988; Hagan 1991; National Research Council 1993; National Research Council and Institute of Medicine 2001). Other research indicates that the most effective treatment programs are found outside custodial institutions and the juvenile justice system, suggesting that confinement disadvantages individuals upon their return (Lipsey 1992). At least one reason is that prison carries a stigma that contributes to suspicions among those who might otherwise employ or assist those released. Still other research has shown that imprisonment does not affect recidivism either way (Cohen and Canela-Cacho 1994). For example, in one six-year study of over five thousand young parolees released from state prisons in twenty-two states, the Bureau of Justice Statistics (Beck and Shipley 1987) found that time served in prison had no consistent impact on recidivism rates: those who served six months or less in prison were about as likely to be rearrested as those who served more than two years.

The National Research Council's Panel on High-Risk Youth (1993) acknowledged the uncertainty of exactly how institutionalization could produce more offending and speculated that imprisonment may both solidify networks of association that support criminality and make job acquisition very difficult. Chung, Little, and Steinberg (chapter 3) argue that the juvenile justice system's inadequacies in trying to treat, protect, and facilitate psychosocial maturation contribute to adverse outcomes. Whatever the dynamics and set of factors involved, the evidence supporting a *specific deterrent effect* of incarceration on offenders is largely lacking.

Based on its review of research, the Panel on High-Risk Youth concluded in 1993 "that the U.S. justice system is overburdened, and that its emphasis on punishment is expensive, unproductive of the desired gains in reducing levels of crime, and probably productive of increased hostility toward itself in ghetto communities" (167). Cautioning that the question concerning the impact of imprisonment on violence cannot be answered unambiguously, the National Research Council's Panel on the Understanding and Control of Violent Behavior (Reiss and Roth 1993) concluded that the increase in the U.S. prison population apparently has had little effect on the country's overall level of violence. Moreover, the panel noted that preventive strategies may be as important as criminal justice responses. Such conclusions support the view that justice sanctions can hinder efforts to support and facilitate social acceptance and the building of skills requisite to successfully transitioning to adulthood.

Another reason why incarceration can be harmful is the absence of continuity of care. Continuity of care is a strategy to foster resilience and promote social inclusions by seeking to sustain gains and benefits attained while in a correctional facility upon return to the community. As the more detailed discussion of continuity of care below demonstrates, a healthy and prosocial transition to adulthood is unlikely in the absence of such continuity.

The lack of continuity of care presents a twofold problem with developmental consequences for adolescents and postadolescents. First, inconsistency between what happens while in a residential facility and what happens back in the community can counteract gains made in the facility. Second, integrating juvenile justice and treatment programs more generally has proven imposing, largely because correctional systems tend to emphasize punishment at the expense of treatment and service. Taken together, these two challenges present a formidable set of barriers that has bedeviled efforts to create a "seamless system" that spans corrections and treatment on the one hand and facility- and community-based interventions on the other hand. Understanding the barriers to such integration is essential for building a system that helps youth obey the law, obtain employment, and develop prosocial relationships with law-abiding peers and adults. While the process of developing these skills and values can begin while in correctional facilities, that process requires positive reinforcement and continuity in community settings.

TRADITIONAL PROBATION AND PAROLE PRACTICE

Young people under correctional authority who are living in the community (rather than in residential placement) have several legal statuses. As already discussed, age by itself is steadily being eclipsed by other factors in determining whether juvenile or criminal justice will assume authority. Young offenders in the midst of transition from adolescence to adulthood can be on some form of probation, either as a sanction in its own right or as a formal diversion from a residential institution. Alternatively, juvenile offenders in the community may be on some form of aftercare or parole status.

Offenders in the community are part of a dramatically increasing population that has been swamping the capacity of probation and parole. From 1987 to 1996, the total number of delinquency cases receiving formal or informal probation increased 46 percent, from 435,200 to 634,100 (Snyder and Sickmund 1999). In addition, probation departments also screened most of the nearly 1.5 million delinquency cases handled by juvenile courts in 1993, made detention decisions on some, prepared investigation reports on most, and delivered aftercare services to many of the juveniles released from institutions (Torbet 1996). Probation has and continues to be the overwhelming sanction of choice for the nation's juvenile courts, where 56 percent of all cases adjudicated for a delinquency offense received probation, 28 percent were placed in some type of residential facility, and 12 percent received some other disposition (e.g., restitution).

As juvenile probation receives more cases overall and more serious cases in particular, one must question probation's capability and capacity to provide not only traditional probation supervision (including so-called intermediate sanctions such as electronic monitoring, drug and alcohol testing, intensive supervision, boot camps, day reporting centers, community service, and restitution) but also the kinds of developmentally appropriate experiences outlined by Chung, Little, and Steinberg (chapter 3). While facing many of the same challenges as probation, aftercare must bridge the gap between the institution and the community. Integrating and coordinating institutional and parole services directly affects how two very distinct parts of the juvenile justice system (institutions and parole) operate. Both have resisted change (Altschuler and Armstrong 1995). When institutions and parole reside within the same agency, their cultures and orientations are often fundamentally at odds. Consequently, even when the treatment and services most needed for a successful transition to adulthood are provided at a residential facility, their continuation in the community is by no means assured.

Caught up in the nexus of institutional and community corrections and in the respective bulging populations is the type of supervision and intervention provided to offenders. In practice most sanction programs—those for juveniles and adults—are first and foremost surveillance and control oriented. Surveillance-oriented approaches dominate even juvenile intensive probation programs, which in theory should equally emphasize counseling and rehabilitation (Armstrong 1991). This imbalance is problematic because research suggests (see, for example, Byrne and Pattavina 1992) that positive impacts are unlikely when intensive supervision is predominantly surveillance oriented and provides few services focused on factors predictive of reoffending (e.g., combating family dysfunction, negative peer influences, school disciplinary problems, and substance abuse). Consequently, corrections programs often do not address the very qualities associated with a successful transition to adulthood. Little can therefore be expected to change.

PROGRAMS THAT SHOW PROMISE

The realization that punishment alone cannot reverse antisocial conduct has led numerous researchers and scholars to identify services and treatments that are promising candidates for use in young offender programs. Particularly important is research suggesting that the most effective institutional programs resemble the most effective noninstitutional community treatment programs.

Recently, programs incorporating cognitive-behavioral approaches and interpersonal social skill training have drawn attention (Lipsey, Chapman, and Landenberger 2001; Pearson et al. 2002). While this research involves small demonstration programs, it offers the best evidence to date on promising direction. This recent work builds on earlier research that came to similar conclusions. Meta-analysis conducted by Lipsey and Wilson (1998) found that among *noninstitutional* programs for juveniles, those exhibiting the greatest reductions in recidivism emphasized interpersonal skill training (Chandler 1973; Delinquency Research Group 1986), behavioral contracting (Barton et al. 1985; Gordon, Graves, and Arbuthnot 1987; Jesness et al. 1975; Kantrowitz 1980; Schwitzgebel and Kolb 1964), and cognitive-behavioral counseling (Bean 1988; Borduin et al. 1990; Kemp and Lee 1975; Lee and Haynes 1978a,b; Lee and Olejnik 1981; Moore 1978; Moore and Levine 1974; Piercy and Lee 1976). Examining a set of *institutional* juvenile offender programs, Lipsey and Wilson identified those providing interpersonal skill training and cognitive behavioral approaches to be most effective (Glick and Goldstein 1987; Shivrattan 1988; Spence and Marzillier 1981; Guerra and Slaby 1990; Schlicter and Horan 1981). Such programs develop prosocial patterns of reasoning by maintaining a focus on managing anger, assuming personal responsibility for behavior, taking an empathetic perspective, solving problems, setting goals, and acquiring life skills.

The overlap of effective treatment types between the institutional and noninstitutional programs suggests the potential for stronger effects of aftercare programs built on skills developed by institutional programs (Altschuler, Armstrong, and MacKenzie 1999). The overlap of treatment types also suggests integrating aftercare programs and their staff into planning and treatment activities in the institutional setting.

CONTINUITY OF CARE AND ITS CONTRIBUTION TO SUCCESSFUL TRANSITION

Whether measured by recidivism, relapse, or both, the failures experienced by juvenile corrections and adolescent drug treatment are frequently attributed, at least in part, to discontinuity. Even the terminology adds to the confusion. The terms "aftercare," "reentry," and "relapse prevention" are often defined or understood as largely referring to what happens after adolescents return to the community. A more expansive definition includes treatment and discharge planning prior to release.

Continuity of care includes several very distinctive components that represent a truly reintegrative approach. It includes five components (Frederick 1999): continuity of (1) control, (2) range of services, (3) service and program content, (4) social environment, and (5) attachment.

Continuity of control involves the extent and nature of the structure and rigidity experienced by adolescents as they move through a program or system. Adolescents returning to the community from residential care sometimes face an abrupt and disorienting reentry experience. High levels of structure and control that are not gradually reduced can produce anxiety and stress as well as excessive and extreme behaviors. A gradual transition process is often recommended with decompression explicitly built in to the reentry (see, for example, Altschuler and Armstrong 1997; Center for Substance Abuse Treatment 1998).

Continuity in the range of services involves services youth may have received while in residential placements. As noted above, such services are often not available in the community (Dembo, Livingston, and Schmeidler forthcoming; Center for Substance Abuse Treatment 1999a). For example, when appropriate schooling, vocational training, or employment are not provided, housing or food is inadequate, or psychotropic medication is not maintained, the risks for failure are elevated. Adolescents with co-occurring disorders (also known as dual diagnosis) especially require attention on multiple fronts (GAINS Center 1997; Altschuler and Armstrong 1994). The lack of available services may be driven by funding restrictions and levels, governmental policy and insurance limitations, availability of providers, access to treatment, and treatment appropriateness or quality.

Continuity of service and program content is also a concern. Such continuity is critically important when it involves education, vocational and social skills, treatment/behavioral management approaches and principles, medications prescribed, and special needs addressed (e.g., treatment for mental health disorders, sex offending interventions). Employing the same treatment approach after offenders are released can reinforce positive skills learned while in placement and thus increase the likelihood of success in the community (Altschuler 1984; Coates, Miller and Ohlin 1978; Empey and Lubeck 1971; Haley 1980; Whittaker 1979; Wolfensberger 1972). Such skills allow the youth to resist or avoid triggers, negative influences, and temptations readily found in the community.

Continuity of social environment requires that the engagement and involvement of an adolescent's social network (e.g., family, antisocial and prosocial peers in the community, neighborhood hangouts, school, and/or job) not be ignored or given short shrift, either during residential care or upon return to the community. Thus, the participation of family, peers, neighborhood, and school has become a central feature of several promising approaches (Altschuler and Armstrong 1994; OJJDP 2001; Center for Substance Abuse Treatment 1998; Center for Substance Abuse Treatment 1999b; Lipsey and Wilson 1998).

Continuity of attachment entails the adolescent's developing a trusting relationship with responsible people in the community. Such relationships may require staff to locate prospects and assist in making those connections. These efforts may involve nothing more than identifying who among the network of people already involved with the youngster may be willing and able to build such relationships (Altschuler and Armstrong 2001).

These five components establish benchmarks around which strategic planning at the policy level and program development at the implementation level can proceed thoughtfully. It is worth remembering that the closing of many state mental health institutions, which began in the 1960s, was predicated on the development and implementation of community mental health clinics, which to a large extent never materialized. In turn, this development resulted in mentally ill people left on the streets with virtually no services or help (Burt and

Pittman 1985). Policy planning (including financing and managed care) and program development for juvenile offenders should consider the meaning of continuity of care and transition to adulthood and the implications for what it will take to get the job done.

INTEGRATION OF JUVENILE JUSTICE AND ADOLESCENT TREATMENT

Bridging residential care and community-based services is one challenge. Beyond this difference in setting, the other challenge concerns the integration of corrections with noncorrectional adolescent treatment services, such as child welfare, drug treatment, mental health services, education, and youth employment. Achieving the developmental tasks of the transition to adulthood clearly calls for a spectrum of treatments and services. Unfortunately, tensions arise that pit treatment services against deterrence and punishment goals. This long-standing problem is the focus of the recent Reclaiming Futures initiative, sponsored by the Robert Wood Johnson Foundation and housed at Portland State University in Oregon (Reclaiming Futures 2001). The Center for Substance Abuse Treatment is supporting work on this topic as well. It should be noted that juvenile justice agencies (at the federal, state, and local levels) and their relationships with agencies at all three levels focused on education, mental health, child welfare, employment, and substance abuse have been the focus of numerous systems reforms and partnership efforts. Some great achievements have occurred across the country, but overall barriers to communication, coordination, and collaboration between corrections and other agencies remain (Altschuler and Armstrong 1995).

The difficulty in integrating the juvenile justice system and substance abuse treatment is just one example of this fragmentation. A similar point could be made regarding education, mental health, or employment services. Putting aside the divergent perspectives and contradictory priorities regarding sanctions, punishment, and rehabilitation that can be found among the police, public defenders, prosecutors, judges, probation, institutional corrections, parole, and aftercare (all part of the justice "system"), a great deal of buck passing and finger pointing often occurs between corrections agencies and treatment programs. This problem can be traced to differences involving (1) the role of punishment versus treatment, (2) which agency has authority over and responsibility for various decisions, (3) which agency has to pay and how much, (4) who will have to do most of the work and whether it can be accomplished with current staffing and personnel, and (5) which agency believes that it can handle the type of adolescent involved.

With regard to drugs, one should note that the response to substance abuse cannot be separated from the larger debate in America on the war on drugs. Underlying this debate is the issue of whether substance abuse is a public health problem where treatment is the priority or a justice system problem where deterrence predominates (Zimring and Hawkins 1992). That this is more than a policy abstraction can easily be illustrated. For example, should an adolescent's relapse—as shown by a positive drug screen for the third time in a month—be handled as a crime punishable by revocation or as an expected recovery setback meriting an intensification or adjustment in drug treatment?

The increasing scarcity of drug treatment both in correctional facilities and in the community further complicates rehabilitation and the successful transition to adulthood. Judges sometimes place adolescents under correctional authority because doing so makes drug treatment available. Such judicial decisions can have the negative effect of widening the net of justice system control. Additionally, rapid advances in drug-testing technology have far outpaced the availability of suitable drug treatment. In effect, then, drug testing becomes the only drug "treatment" provided, making it nothing more than a deterrence strategy.

CRITICAL CHANGES FOR POLICY AND IMPLEMENTATION

As argued above, juvenile justice needs to shift its emphasis from deterrence and punishment to treatment and the psychosocial maturation needed for a successful transition to adulthood. Such a shift will require attention focused on three aspects of organizational structure and program operation.

Organizational Structure and Decision Making

Young people placed on probation or committed to state corrections face distinctly different situations, and the contrast between them varies across states. In thirty-six states, probation is administered by the county (mostly under the judiciary) or a combination of county and state government. Juvenile aftercare services are in most cases provided by the same state executive department that oversees the state juvenile facilities (Griffin 2000). Juvenile aftercare is administered by a state executive agency in thirty-seven states; by a local executive agency in two jurisdictions (District of Columbia and Idaho); by a combination of local and state executive agencies in two states; judicial agencies in four states; and a combination of judicial and executive agencies in six states. Implementing a unified approach across probation and corrections can be difficult when the administrative structures involve numerous agencies or levels of government. Authority in decisions regarding the length and type of placement also varies. Moreover, in many states, services are contracted to private providers, referrals are made to other public sector agencies, and an assortment of other interested parties get involved, including prosecutors, defense attorneys, legislators, victims, families, child advocates, unions, civil service, and the media.

The net effect is a kind of organizational fragmentation that, if not very consciously, carefully, and properly treated, results in chaos, finger pointing, and scapegoating. Public accountability is often lacking (Altschuler 1998; Altschuler and Armstrong 1995). Senior management can overcome these differences only by gaining the support of both the midlevel manager and the line staff. One strategy has been to establish special interagency teams representing all parties with decision-making authority and jurisdiction over targeted offenders, from the point of first contact with the system all the way to official termination (Altschuler and Armstrong 1997; Wiebush, McNulty, and Le 2000). Vesting such teams with authority and flexible resources to cover the full range of organizational functions, both surveillance and treatment, can create improved cooperation, mutual support, and a collective interest in promoting community protection through offender change. In short, a successful development and implementation effort likely will require strong leadership within the program, coupled with the involvement of key stakeholders both inside and outside the program and ties to the wider political and bureaucratic structure within which the program operates.

Probation and Parole Conditions, Technical Violations, and Graduated Responses

Young offenders on probation or parole are usually bound by a variety of conditions and rules. Violation can result in a revocation of the probation or parole status and a period of incarceration. The conditions usually are the same for everyone, and probation officers determine the extent and nature of enforcement. When youth are closely monitored, technical violations are common because behavior change takes time and practice, the proper services are not provided, and sanctions alone are insufficient. Thus, efforts to work with such offenders should incorporate a graduated incentive and consequence system as a formal part of the program (Altschuler and Armstrong 1994).

As many probation officers know, the problem is that some conditions and rules are unrealistic and/or largely unenforceable (Altschuler and Armstrong 1994; Krisberg et al. 1989). Frequently, violations do not influence the likelihood of offenders' committing additional crimes (Lurigio and Petersilia 1992; Turner and Petersilia 1992; Petersilia and Turner 1991). Classic examples include a positive drug test when no drug treatment was made available and failure to attend school when that environment is clearly unresponsive to the offender's educational needs. With some notable exceptions, probation officers are left either to ignore some violations or to respond disproportionately to them. Either response is obviously counterproductive. As rare as graduated sanctions are, recognition of the achievements of youth on probation or parole is even more rare (Altschuler and Armstrong 2001).

Therefore, a graduated response that can encourage compliance (i.e., using incentives and positive motivators) and penalize noncompliance (i.e., using a sanction) is critical. Probation and parole are much more accustomed to sanctions than to using positive incentives. Alternatives include the use of a structured system of phases that ties privileges, status, and/or rewards to progress and ties losses of earned privilege and status to infractions, noncompliance, or violations (Altschuler and Armstrong 1994).

Staffing, Training, and Workload

Some jurisdictions have reduced certain caseloads, have required more contact with offenders, and have developed risk assessments (Altschuler, Armstrong, and MacKenzie 1999). Unfortunately, however, such programs often proceed without clarifying the role of staff or properly training staff to handle the resulting responsibilities and expectations. Debates on the role of probation and parole agents are not new. Should the probation officer serve as case manager or direct service provider, law enforcement officer or counselor, tracker/community outreach worker, or traditional office-based, standard-hours worker? These distinctions are important for programs concerned with the transition to adulthood. Staff should move beyond deterrence-based corrections to consider the treatment and service needs associated with the transition to adulthood. The various roles assumed by staff must be carefully and thoughtfully delineated. Interagency, cross-disciplinary, and multifaceted efforts will require openness, creativity, and flexibility. Consequently, job descriptions that specify day-to-day responsibilities and role expectations should establish the criteria for hiring, retention, and promotions.

Both potential staff and employers must understand the extreme demands that continuity of care and transition to adulthood concerns place on the staff involved and the difficulties encountered in the workplace (Altschuler and Armstrong 1995). Therefore, the recruitment, screening, training, and performance review process needs to emphasize hiring and retaining individuals committed to the goals and approaches of a continuity-of-care and transition-to-adulthood perspective. Workplace and staff rules, regulations, and job protection often complicate the selection of qualified and committed staff. Some civil service and unionized environments, as well as procurement and contracting procedures, have excessively rigid rules and policies regarding hiring, job responsibilities, transfer, and firing. However, continuity-of-care services focused on transition-to-adulthood considerations, particularly with their implications for highly coordinated teamwork, require flexibility and accommodation. Operational issues that must be addressed include job classification, lines of authority, performance reviews, privatization, and use of volunteers, paraprofessionals, and contract workers.

Earlier research does not indicate that smaller caseloads increase contacts between probation officers and clients (see, for example, Banks et al. 1977) or that increased contacts improve the treatment actually provided. Thus, staffing strategies clearly cannot consider only caseload size and number of contacts. It is also important to clarify the purpose of contacts and services provided, time and place of contacts, and the skills and qualifications staff need. Interdisciplinary and interagency teams must monitor how members function collectively, share authority, and provide feedback. Staff qualifications may vary depending on the role and responsibility of the particular team members. Requirements for credentials, training, experience, and aptitude likely will differ across positions. Personnel policy must accommodate such differences. In fact, some team members may be paraprofessionals or volunteers, and some needed services may be available through contract or agreement with other public and private agencies. Regardless of the staffing and agency mix, the division of labor and sharing of authority must be carefully delineated to avoid confusion, discontinuity, and mixed messages.

CONCLUSION

Even well-adjusted adolescents have trouble making a smooth transition to adulthood. Adolescents involved in the juvenile justice system and those moving from the juvenile justice to the criminal justice system face additional obstacles. They must contend not only with the underlying problems that may have contributed to delinquency in the first place but also with barriers created by the sanctioning system itself. Philosophically and conceptually, some believe that most forms of service provision, competency development, and treatment only undermine deterrence and punishment policy. Consistent with such get-tough policies are requirements that do not support social inclusion or building resilience. To that extent, the transition to adulthood may become far more difficult due to increasing marginalization and stigma. Efforts to temper punishment and deterrence with skill building and to address needs and strengths associated with lowering the risk of reoffending represent a more balanced approach to crime control and prevention.

Promising programs incorporate cognitive-behavioral principles and continuity of care between facility and aftercare. Domains of concern include education, vocational training and workforce development, mental, physical and behavioral health, peer group relationships, family matters and living arrangements, substance abuse, and leisure time. Particularly encouraging is the overlap of effective approaches that has been demonstrated by both institutional and community programs. As shown, however, thus far Lipsey and his colleagues have examined research on institutional and community corrections programs functioning largely in isolation from one another. In order to have a true test of continuity of care for particular offenders reentering the community from institutional facilities, there must be direct collaboration between those who deal with these offenders both before and after community reentry. Nevertheless, the overlap of demonstrated effectiveness in institutional and community programs provides grounds for optimism.

Complex organizational structures and decision making by authorities that impede continuity, consistency, and collaboration require fine tuning and modification. Delivering services through interagency teams with authority and flexible resources directed toward particular types of offenders hold promise in directing the most attention to where the public safety payoff would potentially be the greatest. Staff who are well-trained in the correctional philosophy and approach advocated here, and who are assigned the number of cases commensurate with clearly defined roles and responsibilities, would likely lead to a much more disciplined and efficient operation. Administrative control of the handling of technical violations coupled with the development of a structured graduated response capability also would help parole and probation officers respond more appropriately to offenders' actions.

Recognizing the importance of social inclusion and resilience can assist policy makers in assessing how to prepare adolescents for their transition to adulthood. While deterrence and punishment have an important place in sanctioning policy, so too does providing young people with the tools and skills they need to transition to adulthood in ways that promote prosocial, legitimate, and constructive behavior. All of this can be done, but not without a concerted effort to maintain the delicate balance.

REFERENCES

Altschuler, D. M. 1984. Community reintegration in juvenile offender programming. Pp. 365–376 in *Violent juvenile offenders: An anthology.* Edited by R. Mathias, P. DeMuro, and R. Allinson. San Francisco: National Council on Crime and Delinquency.

Altschuler, D. M. 1998. Intermediate sanctions and community treatment for serious and violent juvenile offenders. Pp. 367–385 in *Serious and violent juvenile offenders: Risk factors and successful interventions.* Edited by R. Loeber and D. P. Farrington. Thousand Oaks, CA: Sage.

Altschuler, D. M. 1999. Trends and issues in the adultification of juvenile justice. Pp. 233–271 in *Research to results: Effective community corrections.* Edited by P. M. Harris. Lanham, MD: American Correctional Association.

Altschuler, D. M. 2001. Community justice initiatives: Issues and challenges in the U.S. context. *Federal Probation* 65: 28–32.

Altschuler, D. M., and T. L. Armstrong. 1994. *Intensive aftercare for high-risk juveniles: A community care model.* Washington: Office of Juvenile Justice and Delinquency Prevention, Office of Justice Programs, U.S. Department of Justice.

Altschuler, D. M., and T. L. Armstrong. 1995. Managing aftercare services for delinquents. Pp. 137–170 in *Managing delinquency programs that work.* Edited by B. Glick and A. P. Goldstein. Lanham, MD: American Correctional Association.

Altschuler, D. M., and T. L. Armstrong. 1997. Reintegrating high-risk juvenile offenders from secure correctional facilities into the community. *Corrections Management Quarterly* 1: 75–83.

Altschuler, D. M., and T. L. Armstrong. 2001. Reintegrating high-risk juvenile offenders into communities: Experiences and prospects. *Corrections Management Quarterly* 5: 72–88.

Altschuler, D. M., T. L. Armstrong, and D. L. MacKenzie. 1999. *Reintegration, supervised release, and intensive aftercare.* Juvenile Justice Bulletin. Washington: Office of Juvenile Justice and Delinquency Prevention, Office of Justice Programs, U.S. Department of Justice.

Armstrong, T. L. 1991. Introduction. Pp. 1–28 in *Intensive interventions with high-risk youth: Promising approaches in juvenile probation and aftercare.* Edited by T. L. Armstrong. Monsey, NY: Criminal Justice Press.

Banks, J., A. L. Porter, R. L. Rardin, T. R. Silver, and V. E. Unger. 1977. *Phase I evaluation of intensive special probation projects.* Washington: U.S. Department of Justice.

Barton, C., J. F. Alexander, M. Waldron, C. W. Turner, and J. Warburton. 1985. Generalizing treatment effects of functional family therapy: Three replications. *American Journal of Family Therapy* 13: 16–26.

Bazemore, G., and C. T. Griffiths. 1997. Conferences, circles, boards, and mediations: The "new wave" of community justice decisionmaking. *Federal Probation* 61: 25–37.

Bazemore, G., and M. Umbreit. 1995. Rethinking the sanctioning function in juvenile court: Retributive or restorative responses to youth crime. *Crime and Delinquency* 41: 296–316.

Bean, J. S. 1988. *The effect of individualized reality therapy on the recidivism rates and locus of control orientation of male juvenile offenders.* Doctoral dissertation, University of Mississippi. Dissertation Abstracts International 49(6), 2370B. University Microfilms No. 88-18138.

Beck, A. J., and B. E. Shipley. 1987. Recidivism of young parolees. *Criminal Justice Archive Information Network.* http://webapp.icpsr.umich.edu/cocoon/NACJD-STUDY/08673.xml.

Bernard, T. J. 1992. *The cycle of juvenile justice.* New York: Oxford University Press.

Borduin, C. M., S. W. Henggeler, D. M. Blaske and R. J. Stein. 1990. Multisystemic treatment of adolescent sexual offenders. *International Journal of Offender Therapy and Comparative Criminology* 34: 105–113.

Burt, M. R., and K. J. Pittman. 1985. Testing the social safety net: The impact of changes in support programs during the Reagan administration. Washington: Urban Institute Press.

Byrne, J. M., and L. Kelly. 1989. Restructuring probation as an intermediate sanction: An evaluation of the Massachusetts intensive probation supervision program. Unpublished final report to U.S. National Institute of Justice.

Byrne, J. M., and A. Pattavina. 1992. The effectiveness issue: Assessing what works in the adult community corrections system. Pp. 281–303 in *Smart sentencing: The emergence of intermediate sanctions.* Edited by J. M. Byrne, A. J. Lurigio, and J. Petersilia. Thousand Oaks, CA: Sage.

Catalano, R. F., E. A. Wells, J. M. Jenson and J. D. Hawkins. 1989. Aftercare services for drug-using adjudicated youth in residential settings. *Social Service Review* 63: 553–577.

Center for Substance Abuse Treatment. 1998. *Continuity of offender treatment for substance use disorders from institution to community.* Treatment Improvement Protocol (TIP) Series, no. 30. Washington: Center for Substance Abuse Treatment, Substance Abuse and Mental Health Services Administration, U.S. Department of Health and Human Services.

Center for Substance Abuse Treatment. 1999a. *Strategies for integrating substance abuse treatment and the juvenile system: A practical guide.* Washington: Center for Substance Abuse Treatment, Substance Abuse and Mental Health Services Administration, U.S. Department of Health and Human Services.

Center for Substance Abuse Treatment. 1999b. *Treatment of adolescents with substance use disorders.* Treatment Improvement Protocol (TIP) Series, no. 32. Washington: Center for Substance Abuse Treatment, Substance Abuse and Mental Health Services Administration, U.S. Department of Health and Human Services.

Chandler, M. J. 1973. Egocentrism and antisocial behavior: The assessment and training of social perspective-taking skills. *Developmental Psychology* 9: 326–333.

Coates, R. B., A. D. Miller and L. E. Ohlin. 1978. *Diversity in a youth correctional system: Handling delinquents in Massachusetts.* Cambridge: Ballinger.

Cocozza, Joseph J., and K. Skowyra. 2000. Youth with mental health disorders: Issues and emerging responses. *Juvenile Justice* 7: 3–13.

Cohen, J., and J. A. Canela-Cacho. 1994. Incarceration and violent crime: 1965–1988. Pp. 296–388 in *Understanding and preventing violence,* vol. 4: *Consequences and controls.* Edited by A. J. Reiss, Jr., and J. A. Roth. Washington: National Academy Press.

Delinquency Research Group. 1986. *An evaluation of the delinquency of participants in the Youth at Risk program.* Claremont Graduate School, Center for Applied Social Research, Claremont, CA.

Dembo, R., S. Livingston, and J. Schmeidler. Forthcoming. Treatment for drug involved youth in the juvenile justice system. In *Clinical and policy responses to drug offenders.* Edited by C. Leukefeld, F. Tims, and D. Farabee. New York: Springer.

DiIulio, J. 1995. *Arresting ideas.* Washington: Heritage Foundation.

Empey, L. T., and S. G. Lubeck. 1971. *The silverlake experiment: Testing delinquency theory and community intervention.* Chicago: Aldine.

Feld, B. C. 1997. Abolish the juvenile court: Youthfulness, criminal responsibility, and sentencing policy. *Journal of Criminal Law and Criminology* 88: 68–136.

Frederick, B. 1999. *Factors contributing to recidivism among youth placed with the New York State Division for Youth.* Albany: Office of Justice Systems Analysis, New York State Division of Criminal Justice Services.

GAINS Center. 1997. *Screening and assessment of co-occurring disorders in the justice system.* Delmar, NY: GAINS Center.

Glick, B., and A. P. Goldstein. 1987. Aggression replacement training. *Journal of Counseling and Development* 65: 356–362.

Gordon, D. A., K. Graves, and J. Arbuthnot. 1987. Prevention of adult criminal behavior using family therapy for disadvantaged juvenile delinquents. Unpublished manuscript, Ohio University.

Griffin, P. 2000. *National overviews: State juvenile justice profiles.* Pittsburgh: National Center for Juvenile Justice.

Guarino-Ghezzi, S., and E. J. Loughran. 1996. *Balancing juvenile justice.* New Brunswick, NJ: Transaction Publishers.

Guerra, N. G., and R. G. Slaby. 1990. Cognitive mediators of aggression in adolescent offenders: 2. Intervention. *Developmental Psychology* 26: 269–277.

Hagan, J. 1991. Destiny and drift: Subcultural preferences, status attainments, and the risks and awards of youth. *American Sociological Review* 56: 567–582.

Haley, J. 1980. *Leaving home: The therapy of disturbed young people.* New York: McGraw-Hill.

Harrison, P. M., and J. C. Karberg. 2003. Prison and jail inmates at midyear 2002. Bureau of Justice Statistics Bulletin. Washington: Bureau of Justice Statistics, Office of Justice Programs, U.S. Department of Justice.

Jesness, C. F., F. S. Allison, P. M. McCormic, R. F. Wedge, and M. L. Young. 1975. *Evaluation of the effectiveness of contingency contracting with delinquents.* Sacramento: California Youth Authority.

Kantrowitz, R. E. 1980. *Training nonprofessionals to work with delinquents: Differential impacts of varying training/supervisions/intervention strategies.* Doctoral dissertation, Michigan State University. Dissertation Abstracts International 40(10), 5007B. University Microfilms no. 80-06139.

Kemp, M., and R. Lee. 1975. *Project Crest: A third year experimental study.* Gainesville, FL: Project Crest.

Krisberg, B., O. Rodriguez, A. Bakke, D. Neuenfeldt, and P. Steele. 1989. *Demonstration of post-adjudication non-residential intensive supervision programs: Assessment report.* San Francisco: National Council on Crime and Delinquency.

Lee, R., and N. M. Haynes. 1978a. Counseling delinquents: Dual treatment revisited. *Rehabilitation Counseling Bulletin* 22: 130–133.

Lee, R., and N. M. Haynes. 1978b. Counseling juvenile offenders: An experimental evaluation of Project Crest. *Community Mental Health Journal* 14: 267–271.

Lee, R., and S. Olejnik. 1981. Professional outreach counseling can help the juvenile probationer: A two-year follow-up study. *Personnel and Guidance Journal* 59: 445–449.

Lipsey, M. 1992. Juvenile delinquency treatment: A meta-analytic inquiry into the variability of effects. Pp. 83–127 in *Meta-analysis for explanation: A casebook.* Edited by T. D. Cook, H. Cooper, D. S. Cordray, H. Hartmann, L. V. Hedges, R. J. Light, T. A. Louis, and F. Mosteller. New York: Russell Sage Foundation.

Lipsey, M., and D. B. Wilson. 1998. Effective intervention for serious juvenile offenders: A synthesis of research. Pp. 313–345 in *Serious and violent juvenile offenders: Risk factors and successful interventions.* Edited by R. Loeber and D. P. Farrington. Thousand Oaks, CA: Sage Publications.

Lipsey, M., G. Chapman, and N. Landenberger. 2001. Cognitive-behavioral programs for offenders. *Annals of the American Academy of Political and Social Science* 578: 144–157.

Lurigio, A. J., and J. Petersilia. 1992. The emergence of intensive probation supervision programs in the United States. Pp. 3–17 in *Smart sentencing: The emergence of intermediate sanctions.* Edited by J. M. Byrne, A. J. Lurigio, and J. Petersilia. Newbury Park, CA: Sage Publications.

Mears, D. 2001. Critical challenges in addressing the mental health needs of juvenile offenders. *Juvenile Policy Journal* 1: 41–61.

Moore, R. H. 1978. Effectiveness of citizen volunteers functioning as counselors for high-risk young male offenders. *Psychological Reports* 61: 823–830.

Moore, R. H., and D. Levine. 1974. *Evaluation research of a community-based probation program.* Lincoln: University of Nebraska at Lincoln, Department of Psychology.

National Institute of Justice. 2000. *1999 annual report on drug use among adult and juvenile arrestees.* Washington: U.S. Department of Justice.

National Research Council. 1993. *Losing generations: Adolescents in high risk settings.* Panel on High Risk Youth, Commission on Behavioral and Social Sciences and Education. Washington: National Academy Press.

National Research Council and Institute of Medicine. 2001. *Juvenile crime, juvenile justice.* Washington: National Academy Press.

OJJDP. 2001. *Blueprints for violence prevention.* Juvenile Justice Bulletin. Washington: Office of Juvenile Justice and Delinquency Prevention, Office of Justice Programs, U.S. Department of Justice.

Pearson, F., D. Lipton, C. Cleland, and D. Yee. 2002. The effects of behavioral/cognitive-behavioral programs on recidivism. *Crime and Delinquency* 48: 476–495.

Petersilia, J. and S. Turner. 1991. An evaluation of intensive probation in California. *Journal of Criminal Law and Criminology* 82: 610–658.

Piercy, F., and R. Lee. 1976. Effects of a dual treatment approach on the rehabilitation of habitual juvenile delinquents. *Rehabilitation Counseling Bulletin* 19: 482–492.

Reclaiming Futures. 2001. Call for proposals: Building community solutions to substance abuse and delinquency. Reclaiming Futures National Program Office, School of Social Work, Portland State University (www.reclaimingfutures.org).

Reiss, Jr., A. J., and J. A. Roth. 1993. *Understanding and preventing violence.* Washington: National Academy Press.

Schlicter, K. J., and J. J. Horan. 1981. Effects of stress inoculation on the anger and aggression management skills of institutionalized juvenile delinquents. *Cognitive Therapy and Research* 5: 359–365.

Schwitzgebel, R., and D. A. Kolb. 1964. Inducing behaviour change in adolescent delinquents. *Behavior Research and Therapy* 1: 297–304.

Shannon, L. W., J. L. McKim, J. P. Curry, and L. J. Haffner. 1988. *Criminal career continuity: Its social context.* New York: Human Sciences Press.

Shivrattan, J. L. 1988. Social interactional training and incarcerated juvenile delinquents. *Canadian Journal of Criminology* 30: 145–163.

Sickmund, M., and Y. Wan. 2001. Census of juveniles in residential placement databook. http://ojjdp.ncjrs.org/ojstabb/cjrp.

Snyder, H. N., and M. Sickmund. 1999. Juvenile offenders and victims: 1999 national report. Washington: Office of Juvenile Justice and Delinquency Prevention, U.S. Department of Justice.

Spence, S. H., and J. S. Marzillier. 1981. Social skills training with adolescent male offenders. 2: Short-term, long-term, and generalized effects. *Behavior Research and Therapy* 19: 349–368.

Stahl, A., T. Finnegan, and W. Kang. 2002. Easy access to juvenile court statistics: 1985–2000. http://www.ojjdp.ncjrs.org/ojstatbb/ezajcs.

Torbet, P. M. 1996. *Juvenile probation: The workhorse of the juvenile justice system.* Washington: Office of Juvenile Justice and Delinquency Prevention, Office of Justice Programs, U.S. Department of Justice.

Travis, J., A. L. Solomon and M. Waul. 2001. *From prison to home: The dimensions and consequences of prisoner reentry.* Washington: Urban Institute.

Turner, S., and J. Petersilia. 1992. Focusing on high-risk parolees: An experiment to reduce commitments to the Texas Department of Corrections. *Journal of Research in Crime and Delinquency* 29: 34–61.

Whittaker, J. K. 1979. *Caring for troubled children: Residential treatment in a community-based context.* San Francisco: Jossey-Bass.

Wiebush, R. G., B. McNulty, and T. Le. 2000. *Implementation of the intensive community-based aftercare program.* Washington: Office of Juvenile Justice and Delinquency Prevention, Office of Justice Programs, U.S. Department of Justice.

Wolfensberger, W. 1972. *Normalization.* New York: National Institute on Mental Retardation.

Zimring, F. E. 1978. *Confronting youth crime: Report of the Twentieth Century Fund task force on sentencing policy toward young offenders.* New York: Holmes & Meier.

Zimring, F. E. 1981. Toward a jurisprudence of waiver. Pp. 193–205 in *Major issues in juvenile justice information and training: Readings in public policy.* Edited by J. C. Hall, D. M. Hamparian, J. M. Pettibone, and J. L. White. Columbus, OH: Academy for Contemporary Problems.

Zimring, F. E. 2000. *American youth violence.* New York: Oxford University Press.

Zimring, F. E., and G. Hawkins. 1992. *The search for rational drug control.* New York: Cambridge University Press.

CHAPTER FIVE

Young Adults Reentering the Community from the Criminal Justice System: The Challenge of Becoming an Adult

CHRISTOPHER UGGEN AND SARA WAKEFIELD

We thank the editors, Mark Courtney, and Larry Steinberg for helpful comments on an earlier draft.

In a recent literature review, Michael Shanahan (2000, 685) describes the transition to adulthood in the contemporary United States as less predictable and more precarious than ever before. If the transition to adulthood is more variable and more difficult for the general population, what difficulties are faced by adults who spend their late teens and early twenties in prison or under correctional supervision? In this chapter we consider the vulnerability and resilience of young adults who return to the community from the criminal justice system across various domains of adjustment, including work, family, civic life, mental health, and substance use.

Illustrative of this transition is Dylan, a white Minnesota inmate incarcerated at age sixteen who had been imprisoned for more than half his life when interviewed at age twenty-nine for Uggen's study of the political life of convicted felons. Although Dylan had attained none of the standard markers of adult status when he entered prison, thirteen years later he appeared to be a mature, accomplished, and well-educated adult. Yet, Dylan is also keenly aware of the difficulties he will face when he is released from prison because he is "off-time" relative to his age cohort with regard to the assumption of adult roles (Caspi, Elder, and Herbener 1990; Hagestad and Neugarten 1985).

> I have this feeling of I have so much to make up for, like lost time, and I have nothing to show for it. I'll get out when I'm 34. I have no house, no car, no

anything. So I'm going to have to spend a lot of my time working just to get my feet on the ground.

Pamela, a female inmate incarcerated for prescription drug abuse, suggested that it is difficult to view her fellow inmates as full-fledged adults, no matter their age:

That's how the women are here, just beaten up. Beaten up little kids who grew up. They're like little kids walking around in woman bodies.

These comments raise questions about the links among crime, punishment, and adulthood. Can people "grow up" in prison? (See chapter 3 by Chung, Little, and Steinberg for a discussion of how incarceration arrests normal psychosocial development.) Are correctional facilities and detention centers necessarily holding pens that hinder development, or do they have the potential to help their clients assume stable adult roles? In this chapter we first describe the young adult correctional population in the United States. We then detail the life course delays and disadvantages of young offenders prior to entering the criminal justice system. Next, we describe the consequences of punishment on the transition to adulthood for ex-offenders. Finally, we consider social context and variation in crime, punishment, and the transition to adulthood.

THE U.S. CRIMINAL JUSTICE SYSTEM AND ITS DEFINITION OF THE POPULATION

The U.S. criminal justice system can be divided into a rough sequence of police, court, and correctional functions. The further people are drawn into this sequence—from initial police contact, to arrest, to booking, to charging, to conviction, to sentencing, and ultimately to placement in a secure facility—the greater the potential for stigma, social exclusion, and disruption in life course transition processes. Our primary concern here is with the back end of this system and the young adults who reenter the community after being placed by courts under the supervision of one or more correctional agencies. In particular, we consider the challenge of the transition to adulthood for those serving time as probationers, prisoners, and parolees.

Probation

Probation is a criminal sentence that allows an individual to remain in the community under the supervision of the court for a specified period of time. If the probationer breaks the law or fails to abide by the terms of the probation agreement (which may involve conditions such as drug testing, work requirements, and travel restrictions) for the duration of the sentence, probation may be cancelled or revoked and a more severe sentence imposed. About four million adults were under probation supervision in 2002 (U.S. Department of Justice 2003a). The most recent estimate available suggests that about 26 percent of probationers (about one million individuals) are aged eighteen to twenty-four (Bonczar 1997). Although probation is often applied to first-time offenders or those convicted of nonviolent offenses, it is important to note that about 50 percent of all probationers have been convicted of felonies, or crimes that are punishable by one year or more in prison.

Prison

While probationers are generally permitted to retain work, family, and community ties, prisoners are physically removed from these domains. Because a prison term is likely to have the strongest implications for the transition to adulthood, our discussion relies heavily on interview and survey data from prison inmates (U.S. Department of Justice 2001b; Uggen, Manza, and Behrens 2003b). Roughly 1.4 million offenders were serving time in state or federal prisons in 2002, with an additional 665,000 held in local jails (U.S. Department of Justice 2003b). In contrast to prisons, jails confine people before as well as after they have been sentenced. About 60 percent of the 2002 jail population consisted of persons awaiting trial, and most jail inmates who have been convicted are sentenced to jail terms of less than one year (U.S. Department of Justice 2003b). Overall, about 100,000 young adults aged eighteen to twenty-four will be released from prison this year.

Parole

In addition to probation and incarceration, parole represents a third correctional population of interest that poses challenges in the transition to adulthood. Parole is the planned conditional release and supervision of prisoners before the expiration of their prison sentences. Parolees are subject to similar conditions as probationers and they may be returned to prison for new offenses or for technical violations of parole rules (such as leaving the local area). In contrast to previous years, a greater percentage of parolees enter supervision today as a result of mandatory release dates rather than through discretionary decisions of parole boards. In 1990, about 59 percent of prisoners were released by parole boards; in 2001, only 36 percent. Currently, approximately 16 percent of those released to parole are between the ages of eighteen and twenty-four, about 90 percent are male, and about 65 percent are members of racial minority groups (U.S. Department of Justice 2001a). About 41 percent of the approximately 750,000 people within the total parole population were returned to prison as a result of technical violations or new offenses in 2002 (U.S. Department of Justice 2003a).

All together, a record 6.7 million people were serving time in prison, on probation, or on parole in 2002, representing about 3.1 percent of the total U.S. adult population and a far greater proportion of the young adult population (U.S. Department of Justice 2003a). In recent years, approximately 600,000 people have been released from prison annually, 500,000 complete parole, and 2 million exit probation supervision (U.S. Department of Justice 2003a,b). Many of these individuals are young adults who face a multitude of roadblocks to assuming stable adult roles.

To provide some basic descriptive data on the young adults who face the greatest barriers in entering or resuming work, family, and community roles, we will draw upon data from a large-scale nationally representative survey of young adults in prison. The 1997 Survey of Inmates in State and Federal Correctional Facilities is based on personal interviews conducted by the U.S. Bureau of the Census with approximately 14,000 state prisoners and 4,000 federal prisoners (U.S. Department of Justice 2001b).

As further illustrations, we also reference qualitative interviews conducted in Minnesota as part of a project on the scope and impact of political restrictions on convicted felons in the United States (Manza and Uggen forthcoming; Uggen and Manza 2002). Prisoners, parolees, and felony probationers were asked about their participation in political and civic life and their attitudes about crime and community. Each taped interview lasted approximately one hour and took place in a private room at one of two state correctional facilities or one county community corrections office.[1] To protect the confidentiality of those interviewed, we have assigned each respondent a pseudonym when quoting directly from the interview transcripts.

---

1. The volunteer respondents consist of ten female prison inmates, thirteen male prison inmates, seven male felony probationers, and three male parolees. The respondents range from twenty to fifty-four years of age and represent all major offense categories, although most of the interviewees had been convicted of at least one violent crime. Twenty-two of the respondents are white, six are African-American, and five are Native American.

THE TRANSITION TO ADULTHOOD AND
ENTRY INTO THE CRIMINAL JUSTICE SYSTEM

Historically, transition markers such as moving out of the home of origin, completing an education, finding stable work, getting married, and becoming a parent have signaled adult status (Hogan 1981; Shanahan 2000). Becoming an adult is not only a matter of achieving the markers of adult status but also of obtaining them in reasonable sequence at a socially prescribed or normative age.[2] Most young people enter the criminal justice system lagging far behind their age cohort in employment status, socioeconomic attainment, marriage formation, establishment of an independent residence, and other markers of adulthood. Although prisoners may gain marginal increases in human capital while incarcerated, such as attaining a General Equivalency Diploma, the vast majority will reenter their communities with these deficits intact.

Family of Origin Disadvantages and Socioeconomic Attainment

The socioeconomic divide between correctional populations and the general population is visible when people enter the system, and often more pronounced when they exit it. This observation holds across almost all domains of adult adjustment, but is especially true for socioeconomic attainment and disadvantaged family status. We present some descriptive data from the 1997 National Survey of Inmates in State and Federal Correctional Facilities (U.S. Department of Justice 2001b) in figure 5.1. The inmate survey provides nationally representative data on state prisoners. For the purposes of this chapter, we selected only those inmates age twenty-five or younger in order to develop a portrait of the transition to adulthood for young adult former prisoners who return to the community.

Figure 5.1 reveals high rates of disadvantage in prisoners' families of origin as well as a number of continuing deficits that are likely to impact inmates' lives upon release from prison. With regard to socioeconomic background, 24.2 percent of young inmates spent some portion of their childhood in public housing developments, and 46.5 percent reported that their parents or guardians received public assistance. About 16 percent had been placed in foster care or institutional

2. The timing of life course transitions is also culturally specific and structurally determined. For example, becoming a parent for the first time at approximately age twenty-five is considered normative behavior in the contemporary United States, whereas becoming a parent at age fourteen renders a teenage mother "off-time" in relation to her age cohort. Off-time events often have consequences long after they occur and hold the potential to delay or disrupt later transitions. Early pregnancy, for example, is likely to impact later educational and occupational attainment.

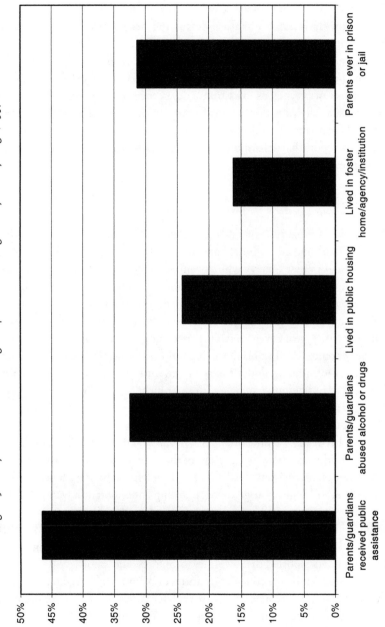

Figure 5.1. Early childhood disadvantages of prison inmates age twenty-five or younger, 1997.

homes at some point during their childhood and about 33 percent reported growing up with parents or guardians who abused alcohol or drugs. (See chapter 2 by Courtney and Heuring for a discussion of youth in the foster care system).

A growing research literature details the deleterious consequences of an incarcerated parent or guardian on their children. Children of incarcerated parents suffer economically from the removal of the parent's legal (and illegal) income (Hagan and Dinovitzer 1999; Johnson and Waldfogel 2004), may be at greater risk of precocious exits from adolescence (Hagan and Wheaton 1993), and are especially vulnerable to involvement in the criminal justice system themselves (Hagan and Palloni 1990). In the inmate survey, 31.3 percent of young prisoners report that at least one parent or guardian spent time in prison or jail while they were growing up.

Juvenile Criminal History

A juvenile criminal history tends to increase later criminal involvement by restricting work and educational opportunities (Hagan 1993; Laub and Sampson 1995). For example, James, a white twenty-four-year-old whom we interviewed in prison, was first charged at age eleven for an assault, was first placed into custody at twelve for auto theft, and had an adult theft conviction at eighteen before his most recent conviction for manslaughter at age nineteen. He noted that "since age 11, I have never been 'off paper' [not serving a probation, prison, or parole sentence] . . . I've been wasting quite a few tax dollars." Overall, about 70 percent of inmates under the age of twenty-five in the survey had a prior criminal record before sentencing for their most recent offense.

Figure 5.2 presents some descriptive statistics on the criminal histories of young adults in the inmate survey (U.S. Department of Justice 2001b). We distinguish between first-time offenders (about 29.9 percent of the sample), nonviolent recidivists (about 25.5 percent of the sample), and recidivists whose past or current offense has involved a crime of violence (about 44.6 percent of the sample). A strikingly clear gradient regarding childhood disadvantage emerges across the three groups. The violent recidivists are most likely to report that one or both parents had been incarcerated, that they lived in foster homes as children, and that they had social ties to delinquent friends while growing up. First-time offenders reported the lowest levels on these indicators.

Focusing on the life course trajectories of delinquents, Hagan (1993) argues that early criminal involvement restricts later education and work opportunities, thereby making continued involvement in crime more likely. As offenders become embedded in criminal networks and entangled in the criminal justice system, barriers to occupational and educational attainment accumulate over

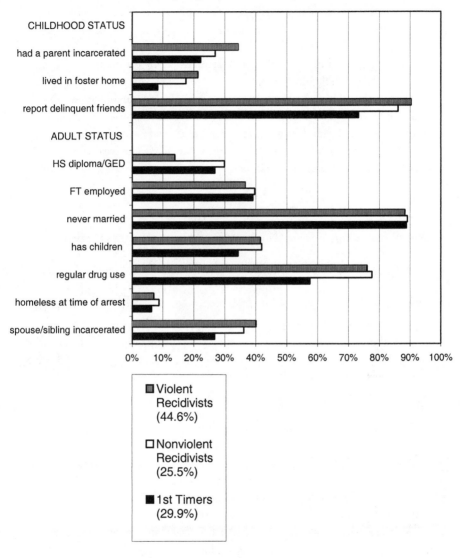

Figure 5.2. Characteristics of prison inmates age twenty-five
or younger by criminal history.

CHILDHOOD STATUS
had a parent incarcerated
lived in foster home
report delinquent friends

ADULT STATUS
HS diploma/GED
FT employed
never married
has children
regular drug use
homeless at time of arrest
spouse/sibling incarcerated

0% 10% 20% 30% 40% 50% 60% 70% 80% 90% 100%

☒ Violent
Recidivists
(44.6%)

☐ Nonviolent
Recidivists
(25.5%)

■ 1st Timers
(29.9%)

time, making major life changes increasingly difficult. (See a similar argument
about homeless youth in Hagan and McCarthy's chapter 7.) As this model suggests, those with more extensive criminal justice contact are also somewhat
more likely to be delayed on several markers of adult status. Violent recidivists
are far less likely to have obtained a high school diploma or GED than the other

groups and somewhat less likely to be working full-time at the time of their most recent arrest. Consistent with criminal embeddedness arguments, violent recidivists are also more likely to report other problems, such as regular use of illegal drugs and homelessness, and to be tied to spouses or siblings who have also been incarcerated.

Looking backward in time, it seems clear that young prisoners who become more deeply embedded in the criminal justice system often have had difficult family backgrounds and ties to delinquent friends and parents in childhood. Looking forward, they are likely to experience greater problems in attaining adult status and greater difficulty in adjustment once they leave prison. In contrast, those entering prison with no prior record are likely to have had a relatively more advantaged background and, perhaps, brighter prospects in the future.

Substance Abuse

When I drink, I always get into trouble. Something always happens.

Kevin, probationer, age 21 (emphasis added)

Currently, about 22 percent of prisoners are incarcerated specifically for drug offenses and the vast majority of prison inmates report prior illegal drug use. About 50 percent of all inmates were drinking or using drugs at the time of their offense; of these, about one in six also report supporting drug use as the primary motivation for their most recent criminal offense (U.S. Department of Justice 1999; see also Uggen and Thompson 2003).

Alex, a thirty-seven-year old prison inmate, says

I thought, "Okay. It's always the other person that gets into trouble." When it finally happened to me—alcohol just makes it easier to do and get into trouble.

Alex was convicted of manslaughter after he stabbed a close family member during an argument. He believes that his alcoholism was a contributing factor to the crime; he now attends an Alcoholics Anonymous program in prison. Despite high rates of substance abuse among prisoners, only 33 percent of inmates using drugs within a month of their arrest have participated in substance abuse treatment since admission to prison. Drug and alcohol abuse is particularly high among younger inmates. Among those aged twenty-five or younger, 71 percent report regular illegal drug use, 63 percent report drug use in the month prior to their arrest, and 33 percent were using drugs at the time of their current offense (U.S. Department of Justice 1999). Drug use is similarly high in the probationer population. In 1995, about 70 percent of probationers reported past illegal drug use, yet only 17 percent of probationers completed drug treatment during their sentence.

Physical, Mental, and Learning Disabilities

Relative to the general population, prison inmates have much higher rates of serious health problems and mental illnesses. Travis and Visher (chapter 6) report that about 20 percent of prison releasees have HIV or AIDS and 38 percent tested positive for tuberculosis. Travis and Visher also report high rates of serious health problems resulting from sustained drug and alcohol abuse.

The prevalence of mental illness in the prison population has also grown substantially since the deinstitutionalization movement of the early 1960s and what some have called the criminalization of mental illness (Lamb and Weinberger 1998; Teplin 1984a). Lamb and Weinberger (1998) note that the number of mentally ill persons in state hospitals has fallen from 559,000 in 1955 to 72,000 in 1998, primarily as a result of closures of state mental hospitals and the shift to the penitentiary as the primary site of mental health care. Mentally ill inmates are more likely than those with no reported mental or emotional conditions to be incarcerated for violent offenses, to have been homeless and unemployed at the time of arrest, or to report a family history of incarceration, substance abuse, or physical or sexual abuse victimization (Ditton 1999; Teplin 1984b). Today, about 10 percent of all prison inmates and 16 percent of probationers report a mental condition or an overnight stay in a mental hospital (Ditton 1999). Such self-reports are likely to significantly underestimate the prevalence of mental illness. Though prisons may not be the most effective site for mental health treatment, about 60 percent of mentally ill inmates and about 50 percent of mentally ill probationers received some form of treatment (medication, counseling, or group treatment program) while serving their sentences.

Although the inmate survey does not formally assess disabilities, respondents reported their mental health and disability status in interviews, as shown in figure 5.3. About 20 percent of young prison inmates reported having some type of disability; 10 percent, a learning disability; 7 percent, a mental or emotional disorder; 5 percent, a physical disability; and 3 percent, a speech disability. Although no directly comparable self-reported disability data are available for the general population, it is likely that the prevalence of disabilities among prison inmates is higher than in other groups. According to the 1997 Survey of Income and Program Participation, for example, 11 percent of the civilian noninstitutionalized population aged fifteen through twenty-one reported any disability, while 5.3 percent reported a severe disability (U.S. Bureau of the Census 2000, 140). The fact that one in five prison inmates report a disability thus

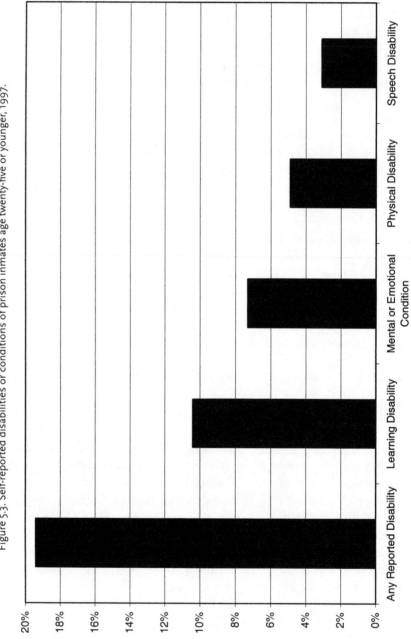

Figure 5.3: Self-reported disabilities or conditions of prison inmates age twenty-five or younger, 1997.

suggests somewhat greater vulnerability among correctional populations to physical, mental, or emotional difficulties.

Moffitt's (1993) developmental research points to neuropsychological deficits as a primary factor for distinguishing between offenders who persist in crime after adolescence and those who leave delinquency behind to adopt conventional adult roles. Adolescents with a childhood history of neuropsychological deficits are more likely to persist in crime into adulthood. Because such problems also tend to be associated with disadvantaged family situations, the deficits experienced by life-course persistent offenders in early childhood are magnified over time, resulting in criminal involvement long after adolescence that hinders adjustment across the domains of school, work, family, mental health, and substance use.

Adult Status Markers: Work, School, and Family Formation

Given the prevalence of early childhood disadvantage, substance abuse, and disability among prison inmates, it is perhaps unsurprising that this group would also lag behind their age cohort in educational and occupational attainment immediately prior to entering prison. Figure 5.4 compares the school, work, and family statuses of young prison inmates with those of males aged eighteen through twenty-four in the general population (U.S. Bureau of Labor Statistics 2003). Most strikingly, the educational attainment of young inmates lags far behind that of their counterparts in the general population. Almost 75 percent of U.S. males aged eighteen to twenty-four have attained at least a high school diploma; less than 20 percent of inmates have done so. At the time of their most recent arrest, inmates were also more likely to have been unemployed than noninmates, and much less likely to be working full-time. The two groups are roughly comparable in terms of marital status, with the vast majority of both populations unmarried in this age range. Some 48 percent of the inmate group, however, reported having at least one child. (Unfortunately, no directly comparable data are available for the general male population.)

All in all, offenders enter prison with a multitude of problems across most domains of adult adjustment. Young offenders, particularly those with juvenile criminal histories, are more likely to have been raised in adverse economic and familial circumstances. A substantial portion have physical health problems, mental health and substance abuse issues, or learning disabilities. When arrested, many young inmates were homeless, unemployed, or undereducated. To what extent can prisons address these deficits? Below, we explore the opportunities and challenges to improving the health, education, and occupational attainment of young offenders while they are serving their sentences.

Figure 5.4. Comparison of inmates age twenty-five or younger and U.S. males age eighteen to twenty-four by adult status markers, 1997.

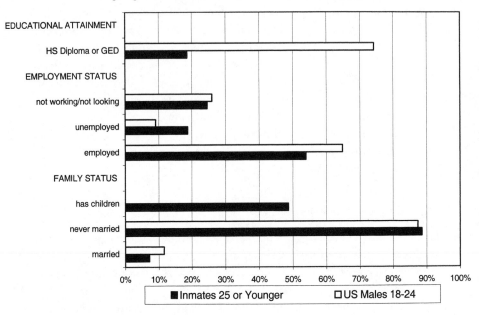

SERVING A SENTENCE: OPPORTUNITIES FOR DEVELOPMENT BEHIND BARS?

Criminal sentences disrupt employment, family arrangements, and civic engagement. While probationers are allowed to complete their sentences in the community, prisoners are removed from most important social contacts for the duration of their sentences. In some cases this may be a positive development, such as when inmates are removed from criminal peer networks or volatile family situations. At the same time, incarceration also cuts inmates off from active participation as parents, community members, and employees. Additionally, inmates may also be subject to serious injury or sexual assault while behind bars (Bell et al. 1999). The Bureau of Justice Statistics reports that in 1997 roughly 20 percent of state prisoners younger than twenty-five were injured in prison; of these, about 10 percent were injured in fights with other inmates (U.S. Department of Justice 2001c).

Current and former inmates now face substantial difficulty entering programs and receiving services that are likely to improve their employment prospects. Many convicted felons are prohibited from receiving financial aid for higher education. Felons on probation or parole are often barred from public assistance programs and access to public housing (Rubenstein and Mukamal 2002). Larry, a thirty-year-old prisoner, expressed displeasure about recent restrictions on inmate access to higher education.

> I think education is underrated. There's not enough of it. They keep taking it away. You know, I was going to [university] through their program and they took the program away. About a year later they brought a smaller version of it back, but still it's not the same as it was.

Larry also doubts the utility of GED-only educational programs for prisoners.

> Well, the G.E.D.'s not gonna do anything. You know, there's all kind of guys in here that have a G.E.D. and they're still running around committin' crime, you know. They need to go to some higher education. A G.E.D. is not going to change anybody's intelligence level. All you got's this little piece of paper saying, "Yeah, I'm *almost like* a high school student."

Offenders also increasingly face the termination of their parental rights as a result of incarceration. For those who retain parental rights, maintaining consistent contact with children is extremely difficult (Travis and Visher, chapter 6). Currently, incarceration rates among women are rising, yielding greater family disruption, since women are more likely to be living with their children prior to incarceration (Hagan and Dinovitzer 1999). Mary, a forty-year-old prisoner, described the difficulties of physical separation from children and the uncertainty of resuming parental duties upon release from prison.

> And it crushes a lot of women. I mean their whole world gets totally shattered in here because they don't have their children nearby. Or their children are in different homes and things like that. There's a lady here who has four children, and they're each in a different foster home. When she gets out is she going to be able to collect her children back? I don't know.

Given the substantial costs associated with removing inmates from community, work, and family life, can prisons release inmates who are better off than when they entered? Whereas prisons generally provide inmates with some degree of education and work experience, jails are much less likely to provide such programming, and jail conditions vary dramatically across jurisdictions. Moreover, though most prisons offer education programs, substance abuse treatment, or vocational training opportunities for inmates, participation in such programs is low and has been declining (Travis and Visher, chapter 6). Inmates are also subject to the long-term trend in U.S. correctional policy emphasizing a punitive rather than a rehabilitative ideology (Altschuler, chapter 4). Our qualitative interviews suggest that inmates are aware of this emphasis as well. Craig, a twenty-two-year-old prisoner, was one of many who felt that the dominance of punitive programs is a direct reflection of the wishes of community members, as opposed to policies imposed by politicians or correctional authorities.

> The general attitude is that, at least with the prison system, is more things are just being taken away. It's getting where it's not so much for politicians, but it's actually the whole community, the whole society is saying, "We want more punishment." "We don't think treatment works. It's not worth it." They just wanna punish. It's real frustrating, it seems like there's not a lot of understanding maybe from the public, or maybe an attempt to work with each other. It seems like a lot of guys in here become angry at the public.

A number of popular biographies have described prison as a transformative experience. For example, *The Autobiography of Malcolm X* and Nathan McCall's *Makes Me Wanna Holler* describe incarceration as a time in which reflection, rest, and growth are possible. Also, despite public skepticism and political resistance, a growing research literature has shown that rehabilitation programs are capable of lowering recidivism rates for those who participate (see Cullen and Gendreau 2000 for a review). Without such programs, the life course perspective, our qualitative interviews, and research on criminal desistance suggest that prison will fail to transform the majority of inmates from immature or disadvantaged offenders into active community members, responsible parents, and stable employees upon release.

REENTERING THE COMMUNITY: CONSEQUENCES OF PUNISHMENT

Perhaps the most important first step to community reengagement and criminal desistance is the adoption of a noncriminal identity. Viewing oneself as a *former* offender is likely to impact an inmate's desire for legitimate employment (and persistence during the job search), chances of successful family reintegration, and resistance to attractive criminal opportunities. Though such a process may begin prior to prison release (e.g., cognitive behavioral treatment programs), the society outside the prison walls will heavily influence how former inmates perceive opportunities for legitimate success and the fate of their developing prosocial identity (Maruna 2001).

Matsueda and Heimer (1997, 167) offer a social-psychological perspective on crime that is useful for understanding the barriers ex-prisoners face in adopting prosocial identities. In this model, self-concept, identity, and the adoption of some roles ("gang member") over others ("computer programmer") are a function of social interaction. The most salient roles are those played repeatedly over time and those that are reinforced in social relationships. This approach suggests that prison reentry programs may be successful only insofar as the social relationships and environment outside of prison reinforces earlier principles learned in prison.

Life course research helps to explain how young adults make their way into the criminal justice system as well as identify the sorts of barriers they are likely to face when returning to their communities (Edin, Nelson, and Paranal 2004; Pettit and Western 2004). Those with early disadvantages are likely to become embedded in problematic life course trajectories with the attendant barriers to work, family, and civic reintegration. Yet it is often the effects of *punishment* rather than offending that disrupt or delay life course transitions. Thus far, we have shown the substantial disadvantages of probationers, inmates, and parolees prior to entering the criminal justice system and discussed the challenges to development while serving their sentences. We next describe the barriers to a successful transition to adulthood that arise from criminal punishment.

Work

Obtaining legitimate and quality employment may powerfully assist in the adoption of a durable noncriminal identity. There is ample evidence that work may be important for explaining both the onset of crime in childhood and adolescence and desistance from crime in adulthood. Although the transition from school to full-time work is a clear marker of adult status in the United States, the effects of employment on crime are likely to be age graded. For example, Uggen (2000) finds that a basic employment opportunity reduces criminal involvement for offenders age twenty-seven and older, a group that is noticeably delayed with respect to adult work transitions. Though evidence suggests that the simple provision of employment is unlikely to impact the criminal behavior of young offenders (Paternoster et al. 2003; Uggen 2000), job quality and earnings are both tied to reductions in crime among offenders (Crutchfield and Pitchford 1997; Uggen 1999; Uggen and Thompson 2003). In contrast, adolescents who work more than twenty hours per week (Bachman and Schulenberg 1993) or in more adultlike work settings (Staff and Uggen 2003) tend to be more involved in delinquency than those who work less or not at all. Such findings may indicate that a precocious transition to adulthood or a "hurried adolescence" (Safron, Schulenberg, and Bachman 2001) is associated with delinquency, substance use, and other risky behaviors. Thus, early as well as late transitions to adult work roles tend to increase criminal involvement because the meaning of work and other important life course transitions is age dependent.

Beyond the impact of work on crime and criminal desistance, a burgeoning research literature is demonstrating strong punishment effects on employment and earnings, showing that imprisonment affects both the quantity and quality of work available to former prisoners (Pager 2003; Western 2002). This pattern of decreased earnings and fewer job opportunities for ex-prisoners has had an especially strong impact on younger workers and African Americans (Pager 2003; Western and Pettit 2000). In our own interviews, several inmates expressed frustration over their inability to get a good job when their criminal record is known to employers. As Karen, a white inmate in her thirties, put it:

> What is it, the fourth question of every job interview? "Have you ever been convicted of a crime?" They ask you that before they ask for your prior work history or education. All that's on the second page, so they read "felon" before they ever read that side.

Similarly, Rita, another female inmate in her forties, had little work experience and few concrete plans for employment. She described a rich network of associates available to assist her in disposing of stolen merchandise, or trading it for drugs that she could sell at a high profit. Her opportunities for legitimate employment, however, paled in comparison:

> I don't know what I'm going to be able to do to make money unless I go out and sell drugs again . . . I mean, I'm gonna get a job that probably, if I'm lucky, makes $8 or $9 an hour, which I can go make a drug deal in a half-hour and make $300, you know?

Michael, a probationer, describes himself as "stuck in streetlife" and explained how his criminal justice experiences have affected his work prospects:

> I'm glad I'm gonna get off probation, and drop my felony. For real. I want a good paying job, 'cause I had a job at [a casino] in '97, I was going to get that job, too. That same day I caught that robbery case . . . that job was gonna pay me like $11 an hour, I had experience as a cook, I went through cooking classes up in the workhouse and got a certificate for like six weeks . . . I was going to be a top chef out at [the casino]. Couldn't do it though, caught that felony,

couldn't even do it, can't work at a casino, you can't get a government job, neither, if you got a felony.

Family

In addition to employment, strong family ties may reduce recidivism and aid in community reintegration of former inmates. Marriage, for example, may reduce crime because spouses provide informal social control for offenders and tend to reduce associations with criminal peers (Laub, Nagin, and Sampson 1998; Warr 1998). As in research on employment, marital quality and commitment, rather than the mere presence of a marital or stable cohabiting union, appears to be critical to inhibiting subsequent crime. Horney, Osgood, and Marshall (1995) report that cohabitation, in the absence of marriage, may even increase offending. Additionally, the presence or even the quality of marriage is less important to future offending when the spouse is also an offender (Giordano, Cernkovich, and Rudolph 2002). Returning prisoners whose spouses are involved in crime may be even *more* likely to continue in crime than unmarried offenders.

Prison inmates increasingly face the formal termination of their parental rights (Braman 2002) and informal barriers to assuming adult family roles. Since 1991, the number of children with an incarcerated parent has increased from about 900,000 to almost 1.5 million (about 2.1 percent of all children under age eighteen). A majority of prison inmates have at least one child under eighteen and almost 50 percent of incarcerated parents were living with their children prior to entering prison. Incarceration also has an impact on a substantial number of very young children—roughly 22 percent of children with an incarcerated parent were under the age of five (U.S. Department of Justice 2000).

Our qualitative interviews suggest that children can have a powerful impact on their parents' offending patterns. For example, Scott, a twenty-six-year-old African-American father on probation, discussed how becoming a "family man" made legitimate work more attractive to him.

> I think being a family man has changed me in that [career] way. To want to be— To get my money right because I don't want to look like a piece of nothing in front of my kids. So stuff like that has to do with pride, too. That helps, man. That helps to have a family.

In contrast, Lori, a thirty-seven-year-old prisoner, describes how losing her parental rights while incarcerated had a dramatic effect on her behavior.

I remember when they took my son from me. Let me tell you something—
I was literally nuts for two years. I didn't give a shit. I did as I pleased when I
pleased, and I didn't give a shit about the consequences.

Unfortunately, sociological research on the impact of children on their parents' criminality and the potentially harmful consequences of reuniting children with criminal parents has only begun to emerge (Hagan and Dinovitzer 1999). Several theories of crime, however, suggest ways in which the presence of children may impact the criminal offending of their parents. Children may reduce parental crime if their presence helps to strengthen family attachments and reinforce a prosocial identity. Alternatively, children may increase the criminal involvement of parents by adding stress and financial strain to an already heavy burden of disadvantages. While more young adults are involved with the criminal justice system, we know very little about the impact the experience may have on the transition to parenthood, parenting skills, and parental attachment (Nurse 2004).

Civic Life

As with parenting, barriers to civic engagement and political participation of ex-inmates have been relatively neglected areas of study (Uggen, Manza, and Behrens 2003a). Civic barriers such as the loss of voting rights and restrictions on community life compound the labor market, educational, and early childhood disadvantages experienced by ex-prisoners, powerfully reinforcing their social isolation. In a recent study of felon disenfranchisement, Uggen and Manza (2002) report that nearly 4.7 million felons and ex-felons are legally disenfranchised in the United States. While this group appears to be more alienated from mainstream politics and community life than the rest of the population (Uggen, Manza, and Behrens 2003a; Uggen and Manza 2002), they have valuable political views to contribute, and their civic inclusion may facilitate their successful adjustment when they return to the community (Uggen and Manza forthcoming).

Regardless of whether felons would exercise the right to vote if given the opportunity, those we interviewed generally viewed voting as fundamental to citizenship. As Lynn, a prisoner in her thirties, put it, voting is a "part of being a citizen and being an adult. Once you reach the age of eighteen, that's something you get to do." Correspondingly, they viewed disenfranchisement as a clear indicator that they were unwanted or unaccepted as full citizens in their communities. This sentiment is clearly expressed by Paul, a male in his thirties who describes himself as "exiled" from his community:

Giving back voting rights is another way to make a person feel part of that community. How can you feel that you're giving back to a community that you're a part of when you're exiled from it by not being able to vote and have a voice in it?

This feeling of exile is especially troubling in light of Matsueda and Heimer's (1997) argument that role adoption is in part a function of the reactions of others and conditioned by social context. Of central concern, then, is Paul's reaction to the denial of voting rights and restrictions placed upon him because of his sex offender status:

When they say, "What are you going to give back to the community for this and for that?" Well, hey, community doesn't want a damn thing to do with me, why should I go back and give anything?

Paul's viewpoint suggests that civil restrictions may inhibit the assumption of other adult roles and undermine the reintegrative goal of encouraging offenders to empathize or identify with other citizens as a strategy for reducing crime (see, e.g., Bazemore 2001; Braithwaite 1989). Moreover, voting at age eighteen may be the first opportunity for civic engagement for many young offenders. When this opportunity is lost, they may be less likely to exercise this right when and if it is regained.

Social Stigma

In addition to substantial disadvantages in the labor market, barriers to family reintegration and educational attainment, and civil penalties, offenders also face heightened stigmatization once they leave prison. Sex offenders, perhaps the most stigmatized group of offenders returning to the community, face especially severe barriers to community reintegration. In the words of Alan, a Minnesota sex offender in his thirties, "We're a step below murderers. People would rather have a murderer living next door than me."

Alan's comments seem to reflect the sentiments of the general public, for a far greater stigma appears to be associated with sex offenses than even violent crimes. In a nationally representative Harris poll conducted in July 2002, about 80 percent of Americans expressed support for the extension of voting rights to convicted felons who have completed their sentences. In a survey experiment in which the offense category was varied, however, sex offenders received a far lower level of support, with only 52 percent for reenfranchisement upon completion of sentence (Manza, Brooks, and Uggen 2004). The increased use of community notification procedures and sex offender registration requirements may increase public safety. Nevertheless, such requirements may also have the unintended effect of increasing sex offender recidivism by removing virtually all routes to the adoption of adult roles, prosocial community involvement, and occupational or educational advancement.

Cumulative Disadvantage and Multiple Barriers

One of the most important findings of life course research on the causes and correlates of criminal offending concerns the interactions among early life disadvantage, later disadvantages, and criminal outcomes. Early life disadvantages such as poverty, criminal parents, and neuropsychological deficits combine to lower later educational and occupational attainment, thereby increasing the likelihood of criminal involvement (Hagan and Palloni 1990; Laub and Sampson 2003; Moffitt 1993). Earlier disadvantages and delayed transitions are magnified over time, resulting in problematic transitions to adulthood and increased criminal offending.

Also, irrespective of gender, race, conviction offense, or correctional status, the felon label acts as a substantial barrier to returning to normal work, family, and civic roles. (See Lyons and Melton's argument about stigma and mental illness in chapter 11). Our respondents suggested important interactions across these domains as well (Uggen, Manza, and Behrens 2003a). For example, barriers to educational attainment or employment impede family reintegration and the assumption of positive parenting roles. Similarly, restrictions on voting, civic participation, and housing limit the ability of offenders to become active citizens. Those ex-inmates who return to their communities will do so with additional challenges, beyond the difficulties that may have brought them to prison. Yet many were optimistic about the prospects for assuming or resuming roles as active citizens. Lynn, whose drug use and criminal activities were widely discussed in her small town, said that "people seen that I changed." She was eager to rejoin that community and establish a new role as a volunteer.

> When I get out I'll be home in time to do whatever I can to help out with [my hometown] centennial. The last two years I've been on house arrest so I couldn't be involved. I had to sit at home. So this will be my first year not [on house arrest], and I plan on, you know, whatever day if they need me to clean up the streets, whatever, I plan on doing it.

In contrast, the young probationer Michael described his trepidation upon returning to a high-crime urban neighborhood after a period of incarceration.

You don't really see progress. I mean people work, they get in stuff, volunteer and stuff, but it's, it's the same cycle . . . Day in, day out, people go to jail, get married, people born, same thing, people get drunk, people get high, it never stops.

Despite these misgivings, Michael also wanted his neighbors to witness his assumption of adult roles:

I want to be there [in my old neighborhood] so people would know, "hey, man, [Mike's] doing something, going to work everyday, family going to church. He was out there wild, look at him now, he's changed" . . . I'd be right there, but, all in all, when you do that, you still have people who might be mad at you, that you made the change, people you used to run with, you know, might not like that.

Although Michael spoke at length about his desire to someday leave crime behind, become involved in his community, and "raise a family like middle-class people," these roles seem to lack salience for him. In particular, he discussed his difficulties making the most of the employment opportunities available to him.

They gave me a chance, you know, working at [a company] making $8 an hour, [it] was a cool job, you know, I was always by myself, can't complain about that. They gave me a chance. It was a white guy, too. They gave me a chance, because I was looking sincere, you know I came to work on time . . . I worked there about six months. Then, I don't know, man, I just stopped going. I don't know why.

In contrast, when asked about where he will live after leaving prison, Dylan references the education he received in prison, describing his work plans in terms of a "career" rather than merely getting a "job."

I don't think I'll live there [my hometown] because of the career I've chosen in prison, I'm a computer programmer. I'm from a small town so I won't be able to have a career necessarily. So I'll probably have to live in the city.

A noticeable difference between Dylan and Michael is in their descriptions of themselves and their work goals. Michael is merely "looking sincere" while expressing doubt about his ability to maintain a legal job, whereas Dylan—who has yet to leave prison and put his plans to a test—describes himself as a computer programmer. Michael, at twenty-three a world-weary probationer, has experienced life on the outside as a felon while Dylan has yet to confront the stigma experienced by those with a criminal history. Combating the reactions and expectations of others when coworkers, neighbors, and friends discover his criminal record is a difficulty Dylan has not yet faced.

Karen, a female inmate, echoed the beliefs of other respondents when she described the labor market consequences of her criminal history. She also argued that her status as a felon would interfere with her ability to remain an involved parent once she returned to her community.

> Even to go into the school, to work with my child's class—and I'm not a sex offender—but all I need is one parent who says, "Isn't she a felon? I don't want her with my child."

Frustration over the inability to be viewed as anything other than a felon was a consistent theme throughout our qualitative interviews. As Karen put it:

> I am more than a felon. I am educated. I am intelligent. I'm hard working, I'm a good mother, I'm dependable, all of those things. I don't have to worry about parole telling me I'm a felon because there's gonna be a ton of other people that are going to say, "You're a felon."

Finally, the barriers described in this chapter impact a historically unprecedented rate and number of young adults in the United States (U.S. Department of Justice 2001b). We conclude by placing the United States in an international context and describing differences in the impact of punishment on the transition to adulthood for various groups within this country.

The U.S. Pattern in Context

To understand U.S. patterns, it is important to consider them in relation to those of other societies. Just as high rates of criminal punishment are exceptional in the U.S., the transition to adulthood for ex-prisoners is also distinctive in American society. Figure 5.5 presents incarceration rates for a wide variety of countries, including the U.S. The United States is increasingly divergent from other nations in both its rate and manner of criminal punishment. To take one example, the U.S. incarceration rate is more than fourteen times that of Japan. Moreover, a sentence to prison is much more common in the U.S. than in Japan for all types of crime. Prison sentences for adults and probation sentences for juveniles are highly unusual in Japan, even for violent crimes (Ministry of Justice 2000; Thornton and Endo 1992; Westermann and Burfeind 1991). In contrast to the U.S., juveniles in particular are rarely confined as a

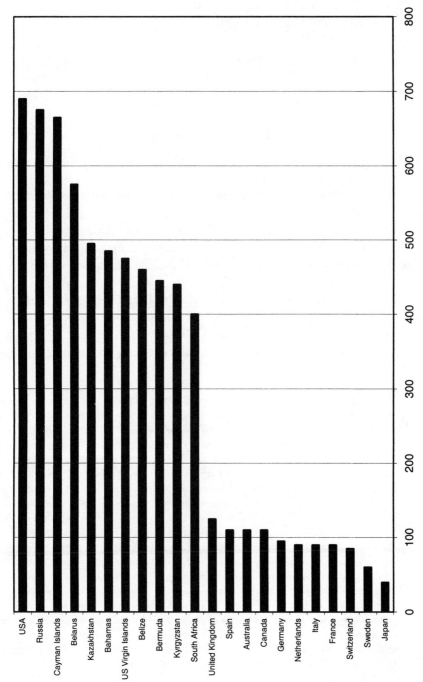

Figure 5.5. Incarceration rates per 100,000 by country, 2000.

result of criminal involvement.[3] In addition to high incarceration rates, the U.S. trend toward community notification, sex offender registries, housing restrictions, and work barriers appears unusually restrictive when placed in international context. For example, political disenfranchisement is rarely applied to nonincarcerated felons in other industrialized nations (Uggen and Manza 2002).

Age, Race, and Gender Disparities

The impact of high incarceration rates and its consequences within this country are not equally apportioned to all U.S. citizens. More young people than ever before are reentering the community from the criminal justice system. As Becky Pettit and Bruce Western (2004) have noted, prison time has become a common event in the life course for young black men. As a result, many of the problems ex-prisoners encounter when returning to the community are disproportionately borne by young African-American males. African-American men are about six times more likely than whites to enter prison at some point during their lifetimes (Bonczar and Beck 1997). Because age, gender, and race are closely correlated with criminal punishment, a high percentage of the young, male, and African-American populations are incarcerated. For example, about 8 percent of all African American males aged eighteen through twenty-

---

3. Although a variety of explanations have been offered to explain Japan's low crime rate and comparatively light sentencing practices, perhaps the most influential argument has been that Japan relies more heavily on informal social control to curb crime (Braithwaite 1989; Westermann and Burfeind 1991). For those young offenders who are incarcerated, community involvement in social reintegration after prison is much greater. For example, community volunteers, rather than professional corrections officers, monitor the majority of Japanese probationers and parolees. In contrast to the experiences of felons in the United States, Japanese offenders are much less likely to experience community "exile." Additionally, prison programs in Japan place an even greater emphasis on work than U.S. prisons and are directed toward repairing educational and occupational deficits of inmates. In contrast, as our qualitative interviews suggested, stigmatizing shaming, or shaming which acts to label offenders as apart from the community, appears to be the norm in the United States. Beyond the greater rate and form of criminal punishment in the United States, differences in the age distribution of crime in the U.S. and Japan impacts the transition to adulthood for ex-prisoners. Criminal involvement in the United States tends to peak at age seventeen or eighteen, whereas crime peaks earlier in Japan, at age fourteen or fifteen, just prior to high school entry (Harada 1995). In the U.S., the crime peak corresponds to a biological age associated with legal adult status. Given that the consequences of punishment are more serious after the age of eighteen (and, today, earlier because of the increased certification of juveniles into adult court), offenders with minimal criminal involvement face harsh consequences and long-term imprisonment in the U.S.

four (and 10 percent of all African-American males aged twenty-five through twenty-nine) were in prison in 2001 (U.S. Department of Justice 2002).

African-American ex-prisoners are disproportionately affected by labor market disadvantages (Western and Pettit 2000) and felon disenfranchisement (Uggen and Manza 2002; Uggen, Manza, and Behrens 2003b). For example, one audit study found that the stigma of a felony conviction was even stronger for African-American job applicants than for whites (Pager 2003). Minority children also face an increased risk of losing their parents to prison. African-American children are about nine times more likely than whites to have an incarcerated parent. Latino children experience parental loss at a rate three times that of white children (U.S. Department of Justice 2000). Finally, because imprisonment disproportionately impacts lower-income African-American communities, the ability of these neighborhoods to develop effective informal social control is increasingly limited (Clear and Rose 1998). African-American men often enter prison with a number of barriers to a successful adult transition, and the prison experience and stigma they face upon release only exacerbate these barriers.

CONCLUSION

There are onerous barriers to the transition to adulthood for young adults with experience in the criminal justice system. Young prisoners in the United States lag far behind their counterparts in the general population across the domains of education, employment, family formation, and behavioral adjustment. Extant research on the transition to adulthood for this group, along with our own qualitative interviews, suggests that disadvantages accumulate across these domains as former felons attempt to assume adult roles when they reenter their communities. We have also emphasized the social-psychological processes that link adult transitions to criminal behavior over the life course. Simply put, those who develop a stable identity of "felon" or "criminal" are unlikely to develop the social relationships and role behavior needed to assume other adult roles (Uggen, Manza, and Behrens 2003a). Since most young people engage in some form of delinquency during adolescence, settling down and aging out of crime may itself be a separate facet of the transition to adulthood (Uggen and Massoglia 2002).

Perhaps the most fundamental question in life course research on crime is whether common life events, such as entering employment, marrying, or establishing an independent residence, are causes of future behavioral trajectories or simply reflections of underlying individual predispositions. Gottfredson and

Hirschi (1990) adopt the latter view, denying the causal significance of life course events and proposing instead a theory of crime based on stable individual differences in self-control. In their view, criminal propensity remains stable over the life course and predicts life course trajectories, events, and criminal involvement. Thus, according to Gottfredson and Hirschi, the relationship among factors such as marriage and work and reduced crime is spurious. Rather, those with low self-control are unlikely to enter stable marital or employment situations in the first place and will remain involved in crime well beyond adolescence. If this position is correct, then policy efforts to facilitate the transition to adult roles are unlikely to affect the future criminal behavior of those involved in the criminal justice system.

If as we believe, on the other hand, life course theories are correct in suggesting that major life transitions play an independent causal role in shaping changes in criminal offending over time, policy efforts to help correctional populations manage adult life and weave them back into the social fabric have great potential to reduce future crime (Laub and Sampson 2003; Sampson and Laub 1990; Uggen 2000). Unfortunately, a significant challenge raised by John Hagan and Bill McCarthy (chapter 7) in their discussion of homeless youth is relevant to the criminal justice population as well—though we can identify potentially significant events that may positively alter the life course of criminal offenders, we cannot predict who will be responsive to these events and who will remain involved in crime. Nonetheless, sociological research and qualitative interview evidence suggest that removing barriers to work, family, and civic engagement may play a role in facilitating the adoption of stable adult roles among young offenders.

It is encouraging that most offenders are aware of these barriers and, at some level, maintain their desire to become active, responsible, productive adult citizens. Moreover, many struggle to make progress toward assuming these roles even while they are incarcerated. We conclude with a brief excerpt from an interview with Larry, a thirty-year-old prisoner, who entered prison at age twenty after a homicide conviction.

LARRY: When I first got locked up I thought, you know, "Life is over." I mean that's it. . . . "I'm not getting out 'til I'm thirty-six, you know, I'm twenty years old." I mean I was just torn to shreds, you know? And I mean, and of course I had guilt over, uh, you know, killing my friend and that, you know, will haunt me for the rest of my life, I'm sure. But, uh, I don't see it anymore as, you know, "I'll never get out," and it's not so far in the future. It's only six years away now. And, you know, thirty-six really isn't that old anymore, you know? And I've grown as a person basically, you know? If you look at any twenty-year-old and any thirty-year-old, you know, there are differences—those are the differences that I've had between when I came in and who I am now."

UGGEN: Some people think that once a prisoner comes in at a certain stage that . . . they sort of get warehoused. You know, put on a shelf and—

LARRY: And then you don't grow or mature until you get out? I think that's bogus.

As Larry suggests, such progress is indeed possible while behind bars, even for those removed from society for serious crimes.

REFERENCES

Bachman, J. G., and J. Schulenberg. 1993. How part-time work intensity relates to drug use, problem behavior, time use, and satisfaction among high school seniors: Are these consequences or merely correlates? *Developmental Psychology* 29: 220–235.

Bazemore, G. 2001. Young people, trouble, and crime: Restorative justice as a normative theory of informal social control and social support. *Youth and Society* 33: 199–226.

Bell, C., M. Coven, J. Cronan, C. Garza, J. Guggemos, and L. Storto. 1999. Rape and sexual misconduct in the prison system: Analyzing America's most "open" secret. *Yale Law and Policy Review* 18: 195–210.

Bonczar, T. P. 1997. *Characteristics of adults on probation, 1995.* Washington: U.S. Government Printing Office.

Bonczar, T. P., and A. J. Beck. 1997. *Lifetime likelihood of going to state or federal prison.* Washington: U.S. Government Printing Office.

Braithwaite, J. 1989. *Crime, shame, and reintegration.* New York: Cambridge University Press.

Braman, D. 2002. Families and incarceration. Pp. 117–135 in *Invisible punishment: The collateral consequences of mass imprisonment.* Edited by M. Mauer and M. Chesney-Lind. New York: New Press.

Caspi, A., G. Elder, and E. Herbener. 1990. Childhood personality and the prediction of life-course patterns. Pp. 13–35 in *Straight and devious pathways from childhood to adulthood.* Edited by L. Robins and M. Rutter. Cambridge: Cambridge University Press.

Clear, T. R., and D. Rose. 1998. Social capital and crime: Explaining the unintended consequences of incarceration. *Criminology* 36: 441–479.

Cullen, F. T., and P. Gendreau. 2000. Assessing correctional policy: Policy, practice, and prospects. *Criminal Justice* 3: 109–175.

Crutchfield, R. D., and S. R. Pitchford. 1997. Work and crime: The effects of labor stratification. *Social Forces,* 76: 93–118.

Ditton, P. M. 1999. *Mental health and treatment of inmates and probationers.* Washington: U.S. Government Printing Office.

Edin, K., T. J. Nelson, and R. Paranal. 2004. Fatherhood and incarceration as potential turning points in the criminal careers of unskilled men. Pp. 46–75 in *Imprisoning America: The social effects of mass incarceration.* Edited by Patillo, M., D. Weiman, and B. Western. New York: Russell Sage Foundation.

Giordano, P. C., S. A. Cernkovich, and J. L. Rudolph. 2002. Gender, crime, and desistance: Toward a theory of cognitive transformation. *American Journal of Sociology* 107: 990–1064.

Gottfredson, M., and T. Hirschi. 1990. *A general theory of crime.* Stanford: Stanford University Press.

Hagan, J. 1993. The social embeddedness of crime and unemployment. *Criminology* 31:465–491.

Hagan, J., and R. Dinovitzer. 1999. Children of the prison generation: Collateral consequences of imprisonment for children and communities. *Crime and Justice* 26: 121–162.

Hagan, J., and A. Palloni. 1990. The social reproduction of a criminal class in working class London, circa 1950–1980. *American Journal of Sociology* 96: 265–299.

Hagan, J., and B. Wheaton. 1993. The search for adolescent role exits and the transition to adulthood. *Social Forces* 71: 955–980.

Hagestad, G. O., and B. L. Neugarten. 1985. Age and the life course. Pp. 35–61 in *Handbook of aging and the social sciences.* Edited by G. Maddox, G. Myers, and J. Schultz. New York: Van Nostrand Reinhold.

Harada, Y. 1995. Adjustment to school, life course transitions, and changes in delinquent behavior in Japan. *Current Perspectives on Aging and the Life Cycle* 4: 35–60.

Hogan, D. P. 1981. *Transitions in the lives of American men.* New York: Academic Press.

Horney, J., D. W. Osgood, and I. Haen Marshall. 1995. Criminal careers in the short-term: Intra-individual variation in crime and its relation to local life circumstances. *American Sociological Review* 60: 655–673.

Johnson, E. I., and J. Waldfogel. 2004. Children of incarcerated parents: Multiple risks and children's living arrangements. Pp. 97–134 in *Imprisoning America: The social effects of mass incarceration.* Edited by Patillo, M., D. Weiman, and B. Western. New York: Russell Sage Foundation.

Lamb, H. R., and L. E. Weinberger. 1998. Persons with severe mental illness in jails and prisons: A review. *Psychiatric Services* 49: 483–492.

Laub, J. H., D. S. Nagin, and R. J. Sampson. 1998. Trajectories of change in criminal offending: Good marriages and the desistance process. *American Sociological Review* 63: 225–238.

Laub, J. H., and R. J. Sampson. 1995. Socioeconomic achievement in the life course of disadvantaged men: Military service as a turning point, circa 1940–1965. *American Sociological Review* 61: 347–367.

Laub, J. H., and R. J. Sampson. 2003. *Shared beginnings, divergent lives: Delinquent boys to age 70.* Cambridge: Harvard University Press.

Manza, J., C. Brooks, and C. Uggen. 2004. Public attitudes toward felon disfranchisement in the United States. *Public Opinion Quarterly* 68: 276–287.

Manza, J., and C. Uggen. Forthcoming. *Locked out: Felon disfranchisement and American democracy.* New York: Oxford University Press.

Maruna, Shadd. 2001. *Making good: How ex-convicts reform and rebuild their lives.* Washington: American Psychological Association Books.

Matsueda, R., and K. Heimer. 1997. A symbolic interactionist theory of role-transitions, role commitments, and delinquency. Pp. 163–213 in *Developmental theories of crime and delinquency.* Edited by T. P. Thornberry. New Brunswick, NJ: Transaction Press.

Ministry of Justice. 2000. *White paper on crime 2000.* Tokyo: Research and Training Institute.

Moffitt. T. E. 1993. Life-course-persistent and adolescence-limited antisocial behavior: A developmental taxonomy. *Psychological Review* 100: 674–701.

Moffitt, T. E., A. Capsi, H. Harrington, and B. Milne. 2002. Males on the life-course-persistent and adolescence-limited antisocial pathways: Follow-up at age 26 years. *Development and Psychopathology* 14: 179–207.

Nurse, A. M. 2004. Returning strangers: Newly paroled young fathers and their children. Pp. 76–96 in *Imprisoning America: The social effects of mass incarceration.* Edited by M. Patillo, D. Weiman, and B. Western. New York: Russell Sage Foundation.

Pager, D. 2003. The mark of a criminal record. *American Journal of Sociology* 108: 937–975.

Paternoster, R., S. Bushway, R. Brame, and R. Apel. 2003. The effect of teenage employment on delinquency and problem behaviors. *Social Forces* 82: 297–335.

Pettit, B., and B. Western. 2004. Mass imprisonment and the life course: Race and class inequality in U.S. incarceration. *American Sociological Review* 69: 151–169.

Rubenstein, G., and D. Mukamal. 2002. Welfare and housing: Denial of benefits to drug offenders. Pp. 37–49 in *Invisible punishment: The collateral consequences of mass imprisonment.* Edited by M. Mauer and M. Chesney-Lind. New York: New Press.

Safron, D., J. Schulenberg, and J. G. Bachman. 2001. Part-time work and hurried adolescence: The links among work intensity, social activities, health behaviors, and substance use. *Journal of Health and Social Behavior* 42: 425–449.

Sampson, R. J., and J. H. Laub. 1990. Crime and deviance over the life course: The salience of adult social bonds. *American Sociological Review* 55: 609–627.

Sampson, R. J., and J. H. Laub. 1993. *Crime in the making: Pathways and turning points through life.* Cambridge: Harvard University Press.

Shanahan, M. J. 2000. Pathways to adulthood in changing societies: Variability and mechanisms in life course perspective. *Annual Review of Sociology* 26: 667–692.

Staff, J., and C. Uggen. 2003. The fruits of good work: Job quality and adolescent deviance. *Journal of Research in Crime and Delinquency* 40: 263–290.

Teplin, Linda A. 1984a. *Mental illness and criminal justice.* Beverly Hills, CA: Sage.

Teplin, Linda A. 1984b. Criminalizing mental disorder: The comparative arrest rate of the mentally ill. *American Psychologist* 39: 794–803.

Thornton, R. Y., and K. Endo. 1992. *Preventing crime in America and Japan.* New York: ME Sharpe.

Uggen, C. 1999. Ex-offenders and the conformist alternative: A job quality model of work and crime. *Social Problems* 46: 127–151.

Uggen, C. 2000. Work as a turning point in the life course of criminals: A duration model of age, employment, and recidivism. *American Sociological Review* 65: 529–546.

Uggen, C., and J. Manza. 2002. Democratic contraction? Political consequences of felon disenfranchisement in the United States. *American Sociological Review* 67: 777–803.

Uggen, C., and J. Manza. Forthcoming. Voting and subsequent crime and arrest: Evidence from a community sample. *Columbia Human Rights Law Review.*

Uggen, C., J. Manza, and A. Behrens. 2003a. Less than the average citizen: Stigma, role transition, and the civic reintegration of convicted felons. Pp. 258–290 in *After crime and punishment: Ex-offender reintegration and desistance from crime.* Edited by S. Maruna and R. Immarigeon. Albany: SUNY Press.

Uggen, C., J. Manza, and A. Behrens. 2003b. Felon voting rights and the disenfranchisement of African Americans. *Souls: A Critical Journal of Black Politics, Culture, and Society* 5: 47–55.

Uggen, C., and M. Massoglia. 2002. Settling down and aging out: Desistance from crime as a turning point in the life course. Paper presented at the annual meeting of the American Society of Criminology, November 15, Chicago.

Uggen, C., and M. Thompson. 2003. The socioeconomic determinants of ill-gotten gains: Within-person changes in drug use and illegal earnings. *American Journal of Sociology* 109: 146–185.

U.S. Bureau of the Census. 2000. *Statistical abstract of the United States.* Washington: U.S. Government Printing Office.

U.S. Bureau of Labor Statistics. 2003. *Current population survey.* Washington: U.S. Government Printing Office.

U.S. Department of Justice. Bureau of Justice Statistics. 1999. *Substance abuse and treatment in state and federal prisoners, 1997.* Washington: U. S. Government Printing Office.

U.S. Department of Justice. Bureau of Justice Statistics. 2000. *Incarcerated parents and their children.* Washington: U.S. Government Printing Office.

U.S. Department of Justice. Bureau of Justice Statistics. 2001a. *Trends in state parole, 1990–2000.* Washington: United States Government Printing Office.

U.S. Department of Justice. Bureau of Justice Statistics. 2001b. *Survey of inmates in state and federal correctional facilities, 1997.* [Computer file]. Compiled by U.S. Dept. of Commerce, Bureau of the Census. ICPSR ed. Ann Arbor, MI: Inter-university Consortium for Political and Social Research [producer and distributor].

U.S. Department of Justice. Bureau of Justice Statistics. 2001c. *Medical problems of inmates, 1997.* Washington: U.S. Government Printing Office.

U.S. Department of Justice. Bureau of Justice Statistics. 2002. *Prisoners in 2001.* Washington: U.S. Government Printing Office.

U.S. Department of Justice. Bureau of Justice Statistics. 2003a. *Probation and parole in the United States, 2002.* Washington: U.S. Government Printing Office.

U.S. Department of Justice. Bureau of Justice Statistics. 2003b. *Prison and jail inmates at midyear 2002.* Washington: U.S. Government Printing Office.

Warr, M. 1998. Life-course transitions and desistance from crime. *Criminology* 36: 183–216.

Westermann, T. D., and J. W. Burfeind. 1991. *Crime and justice in two societies: Japan and the United States.* Pacific Grove, CA: Wadsworth.

Western, B. 2002. The impact of incarceration on wage mobility and inequality. *American Sociological Review* 67: 526–546.

Western, B., and B. Pettit. 2000. Incarceration and racial inequality in men's employment. *Industrial and Labor Relations Review* 54: 3–16.

CHAPTER SIX

Prisoner Reentry and the Pathways to Adulthood: Policy Perspectives

JEREMY TRAVIS AND CHRISTY A. VISHER

The authors thank Asheley Van Ness for her assistance with background research, editing, and the references.

INTRODUCTION

Over 100,000 young adults between the ages of eighteen and twenty-five now leave state or federal prisons each year.[1] Young prisoners who make transitions from incarceration to free society face more daunting hurdles than their older counterparts. Young adults are at higher risk for recidivism and return to prison in the first three years after release than older prisoners (Langan and Levin 2002). They also experience special difficulties making the transition from prison to community because they lack well-established ties to conventional roles and activities prior to their incarceration. Moreover, their recent social and familial history, including ties to delinquent friends, dropping out of school, and parental criminality, makes it more difficult for them to find legitimate employment (Hagan 1993). For young adults, the pathways from prison are distinctive and difficult, contributing even more to challenges faced in the transition to adulthood more generally.

Federal, state, and local governments play a role in defining the framework of policies and programs surrounding prisoner reentry. In recent years, several factors have emerged to focus renewed attention on the problems of prisoner reentry at these levels of government. The federal government has launched a

---

1. In 2002, of the 1.4 million individuals serving prison terms, 89 percent were held in state prisons; the remainder was held in federal or local detention facilities.

funding initiative focused on reentry planning for youthful offenders. State governments, facing unprecedented fiscal constraints, are reconsidering the tough sentencing policies adopted over the past two decades. Local governments are realizing the impact of high rates of incarceration and reentry of young adults on service delivery systems, education programs, and informal networks at the community level. This chapter reviews the general policy environment influencing the transition from prison to community for young adult prisoners and provides an in-depth focus on the policy issues for three important challenges facing these prisoners—work, family, and health—as well as how these challenges impact the transition to adulthood.

THE POLICY CONTEXT FOR RETURNING PRISONERS

The policy environment concerned with young incarcerated offenders in America who eventually will face the challenges of returning home from prison has shifted considerably over the past two decades. The incarceration rate for young adults aged twenty through twenty-four has risen dramatically in the last decade, from 652 to 1,173 per 100,000 (Harrison and Beck 2002), with the simple consequence that many more young adults, especially men, have spent time in prison. As part of a broader "tough on crime" movement, many states have passed laws permitting or mandating that juveniles (generally defined as under age eighteen) charged with serious crimes be prosecuted in the adult criminal justice system (Butts and Mitchell 2000). The result is that more adolescents are coming of age in adult prisons.

The shift in sentencing policy can be attributed in part to a heightened public concern about youth violence. Beginning in the mid-1980s, arrest rates of young adults aged eighteen through twenty-four for violent crimes rose significantly, coinciding with the onset of the crack cocaine epidemic (Blumstein 2000). This increase in violence prompted some commentators to predict a "coming bloodbath" of violent crimes, committed by a new breed of "superpredators." These predictions were soon confounded when, beginning in the early 1990s, arrest rates for young adults fell even more precipitously than they had risen (Butts and Travis 2002). But with rare exceptions, the new low rates of arrests for youth violence have not translated into more lenient sentencing policies. This means that more young adults are in prison, serving longer prison sentences, and then returning home. These policy shifts have had particularly harsh consequences for minorities: at current rates, 28 percent of black males will enter state or federal prison during their lifetime (Bonczar and Beck 1997).

The impact of these stricter enforcement and sentencing policies is felt most acutely in a small number of neighborhoods, predominantly minority neighborhoods, in urban America. Lynch and Sabol (2001), for example, found that less than 1 percent of the block groups in Cuyahoga County, Ohio (which includes Cleveland) accounted for approximately 20 percent of the county's prisoners. In these block groups, between 8 and 15 percent of the young black males are incarcerated on a given day. Cadora and Swartz (2001) conducted a similar analysis in Brooklyn and found that in blocks with high concentrations of incarcerated residents, one in eight parenting-age males (eighteen to thirty-five) is arrested and sent to jail or prison each year.

These shifts in the policy environment also have affected an experience that is as old as prison itself—the experience of leaving prison. Significantly more young adults—mostly men—are being arrested, removed, incarcerated, and returned to a small number of poor, minority communities, with potentially profound effects on their pathways to adulthood. Most of these young adults serve their prison sentences in state facilities;[2] thus, the policies most directly affecting their return are state policies.

The first step in the transition process is the release decision itself. Who decides when someone gets out of prison? Over the past generation, there has been a profound shift in the allocation of responsibility for that decision. Under the classic indeterminate sentencing model, which dominated American jurisprudence for most of the twentieth century, parole boards made that decision (Tonry 1999). Following a generation of sentencing reforms beginning in the 1970s, parole boards no longer play a dominant role in releasing prisoners. In 1976, 65 percent of prisoners were released by parole boards. By 1999, that figure had dropped to 24 percent (Travis and Lawrence 2002). Most prisoners are now released at the conclusion of a fixed sentence, known as mandatory release.

According to earlier procedures, to be eligible for release by a parole board a prisoner typically had to demonstrate, among other things, that he had a job, a place to live, and a social support system. The recent sharp cutback in parole board decisions may have eliminated some of the pressure on prisoners to prepare themselves for release. Moreover, as corrections policy in the U.S. has shifted over the past several decades from a rehabilitative focus on prisoners' needs, problems, and appropriate treatment, to a punishment focus, states have enacted many "tough on crime" measures. Examples include mandatory minimum sentences for certain offenses, automatic and lengthy prison terms for a

2. This estimate is based on a calculation performed by Sara Wakefield, University of Minnesota. Wakefield's calculations were based on the National Corrections Reporting Program data for 1999 (http://www.ojp.usdoj.gov/bjs/dtdata.htm#ncrp), a similar proportion from the Federal Justice Statistics Program for 1999 (http://fjsrc.urban.org/index.cfm) and personal communication from Allen Beck of the Bureau of Justice Statistics, and the estimate of state and federal releases reported in Beck, Karberg, and Harrison (2001).

second or third offense ("three strikes" laws), and requirements that offenders convicted of violent offenses serve 85 percent of their sentence in prison before being eligible for release ("truth in sentencing" laws). In addition, greater local attention to the enforcement of drug law violations (both possession and sale) in the 1990s led to a rapid rise in prison admissions for these offenses, particularly among black men (Travis 2002a). And although overall recidivism rates for released prisoners did not change significantly between 1983 and 1994, drug offenders released in 1994 were more likely to be reconvicted within three years than those released in 1983 (Langan and Levin 2002).

The result of these changes in punishment policy has been less attention to addressing prisoners' needs through education, vocational training, drug treatment, job placement, and mental health services. Most states have not focused on the increasing numbers of prisoners being released and what happens to them once they leave prison. Typically, inmates are released with a small amount of cash (generally under fifty dollars), a set of clothes, a bus ticket, and orders to report to a community supervision officer, if their sentence requires some period of parole or community supervision after release.[3] However, one in five returning prisoners are released back to the community without any supervision or formal oversight by the criminal justice system (Travis and Lawrence 2002). These receive no official attention to their needs for assistance postrelease.

Currently, prerelease programs offered by state correctional agencies provide limited assistance to inmates preparing to make the transition back to the community. Most states have some type of prerelease program that is usually initiated about six months before release, but these programs rarely are available to all inmates (American Correctional Association 2000). Various models include prerelease transition centers and halfway houses, in-prison classes attended by prisoners on a variety of topics, and continuum-of-care programs that initiate treatment (substance abuse, medical, etc.) in prison and continue treatment in the community. Data on prisoner involvement in prerelease programs are difficult to obtain and do not differentiate involvement by age. In a 1997 survey of state inmates within twelve months of release, only 13 percent reported participating in prerelease programs (Lynch and Sabol 2001). Inmates also reported low participation rates in vocational (27 percent) and education (35 percent) programs, which could be seen as preparatory for release. Slightly fewer than 10 percent of all inmates in state prisons had received drug treatment

3. Community supervision can include parole, probation, and some community-based programs administered by correctional institutions (such as electronic monitoring and day reporting). The term "community supervision" is often used interchangeably with the term "parole," as it is with other forms of community-based supervision such as probation.

since their admission (Mumola 1999). Participation in these programs, which has been declining in the last decade (Lynch and Sabol 2001), is heavily dependent on the availability of classes and teachers. Many correctional administrators acknowledge that rising expenditures have forced cutbacks in prison programming in recent years. Programs and services that may reduce the likelihood of a return to prison have been eliminated or seriously curtailed (Petersilia 2003).

Community-based programs—most of which do not have links to the prison system—also play a role in the transition from prison. These service organizations, however, are often focused on a single problem, such as employment assistance or mental health services, and capacity is usually not sufficient to meet demand. Moreover, only a fraction of these programs in a community are targeted specifically to returning prisoners, with most programs targeted generally at disadvantaged populations. Further, the differences in the locations of released prisoners' residences and necessary services may create difficulties for meeting parole obligations (see e.g., La Vigne, Kachnowski et al. 2003; La Vigne, Mamalian et al. 2003; Clear, Rose, and Ryder 2000). Absent a coordinated system to ensure that ex-prisoners are connected to these resources, a state that enforces stringent conditions of release—such as requiring a released prisoner, while under parole supervision, to hold a job, enroll in drug treatment, and meet child support requirements—may very well be setting individuals up for failure.

Policies that foster coordination between state corrections agencies and local community service providers could increase the likelihood of connecting returning prisoners to needed transition services. However, Rossman (2003) identifies a number of barriers to coordinating prison and community-based services. The simple fact that prisons are far removed from the communities to which prisoners return poses considerable logistical difficulties. The missions and cultures of the two service networks are often at odds with a reintegration objective. Prison services have the benefit of being located within one organization, yet the organization has an overriding security objective. Community-based services that might meet the employment, health care, and family welfare needs of returning prisoners are highly fragmented and historically underfunded and place little priority on prisoner reintegration. The neglect of prison programs and the scarcity of services for returning prisoners make it likely that recidivism rates will remain high and that the transition to adulthood is likely to be even more challenging.

Overall, the content of prison and community-based programs designed to facilitate a successful transition from prison to community is not well-documented. Further, these programs vary widely in structure, length, and content. Evaluations of their effectiveness are quite limited and virtually none examine their effectiveness for young adults specifically (Seiter and Kadela 2003). Many evaluations of prisoner reentry programs can be critiqued on methodological grounds because they do not successfully address problems of selection bias (Gaes et al. 1999; Wilson, Gallagher, and Mackenzie 2000). They also place too much emphasis on recidivism as a measure of effectiveness at the expense of measures of adjustment or reintegration, such as employment, family support, or good health. The most effective interventions for returning prisoners appear to be those that develop service plans or initiate treatment in prison and link released prisoners to immediate treatment or services after release (Gaes et al. 1999; Inciardi et al. 1997; Taxman et al. 2002). The lack of a coordinated service delivery system between correctional facilities and communities in most states limits the availability of these interventions (Rossman 2003). Promising interventions for returning prisoners in the areas of employment, family, and health are discussed later in this chapter.

Unfortunately, the roles of some existing institutions in facilitating a successful transition from prison to community have made it more difficult for all ex-prisoners, including younger prisoners, to succeed after release. For example, historically, the role of parole officers in facilitating the transition from prison to community was to provide links to services in the community (Petersilia 2003). In the last decade, parole officers' caseloads have increased dramatically; consequently, their ability to help ex-prisoners find jobs and services has declined (Travis and Lawrence 2002). Moreover, although the majority of returning prisoners are under some form of state supervision after release, whether this supervision helps or hinders a successful reintegration is not yet known. Little research exists on the effects of postrelease supervision and conditions of release on criminal behavior. Parole supervision has not been found to reduce new arrests but has been associated with an increase in technical violations (Petersilia and Turner 1993).[4] Technical violations occur when a parolee does not abide by the conditions of release (e.g., meeting regularly with a parole officer, staying drug free, and avoiding convicted felons). Indeed, an increasing percentage of prison admissions are persons who are parole violators, either for technical violations or for new crimes (Travis and Lawrence 2002).

The federal government has had a significant role in prisoner reintegration through some key pieces of legislation enacted in the last two decades. During the late 1980s and 1990s, Congress passed legislation that made felons inelig-

---

4. Researchers hypothesize that this is a result of more technical violations coming to the attention of the parole officer due to increased supervision, rather than a behavioral response to supervision on the part of the parolee.

ible for a wide array of federal benefits. (In some cases, only certain felons, particularly those convicted of drug offenses, are targeted.) Under these laws, ex-prisoners can be denied public housing, education loans, welfare benefits, the mobility necessary to access jobs that require driving, and parental rights. This network of "invisible punishments" poses significant hurdles for those who are exiting prison and returning home, particularly for the poorest returning prisoners (Travis 2002a).

Local policies also play a critical role in prisoner reentry. City or county policies regarding eligibility for public housing assistance, tenant restrictions, and local enforcement of these regulations may support or undermine the family's ability to play a constructive role at the time of release. In some cases, local governments have been given discretion by the federal government to implement policies that serve as barriers to prisoner reintegration. For example, the housing authorities in some cities have used their discretion to bar ex-felons from visiting friends or relatives in public housing, while in other cities these rules are not strictly enforced (Legal Action Center 2000). Local eligibility rules for participation in drug treatment programs may determine whether a prisoner who has been in treatment while incarcerated is placed at the head of the line, or at the end, when he or she is released from prison (Nelson, Deess, and Allen 1999). Police practices may influence the posture of the police vis-à-vis former prisoners, either as watchful supporters of reintegration or agents of a more aggressive "zero tolerance" policy.

In a more positive direction, recent policy activity at the federal level is designed to increase state and local involvement in and attention to improving the odds of successful prisoner reentry by coordinating service delivery and reducing existing obstacles. In 2002, the U.S. Department of Justice, representing a consortium of five federal agencies, announced $100 million in grants to the states under a new initiative titled Going Home. Building on funds first proposed by the Clinton administration, the Bush administration brought together the U.S. Departments of Justice, Labor, Housing and Urban Development, Education, and Health and Human Services to "build on those innovative ideas that reduce the recidivism of these offenders and, thus, reduce the overall amount of violent and other serious crime that is inflicted on our society" (U.S. Department of Justice 2002, 1). Participating states were required to submit plans to develop a partnership between institutional and community corrections agencies to identify and enhance institutionally based programs, community-based transition programs, and community-based long-term support. This initiative is historic for two reasons. It represents the largest federal expenditure ever on behalf of prisoners transitioning back into society. It also embraces, and requires the states to embrace, a multifaceted definition of the ingredients necessary to stay out of prison. A national evaluation of the impact of the federal reentry program is underway with findings expected in 2006.

These shifts in federal, state, and local policy have created a policy environment that is inimical in many ways to the needs of young adults who leave prison. Higher rates of incarceration increase the demands placed on the public service agencies and private support networks that traditionally help returning prisoners make this transition. The "tough on crime" sentiment has increased the level of stigma and social exclusion experienced by convicted felons, particularly young offenders who were identified as "super-predators" when violent crime was on the rise. The focus on transition planning that characterized the indeterminate sentencing philosophy has been lost in the successive waves of stricter sentencing laws. The political imperative to fund more prisons has meant less funding for in-prison programs and less money for community supervision, while at the same time more ex-prisoners are being returned to prison for failing to meet the technical conditions of parole. With these new realities in mind, we turn next to a discussion of the more specific policy challenges of connecting young adult prisoners to the world of work, family relationship networks, and public health systems.

IMPROVING ATTACHMENTS TO WORK

Work can be a life-centering experience, and is certainly an important part of becoming an adult. Yet involvement with the criminal justice system, particularly incarceration, can interrupt the relationships between a young adult and the world of work, with consequences that may affect his or her lifelong employment history. According to Western and colleagues, incarceration is a "punctuating event that can interrupt a young man's transition into stable employment" (Western, Pettit, and Guetzkow 2002, 177). These interruptions are experienced by individuals with varying effects. They are also experienced, in aggregate, by a small number of neighborhoods, with unknown effects on the youthful patterns of finding jobs, connecting with apprenticeships or work mentors, or moving up the ladder of responsibility in a particular work setting. Recall, for example, the Brooklyn neighborhood described above, where on certain blocks one in eight men aged eighteen to thirty-five is arrested and sent to jail or prison each year (Cadora and Swartz 2001). On those blocks, the intersections between criminal justice policies and the pathways to adulthood are deeply intertwined. In this community, and others like it around the country, traditional notions about the relationship between work and adulthood rarely apply.

In this section, we examine the ways that correctional policy attempts (or fails to attempt) to prepare inmates for connecting to the world of work upon release and the efforts of criminal justice institutions and employment service agencies to find work for those who leave prison without jobs. We adopt a life course perspective on these issues, asking how involvement in the criminal justice system influences the pathways of young adults as they seek and maintain work. We also offer some thoughts on opportunities for policy innovations that might improve the employment and earnings prospects of these young adults and thereby the economic viability of their neighborhoods.

Employment Programs and Work in Prison

As noted by Uggen and Wakefield in chapter 5, young adults who end up in prison face a number of hurdles in terms of their future employability. Prior to their arrival in prison, they may have been engaged in legitimate work, typically at low levels compared to their peers not involved in the criminal justice system. They are frequently involved in illicit avenues of employment—indeed, this criminal activity may have led to their arrest. Overall, they have low levels of educational attainment and literacy. They are burdened by high rates of medical, mental, and physical impairments that may also limit their ability to work.

Prison reformers and correctional administrators have long subscribed to the view that prisons should be places that improve the employment prospects of inmates upon their departure. In the late eighteenth century, the Quakers promoted the notion of work in prison as rehabilitation. In the late nineteenth century, reformers who designed the modern parole system viewed work as central to successful reintegration. In their view, prisoners should be given incentives to take on greater work responsibilities while in prison. Successful work experiences would be rewarded with early release, which in turn would be followed by work under parole supervision in the community (Petersilia 2003). These efforts, and their modern day equivalents, reflect the commonsense notion that having a job reduces one's participation in criminal activity, a notion now broadly supported by social science research (Bushway and Reuter 2002; Sampson and Laub 1993; Uggen and Thompson 2003).

The dominant policy strategy has been to improve a prisoner's employment prospects by offering programs and other opportunities that enhance his or her human capital. Virtually every prison provides such programs, although they serve only a small portion of the prisoner population. In some cases—skill-building programs and vocational programs—the link between the program and future employability is explicit. In others—drug treatment programs, prison industries, and GED programs—the link is more attenuated. These activities are expected to enhance the prisoner's human capital, and thus indirectly improve his or her job prospects.

The efficacy of these interventions has traditionally been measured by their impact on recidivism. Over the past two decades, the weight of research on program effectiveness has shifted from the "nothing works" conclusion of the mid-1970s (Martinson 1974) to a more hopeful conclusion that prison-based programs can reduce crime. In one of several meta-analyses conducted in recent years, Gaes and his colleagues found that, "despite methodological shortcomings and challenges, the evidence suggests that carefully designed and administered education and work programs can . . . reduce recidivism and promote involvement in pro-social activities after release" (Gaes et al. 1999, 398; see also Wilson, Gallagher, and Mackenzie 2000). Although this meta-analysis does not distinguish between younger and older prisoners, a random assignment evaluation of a vocational rehabilitation program targeting eighteen- to twenty-two-year-old males convicted of property offenses found similar effects. Lattimore, Witte, and Baker (1990) found that participants in the North Carolina Vocational Delivery System (VDS), which integrated training and employment services provided by a variety of agencies into one program, had rearrest rates of 36 percent during the two years following release, compared to 46 percent within the control group.

The evaluation literature also identifies the characteristics of effective prison-based programs. Cullen and Gendreau (2000), for example, stress, among other factors, the importance of focusing on skills that are applicable to the job market, ensuring that program participation is timed to be close to the inmate's release date, sustaining programming for at least several months, providing continuity between prison programs and community-based services and treatment following release from prison, and working on those offender needs that are dynamic and may contribute to criminal activity.

The recent meta-analyses that have identified effective programs, and the characteristics of those programs, have provided the basis for cost-benefit studies that translate an individual program's effect size (how much did the desired outcome, reductions in recidivism, change in the desired direction), program cost (the per-participant cost), and future savings (particularly savings attributable to reductions in criminal activity by program participants) into an overall assessment of the value of a societal investment in each intervention. Aos, Phipps, Barnoski, and Lieb of the Washington State Institute for Public Policy conducted such a cost-benefit analysis at the direction of the Washington State legislature. In examining about three hundred studies that met minimum research design criteria, they developed an "investment portfolio" of programs that would reduce crime and yield savings greater than the original program costs (Aos et al. 2001).

That this analysis yielded mixed results is of particular interest for this discussion regarding pathways to work for incarcerated young adults. Work release programs, for example, were relatively inexpensive to operate ($456 per offender), but had small effect sizes and produced only modest net savings in reduced criminal justice expenditures. Adult basic education programs were more expensive ($1,972 per participant), but had larger effect sizes, and therefore yielded net savings of $1,852. In-prison vocational programs cost about as much ($1,960 per participant), were slightly more effective, and therefore yielded greater savings ($2,835) in subsequent criminal justice costs. Counseling and job search programs for inmates leaving prison were relatively inexpensive ($772 per participant), were modestly effective, and produced a net savings to the taxpayers of $625 per participant (Aos et al. 2001). This analytical approach is useful to policy makers who are ready to move beyond the question "what works?" to address the question "which effective programs warrant investment of taxpayer dollars?"

The Washington State Institute for Public Policy study uses only one measure of program effectiveness, crime reduction, as the yardstick for success and cost savings. Adding two other measures—increases in employment levels and earnings—would provide policy makers with another basis for deciding whether to invest public funds in preparing young adults for work after prison. Yet few studies track postrelease employment levels for participants in prison-based programs, a weakness in the literature attributable in part to the overriding interest in rearrest rates and in part to the difficulty in tracing employment rates of released prisoners. A 1994 meta-analysis concluded that in three of the four studies investigated, prison education programs significantly increased chances of securing employment following release from prison (Gerber and Fritsch 1994). A study conducted in the federal prison system found that prisoners who had participated in training and work experiences in prison had higher rates of employment twelve months after release than a comparison group (71.7 vs. 63.1 percent) (Saylor and Gaes 1992), but this study did not distinguish between young adults and older prisoners.

Yet, as discussed earlier in this chapter, the more important, overarching observation is that these programs serve few prisoners. An Urban Institute survey of seven state correctional systems found that only 10 percent of inmates participated in educational, vocational, or treatment programs on any given day (Lawrence et al. 2002). An analysis of national data found that program participation levels declined from 1991 to 1997 (Lynch and Sabol 2001). These cutbacks in program participation, covering a time frame in which the number of prisoners being released from prison increased substantially, can only weaken the employment and reintegration prospects of large numbers of individuals. The current fiscal crisis in the states has resulted in deeper cuts in prison programs and thus is likely to exacerbate this shortfall in prerelease preparation.

A focus on the efficacy of in-prison programs, essentially a human capital framework, captures only one dimension of the nexus between incarceration and employability. Time in prison can also be viewed as time removed from social networks, resulting in a decrease in social capital (Western, Pettit, and Guetzkow 2002). In this framework, connections to the world of work are facilitated by personal contacts, referrals to apprenticeships, mentor relationships, and daily opportunities to interact with people and institutions that can advance one's employment prospects. Yet little is done (and perhaps little can be done) to militate against the loss of social capital during imprisonment. A more modest policy goal may be to guard against the magnetic attractions of antisocial and criminogenic networks, such as gangs, that serve to facilitate continued "embeddedness" in criminal behavior upon release (Hagan 1993).

Some prison administrators have explicitly embraced the goal of improving prosocial behaviors while in prison, striving to create what one prison reformer called a "parallel universe" within the prison walls (Schriro 2000). In this view, prisons should emulate, to the extent possible, the life and work rhythms of the free society. Inmates should be expected to work, apply for prison jobs, be promoted on a merit basis, develop résumés with references from prison supervisors to present to future employers, and earn points for good behavior that can be translated into a modest bank account. In Oregon, the voters passed an initiative (by 72 percent) requiring that inmates work a full week or participate in programs. In 2002, 78 percent of the eligible prison workforce was counted as either working full-time or participating in a program (Oregon Department of Corrections 2002). Some prisons invite private businesses inside the prison walls to interview inmates as potential employees (Finn 1998a). Yet despite these broad-scale reform efforts, only about half of the state prisoners in America work while they are in prison (Government Accounting Office 2001). The high rate of idleness in America's prisons represents a lost opportunity to teach concrete work skills and impart the value of the work ethic to a population with few skills and spotty work histories.

Employment Prospects after Prison

Little is known about the job-seeking patterns of former prisoners. Yet, according to a Vera Institute of Justice study documenting the experience of leaving prison, the search for work is important among all age groups: "The number one concern for most people in the study was landing a job. Throughout the first month after release from prison, people consistently were more preoccupied with finding work than avoiding drugs and other illegal activity or staying in good health" (Nelson, Deess, and Allen 1999, 13). Some of this pressure to find work comes from the parole agencies that supervise the release of most returning prisoners. According to a 1991 survey of state parole agencies, forty of the fifty-one reporting jurisdictions required parolees to "maintain gainful employment" (Rhine, Smith, and Jackson 1991). But, according to a three-state study, fewer than half of released prisoners had a job lined up on their return to the community (Stuerer, Smith, and Tracy 2001).

Finding a job can be difficult for returning prisoners, due both to legal obstacles and to discrimination. Young adults leaving prison not only carry an adult conviction; in some states, any juvenile record is also available to the public. Their felony convictions serve as an explicit bar to a long list of jobs (Mukamal 2001). Fewer than 40 percent of employers responding to a recent survey said they would "definitely" or "probably" hire someone with a criminal record for an unskilled, noncollege position. They were far more likely to hire someone on welfare (92 percent), with a GED (96 percent), with a spotty work history (59 percent), or unemployed for a year (83 percent) (Holzer, Raphael, and Stoll 2002). In a study involving matched pairs of applicants for the same job—one with a criminal record, one with none—white applicants with criminal records were 50 percent less likely than other whites to get job offers. African-American applicants with criminal records were 64 percent less likely than African-Americans with no record to receive an offer (Pager 2002).

Many state and local jurisdictions offer transitional assistance programs for individuals leaving prison. These programs span a variety of activities designed to improve employment outcomes and reduce crime—assistance with locating a job, skill development, on-the-job training, or work experience in general or for a specific employer. Evaluations of these programs have not been encouraging (see Bushway and Reuter 2002 for an excellent review). The exception to this bleak assessment is the finding by Uggen (2000), who reanalyzed the findings from the supported work experiments of the 1970s and found that transitional work programs for ex-offenders had significant success at reducing crime and improving work outcomes for male participants over the age of twenty-six. For the young adults who are the focus of this volume, however, there is precious little evidence that transitional work programs located in the community will reverse the adverse effects of imprisonment on their attachments to the world of work.

Bushway and Reuter (2002, 219) explain the successful outcomes for older

offenders by underscoring the central role of motivation: "The growing literature on desistance from crime emphasizes that the first step in the process involves some type of personal change in motivation away from crime and towards more pro-social goals (Fagan 1989; Maruna 2000; Shover 1996). After
this change has occurred, outside forces such as relationships or work can help
the individual maintain this change in orientation." The challenge, then, for
programs geared to young adults is to discern and leverage the factors that
might motivate them to change. Ironically, programs designed explicitly to
improve employment outcomes might be less effective for this particular age
group. Training, education, mentoring, apprenticeship, and positive peer group
experiences might be more age-appropriate strategies that can counter the attractions of antisocial lifestyles and promote a more positive attitude toward
work. Demonstrating the efficacy of these strategies would require rigorous
long-term evaluations of complex interventions.

Policy Opportunities

Three policy rationales might justify the design and implementation of new
interventions, whether in prison or after prison, to improve the employment
prospects for young adults coming out of prison. Research has underscored the
importance of work in the process of desistance (Sampson and Laub 1993). Former prisoners who are able to reconnect to the labor market through previous
employers or contacts from family or friends are more likely to have successful
outcomes after release. According to Wilson and colleagues, the two outcomes
are linked. In reviewing evaluations of prison education, vocation, and work
programs for adult offenders, they found that programs with the largest effect
on employment rates to also be most likely to have the largest reduction in recidivism (Wilson, Gallagher, and Mackenzie 2000). For this reason alone, we
might imagine that policy makers would be focused squarely on the need to
connect or reconnect returning prisoners to jobs. The policy rationale would
be deceptively straightforward: helping returning prisoners get jobs will bring
crime rates down. But for young adults, the pathways to employment are not
as straightforward as for older, motivated adults, so the successful intervention
may be more complex than simply providing work opportunities. Training,
education, mentoring, and peer group supports would seem to be required.

Another argument for a policy focus on securing work for this population
might be a labor market rationale. For a variety of reasons, having a felony conviction, especially having served time in prison with a felony conviction, has
the effect of diminishing one's employment prospects. According to some estimates, time in prison imposes a "wage penalty" of between 10 and 30 percent

(Western and Pettit 2000). The longer the prison sentence, the lower the like-lihood of finding legitimate employment after release (Hagan and Dinovitzer 1999) and these negative effects on employability are not evenly distributed. They fall particularly harshly on the already hard-pressed inner-city communi-ties where rates of crime, imprisonment, and reentry are highest, the commu-nities where "work has disappeared" (Wilson 1996). Accordingly, if policy makers were interested in addressing the issue of decreasing wage rates among low-skilled men, particularly minority men, they would focus on the process of connecting returning prisoners to jobs. An even sharper focus on young adults coming out of prison, developing the multifaceted service interventions that would overcome the negative consequences of imprisonment (what Western, Pettit, and Guetzkow [2002] termed the "punctuating event" in the pathway to employment) could have long-term payoffs in reversing the aggregate labor market effects of our incarceration policies.

A third reason would be a social inclusion rationale. In an era of mass im-prisonment, we have more than quadrupled the per capita rate of incarceration over the past generation, with incalculable social costs (Mauer and Chesney-Lind 2002). More than thirteen million Americans have felony convictions— 7 percent of the adult population, 12 percent of the men. Approximately three million Americans have served time in prison (Uggen, Manza, and Thompson 2000). As mentioned above, our penal policies have profound consequences for racial minorities: An African-American man now faces a 28 percent lifetime probability that he will spend at least a year in prison (Bonczar and Beck 1997). Perhaps the nation wishes to absorb the marginalizing effects of these policies as an acceptable cost of our "get tough" era. Alternatively, if policy makers wished to find ways to encourage the reintegration of ex-offenders, helping them work—become taxpayers, contribute to their families, gain economic sta-bility—would seem a wise investment. (For a fuller discussion of social inclu-sion, see chapter 14.)

Yet remarkably little attention is paid to the employment needs of this pop-ulation. Granted, a number of workforce development programs for the hard-to-employ also serve ex-offenders. But given the risks (and therefore opportu-nities) inherent in the moment of release from prison (when the needs for housing, income, subsistence, and relapse avoidance are highest), and given the priority attached by returning prisoners to securing a job (in part to make those other transitions more likely to succeed), what is striking is the lack of system-atic efforts to improve the chances that returning prisoners, particularly young adults, will connect to work, and activities leading to work, in the community.

There are noteworthy exceptions to this bleak assessment, such as Project RIO in Texas, the Safer Foundation in Illinois, and the Center for Employment

Opportunities in New York (Finn 1998a,b,c; Travis, Solomon, and Waul 2001). But even these large, well-established programs serve small numbers of returning prisoners and struggle to stay afloat. Perhaps the research findings on transitional work programs in the 1970s—that supported work programs did not reduce recidivism (see, e.g., Piliavin and Masters 1981)—convinced policy makers that interventions with this population are too risky. More likely, the "tough on crime" attitudes of the public and our elected officials have made it difficult to build support for programs designed to help those who have violated the law, particularly when the law-abiding poor are still underserved. But given the magnitude of the incarceration and reentry phenomenon in modern America, the life-long negative consequences for earnings levels of millions of poor, mostly male ex-offenders and the potential payoff in terms of crime reduction, strong arguments can be made for a new generation of demonstration programs that would test and evaluate new multifaceted intervention strategies. These interventions would begin in the prisons, capitalize on the moment of release, and transition returning prisoners to private-sector jobs in the community. These interventions would seem particularly apt for young adults who have a lifetime ahead of them that could, with the right investments targeted to their distinctive needs, be highly productive.

IMPROVING ATTACHMENTS TO FAMILY

Young adults who are returning to the community after release from prison are likely to quickly turn to family members to help them in the process of reentry and reintegration. Family members may provide returning prisoners immediate transportation after release, a place to stay for days, weeks, or months, help in finding a job, financial assistance, and emotional support. Although substance abuse treatment, educational programs, or job skills may enhance a returning prisoner's likelihood of a successful transition from prison to community, probably most important is for these individuals to have someone who will provide support and guidance after release.

Strong family attachments during prison and after release appear to significantly improve postrelease outcomes (Laub and Sampson 2001; Nelson, Deess, and Allen 1999; Uggen, Manza, and Behrens 2004; Visher and Travis 2003), although rigorous evaluations of family-focused interventions are quite limited. In fact, it is likely that certain attributes of offenders lead to both strong attachments and successful postrelease outcomes. Unfortunately, we know little about whether planned interventions either in prison or after release can, in themselves, strengthen family relationships. Moreover, many impediments exist to reestablishing family relationships after release from prison. Attachments to family may have been significantly weakened by the length of the prison term and infrequent communication. Some families may want only limited contact until the former prisoner has shown that he or she is intent on staying out of trouble. And some persons return to families that are themselves immersed in dysfunctional behaviors, such as criminal activity and drug use, which would create an environment detrimental to successful reintegration.

As Uggen and Wakefield noted in chapter 5, these potential impediments to family reintegration are particularly serious for young adults leaving prison. Moreover, the general population of young adults aged eighteen to twenty-four rely heavily on family for housing, financial assistance, and emotional support. Absent these supports, young adults facing a transition from prison to community are at a serious disadvantage for a successful transition to full adulthood. This section reviews what we know about the policies, programs, and social service arrangements—primarily at the state and local levels—that affect family attachment among prisoners and members of their families.

Family Attachment in Prison

Prison policies impose significant challenges to family attachment. Prison assignments are rarely made to accommodate proximity to family members. Exceptions may occur for mothers with young children (but not fathers) or if the sentencing judge explicitly requests that an offender be placed in a facility near family members. Prisons are often in remote areas of the state, hundreds of miles from the major urban areas where family members are located, making a visit time-consuming and expensive. Other obstacles include inadequate information on visiting procedures, little help from correctional facilities about visiting arrangements, and visiting procedures that are uncomfortable or humiliating (Travis and Waul 2003). The only means of staying in touch with family members may be a weekly or monthly telephone call. However, correctional facilities often set higher-than-average rates for telephone use to generate revenue for prison operations and prisoners and family members frequently complain about the high cost of telephone calls (Florida House of Representatives 1998; Ross and Richards 2002). Correctional facilities also may impose other restrictions on telephone use including withholding use as punishment, approving calling lists, and limiting duration of phone calls.

Most policy makers would view prison primarily as performing a public safety function for the community, and secondarily as a corrective function for the offender. As discussed earlier, in the last decade the emphasis in the majority of states has been on the former. Notably absent from the standard array of in-prison programs (e.g., GED, vocational training, substance abuse recovery) has been any attempt to develop programs designed to help prisoners connect or reconnect with family members (Florida House of Representatives 1998). Some correctional facilities do offer parenting programs but waiting lists for these programs are common because states cannot afford to pay for the staff required to operate them. Moreover, correctional policies regarding visitation programs and telephone calls have been designed to reduce security threats rather than to maintain family connections. (Whether family visitors pose serious security risks is a reasonable question. A study in Florida found that the typical visitor to a correctional facility was a fifty-year-old mother visiting her son.)

The types of programs available to prisoners and their families to facilitate family relationships are primarily offered in the six to twelve months prior to release, when both the prisoner and family members are reestablishing connections in preparation for release and return home. State correctional facilities offer a variety of prerelease programs, including transfers to facilities closer to eventual residence (and thus, family members), home furloughs, and transfers to halfway house or work release facilities (American Correctional Association 2000). Other nongovernmental resources for prisoners and their families have also emerged. For example, some community groups sponsor transportation programs to help family members visit relatives in prisons that are not accessible by public transportation. In 1983, the Family and Corrections Network (http://www.fctnetwork.org) was created to provide a forum for families of prisoners, policy makers, and service providers and to advocate for greater policy attention to the families of prisoners and their needs.

States are beginning to recognize the importance of creating programs and policies to improve family contact when a family member goes to prison. In Florida, a report by the Committee on Corrections of the House of Representatives recommended a series of changes designed to enhance family attachment, including creating an Office of Family Services within the Department of Corrections and requesting several feasibility studies of policies to improve family contacts (Florida House of Representatives 1998). Subsequently, the Florida Department of Corrections (FDOC) did create an Office of Citizens' Services, and the FDOC web site now prominently displays information for family members about contacting prisoners, visitation policies, and other matters of interest to them. These policy changes are likely to be low cost and may improve the ability of family members to stay connected. In order to determine whether such programs might benefit young adult prisoners, rigorous evaluations are needed that examine postrelease outcomes (e.g., stable employment or reductions in rearrests) and carefully estimate program costs.

Family Attachment after Release

Returning prisoners face many challenges upon their release from prison and return home, and family attachments (or lack thereof) may make the difference between a successful transition and an unsuccessful one (Uggen and Wakefield, chapter 5). Housing polices and practices are especially critical to a successful transition out of prison and to adulthood more generally, as many young adults leaving prison often rely on help from family members; otherwise, they may face living in a shelter or on the street. Not surprisingly, many young adults leaving prison are returning to disadvantaged urban areas and family members who live in public housing. But living with these family members in public housing may not be an option because federal housing policies permit public housing authorities to deny housing to individuals who have engaged in certain criminal activities or to even visit family members in public housing (Mukamal 2001). And access to other forms of public assistance, including food stamps and welfare benefits, may be limited because of their criminal record (see, e.g., Hirsch et al. 2002).

As mentioned earlier, family attachment has not been a priority program area for state correctional operations, and few programs exist at the state or local level to help returning prisoners reconnect with their family. Eligibility for these programs varies considerably by state and some programs are comanaged with community organizations. There are very few experienced, community-based institutions with the capacity to serve adequately and efficiently the growing number of adults and families touched by the transition from prison to home. In a report on promising prisoner reentry programs nationwide, only nine "family intervention" programs were identified; only one program had reliable information on program effectiveness (Waul et al. 2003).

The one notable program with outcome data targets drug offenders on parole and their family members. The premise of La Bodega de la Familia, a community organization in Lower Manhattan, is that involving families of drug users under criminal justice supervision can change drug treatment and parole outcomes (Shapiro and Schwartz 2001). Services include case management for the family to determine needs and obtain referrals for community services, support groups, and a twenty-four-hour crisis support for drug-related emergencies. The evaluation found that illegal drug use and criminal justice involvement declined among those in the Bodega program as compared with those in a control group. The Bodega group's reported use of illegal drugs in the previous month declined from 80 to 42 percent after six months of program participation compared with a reduction from 61 to 48 percent for the comparison group (Sullivan et al. 2002). In the six months following the program, 11 percent of Bodega participants were rearrested compared to 18 percent of the comparison group. Moreover, family members in the program for six months reported fewer unmet needs for medical, social, housing, and mental health services: after six months in the program, 9 percent of the Bodega family members reported a need for services compared to 28 percent of the comparison family members (Sullivan et al. 2002). The average age of program participants was thirty-six years; the evaluation did not examine outcomes separately for younger drug users.

Policy Challenges

Taken together, life course research on crime (see Uggen and Wakefield, chapter 5; Laub and Sampson 2001) and general studies of youth-to-adult transitions point to important policy directions for improving postrelease outcomes for young adult ex-prisoners returning home. In order for young adults released from prison to successfully navigate the transition from prison to families and communities, they will need economic and social support, acceptance, and strong encouragement for maintaining a conventional lifestyle, however difficult (Maruna 2000; Nelson, Deess, and Allen 1999). For young adults eighteen to twenty-five, these kinds of support are most likely to be found in one's primary family. For former prisoners, family is also likely to be the source for postrelease support of varying types. Family members are also well-positioned to exert methods of informal social control to prevent relapse to criminal activity or illegal drug use.

An important first step for correctional prerelease programs and discharge policies would be to assess the capability of the prisoner's family to provide postrelease support and assistance. If families of returning prisoners are themselves involved in criminal activity and drug use, then the prerelease preparation should include a discharge plan that would provide a supportive postrelease environment (i.e., halfway house, transition center, day reporting center). If the family is available, then correctional programs and policies need to facilitate and encourage support for young adults returning home. This approach might include arranging for prerelease meetings with family members and family counselors; involving the family in a postrelease program such as La Bodega; or providing other community support for families of returning prisoners. Unfortunately, the intervention literature on family programs for ex-prisoners is virtually nonexistent and no research has examined the effectiveness of involving family members in the prison-to-community transition for young adults. Thus, there is a clear need for a series of planned demonstration programs to test hypotheses about the role of family in the lives of young adults leaving prison, and to identify the most effective policies and programs that would increase the likelihood of their successful transition from prison to community.

HEALTH POLICIES AND TRANSITIONS FROM PRISON

As documented by Uggen and Wakefield in chapter 5, prisoners are, relatively speaking, very unhealthy. Their rates of HIV and AIDS, tuberculosis, hepatitis C, and mental illness are two to ten times as great as those of the general population (National Commission on Correctional Health Care 2002). A large majority of prisoners have histories of alcohol and substance use and abuse (Mumola 1999). When they enter prison, they come under the care of a vast network of prison health care providers, mostly government employees but including an increasing number of private-sector health professionals paid for by state and federal governments (McDonald 1999). Within the first few weeks of their arrival, they undergo a detailed health appraisal, including a review of their health history, a physical exam, and screening tests to detect communicable diseases. They are checked for dental needs and unusual health concerns (e.g., mental illness, substance abuse). While in prison, they can call upon this health care system to respond to health needs ranging from routine illnesses to kidney dialysis and even heart surgery (Anno 2002). For many prisoners, this is the best health care they have received in their life time, but at the same time, the quality of prison health care is often below that provided in community health facilities (Anno 2002).

When young adults enter the prison system, they bring with them a range of health issues different, in important ways, from those of their older counterparts. They are unlikely to be concerned about onset of cancer, dementia, or arthritis. Given their place in the cycle of human development, they may be more concerned about issues of sexuality, including sexually transmitted diseases, early experimentation with drug use, mental health disorders, and ways to reduce their exposure to violence. For young adults, the issues of health policy during their time of incarceration reflect the overlay of traditional concerns—attending to their daily health needs—and recognition of their stage of development.

This section reviews the health dimensions of the transition from prison to community. We begin by briefly describing the health profile of the prison population, building on the Uggen and Wakefield presentation, but our emphasis is on the long-term implications of the period of imprisonment for the health status of a young man or woman who passes through our prisons. This longer view squares nicely with a public health approach to policies regarding prison health care. Under this approach, which we explore at the end of this section, prisons are opportunities to intervene to improve the health outcomes of a population of great concern, as well as those of their families and communities.

Health Profile of Prisoners

In 2002, the National Commission on Correctional Health Care (NCCHC) released a report to Congress on the health status of soon-to-be released inmates. The commission estimated that the level of infectious diseases in the prison population was significantly higher than that of the general population (the report covers the jail population as well). Among prisoners, the rate for confirmed AIDS cases is five times greater; for positive HIV tests, five to seven times greater; for TB infection, nine to ten times greater; and for active TB, four times greater (National Commission on Correctional Health Care 2002). In the category of chronic diseases, the commission found that the prevalence of asthma was slightly higher than in the U.S. population, while the rates for diabetes and hypertension are somewhat lower, reflecting the younger age of the prison population (Davis 2002).

The prison population also presents high levels of physical and mental impairment. According to the Bureau of Justice Statistics (BJS), nearly 33 percent of all state prisoners report a physical impairment or mental condition (Maruschak and Beck 2001); 10 percent a learning disability (e.g., attention deficit disorder or dyslexia); and 16 percent a mental condition, or at least one night in a mental hospital or mental health facility (Ditton 1999). Because these findings were based on self-reports, they likely understate the extent of mental illness in state prisons (Veysey and Bichler-Robertson 2002).

A high percentage of the prison population—80 percent—report a history of substance abuse, including alcohol and drug use (Mumola 1999). According to BJS, 25 percent of state prison inmates fit a validated profile of alcohol dependence (Mumola 1999). At least 33 percent of state prisoners had taken part in a substance abuse treatment program, an indication of a personal need for help in stopping drug use. More than 50 percent of state prisoners report using drugs and/or alcohol at the time of their arrest (Mumola 1999).

The portrait that emerges from these data is of a population with a significant amount of health problems. For many state prisoners, these health conditions overlap, and dual and triple diagnosis is a frequent occurrence. As important, these health conditions are deeply intertwined with behavioral dimensions of the prisoners' lives in the community so that, for example, intravenous drug use can increase the chances of HIV infection, which can in turn lead to increased risk of other opportunistic diseases.

Table 6.1. Percentage of total burden of infectious disease among people soon to be released from correctional facilities, 1997

Condition	Est. number of releases with condition, 1997	Total number in U.S. population with condition	Releases with condition as percentage of total population with condition
AIDS	39,000	247,000	16
HIV infection	112,000–158,000	503,000	22–31
Total HIV/AIDS	151,000–197,000	750,000	20–26
Hepatitis B infection	155,000	1–1.25 million	12–16
Hepatitis C infection	1.3–1.4 million	4.5 million	29–32
Tuberculosis disease	12,000	32,000	38

Source: Hammett 2000.

Prison Health Care through a Reentry Lens

Given this health profile of the prison population, and the reality that, with the rare exception of those who die in prison, every prisoner returns to live in the community, a clear policy question comes into focus: Should the time in prison be used to improve the health status of those who pass through prison's gates? As table 6.1 shows, this question takes on significance far beyond a concern for the well-being of the individual prisoner. Rather than view a particular health condition in terms of its prevalence within the prison or jail (note that the table presents data for both prison and jail releases), this perspective frames the prevalence measure in societal terms and presents data on the percentage of the U.S. population with that condition who pass through a correctional facility each year.

This perspective presents new policy challenges to corrections officials (particularly prison health care providers) and to public health officials generally. We use HIV/AIDS to illustrate the scope of the policy challenge and to highlight recent innovations, although a similar analysis for other health conditions could readily lead to the same conclusion—that policy makers have paid little attention to the health care needs of returning prisoners.

If, as the NCCHC report documents, 20 to 26 percent of the U.S. population with HIV/AIDS passes through a correctional facility each year, then the policy question is how best to exploit the time of their incarceration to combat the HIV/AIDS epidemic. Following this logic, prison administrators should use the time in prison, at a minimum, to treat those sick and infected, but also to educate inmates about the risks of HIV/AIDS, prevention strategies and ways to reduce transmission of the virus.

The current approach to addressing the health care needs of those inmates with HIV/AIDS who are about to return home falls far short of this goal. A review of discharge planning for HIV-infected inmates in ten large state correctional systems undertaken between 1999 and 2001 by Abt Associates, under contract to the Centers for Disease Control and Prevention (CDC), found the system to be "seriously deficient" (Roberts et al. 2001). At one end of the spectrum, four states provided all HIV-infected inmates with comprehensive linkages to medical and social services. At the other end, the survey found that one state provided no discharge planning, although it had recently implemented a pilot program for some inmates. Two states simply referred released prisoners for appointments with medical or service providers. Building on these troubling survey results, the CDC and the Health Resources and Services Administration (HRSA) selected six states and one city to participate in a Corrections Demonstration Project. These jurisdictions were awarded five-year grants to expand or implement discharge planning, case management in the community, and other services to assist prisoners infected with HIV make better connections with the community health systems treating this infection.

Although findings from the CDC-HRSA demonstration project are still years away, the evaluation of the implementation stages sheds light on the broader challenges of linking health care in prison with health services in the community. One difficulty stems from the fact that health care professionals and corrections professionals come from different organizational cultures, with different social missions. In addition, funding streams for health benefits and insurance coverage are not readily transferred from a prison setting to a community setting; Medicaid enrollment typically ends when someone is sent to prison and getting back on the Medicaid list requires time and persistence. Federal funding such as that provided by CDC and HRSA may help bring these agencies together in common purpose, but what happens when the demonstration project is over? The challenges here are formidable (Roberts et al. 2001).

These challenges must be weighed against the potential benefits to the health status of returning prisoners, their families, and the broader society. Recognizing the potential for intervening effectively in a variety of critical disease categories, several public health researchers and analysts have called the criminal justice system a "public health opportunity" (Glaser and Greifinger 1993; Polonsky et al. 1994; Gaiter and Doll 1996). Seizing this opportunity would require an expansion of the prison health care mission to include responsibility for reducing the prevalence of those diseases within the broader community.

This shift has important operational implications. The case of hepatitis C provides a clear example. There is no vaccine to prevent hepatitis C. Treatment for those with symptoms is effective only about 40 percent of the time, is very expensive (between $5,000 and $13,000 per patient per year), and must be continued for a long time. For these reasons, most corrections agencies will not treat an inmate infected with hepatitis C unless he or she will be incarcerated for at least fifteen months (Positive Populations 2000, 4). Viewing prison as a public health opportunity, one would arrange treatment for hepatitis C to begin in prison and continue upon release for every infected inmate. Now, most prisons do not even screen for the disease (Anno 2002).

Even if prison health care systems took greater responsibility for society's health challenges, carrying out this mandate would require creating linkages with community-based health care delivery systems. Those systems are underfunded, struggle with cutbacks mandated by the operation of managed care systems, and are facing unmet demands by other groups needing medical services, groups that have not had the "benefit" of health care in prison (Freudenberg 2002). Without a system of universal health coverage, it would be difficult to argue that prisoners should get preferential health care in the community, as they did by virtue of their legal status in prison. A strategy that increases the share of public health resources for the returning prisoner population, at the expense of other equally deserving populations, would face difficult issues of equity.

Policy Challenges

We have presented an argument for rethinking the role of prison health care in assisting individuals, and by extension the broader society, in improving their health status when they make the transition back home. For young prisoners, the yield from this new policy strategy might not be realized for decades. But other aspects of this strategy could have short-term results. For example, intervening successfully to interrupt the cycle of drug use in the community, forced abstinence in prison, and relapse soon after release could significantly reduce drug use and crime in the communities to which prisoners return (Inciardi et al. 1997). These positive outcomes would have important health benefits in reduced intravenous drug use and lower rates of HIV infection, as well as lower costs.

In a time of severe fiscal constraints, we need to ask which dimension of this new strategy might warrant additional public investment. Which one would have greatest payoff for both the short and long term? From a public health perspective, one could argue that intervening to reduce the spread of infectious disease would be the wisest strategy (Howell, Greifinger, and Sommers 2002). In this analysis, correctional health care systems should focus squarely on diseases such as HIV, sexually transmitted diseases, and tuberculosis, with broad-based programs of education and screening. These interventions are also likely to be a good investment. In their review of the literature on cost-effectiveness of health services for returning prisoners, Howell, Greifinger, and Sommers (2002, 9) concluded that "well-designed HIV education programs for returning prisoners could be cost-effective and possibly cost-saving." The screening of 10,000 inmates for syphilis and treating identified infections would avert $1.6 million in future treatment costs; screening 10,000 prisoners for latent TB infection and providing treatment where necessary would avert $7.1 million in future costs. The public health rationale for these interventions seems compelling but requires the investment of scarce resources today, on a population that is not favored in policy circles, to yield a savings that cannot be realized for years to come.

From a public safety perspective, intervening to address issues of mental illness and addiction might be the wisest investment because this strategy would result in the greatest reductions in crime, particularly among young adults. Our policy makers generally shy away from investing public dollars to treat addiction and mental illness, particularly when those conditions are found in the crime-involved population. Overcoming these obstacles will require more than solid research linking crime reductions with these health interventions.

From a youth development perspective, a successful policy argument would be grounded in the fact that young adults in prison are still too early in their development to have earned the public opprobrium directed at their older counterparts. In their case, one might argue that the time in prison should be used to inculcate, through a variety of techniques, a sense of self-worth, an awareness of health risks of various behaviors, and an ability to manage interpersonal conflict without resort to violence—in short, a health-focused resiliency that could serve them well when they return home and throughout their life.

Developing policies to take advantage of this public health opportunity would require a significant realignment of health services, both in prison and in the community. Prisons would have to focus on universal health screening, treatment of identified health conditions, education, and discharge planning that links released prisoners with health care in the community. Policies should be implemented to establish Medicaid and other benefits at the moment of release. Community supervision by parole agencies should include requirements that former prisoners participate in drug treatment programs, keep appointments with mental health providers, take medication, and generally access the health care system. Aligning the corrections and health care systems to meet these goals has proven difficult (Roberts, Kennedy, and Hammett 2002; Rossman 2003). Increasing compliance and participation by former prisoners with these health regimes is at least equally formidable.

CONCLUSION

Youthful prisoners who are making the transition from prison to community experience many challenges, not only with respect to work, family, and health issues, but also with finances, housing, transportation, and peer relationships (see also Travis, Solomon, and Waul 2001; Uggen and Wakefield, chapter 5; Visher and Travis 2003). However, these challenges are not being met by current policies. Recent research substantiates the need for individualized transition planning and support that would begin prior to release and extend afterwards. Delivering such services requires a commitment to a joint plan of action coupled with intensive coordination of efforts between the justice system and community-based social services organizations. Many states and communities are beginning to embrace the former, but the latter brings a host of challenges and obstacles towards improving transitions from prison to community (Rossman 2003).

Ideally, an integrated service network would connect correctional institutions with community organizations. In recognition of the reality of reentry, particularly the high risks that attend the "moment of release" (Travis, Solomon, and Waul 2001), these services would preferably be aligned to provide a continuum of care between prison and community. In this model, corrections agencies and local institutions—housing agencies, faith institutions, schools, and youth-serving entities—would focus squarely on the complex dynamics of the family reunion that occurs upon a prisoner's release. Prisoners who return to live with extended families, and those family members, would have opportunities to plan for the dynamics, both positive and negative, associated with reunification. Public and private institutions within the community could be mobilized around these goals.

Similarly, the private business sector, local employment agencies, and public-sector work programs could be realigned with a new mission of improving the employment prospects of returning prisoners. In an ambitious version of this model, transitional employment would be provided for a few months to every returning prisoner, and work would be required as a condition of release (Travis 2002b). Drawing lessons from the history of welfare reform, this policy initiative would be justified principally as a part of a national initiative to reverse the debilitating negative effects of imprisonment on the lifetime employment prospects of millions of low-skill, mostly minority, men who pass through our prisons.

Finally, this model would envision a new approach to linking prison health care with community-based health delivery systems. A continuum-of-care model is particularly compelling for those prisoners with infectious diseases. A shift in public health policy that capitalizes on the high numbers of individuals in prison with HIV/AIDS, tuberculosis, hepatitis, and other serious health burdens could be justified solely on public health grounds, with considerable savings in health care costs. Yet a similar approach to other health conditions, particularly mental illness and addiction, could be justified on public safety grounds. Ensuring that mentally ill prisoners have continuing medication and health care, and that prisoners with serious histories of substance abuse are provided treatment in the community as they confront the realities of relapse risk, could potentially avert patterns of criminal behavior.

As Rossman (2003) points out, these policy shifts would require realignment of organizational missions, agency operations, and public expenditures. However, the recognition of the impact of mass incarceration on our society, and particularly on the life trajectories of young adults who now pass through our prisons in record numbers, may provide the impetus for a new policy consensus. Thus, an innovative strategy would align the delivery of family services, workforce development activities, and health care to meet a broader social goal of reintegration for those who have violated our criminal laws and spent years in our prisons.

REFERENCES

American Correctional Association. 2000. Survey summary: Prerelease/reintegration. *Corrections Compendium* 25(8): 7–25.

Anno, B. J. 2002. Prison health services: An overview. A paper prepared for the Urban Institute's Public Health Reentry Roundtable, Los Angeles.

Aos, S., P. Phipps, R. Barnoski, and R. Lieb. 2001. *The comparative costs and benefits of programs to reduce crime.* Olympia: Washington State Institute for Public Policy.

Beck, A., J. Karberg, and P. Harrison. 2001. *Prisons and jails at midyear.* Washington: U.S. Department of Justice, Bureau of Justice Statistics.

Blumstein, A. 2000. Disaggregating the violence trends. Pp. 13–44 in *The crime drop in America.* Edited by A. Blumstein and J. Wallman. Cambridge: University of Cambridge Press.

Bonczar, T. P., and A. J. Beck. 1997. *Lifetime likelihood of going to state or federal prison.* Washington: U.S. Department of Justice, Bureau of Justice Statistics.

Bushway S., and P. Reuter. 2002. Labor markets and crime. Pp. 191–224 in *Crime: Public policies for crime control,* 2nd ed. Edited by J. Q. Wilson and J. Petersilia. San Francisco: ICS Press.

Butts, J., and O. Mitchell. 2000. Brick by brick: Dismantling the border between juvenile and adult justice. Pp. 167–213 in *Criminal justice 2000 (2): Boundary changes in criminal justice organizations.* Edited by C. M. Friel. Washington: National Institute for Justice.

Butts, J., and J. Travis. 2002. *The rise and fall of American youth violence: 1980 to 2000.* Washington: Urban Institute/Justice Policy Center.

Cadora, E., and C. Swartz. 2001. Analysis for the community justice project at the Center for

Alternative Sentencing and Employment Services (CASES). http://www.communtyjustice project.org

Clear, T. R., D. R. Rose, and J. A. Ryder. 2000. Coercive mobility and the community: The impact of removing and returning offenders. A paper prepared for the Urban Institute's Reentry Roundtable, Washington.

Cullen, F. T., and P. Gendreau. 2000. Assessing correctional rehabilitation: Policy, practice, and prospects. Pp. 109–173 in *Criminal justice 2000 (3): Policies, processes, and decisions of the criminal justice system.* Edited by J. Horney. Washington: National Institute of Justice.

Davis, L. 2002. Health profile of the state prison population and returning offenders: Public health challenges. A paper prepared for the Urban Institute's Public Health Reentry Roundtable, Los Angeles.

Ditton, P. M. 1999. *Mental health and treatment of inmates and probationers.* Washington: U.S. Department of Justice, Bureau of Justice Statistics.

Fagan, J. A. 1989. Cessation of family violence: Deterrence and dissuasion. *Crime and Justice: A review of research* 11: 377–426.

Federal Justice Statistics Program. *Federal Justice Statistics Resource Center.* http://fjsrc.urban.org/index.cfm.

Finn, P. 1998a. *Texas' Rio Project: Reintegration of offenders.* Washington: U.S. Department of Justice.

Finn, P. 1998b. *Chicago's Safer Foundation: A road back for ex-offenders.* Washington: U.S. Department of Justice.

Finn, P. 1998c. *Successful job placement for ex-offenders: The Center for Employment Opportunities.* Washington: U.S. Department of Justice.

Florida House of Representatives. 1998. *Maintaining family contact when a family member goes to prison: An examination of state policies on mail, visiting, and telephone access.* Tallahassee: Committee on Corrections.

Freudenberg, N. 2002. Community health services for returning jail and prison inmates. A paper prepared for the Urban Institute's Public Health Reentry Roundtable, Los Angeles.

Gaes, G., T. Flanagan, L. Motiuk, and L. Stewart. 1999. Adult correctional treatment. Pp. 361–426 in *Prisons: Crime and justice: A review of research.* Edited by M. Tonry and J. Petersilia. Chicago: University of Chicago Press.

Gaiter, J., and L. S. Doll. 1996. Editorial: Improving HIV/AIDS prevention in prisons is good public health policy. *American Journal of Public Health* 86: 1201–1203.

Gerber, J., and E. Fritsch. 1994. *The effects of academic and vocational program participation on inmate misconduct and reincarceration.* Prison education research project, final report. Huntsville, TX: Sam Houston State University.

Glaser, J. B., and R. B. Greifinger. 1993. Correctional health care: A public health opportunity. *Annals of Internal Medicine* 118: 139–145.

Government Accounting Office. 2001. *Prisoner release: Trends and information on reintegration programs.* Washington: Government Accounting Office.

Hagan, J. 1993. The social embeddedness of crime and unemployment. *Criminology* 31: 465–491.

Hagan, J., and R. Dinovitzer. 1999. Collateral consequences of imprisonment for children, communities, and prisoners. Pp. 121–162 in *Prisons: Crime and justice: A review of research.* Edited by M. Tonry and J. Petersilia. Chicago: University of Chicago Press.

Hammett, T. M. 2000. Health-related issues in prisoner reentry to the community. Paper prepared for the Urban Institute Reentry Roundtable, Washington.

Harrison, P. M., and A. J. Beck. 2002. *Prisoners in 2001.* Washington: U.S. Department of Justice, Bureau of Justice Statistics.

Hirsch, A. E., S. M. Dietrich, R. Landau, P. D. Schneider, I. Ackelsberg, J. Bernstein-Baker, and J. Hohenstein. 2002. *Every door closed: Barriers facing parents with criminal records.* Washington: Center for Law and Social Policy.

Holzer, H., S. Raphael, and M. Stoll. 2002. Can employers play a more positive role in prisoner reentry? A paper prepared for the Urban Institute's Reentry Roundtable, Washington.

Howell, E., R. Greifinger, and A. Sommers. 2002. What is known about the cost-effectiveness of health services for returning prisoners? A paper prepared for the Urban Institute's Public Health Reentry Roundtable, Los Angeles.

Inciardi, J. A., S. S. Martin, C. A. Butzin, R. M. Hooper, and L. D. Harrison. 1997. An effective model of prison-based treatment for drug-involved offenders. *Journal of Drug Issues* 27: 261–278.

Langan, P. A., and D. J. Levin. 2002. Recidivism of prisoners released in 1994. Washington: U.S. Department of Justice, Bureau of Justice Statistics.

Lattimore, P., A. D. Witte, and J. R. Baker. 1990. Experimental assessment of the effect of vocational training on youthful property offenders. *Evaluation Review* 14: 127–141.

Laub, J. and R. Sampson. 2001. Understanding desistance from crime. Pp. 1–69 in *Crime and justice: A review of research 28.* Edited by M. Tonry. Chicago: University of Chicago Press.

La Vigne, N. G., and V. Kachnowski, with J. Travis, R. Naser, and C. Visher. 2003. *A portrait of prisoner reentry in Maryland.* Washington: Urban Institute/Justice Policy Center.

La Vigne, N. G., S. Lawrence, V. Kachnowski, and R. Naser. 2002. *COR Process evaluation: Programming for successful community reintegration.* Washington: Urban Institute/Justice Policy Center.

La Vigne, N. G., and C. A. Mamalian, with J. Travis and C. Visher. 2003. *A portrait of prisoner reentry in Illinois.* Washington: Urban Institute/Justice Policy Center.

Lawrence, S., D. Mears, G. Dubin, and J. Travis. 2002. *The practice and promise of prison programming.* Washington: Urban Institute/Justice Policy Center.

Legal Action Center. 2000. *Housing laws affecting individuals with criminal convictions.* http://www.lac.org/pubs/pubs_top.html.

Lynch J. P., and W. J. Sabol. 2001. *Prisoner reentry in perspective.* Washington: Urban Institute/Justice Policy Center.

Martinson, R. 1974. What works? Questions and answers about prison reform. *Public Interest* 35: 22–54.

Maruna, S. 2000. *Making good: How ex-convicts reform and rebuild their lives.* Washington: American Psychological Association.

Maruschak, L. M., and A. J. Beck. 2001. *Medical problems of inmates, 1997.* Washington: U.S. Department of Justice, Bureau of Justice Statistics.

Mauer, M., and M. Chesney-Lind, eds. 2002. *Invisible punishment: The collateral consequences of mass imprisonment.* New York: New Press.

McDonald, D. 1999. Medical care in prisons. Pp. 427–478 in *Prisons: Crime and justice: A review of research.* Edited by M. Tonry and J. Petersilia. Chicago: University of Chicago Press.

Mukamal, D. 2001. *From hard time to full time: Strategies to help move ex-offenders from welfare to work.* Washington: U.S. Department of Labor.

Mumola, C. J. 1999. *Substance abuse and treatment: State and federal prisoners, 1997.* Washington: U.S. Department of Justice, Bureau of Justice Statistics.

National Commission on Correctional Health Care. 2002. *The health status of soon-to-be-released inmates: A Report to Congress.* http://www.ncchc.org/pubs_stbr.html.

National Corrections Reporting Program. *Spreadsheets.* http://www.ojp.usdoj.gov/bjs/dtdata .htm#ncrp.

Nelson, M., P. Deess, and C. Allen. 1999. *The first month out: Post-incarceration experiences in New York City.* New York: Vera Institute of Justice.

Nelson, M., and J. Trone. 2000. *Why planning for release matters.* New York: Vera Institute of Justice.

Oregon Department of Corrections. 2002. Ballot measure 17 compliance source data. http:// www.doc.state.or.us.

Pager, D. 2002. The mark of a criminal record. Paper presented at the annual meeting of the American Sociological Association, Chicago.

Petersilia, J. 2003. *When prisoners come home: Parole and prisoner reentry.* New York: Oxford University Press.

Petersilia, J., and S. Turner. 1993. *Evaluating intensive supervision probation and parole: Results of a nationwide experiment.* Washington: National Institute of Justice.

Piliavin, I., and S. Masters. 1981. *The impact of employment programs on offenders, addicts, and problem youth: Implications from supported work.* Madison: University of Wisconsin, Institute for Research and Poverty Discussion.

Polonsky, S., S. Kerr, B. Harris, J. Gaiter, R. R. Fichtner, and M. G. Kennedy. 1994. HIV prevention in prisons and jails: Obstacles and opportunities. *Public Health Reports* 109: 615–625.

Positive Populations. 2000. Correctional systems grapple with dual epidemics: HIV and Hepatitis C. *Positive Populations* 2(2): 4.

Rhine, E., W. R. Smith, and R. Jackson. 1991. *Paroling authorities: Recent history and current practice.* Laurel, MD: American Correctional Association.

Roberts, C. A., S. S. Kennedy, and T. M. Hammett 2002. Linkages between in-prison and community-based services. A paper prepared for the Urban Institute's Public Health Reentry Roundtable, Washington.

Roberts C. A., S. S. Kennedy, T. M. Hammett, and N. F. Rosenberg. 2001. *Discharge planning and continuity of care for HIV-infected state prison inmates as they return to the community: A study of ten states.* Cambridge, MA: Abt Associates.

Ross, J., and S. Richards. 2002. *Convict criminology.* Belmont, CA: Wadsworth.

Rossman, S. 2003. Building partnerships to strengthen offenders, families, and communities. Pp. 343–380 in *Prisoners once removed: The impact of incarceration and reentry on children, families, and communities.* Edited by J. Travis and M. Waul. Washington: Urban Institute Press.

Sampson, R. J., and J. H. Laub. 1993. *Crime in the making: Pathways and turning points through life.* Cambridge: Harvard University Press.

Saylor, W., and G. Gaes. 1992. Prep study links UNICOR work experience with successful post-release outcome. *Research Forum* 1(3): 1–8.

Schriro, D. 2000. *Correcting corrections: Missouri's parallel universe series: Sentencing and corrections: Issues for the 21st century.* Washington: National Institute of Justice.

Seiter R. P., and K. R. Kadela. 2003. Prisoner reentry: What works, what doesn't, and what's promising. *Crime and Delinquency* 49: 360–388.

Shapiro, C., and M. Schwartz. 2001. Coming home: Building on family connections. *Corrections Management Quarterly* 5(3): 52–61.

Shover, N. 1996. *Great pretenders: Pursuits and careers of persistent thieves.* Boulder, CO: Westview Press.

Stuerer S. J., L. Smith, and A. Tracy. 2001. Draft report on the three-state recidivism study for Maryland, Minnesota, and Ohio. Lanham, MD: Correctional Education Association.

Sullivan, E., M. Mino, K. Nelson, and J. Pope. 2002. *Families as a resource in recovery from drug abuse: An evaluation of La Bodega de la Familia.* New York: Vera Institute of Justice.

Taxman, F. S., D. Young, J. M. Byrne, A. Holsinger, and D. Anspach. 2002. *From prison safety to public safety: Innovations in offender reentry.* College Park: University of Maryland, College Park, Bureau of Governmental Research.

Tonry, M. 1999. The fragmentation of sentencing and corrections in America. *Sentencing and corrections: Issues for the 21st century, 1.* Washington: U.S. Department of Justice, National Institute of Justice.

Travis, J. 2002a. Invisible punishment: An instrument of social exclusion. Pp. 15–36 in *Invisible punishment: The collateral consequences of mass imprisonment.* Edited by M. Mauer and M. Chesney-Lind. New York: New Press.

Travis, J. 2002b. Thoughts on the future of parole. Lecture at the Vera Institute of Justice, New York, May 22.

Travis, J., and S. Lawrence. 2002. Experimenting with parole. *California Journal* 33 (8): 18–23.

Travis, J., A. Solomon, and M. Waul. 2001. *From prison to home: The dimensions and consequences of prisoner reentry.* Washington: Urban Institute.

Travis, J., and M. Waul. 2003. Prisoners once removed: The children and families of prisoners. Pp. 1–32 in *Prisoners once removed: The impact of incarceration and reentry on children, families, and communities.* Edited by J. Travis and M. Waul. Washington: Urban Institute Press.

Uggen, C. 2000. Work as a turning point in the life course of criminals: A duration model of age, employment, and recidivism. *American Sociological Review* 67: 529–546.

Uggen, C., J. Manza, and A. Behrens. 2004. Less than the average citizen: Stigma, role transition, and the civic reintegration of convicted felons. Pp. 258–290 in *After crime and punishment: Ex-offender reintegration and desistance from crime.* Edited by S. Maruna and R. Immarigeon. Cullompton, UK: Willan.

Uggen, C., J. Manza, and M. Thompson. 2000. Rethinking crime and inequality: The socioeconomic, familial, and civic lives of criminal offenders. Paper presented at the annual meeting of the American Society of Criminology, San Francisco.

Uggen, C., and M. Thompson. 2003. The socioeconomic determinants of ill-gotten gains: Within-person changes in drug use and illegal earnings. *American Journal of Sociology* 109: 146–185.

U.S. Department of Justice. 2002. Going home: The serious and violent offender reentry initiative. Program solicitation issued May 15. Washington: U.S. Department of Justice.

Veysey, B. M., and G. Bichler-Robertson. 2002. Providing psychiatric services in correctional settings. In *The Health status of soon-to-be-released inmates: A report to Congress.* National Commission on Correctional Health Care. http://www.ncchc.org/pubs.

Visher, C. A., and J. Travis. 2003. Transitions from prison to community: Understanding individual pathways. *Annual Review of Sociology* 29: 89–113.

Waul, M., A. Van Ness, M. Funches, and J. Travis. 2003. *Easing the transition from prison to home: A sample of promising reentry programs.* Washington: Urban Institute.

Western, B., and B. Pettit. 2000. Incarceration and racial inequality in men's employment. *Industrial and Labor Relations Review* 54: 3–16.

Western, B., B. Pettit, and J. Guetzkow. 2002. Black economic progress in the era of mass imprisonment. Pp. 165–180 in *Invisible punishment: The collateral consequences of mass imprisonment.* Edited by M. Mauer and M. Chesney-Lind. New York: New Press.

Wilson, D. B., C. A. Gallagher, and D. L. Mackenzie. 2000. A meta-analysis of corrections-based education, vocational, and work programs for adult offenders. *Journal of Research in Crime and Delinquency* 37: 347–368.

Wilson, W. J. 1996. *When work disappears: The world of the new urban poor.* New York: Alfred A. Knopf.

CHAPTER SEVEN

Homeless Youth and the Perilous Passage to Adulthood

JOHN HAGAN AND BILL MCCARTHY

INTRODUCTION

Homeless youth challenge common ideas of the transition to adulthood. Indicators of the end of adolescence typically include completing high school, enrolling in college or university, entering full-time employment, living independently from one's family, and involvement in lifestyle activities that are typically prohibited for young teenagers but common among adults (e.g., nonepisodic sex). Yet many homeless youth begin these transitions before they acquire the skills, credentials, experiences, psychological resources, connections, social support, and other assets that increase the likelihood of success. Moreover, many of these youth skip transitions associated with the beginning of adulthood, embarking upon others that typically occur much later, or they initiate new transitions without completing those that typically precede them. Thus, compared to other youth, a greater proportion of the homeless experience "extended" and "fractured" transitions (Coles and Craig 1999).

Homeless adolescents' transition to adulthood is further compromised by the many risks that characterize living on the street. One of the most prevalent risks in this period of emerging adulthood is the prospect of escalating contact with the juvenile and criminal justice systems. The likelihood of police contact is greatest for homeless youth who are involved in crime, yet others face elevated risks because their homelessness increases the time they spend in public settings (e.g., parks, street corners). Police often focus their patrols on these areas and often arrest homeless youth for an array of illegal but noncriminal activities (e.g., sleeping in a public setting, loitering). Interactions with police can have a self-perpetuating quality: they may lead to formal sanctions that include imprisonment and they can perpetuate feelings of shame, embarrassment, and other emotions that often amplify identification and involvement with street subcultures of crime, in turn preventing or delaying a successful transition to adulthood.

The conditions that characterize contemporary homelessness increase the probability that homeless youth will travel the streets they occupy in one direction—away from adults and peers who can help them form links to employment opportunities that can provide an escape from homelessness. Still, not all homeless youth are enmeshed in the criminal justice system; indeed, some resilient youth are able to reverse the course of their lives by pursuing employment opportunities that lead away from adult criminals and peers connected to high-risk lives on the street. The challenge is to capture the realities of risk and resilience and their relationship to one another and to distinguish those youth who succumb to the street from those who do not. Success will increase our understanding and ideally our leverage over those factors that improve the odds of successful transitions to adulthood.

In this chapter we provide a portrait of homeless youth that draws upon findings from two of the larger, more recent studies of homeless youth in North America. Several similarities may be found between homeless youth and the inner-city youth who are at the heart of a recent controversy about high-risk youth and employment. We review this debate, elaborating upon an aspect of inner-city adolescent life that is emphasized in studies of homeless youth: police contact. Our thesis is that limiting contact with the justice system is a crucial micro-level factor, especially for emotionally vulnerable youth, in preserving the prospects for successfully leaving the street for the more conventional world of legal work. Of course, limiting harmful justice system contacts is important for both homeless youth and other vulnerable populations considered in this volume, such as youthful drug users and mentally ill youth who have been deinstitutionalized. We also suggest that community variation in social welfare and law enforcement policies introduces a further macro-level determinant of the risks of vulnerability and the prospects of resilience for homeless youth as well as other vulnerable youth.

STUDYING THE STREET

Recent figures from the United Nations Children's Fund indicate that more than eighty million "unaccompanied" children and youth live on the streets around the world (van der Ploeg and Scholte 1997). The vast majority of homeless youth congregate in cities in the poorer developing countries of Asia (e.g., Ganesan 1996), Africa (e.g., Mufune 2000), Latin America (e.g., Campos, Raffaelli, and Ude 1994; Mickelson 2000; Wright, Wittig, and Kaminsky 1993), and Eastern Europe (e.g., Stephenson 2001), yet there are many homeless youth in the wealthier countries of Western Europe, Australia, and North America (Avramov 1998; Coles and Craig 1999; Downing-Orr 1996; Shane 1996). The United Nations (UNICEF 1998) defines "youth on the street" as those who engage in street-based activities such as begging or peddling but have a home base to return to, whereas "youth of the street" have weaker ties to their families and live largely on the streets. "Abandoned youth" have no family connections and live nearly exclusively on the streets. An estimated two-fifths of the world's street youth live in Latin America, with a majority of these living "of the streets" of Brazil (Campos, Raffaelli, and Ude 1994). In the United States, recent figures suggest that there could be up to two million runaways each year—many of whom will become "of the streets"—and about a half a million abandoned youth (Shane 1996). Van der Ploeg and Scholte (1997) noted that the number of homeless youth rose throughout the 1990s in most countries, and that the rise was greatest among females, cultural and racial minorities, and younger adolescents.

In the 1990s, several researchers in the United States and Canada surveyed modestly large samples of homeless youth. In the following summary, we draw primarily on the results of two of these studies. Building upon an earlier study we completed in 1985 (McCarthy and Hagan 1992), we gathered information from youth aged sixteen to twenty-four in Toronto and Vancouver over a three-month period in the summer of 1992 (Hagan and McCarthy 1997). The first wave of the study included 482 youth, of whom 376 took part in the second wave a month after the first interview. A month later, 257 finished a third interview. We combine data from both cities in our overview; however, the two cities had dramatically different policy approaches to homeless youth, an issue we develop in a later section of this chapter. A second key study conducted by Whitbeck and Hoyt (1999) involved 602 runaway and homeless adolescents aged twelve to twenty-two from five Midwestern U.S. cities. Other modestly sized surveys of homeless youth in the U.S. and Canada include studies from Hollywood, California (Kipke et al. 1997), Edmonton, Canada (Baron and Hartnagel 1997), and Toronto, Canada (Gaetz and O'Grady 2002).

Most North American youth first live independently from their families when they leave home to attend college or university, establish themselves financially as a result of employment, or begin military service. Most of these transitions occur after youth turn eighteen. In contrast, the majority of the youth we interviewed left home before that age. For example, before they turned eighteen, 54 percent of these youth reported that they had stayed on the street for more than a few days and 34 percent had slept in a hostel. About 33 percent slept on the street before they were sixteen, and 9 percent stayed in a hostel. Whitbeck and Hoyt (1999) reported that 80 percent of the youth they surveyed left home before they were sixteen. On average, these youth first left home before they were fourteen.

Data from the U.S. Census Current Population Survey (U.S. Bureau of the Census 1993) indicate that in 1992, about 80 percent of young people aged eighteen and over completed four years of high school. Meanwhile, National Center for Education Statistics data report that only 11 percent of U.S. youth aged sixteen or over had dropped out of school in that year (McMillen, Kaufman, and Whitener 1994). Canadian data reflect similar patterns; moreover, these rates remained fairy stable in the years since 1992. Together, these data indicate that the great majority of Canadian and U.S. youth successfully navigate the transition out of secondary school. In our study, 85 percent of the homeless youth aged eighteen or older *did not* graduate from high school. Indeed, 30 percent of the youth we spoke with had not completed their first year of high school (i.e., grade nine). Meanwhile, 80 percent of the youth in our sample had to repeat at least one grade. Although difficulties with school material and requirements, as well as family disruptions and residential moves, contributed to their school failures, 80 percent of our respondents reported that they first left school because they were expelled. Their alienation from conventional educational institutions is further reflected in the small number who enrolled in an educational program after leaving home. Of the 257 youth we followed for three months, only 14 percent were attending school at the end of our study. Although the youth interviewed by Whitbeck and Hoyt (1999) are younger on average than those we studied, they also report considerable difficulties with school. For example, 72 percent of these young people had been suspended from school at some point and 36 percent had dropped out. These figures suggest that many of these youth will not graduate from high school.

Employment data for the 1990s indicate that about 80 percent of youth in the United States and Canada were employed at some time during the four years of high school. On average, youth in senior grades worked between eighteen and twenty hours a week (Mortimer 2003, 18). U.S. Bureau of Labor Statistics data and Statistics Canada data indicate that in 1992, unemployment among sixteen- to nineteen-year-olds peaked at just below 20 percent (in the U.S., the African-American rate was almost double) and declined by several points by the end of the decade.

The majority (84 percent) of the homeless youth we surveyed had worked in a full- or part-time job that lasted a month or more. However, this aggregate statistic hides several more disturbing trends. Of those aged eighteen and over, 43 percent never had a job before their eighteenth birthday, suggesting that many left high school without having been employed. Almost 25 percent of the youth who found employment reported that they had been subsequently fired from their jobs, whereas only 6 percent reported leaving a job because they were promoted or found a better one. Focusing on those youth who completed all three waves of our study reveals that in 1992, only 17 percent were working at all three waves, and only 10 percent consistently had full-time work. Whitbeck and Hoyt (1999) reported that only 29 percent of their sample had worked in a nontemporary job (i.e., not as a day laborer).

Not surprisingly, many homeless youth reported receiving a considerable proportion of their income from work outside the legal economy. Popular methods involved begging or panhandling and squeegeeing vehicle windows. Although neither activity was explicitly illegal during our research, local police frequently stop these activities and at times arrest homeless youth for asking for spare change (Coles and Craig 1999) or for requesting money for cleaning vehicle windows (Dachner and Tarasuk 2002; Gaetz and O'Grady 2002). Of the youth we studied, 56 percent reported that they panhandled or squeegeed since leaving home. Other sources of income more clearly involve breaking the law. About 50 percent of the youth we interviewed stole clothing or food, 36 percent shoplifted other goods, 40 percent sold something they knew was stolen, 40 percent sold marijuana, and 36 percent trafficked other drugs. As expected, many of these youth were charged and convicted for an array of offenses from theft, drug selling, and soliciting to more minor infractions associated with homelessness (e.g., trespassing). More than half (56 percent) of the youth with whom we spoke had been charged since they left home and 30 percent had been charged on three or more occasions. Whitbeck and Hoyt (1999) reported that 30 percent of the youth they spoke with sold drugs since leaving home, about 25 percent stole, and just over 15 percent panhandled.

Receiving social assistance represents another transition that often marks the end of adolescence. Although many youth live in families that receive AFDC, food stamps, Medicaid, and other forms of government assistance, few domiciled youth directly receive government support. Yet more than 75 percent of the homeless youth we surveyed had received such support. About one third (32 percent) of the youth we followed across the three waves of our study reported receiving welfare in the final weeks of our research and 21 percent relied on social assistance at each wave of our study. These figures suggest that almost 20 percent of our sample may have begun a transition into chronic or long-term welfare. As noted later in this chapter, welfare assistance is more widely available to street youth in Toronto than in Vancouver, which in this respect is more similar to U.S. jurisdictions.

Data on the transition from virginity to nonvirginity and nonepisodic sex suggest that about 55 percent of U.S. students have sexual intercourse before they leave high school; less than 10 percent reported having sex before their thirteenth birthday, and between 18 (female) and 38 (male) percent indicated having sex with four or more partners (Centers for Disease Control 1996; Besharov and Gardiner 1997). In contrast, 84 percent of the youth interviewed by Whitbeck and Hoyt (1999) were sexually experienced. The median age for the transition to nonvirginity among these youth was thirteen for males and fourteen for females; the median number of sexual partners was five for males and four for females (see also Russell 1998). Homeless youth differ further from nonhomeless youth in that a far greater proportion are molested as their first sexual experience. Self-report surveys likely underestimate the extent of sexual abuse because of the sensitivity and shame that often accompany it; nonetheless, a great many youth report being sexually victimized. In our study, about 20 percent of respondents indicated that a family member attempted to sexually abuse them, the same proportion reported by Whitbeck and Hoyt (1999) but a smaller proportion than the 34 percent reported for a sample of youth studied in Hollywood (Russell 1998).

The sexual lives of many homeless youth are distinguished further by their involvement in "survival sex" and the sex trade. Studies vary in their estimates, but between 10 percent and 30 percent of homeless youth report trading sex for shelter, food, or other resources (Pennbridge, Freese, Mackenzie 1992; Russell 1998). In our study, about one-third of the youth we interviewed said that they had sold sex at some point since leaving home. As expected, homeless youth who participate in the sex trade reported higher levels of violent victimization than other youth and had a greater risk of contracting a sexually transmitted disease (STD). For example, Whitbeck and Hoyt (1999) reported that about 20 percent of the youth they interviewed had been diagnosed with a STD (see also Russell 1998; De Rosa et al. 2001).

Two broad sets of factors further complicate the transition to adulthood for homeless youth: their family backgrounds and their current living situation and lifestyle. Almost one third of the youth we interviewed had never lived with both their biological parents and the majority had lived in several family situations. For example, approximately 60 percent had lived in three or more different family settings and 20 percent had lived in six or more. Most homeless youth are estranged from their parents. In our study, 62 percent had been bruised or bloodied by an assaultive parent (22 percent reported that they were frequently victimized). Not surprisingly, only 32 percent had spoken to their father at least once a month since they last lived at home, 58 percent had spoken with their mothers on the phone, but only 23 percent had seen them at least once a month since they left home. As a result, few of these youth are able to draw on their parents' or relatives' financial, emotional, or psychological support or their parents' social capital in their search for work, school, and housing.

Most homeless youth spend a considerable amount of their time, especially when they first move to the street, searching for food, stable shelter, and the means to obtain these. The instability of shelters and other more precarious housing (e.g, abandoned buildings and public parks) increases the difficulties associated with trying to attend school or find and keep a job. The challenges associated with these transitions are exacerbated further by a lifestyle that involves considerable "partying" and trouble with the police. Many homeless youth have serious substance use problems. Almost 80 percent of the homeless youth we spoke with reported having smoked marijuana, 57 percent had ingested hallucinogens, and 43 percent had used crack or powder cocaine more than twice since leaving home. Whitbeck and Hoyt (1999) found that 80 percent of their sample used alcohol in the last year, about 70 percent smoked marijuana, about 20 percent took hallucinogens, and 15 percent ingested cocaine. Many of these youth were regular users, with about 40 percent reporting that they drank alcohol or smoked marijuana monthly or more frequently, and about 10 percent revealing that they used hallucinogens that often.

The descriptive research paints a mostly grim picture of the daily lives of urban street youth in the period when their home- and school-oriented peers are taking their first steps toward adulthood. While most young people invest the largest part of their daily energies in benign settings, homeless youth spend most of their time less profitably and more dangerously on the street and in parks, social assistance offices, shelters, and abandoned buildings. Together with friends acquired on the street, they spend a large part of their time looking for food, shelter, and money. Most remain unemployed, spending their time hanging out, panhandling, partying, and foraging in the shadow of the street.

Yet as we noted above, some of these youth have some success in the legal labor market. Although only 17 percent of the youth we surveyed were employed across all three waves of our study, 27 percent were working at the time of the second wave. In the third wave, toward the end of the summer, nearly 29 percent were legally employed. Meanwhile, among those who were unemployed, 59 percent were searching for work, checking want ads, and visiting agencies and prospective employers. And almost half (47 percent) of those without work indicated that they had applied for at least one job in the two weeks prior to the second interview. Even though the latter applications rarely resulted in employment, the combination of the 25 to 33 percent of these homeless youth who were working, and the majority of the remaining who were looking for work, indicate that the prospect of work was a major part of their everyday lives. Not surprisingly, many of those homeless youth who fail to find work ultimately abandon the search. By the time of the third interview, the proportion of unemployed youth still searching the want ads for work dropped from 59 percent to 44 percent. The proportion who applied for work also fell, from 47 percent to over 38 percent. Yet by the third wave of the summer panel, nearly 33 percent of the youth were still employed. The majority of jobs were low-skill service work. However, a wide range of jobs were involved. In addition to the conventional fast-food, janitorial, and retail work characteristic of youth-oriented "McJobs," respondents found jobs as rickshaw pullers, participants in research experiments, crossing guards, chicken catchers, and live-bait procurers. Several respondents successfully found employment in skilled jobs less typical of youth work. They worked as welders, meat cutters, carpenters, mechanics, and in other trades; some found employment in offices working as receptionists, title searchers, and counselors; and a few worked in entertainment as disc jockeys, piano players, models, and dancers.

HOMELESS YOUTH AND RESEARCH
ON THE LIVES OF THE URBAN POOR

The risk and resilience that characterize the lives of street youth place them in the middle of a recent critique by Wacquant (2002) of urban street field research. The most notable target of Wacquant's critique is, for our purposes, Newman's *No Shame in My Game: The Working Poor in the Inner City* (1999). While Newman's study does not focus on homeless youth, it addresses an apparent issue among these young people, namely, that against all odds, some socially and economically disadvantaged youth are anxious and able to find and pursue legal employment during the transition to adulthood.

According to Newman, paid legal work is an important part of life in even the most impoverished African-American communities. This attention to the working poor is intentionally contrasted in Newman's work with the focus on the jobless underclass that is central to the writing of Wacquant and his mentor, William Julius Wilson (e.g., Wacquant and Wilson 1989). Newman points out that Wacquant is so focused on what we have identified as the first theme above—the risks that link poverty to crime and arrest—that he does not consider a second theme that characterizes life in the inner city—the resilience of the working poor. As Newman (2002, 1578–1579) explains:

[W]ork on the inner city has fixated on deviant behavior. However, a central contention of my book is that life in the African-American inner city is not predominately focused on Wacquant's under-class end of the street. Sociologists have so emphasized the presence of gangs, drugs, and hustlers that they have forgotten that paid work has been and remains a central and defining activity for many African-American residents of the ghetto. Even in the most impoverished neighborhoods in the Urban Family Life Survey at the University of Chicago to which Wacquant contributed, more than one-third of the respondents in the poorest neighborhoods were working and over half were either in the labor force or in school.

The same point can and should be made about homeless but working street youth, because some homeless youth successfully find legal work and avoid all contact with the justice system. Variation in their success across individuals and social settings needs to be noted and explained.

Wacquant's (2002, 1512) response is that Newman is narrowly focused on the choices and possibilities that Western, postindustrial labor markets present poor and minority youth. The concern is both methodological and theoretical, with Wacquant noting (2002, 1504) that by focusing on employed youth, Newman in effect samples on the dependent variable and thereby occludes the source of variation in employment outcomes that is necessary to test the mechanisms and conditions that lead away from the street and joblessness.

Newman actually does give attention to youth who do not get jobs and she is aware of the constraints as well as the choices confronted by poor youth. What most clearly distinguishes Newman from Wacquant is the focus on resilience in the lives of the young working poor and the possibility that these young people at least sometimes can find routes that lead away from the alternative risks of urban street life. Newman (2002, 1579) insists that these youth are a crucial part of the story of the streets:

> Their inclusion is critical because the workplace is one of the sites where the intersection between middle- and working-class people and the ghetto poor—alleged to have disappeared—actually takes place. Working, even at minimum wage jobs, encourages mainstream models of behavior, in part because the workplace creates a social space and friendships that buttress and intensify conventional aspirations and mores. In addition, the long hours and exhausting schedules of low-wage jobs draw low-wage workers away from "street" friends, partying, and hanging out. Being ridiculed by street acquaintances for working at a "chump change" job reinforces that distance.

It is the latter focus on staying away from, resisting, and leaving the street behind that is especially crucial for our purposes. The title of Newman's book, *No Shame in My Game,* with its resilient rejection of the ridicule, stigma, and shame of the McJobs she studies, speaks powerfully, albeit not yet completely, to the analytic questions of who and why youth take and reject these jobs.

THE INFLUENCE OF DISSONANT CONTEXTS

Several processes may help explain why some experiences can change the direction of youthful lives, including those of homeless youth, in positive as well as negative ways. Rosenberg's (1975) theory of dissonant contexts offers one possibility beyond the basic and often meager economic returns provided by entry-level employment. According to Rosenberg, social locations act as powerful frames of reference for people. These contacts include one's place in the larger social structure and cultural milieu, as well as the more specific contexts, such as the networks and neighborhoods, that people inhabit. Rosenberg noted further that people often find themselves in conflicting contexts, situations that are not inherently dissonant but that become incompatible because of a person's experiences.

For example, Rosenberg suggests that the self-esteem of black youth who enter integrated schools declines only if such youth represent a small fraction of the overall school population. In these cases, the lack of black peers means that the integrative experience is dissonant with the youth's previous schooling. Conversely, youth who enter settings where black and white youth are more equally represented encounter less conflicting social milieus; thus, they experience considerably less dissonance. The goal is to build on rather than diminish existing strengths and to encourage further movement into constructive contexts. Homeless youth may be most likely to traverse the perilous passage to adulthood in community settings that promise to include rather than threaten to exclude them.

In general, Rosenberg's theory suggests that people who experience contextual dissonance resolve it in three ways: (1) by changing their views of themselves; (2) by modifying their perceptions of their environment; and (3) by exiting the dissonant context and increasing their involvement in less dissonant or nondissonant situations. Those whose reactions include the third path resolve their dissonance by withdrawing from the situation that has the fewest social, psychological, or economic rewards, security, and status.

The demands of a job are often inconsistent or discordant with a homeless lifestyle. Although some homeless youth create work on the street, through panhandling or by squeegeeing or providing other services, this work is inconsistent and relatively unstructured and often invites police attention (Dachner and Tarasuk 2002; Gaetz and O'Grady 2002). In contrast, extended involvement in conventional work requires a commitment to scheduling, a continual delay of gratification, and a responsiveness to the authority and demands of others; these are sharp contrasts to the relatively unconstrained use of time, alcohol, and drugs that characterize street life. Thus, as street youth's awareness of and exposure to employment opportunities increase, through contacts with employed friends, for example, they may experience dissonance from their simultaneous locations in the two opposing worlds of work and the street and gain a sense of inclusion and acceptance in the world of work (Rosenbaum et al. 1990).

Furthermore, friends who are employed in legal work can provide important information about job openings or connections for future employment opportunities (Granovetter 1974), thereby increasing one's prospects of inclusion in the work world (Hagan 1993). As well, these personal ties can establish obligations and connections to conventional employment frameworks and the settings in which they are located. Thus, there are opportunities and incentives, even on the street and available to homeless youth, that represent dissonant contexts favoring employment and toward which these youth may be drawn and move.

THE SHAME IN THEIR GAME

Employment can clearly improve the economic conditions of homeless youth and other disadvantaged youth, but Wacquant (2002) reminds us that we cannot ignore the emotional context of many low-level jobs. Indeed, he refuses to relieve Newman and like-minded writers from the implications of the fundamental insight that the pursuit of low-end legal work involves overcoming and counteracting humiliation and resulting feelings of shame. In the face of what he calls Newman's "relentless cheerfulness," Wacquant (2002, 1506) insists that "fast-food work is widely reviled not only because it is precarious, dull, soiling, and pays a pittance, but also because those who hold such jobs must display subservience to management and servility toward customers even when the latter are rude, scornful, and aggressive."

This sobering reality takes us back to the question of why some impoverished youth accept such jobs, and its predictable but crucial answer about which Newman and Wacquant agree: "that ghetto youths pursue paid employment in clothing outlets, pharmacies, and bodegas, cosmetics and sporting goods stores, as well as security firms and fast-food establishments, first and foremost, to gain protection from *the pressures of the street and to escape trouble at home and in the neighborhood*" (Wacquant 2002, 1505; emphasis added).

Most homeless youth stand precisely at the crossroads of home, street, and neighborhood pressures, where they confront the unappealing prospect of low-end legal work. The emotional divide that must be crossed in accepting what is often demeaning work prominently includes feelings of humiliation and shame that may often already have been oppressively prevalent at home as well as on the street and its neighborhoods. The result is that although for most homeless street youth, low-end jobs are the most promising of the unwelcoming legal routes to temporarily if not more permanently leaving the street, their access to this work is practically and emotionally limited because in addition to the obstacles already noted, standing at the gates to this unappealing escape route is one more fundamental barrier that Wacquant (2002, 1471) demands we acknowledge and engage: "the ongoing construction of the *neoliberal* state and its 'carceral-assistential complex' for the management of the poor, on and off the street." Wacquant uses the term carceral-assistential complex to refer to monitoring and controlling persons in and outside of institutions, through, for example, probation and parole.

The iron fist of the state-based carceral complex is first and frequently wielded by the police, who may, essentially at will, arrest homeless street youth in their sometimes willful and often aimless wanderings through the public spaces of our urban lives. The police may in this sense be the explanatory factor that Wacquant argues Newman neglects in explaining who "chooses" to do low-paid, low-end legal work as a means of leaving and/or staying off the street. Of course, the police do not act alone or in a vacuum.

Homeless youth encounter two front-line, institutional sources of social control in their early lives—their parents and the police—both of whom can be exclusionary not only in an instrumental sense, but also in the subjective and symbolic sense of creating intense feelings of shame. But this is not the full story. Braithwaite (1989) more optimistically noted that family and criminal sanctions can potentially be sources of reintegration as well as rejection. We can refer to these alternative possibilities as involving inclusive and exclusive shaming. Braithwaite observed that inclusive shaming occurs when reacceptance follows expressions of disapproval of deviance, for example, in benign family settings and in certain legal systems such as that of Japan. Alternatively, exclusive shaming is typical of abusive families and criminal sanctioning in North America, where the person is punished and stigmatized as much or more than the behavior. In these environments, there is usually little or no provision for reintegration or inclusion, and the shame of being sanctioned is unabated.

The key to Braithwaite's distinction is that reintegrative shaming includes rituals of reincorporation and inclusion, whereas stigmatic shaming is an unremitting source of exclusion. Thus inclusion and the transition to legal work may require successfully eluding the damaging effects of family and state shaming processes, so that the added humiliating conditions of the available jobs can be further tolerated. Most homeless youth do not escape their homes and the street emotionally unscathed, and so they may be poorly prepared in emotional terms to withstand the further humiliation of menial low-end legal work. This is the importance of the social inclusion perspective, which, as noted at the outset of this volume, pushes us beyond the question addressed initially in this chapter, "who is vulnerable and what do they need to make a successful transition to adulthood?," to later ask in the second part of this chapter, "what policies would level the playing field and enable groups who are otherwise left out to participate fully as adult citizens?"

Scheff and Retzinger (Scheff 1988; Scheff and Retzinger 1991) added further micro-level detail to our initial understanding of feelings of shame and sanctioning by analyzing their impact on interpersonal bonds. The core of Scheff and Retzinger's theoretical contribution builds on Lewis's (1971) premise that disapproval that leads to unconfronted or unacknowledged shame (i.e., shame unresolved through reintegration) results in anger. Lewis called this a "feeling trap." Scheff (1988, 397) noted that such shame-induced feeling traps have inter- as well as intrapersonal implications:

> When there is a real and/or imagined rejection on one or both sides . . . the deference-emotion system may show a malign form, a *chain reaction* of shame and anger between and within interactants. This explosion is usually brief, perhaps a few seconds. But it can also take the form of bitter hatred and can last a lifetime. . . . I refer to such explosions as *triple spirals* of shame and anger (one spiral within each party and one between them).

Scheff suggested that this kind of shaming can be especially persistent, observing that "the unlimited fury of shame/rage in a triple spiral may explain why social influence can be experienced as absolutely compelling."

Scheff and Retzinger (1991, 30) noted the direct connection between their formulation and the work by Lewis and Braithwaite. They observed that although Braithwaite considers punishment at the state-based macro-level, they reached the same conclusion: "We will call it the Lewis-Braithwaite hypothesis: that normal shame and shaming produce social solidarity, whereas pathological shame and shaming produce alienation." Our further point is that there is likely a sequential and consequential connection between the experience of unresolved and personally experienced shame and rejection within the family and unmitigated state stigmatization. That is, this combination of family and state shaming contains the seeds of powerful alienating feelings that, for example, make benign inclusion in menial and demeaning employment environments unlikely.

In particular, the physical and sexual abuse that street youth have often experienced in the families they have fled may make them especially sensitive to further humiliation. Thus youth who have experienced repeated abuse at home may be tracked on the street to continually escalating shame-rage spirals that are exacerbated by subsequent societal reactions, by legal authorities as well as prospective employers. Braithwaite anticipated (1989, 80) this kind of possibility when he noted that "just as the evidence shows that aggression and delinquency are the reaction to excessive use of punishment and power assertion as the control strategy within the family, we might expect rebellion against a demeaning punitiveness on the street to be all the more acute when families have eschewed authoritativeness in favor of authoritarianism."

Scheff and Retzinger (1991, 164) brought this point directly into the employment context by noting that employers, as well as parents and teachers, increasingly recognize large numbers of highly "touchy," angry young people ready to punish any available target for the sins of their past insulters, starting with the shame they felt as children from rejection by caretakers. An implication is that police-imposed sanctions may often be the sequelae that set off spirals or sprees (see also Katz 1988) of criminal activity by youth previously subjected to brutal and/or arbitrary family punishment, making these youth especially unlikely prospects for successful employment in low-end menial and demeaning jobs.

Sherman (1993) also emphasized the explosive and persistent nature of youthful reactions to criminal sanctions and drew on the work of Lewis, Braithwaite, and Scheff and Retzinger in developing what he called a defiance theory of the criminal sanction. Sherman began by observing that similar criminal sanctions often have opposite or varying effects in different social settings, on different kinds of offenders and offenses, and at different levels of analysis. He suggested that this heterogeneity of outcomes can be explained by closer attention to connections between kinds of offenders and sanctions.

In a key part of his formulation, Sherman (1993, 458–459) drew on Braithwaite and on Scheff and Retzinger to identify interactions that involve the defiant recidivist reactions of sanctioned criminal offenders. He reasons that the question of when criminal sanctions lead to defiant responses is addressed by Scheff and Retzinger's sociology of emotions, and that "a great deal of evidence suggests the best name for this proud and angry emotion—and the retaliation it causes vicarious victims—is defiance." The implication is that when the kind of unresolved personal shame emphasized by Scheff and Retzinger interacts with the unremitting criminal stigma emphasized by Braithwaite, a defiant criminal response is likely to follow. That is, family-based experiences of shame and rejection can interact with state-imposed criminal stigma to provoke what earlier labeling theory referred to as secondary deviance. This kind of background experience may therefore be especially likely to lead street youth into secondary behaviors that direct them away from adults and peers who can link them to opportunities to leave the street and find employment.

LINKS IN THE LIFE COURSE

The kind of chain reaction postulated by Scheff and Retzinger (1991) parallels Rutter's (1989) further discussion of chains of adversity in the life cycle (see also Caspi and Elder 1988) that can stretch from childhood through adulthood, including long-term employment outcomes. Rutter (1989, 27) wrote that "the impact of some factor in childhood may lie less in the immediate behavioral change it brings about than in the fact that it sets in motion a chain reaction in which one 'bad' thing leads to another." Rutter further observed that "antisocial behavior . . . will influence later environments through the societal responses it induces—such as custodial or correctional actions that may serve both to 'label' and to strengthen antisocial peer group influences" (42). As noted, these antisocial peer group influences likely include diversion away from links to employment possibilities.

Thoits (1983) also pointed to the multiplicative chain effects of stressful life events. She observed that "a person who has experienced one event may react with even more distress to a second . . . ; to the person, life might seem to be spiraling out of control. This would produce . . . [an] interaction between event occurrences; two or more events would result in more distress than would be expected from the simple sum of their singular effects" (Thoits 1983, 69). Thoits offers a vulnerability model of interaction in which early stressful events set the foundation for adverse reactions to subsequent events. In this model, "predispositions are remote, enduring physiological and psychological characteristics that . . . enhance . . . the impacts of current life experiences" (80). Again, childhood and adolescent experiences can accumulate to create long-term scenarios in which trajectories that include diversion from employment become likely.

The work we have reviewed supports our thesis that childhood experiences of parental abuse and violence, and the resulting shame spirals produced by these incidents, may be predisposing life experiences that interact with later criminal justice sanctions to intensify involvements in crime and diversion from legal work. This is a model of secondary deviance—that is, the deviant behavior that follows official sanctions—in which childhood victimization constitutes a family context and a set of informal sanctioning experiences that interact with later formal sanctions imposed by the criminal justice system. Drawing on the theoretical leads of Lewis, Black, Braithwaite, Sherman, Sampson and Laub, and Scheff and Retzinger, we propose that these violent childhood events can initiate sanction sequences that, combined with police encounters, can increase the likelihood of defiantly persistent criminal behavior and legal unemployment. This notion of interaction and cumulation is consistent with the kinds of feeling traps, chain reactions, and resulting crime sprees and spirals depicted in a diverse set of recent formulations.

SOCIAL POLICIES AND THE STREETS OF TWO CITIES

An array of social services have been introduced to help runaway and homeless youth in North America. Private donations and provisions under the Runaway and Homeless Youth Act (1977), the Stewart B. McKinney Homeless Assistance Act (1987), and other government and private organizations have helped create a network of emergency shelters that extends over most regions and have funded educational programs for homeless youth. In addition, a great number of federally, state, municipally, and privately supported programs offer counseling, medical and legal aid, and job training. Yet services for the homeless are uneven and serve a relatively small number of youth at any one time. Many programs have yearly budgets in the mere tens of thousands of dollars and rely on funds for which there is no long-term commitment. The general educational standards, pay, and benefits for program workers are low for professional work and there is considerable staff turnover; public support is inconsistent; and many youth avoid or refuse to make use of available social services (Shane 1996; Wincup and Bayliss 2001).

Critics have noted important flaws in the social services available to the homeless, from shortcomings associated with educational programs (Epstein 2000; Mickelson 2000), the inadequacies of shelters, their philosophy and restrictions (Carlen 1994; Ruddick 1996; Shane 1996; Smart 1991), and the problems that arise from treatment models that move difficult youth from one social service agency to the next (van der Ploeg and Scholte 1997), to the negative consequences that occur when government bureaucracies redefine who is and is not officially homeless (Carlen 1994). Several writers note, for example, that the conditions for homeless youth worsened dramatically in the United Kingdom in 1988 when those under age seventeen lost their entitlement to income support and those aged eighteen through twenty-four received less than those twenty-five and older (Coles and Craig 1999; Fitzpatrick 2000). Almost no studies, however, systematically evaluate the effectiveness of programs for homeless youth, especially from a comparative or longitudinal perspective. One exception, a study in Glasgow, followed twenty-five youth for a one-year period (Fitzpatrick 2000). Findings showed that youth who avoided the "homeless subcultures" of city centers and stayed in youth-specific shelters where they were able to take advantage of social services had better employment outcomes; they were better able to avoid the "downward spiral" experienced by youth who stayed in adult-dominated hostels and who spent much of their time hanging out on street corners with other homeless youth.

Our research did not have an explicit policy evaluation component; however, the two cities in which we conducted our research, Toronto and Vancouver, adopted considerably different approaches in their response to problems such as homelessness and crime. These macro-level differences influence the ways in which individual variations in risk factors and potential for resilience among the homeless are expressed. At the time of our study, Toronto's orientation to street youth had many features of a social welfare model. Provincial family and welfare legislation defined the age of majority as sixteen. As a result, youth of that age who lived apart from their families could receive emergency and longer-term welfare support from the province. Perhaps more significantly, this legislation allowed a framework in which the province, municipalities, and philanthropic organizations could provide shelter for youth without requiring parental consent. In the 1990s, there were four hostels in Toronto exclusively for youth aged sixteen through twenty-one. Although hostels have their problems and some youth prefer the streets, the shelter and other services provided were clearly valued by most street youth. One youth in our Toronto sample observed that "there's enough hostels here, there's always somewhere to go. I mean, it's not going to be pleasant, but they're there."

The situation was much different in Vancouver. Provincial family and welfare legislation mandated that under most statutes, a youth in British Columbia was legally a "child" or "infant" until the age of nineteen. This definition made parents legally and financially responsible for their children until the latter turned nineteen. Until then, unmarried youth living apart from their families in Vancouver could receive public welfare support only in unusual circumstances. Moreover, care providers could offer shelter to those younger than nineteen only if they first had parental permission, a condition hard to fulfill when providing services to homeless youth. At the time of our research, there was no developed system of hostels, shelters, or safe houses for the short-term housing of street youth in Vancouver. Few places provided support for them on the street (Baxter 1991). The potential significance of the disparity between the social services of the two cities is captured in the comments of several youth in our Vancouver sample, one of whom had previously been in Toronto.

After being homeless in Toronto, a youth we called Julia hitchhiked to Vancouver, eventually moving into an abandoned building, or "squat," in the Granville Street area. She said that she was shocked at the differences between Toronto and Vancouver, adding that

> it was tough because of the lack of services in Vancouver, like not having safe houses and shelters. I think that does make a difference. And the availability of welfare, and food and job-training programs, and all those things can make a difference. I mean, it's true that people won't use them unless they really want to, but what if they do and they're not there? They should be available. . . . That's what I first noticed when I came out here . . . , there was nothing to help me.

Another youth, Jordy, who also lived on the streets in both cities, remarked that "I liked Vancouver way better than Toronto. But Vancouver doesn't have as many things for youth—services and programs like to get back into school, work, housing. I liked Vancouver better, but there's more opportunities here in Toronto."

A related observation by Alan made the connection between the availability of programs and services and vulnerability to the attention of the police: "Vancouver's . . . worse off than any other city because they have no, like, drop-in center really for kids to go hang out at. . . . So, there's no safe haven away from the police." Alan's point is telling because it reflects the nature of the Vancouver law enforcement/crime control model for dealing with street youth. Vancouver street youth who were picked up by the police could not be taken to a youth hostel. Instead, many faced one of several less desirable consequences: they were returned to their families, who were liable to criminal prosecution if they refused to accept and promise to support their children; they were placed in government care and sent to a foster or group home; or they were arrested and jailed. These options do not offer promising solutions to problems that cause youth to leave home in the first place.

Our analyses confirmed that city settings and policy models make a difference. This was reflected most clearly in our data by a strong effect of being in Vancouver as contrasted with Toronto, on involvement in crimes of theft, drugs, and prostitution. Our results also highlighted another key difference between these cities, one that further diminished involvement in street crimes. Toronto's social welfare model of providing access to overnight shelters and social services reduced exposure to criminal opportunities, whereas Vancouver's crime control model and absence of assistance made it more common. This heightened exposure to the street and its criminal opportunities intensified a movement toward criminal embeddedness among criminally engaged associates and away from legally employed peers. Vancouver youth were also more likely to be charged by the police for their involvement in street crime, which is, of course, also consistent with a crime control model and inconsistent with finding and keeping jobs. More generally, the direct and indirect effects of taking to the streets in these different cities illustrate the significant roles that macro-level policy variation plays in determining paths that lead further into and away from the criminal subculture of the street.

THE PERILOUS PASSAGE

Ethnographies of inner-city communities and studies of the homeless reveal that, notwithstanding high unemployment rates, a solid minority of these youth are working and that a majority continue to look for jobs. We add that the monetary benefits of a job notwithstanding, a more important consequence is the exposure to the network of contacts and primary friends that increases the odds of finding and keeping a job. As the proportion of one's friends who work increases, the opportunities and incentives to become and stay employed increases, as do the prospects of leaving the culture of the street behind. However, service and related jobs are often the only employment opportunities available to homeless and inner-city youth. Crossing over into this world of legal work involves overcoming the barrier of humiliation and potential feelings of shame that holding low-end McJobs involves. As one of our respondents who was holding on to his service job put it, "I wasn't treated like a human being, I wasn't paid like a human being, but I stuck with it, just to get a little bit further ahead. . . . It's just one notch out."

However, a sizable number have ceased their search for work and are moving away from networks and opportunities of legal employment. Wacquant (2002) proposed that the carceral-assistential complex, whose gatekeepers are the police, add injury to insult with regard to the motivation to search for work. We agree. Drawing on the writings of the new sanction theorists, we argue that youth who have experienced humiliation and shame in their family histories, and who experience further feelings of humiliation and shame at the hands of authorities such as the police, may be especially ill-disposed to endure the further humiliation and shame of low-end work and may pursue street crime. These are the competing possibilities of risk and resilience to which homeless youth are exposed. Yet, as noted at the outset of this chapter, the language of risk and resilience is individual in the focus of its attention, while the perils and possibilities of the passage of homeless youth to adulthood as well has a state-based policy dimension of exclusion and inclusion.

The initial thesis of this chapter was that contact with the justice system is a crucial risk factor that decreases the likelihood of emotionally vulnerable homeless youth leaving the street for the more conventional world of legal work. Yet a significant number of resilient homeless youth do traverse the perilous passage of their teen years on the street, at least to the extent that they find and hold legal employment. Our subsequent thesis was that this indication of success is not simply a matter of individual-level resilience, but that the probabilities of avoiding street crime and entering the conventional work of legal employment are increased by community-level social programs that provide opportunities and limit the exposure of homeless youth to police contacts. Why and how is this so?

Based on our research in Toronto and Vancouver, we conclude that communities that rely on law enforcement instead of social welfare programs lead homeless youth away from employed peers and into a subculture of street crime where conventional employment is uncommon and disdained. Our research suggests that homeless youth are especially prone to an exclusive shaming process that begins often with their parents, including fathers who have been caught up in the criminal justice system and mothers who may physically and abusively punish their children. Our work suggests that both kinds of family backgrounds interact with the experience of homeless youth being charged by the police and becoming further involved in criminal behavior, which in turn leads to further police charges. This scenario is most common in communities, like Vancouver, that rely on law enforcement policies.

Yet a minority of homeless youth are able to escape police contact, and the size of this minority is enhanced in communities, like Toronto, that make social welfare programs available to homeless youth. Our point is that these homeless youth are most likely to move along an avenue of escape that can lead to legal employment and away from the street. A key aspect of this escape route from the street involves contacts with employed peers and the context and contacts they provide. In this respect, it may be important to add to this picture a further point about the employed peers themselves: these latter youth may intentionally avoid homeless youth who have been charged by the police because they are so intent on resisting the same criminal fate. Newman (1999) makes this point in detailed descriptions of the strategies followed by three young people in her sample.

Newman describes Jamal as a popular young man in his neighborhood who avoids involvements with a group he systematically evades, saying "his 'associates' from the neighborhood like him and invite him along on their escapades, but Jamal resists because he knows that is a road to trouble with the law." Stephanie is described as a young woman who is striving through her work to stay away from the "heat" of the drug trade, reasoning "that an honest job for low pay is preferable to getting mixed up with people in the illegal sector." Juan is described as a youth who is determined to remain apart from his peers who have wound up "on the wrong side of the law": "what Juan does is try to maintain a cordial relationship with these guys, but put as much distance between himself and them as he can without giving offense."

Newman's point is not that the youth in her legally employed sample dislike their peers who have run afoul of the law. Indeed, the two groups have much in common and may often have experimented with many of the same illegal behaviors. Yet becoming known to the police as a part of this criminal underworld places their persistent efforts at staying legally employed at risk. This kind of reaction from employed peers may become another powerful part of the exclusionary shaming process that keeps homeless youth out of the legal labor market. If this is so, then everyday risks and background imperatives that commonly lead homeless youth into conflict with the law may make it that much more remarkable that such a large minority do find legal employment and display a resilience that can elude or overcome feelings of shame and lead away from the street and into a more promising adulthood. Oppressive police charging practices, like those in Vancouver, are the opening gates to the carceral-assistential complex described by Wacquant. This law enforcement complex is an obstacle to be avoided in the perilous passage from the street to a chance at successful passage to adulthood.

REFERENCES

Avramov, D. 1998. *Youth homelessness in the European Union.* Brussels: Feantsa.

Baron, S. W., and T. F. Hartnagel. 1997. Attributions, affect, and crime: Street youths' reactions to unemployment. *Criminology* 35: 409–434.

Baxter, S. 1991. *Under the viaduct: Homeless in beautiful B.C.* Vancouver: New Star Books.

Besharov, D., and K. Gardiner. 1997. Trends in teen sexual behavior. *Children and Youth Services Review* 19: 341–367.

Braithwaite, J. 1989. *Crime, shame, and reintegration.* Cambridge: Cambridge University Press.

Campos, R., M. Raffaelli, and W. Ude. 1994. Social networks and daily activities of street youth in Belo Horizonte, Brazil. *Child Development* 65: 319–330.

Carlen, P. 1994. The governance of homelessness: Legality, lore, and lexicon in the agency-maintenance of youth homelessness. *Critical Social Policy* 41: 18–35.

Caspi, A., and G. Elder. 1988. Emergent family patterns: The intergenerational construction of problem behaviors and relationships. Pp. 218–240 in *Relationships within families: Mutual influences.* Edited by R. Hinde and J. Stevenson-Hinde. Oxford: Clarendon Press.

Centers for Disease Control. 1996. Youth risk behavior surveillance—United States, 1995. *Morbidity and Mortality Weekly Report* 45: 1–86.

Coles, B., and G. Craig. 1999. Excluded youth and the growth of begging. Pp. 63–82 in *Begging questions: Street-level economic activity and social policy failure.* Edited by H. Dean. Bristol: Policy Press.

Dachner, N., and V. Tarasuk. 2002. Homeless "squeegee kids": Food insecurity and daily survival. *Social Science and Medicine* 54: 1039–1049.

De Rosa, C. J., S. B. Montgomery, J. Hyde, E. Iverson, and M. D. Kipke. 2001. HIV risk behavior and HIV testing: A comparison of rates and associated factors among homeless and runaway adolescents in two cities. *AIDS Education and Prevention* 13: 131–148.

Downing-Orr, K. 1996. *Alienation and social support: A social psychological study of homeless young people in London and in Sydney.* Brookfield, VT: Aldershot.

Epstein, I. 2000. Dependency served: Rhetorical assumptions governing the education of homeless children and youth in the United States. Pp. 99–107 in *Children on the streets of the Americas: Homelessness, education, and globalization in the United States, Brazil, and Cuba.* Edited by R. A. Mickelson. New York: Routledge.

Fitzpatrick, S. 2000. *Young homeless people.* New York: St. Martin's Press.

Gaetz, S., and B. O'Grady. 2002. Making money: Exploring the economy of young homeless workers. *Work, Employment, and Society* 16: 433–456.

Ganesan, A. 1996. *Police abuse and killings of street children in India.* New York: Human Rights Watch.

Granovetter, M. 1974. *Getting a job: A study of contacts and careers.* Cambridge: Harvard University Press.

Hagan, J. 1993. The social embeddedness of crime and unemployment. *Criminology* 31: 465–491.

Hagan, J., and B. McCarthy. 1997. *Mean streets: Youth crime and homelessness.* New York: Cambridge University Press.

Katz, J. 1988. *Seductions of crime: Moral and sensual attractions in doing evil.* New York: Basic Books.

Kipke, M. D., T. R. Simon, S. B. Montgomery, J. B. Unger, and E. Iverson. 1997. Homeless youth and their exposure to violence while living on the streets. *Journal of Adolescent Health* 20: 360–367.

Lewis, H. 1971. *Shame and guilt in neurosis.* New York: International Universities Press.

McCarthy, B., and J. Hagan. 1992. The theoretical significance of situational delinquency among homeless youth. *American Journal of Sociology* 98: 597–627.

McCarthy, B., and J. Hagan. 1997. Surviving on the street: The experiences of homeless youth. *Journal of Adolescent Research* 7: 412–30.

McMillen, M. M., P. Kaufman, and S. D. Whitener. 1994. *Drop-out rates in the United States: 1993.* U.S. Department of Education, National Center for Education Statistics.

Mickelson, R. A., ed. 2000. *Children on the streets of the Americas: Homelessness, education, and globalization in the United States, Brazil, and Cuba.* New York: Routledge.

Mortimer, J. 2003. *Working and growing up in America.* Cambridge: Harvard University Press.

Mufune, P. 2000. Street youth in Southern Africa. *International Social Science Journal* 164: 233–243.

National Research Council. 1993. *Losing generations: Adolescents in high risk settings.* Washington: National Academy Press.

Newman, K. 1999. *No shame in my game: The working poor in the inner city.* New York: Russell Sage Foundation; New York: Knopf.

Newman, K. 2002. No shame: The view from the left bank. *American Journal of Sociology* 107: 1577–1599.

Pennbridge, J., T. Freese, and R. Mackenzie. 1992. High risk behaviors among male street youth in Hollywood, CA. *AIDS Education and Prevention* Supplement 24–33.

Rosenbaum, J., T. Kariya, R. Settersten, and T. Maier. 1990. Market and network theories of the transition from high school to work: Their application to industrialized societies. *Annual Review of Sociology* 16: 263–99.

Rosenberg, M. 1975. The dissonant context and the adolescent self concept. Pp. 97–116 in *Adolescence in the life cycle: Psychological change and social context.* Edited by S. Dragastin and G. Elder. New York: Halstead Press.

Ruddick, S. M. 1996. *Young and homeless in Hollywood: Mapping social identities.* New York: Routledge.

Russell, L. A. 1998. *Child maltreatment and psychological distress among urban homeless youth.* New York: Garland.

Rutter, M. 1989. Pathways from childhood to adult life. *Journal of Child Psychology and Psychiatry and Allied Disciplines* 30: 23–51.

Scheff, T. 1988. Shame and conformity: The deference-emotion system. *American Sociological Review* 53: 395–406.

Scheff, T., and S. Retzinger. 1991. *Emotions and violence: Shame and rage in destructive conflicts.* Lexington, MA: Lexington.

Shane, P. G. 1996. *What about America's homeless children? Hide and seek.* Thousand Oaks, CA: Sage.

Sherman, L. 1993. Defiance, deterrence, and irrelevance: A theory of the criminal sanction. *Journal of Research on Crime and Delinquency* 30: 445–473.

Smart, D. H. 1991. Homeless youth in Seattle: Planning and policy-making at the local government level. *Journal of Adolescent Health* 12: 519–527.

Stephenson, S. 2001. Street children in Moscow: Using and creating social capital. *The Sociological Review* 49: 530–547.

Thoits, P. 1983. Dimensions of life events that influence psychological distress: An evaluation and synthesis of the literature. Pp. 33–103 in *Psychosocial stress: Trends in theory and research.* Edited by H. Kaplan. New York: Academic Press.

UNICEF. 1998. *Progress of nations report.* New York.

U.S. Bureau of the Census. 1993. *School enrollment—social and economic characteristics of students: October 1992.* Washington: U.S. Government Printing Office.

van der Ploeg, J., and E. Scholte. 1997. *Homeless youth.* London: Sage.

Wacquant, L. 2002. Scrutinizing the street: Poverty, morality, and the pitfalls of urban ethnography. *American Journal of Sociology* 107: 1468–1532.

Wacquant, L., and W. J. Wilson. 1989. Poverty, joblessness, and the social transformation of the inner city. Pp. 70–102 in *Welfare policy for the 1990s.* Edited by P. H. Cottingham and D. T. Ellwood. Cambridge: Harvard University Press.

Whitbeck, L. B., and D. R. Hoyt. 1999. *Nowhere to grow: Homeless and runaway adolescents and their families.* New York: Aldine de Gruyter.

Wincup, E., and R. Bayliss. 2001. Problematic substance use and the young homeless: Implications for health and well-being. *Youth and Policy* 71: 44–58.

Wright, J. 1991. Health and the homeless teenager: Evidence from the national health care for the homeless program. *Journal of Health and Social Policy* 2: 15–35.

Wright, J., M. Wittig, and D. Kaminsky. 1993. Street children in North and Latin America: Preliminary data from Projecto Alternativos in Tegucigalpa and some comparisons with the U.S. case. *Studies in Comparative International Development* 28: 81–92.

CHAPTER EIGHT

Transition for Young Adults Who Received Special Education Services as Adolescents: A Time of Challenge and Change

PHYLLIS LEVINE AND MARY WAGNER

We gratefully acknowledge our colleagues Lynn Newman, Renee Cameto, Camille Marder, and Jose Blackorby, and the staff of SRI International Center for Education and Human Services. This project has been funded at least in part with Federal funds from the U.S. Department of Education under contract number ED-01-CO-0003. The content of this publication does not necessarily reflect the views or policies of the U.S. Department of Education nor does mention of trade names, commercial products, or organizations imply endorsement by the U.S. government.

Life is not so much a matter of holding good cards,
but sometimes of playing a poor hand well.

Robert Louis Stevenson

INTRODUCTION

Adolescents undergo enormous developmental changes in the physical, psychological, social, and emotional domains. Along with the physical and maturational changes that accompany puberty comes a heightened awareness of self, as viewed personally in relation to others and within the larger society. This developmental period is characterized by a focus on individuality as well as a strong tendency toward ethnic identity, group membership, fitting in, and belonging. At the same time, adolescents have an increased drive for independence and separation from family. Body image is especially important during these years, an importance heightened by peer pressure, strong media presence, and an intensified desire for acceptance and intimacy. Successfully negotiating the changing adolescent landscape and transitioning to adulthood is shaped by myriad factors, including family constellation and expectations, community demographics and practices, the ebb and flow of relationships, and stressful vocational and personal choices.

For youth with disabilities sufficient to qualify for special education services, adolescence and the transition to young adulthood can bring additional challenges. In many ways the disparities between youth with and without disabilities become greater during these turbulent years. For example, the cognitive limitations of mental retardation can have cumulative impacts on learning, so that by late adolescence there can be a cavernous gap between what youth with mental retardation and other youth know and can do. Options for postsecondary education and training or employment are limited accordingly. Youth whose disabilities have powerful impacts on social adjustment or interaction, such as emotional disturbances or autism, can find themselves left out of the kinds of social relationships that are common for most teens and that are a crucial foundation for healthy friendships and romantic relationships in young adulthood. Learning disabilities often are referred to as a "school disability" because deficits associated with this disability category primarily manifest in educational settings or in circumstances that require academic tasks. Many youth with learning disabilities who are streetwise will avoid the failures associated with academic settings by avoiding postsecondary education, often resulting in less than optimal employment options (e.g., entry-level jobs with few opportunities for economic and career mobility).

This chapter presents an overview of the challenges faced in the transition to adulthood for youth with disabilities who received special education services as adolescents (and more often than not, as young children).[1] The discussion focuses on their struggles, strengths, and experiences in light of the variability among youth identified with different disability categories. The chapter begins with a discussion of the characteristics of youth who receive special education services in secondary school, including their disabilities and demographic factors known to influence later outcomes. It then describes the seeds of the later transition experiences that are sown in high school, highlighting the challenges youth with disabilities face in their high school careers. We then summarize what is known about the success with which youth with disabilities transition

1. According to parents of youth in the National Longitudinal Transition Study-2, 32 percent of youth with disabilities begin receiving special education services at age of school entry, five or six, 28 percent start at age seven or eight, and 41 percent at age nine or older. The average age at which children begin receiving special education services is just over eight. Among the approximately 30 percent of youth whose disabilities were identified before age five, the majority are reported to have participated in early intervention programs or preschool special education (Wagner 2003a).

to early adulthood. Finally, the chapter looks ahead and outlines emerging factors in both high school and in the postschool world that have the potential to influence the transition of youth with disabilities in the future.

The chapter describes the challenges facing youth with disabilities as a group, as well as youth with specific disabilities. It places special focus on students with learning disabilities, emotional disturbances, or mental retardation. Those with learning disabilities are the dominant group among youth receiving special education in high school. Youth with emotional disturbances or mental retardation represent two major forms of disability—those that affect social adjustment and cognitive ability—and are youth who are particularly vulnerable to transition failures that can have serious repercussions for long-term adult adjustment.

CHILD-BASED LONGITUDINAL DATA

Transition planning became a focus of federal policy for students with disabilities in the mid-1980s, when it was conceptualized as a "bridge" from school to young adulthood (Will 1984). A series of studies demonstrating the lack of adequate transition planning in secondary school and generally poor postschool outcomes for young people with disabilities generated heightened attention to the transition experiences of this population (Hasazi, Gordon, and Roe 1985; Edgar and Levine 1987; Mithaug, Horiuchi, and Fanning 1985; Neel et al. 1988; Sitlington and Frank 1989). At the same time, Congress mandated that the U.S. Department of Education Office of Special Education Programs (OSEP) conduct a longitudinal study of secondary school students with disabilities in transition to adulthood to provide the first national picture of their experiences. SRI International conducted the National Longitudinal Transition Study of Special Education Students (NLTS) from 1984 through 1993. This study provided the first in-depth national view of the school programs, transition issues, and postschool outcomes of youth served by special education.

Following the success of NLTS, OSEP designed a comprehensive program of child-based longitudinal studies including children with disabilities from birth and early childhood (National Early Intervention Longitudinal Study, NEILS) through the elementary and middle school years (Special Elementary Education Longitudinal Study, SEELS), to the transition years from high school to early adulthood (National Longitudinal Transition Study-2, NLTS2). These studies, which are being conducted by SRI International, provide a unique database that characterizes the school programs, nonschool influences, and long-term outcomes for nationally representative samples of children and youth with disabilities receiving special education services. Most pertinent to this chapter are data from NLTS2, a ten-year study of a nationally representative sample of more than 11,000 youth who were ages thirteen through sixteen and receiving special education services in grade seven or above when the study began in 2001. It revisits many of the features of the original NLTS, and also delves deeper into school characteristics, specific programming, access to the general education curriculum, direct assessments of youth, and the spectrum of student behavioral and social influences on postschool success.

Youth Served by Special Education

Understanding the characteristics of youth who receive special education services is crucial to understanding how they fare in the transition to young adulthood. Clearly, the disabilities and limitations that make youth eligible for this "school-defined" population also shape youth's transition and postschool experiences. In addition to their disabilities, youth bring to their experiences a complex history and background that is shaped by demographic characteristics (e.g., gender and ethnicity) and by family background (e.g., household income). These factors and their potential implications for youth's transition experiences are described below.

Disability

Although we refer to students receiving special education as "youth with disabilities," the population of those with disabilities is larger than those receiving special education (National Center for Health Statistics 2001).[2] Students with disabilities go through an identification and diagnostic process that determines their eligibility for special education services. Some students have a degree of disability that does not pose a significant challenge to their ability to learn in typical school settings and are not qualified for special education (e.g., mild speech, visual, or hearing impairments). Others are determined to need special education or related services to benefit from their education. The Individuals with Disabilities Education Act (IDEA) expanded the option for students with disabilities to remain in school and receive special education services to age twenty-one. Part B of IDEA also mandates states to offer early childhood special education services to eligible children ages three to five. In the 2003–2004 school year, the eligibility determination process resulted in more than 6.7

2. In this chapter and the following chapter on policy, "children and youth with disabilities" is used interchangeably with "children and youth receiving special education services," with the recognition that the population with disabilities is considerably larger.

Table 8.1. Federal child count of students receiving special education services under IDEA, Part B, in the 2003–2004 school year, by age group

Age group	Number	Percentage
3–5	680,142	10.1
6–11	2,770,084	41.2
12–17	2,970,267	44.2
18–21	305,700	4.6
Total	6,726,193	100.1

Source: Office of Special Education Programs 2003.

Data based on the December 1, 2003, count, updated as of July 31, 2004. The total percentage differs from 100 due to rounding error.

million children and youth ages three to twenty-one receiving special education services under IDEA, Part B (table 8.1), which constituted 12 percent of the school population in the fifty states and Puerto Rico (Office of Special Education Programs 2003). (See chapter 9 for a fuller discussion of special education legislative and policy decisions.)

In any discussion of challenges faced by youth receiving special education services, it is critical to point out the tremendous variability in this sizable population of children and youth. In many ways, these students differ as much (or more) from each other as they do from their peers in general education. The special education eligibility process in most jurisdictions results in assignment of a primary disability classification. These classifications capture in broad strokes differences in physical, sensory, cognitive, social/emotional, and communication functioning. Functional abilities influence youth's ability to learn, interact with others, participate successfully in the education process, and experience a stable and satisfactory adult life.

Table 8.2 depicts the primary disability classifications assigned by schools to students ages twelve through seventeen, and students ages eighteen through twenty-one who received special education services in the 2003–2004 school year (Office of Special Education Programs 2003).

Overall, 59 percent of students ages twelve through seventeen who receive special education services are classified as having a learning disability, 11 percent are classified with mental retardation, and 11 percent are classified with emotional disturbances as their primary disability. These also are the three largest categories among youth ages eighteen through twenty-one who are receiving special education services. Thus, when data are presented for youth with dis-

Table 8.2. Disability category distribution of youth receiving special education services, IDEA, Part B, in the 2003–2004 school year, by age group

Primary Disability Classification	Ages 12–17		Ages 18–21	
	Number	Percentage	Number	Percentage
Specific learning disability	1,749,494	58.9	146,319	47.9
Speech/language impairment	149,611	5.0	5,219	1.7
Mental retardation	317,302	10.7	70,635	23.1
Emotional disturbances	312,503	10.5	28,482	9.3
Multiple disabilities	61,674	2.1	17,451	5.7
Hearing impairment	34,912	1.2	4,634	1.5
Orthopedic impairment	30,211	1.0	4,952	1.6
Other health impairment	242,247	8.2	15,690	5.1
Visual impairment	12,205	0.4	1,906	0.6
Autism	46,999	1.6	8,028	2.6
Deaf-blindness	767	0.0	214	0.1
Traumatic brain injury	12,342	0.4	2,170	0.7
Total	2,970,267	100.0	305,700	99.9

Source: Office of Special Education Programs 2003.

Data based on the December 1, 2003, count, updated as of July 31, 2004. The total percentage for the 18–21 age group differs from 100 due to rounding error.

abilities as a whole in either age group, they represent largely the experiences of those with learning disabilities, mental retardation, or emotional disturbances.

However, it is important to note the differences in the relative size of these disability categories in the two age groups. Youth with learning disabilities constitute fewer than half of the older age group; youth with mental retardation increase to almost one fourth of eighteen- to twenty-one-year-olds receiving special education. Youth with emotional disturbances decrease only slightly to 9 percent of those in the older group. The relative sizes of some other categories also change. Youth with multiple disabilities are only 2 percent of twelve- through seventeen-year-olds, but are almost three times that proportion of those ages eighteen through twenty-one. In contrast, youth with other health impairments (which includes a large number of youth whose primary disability is attention deficit hyperactivity disorder, or ADHD) decreases from 8 percent of the younger age group to 5 percent of the older group. These changes demonstrate that youth with disabilities who remain in secondary school after age seventeen are more seriously impaired, as a group, than their younger peers.

As youth progress through school and into adulthood, the nature of the disability for which they receive special education services and the degree of their functional limitations can be a powerful influence on their transition and postschool experiences. We now highlight this variability by focusing the discussion on youth in three disability categories: learning disabilities, emotional disturbances, and mental retardation.

Learning disabilities. As mentioned above, youth with learning disabilities are the largest category of adolescents and young adults with disabilities. Learning disabilities are lifelong conditions that are neurologically based and manifest in a wide variety of academic and social behaviors. Usually children and youth identified with learning disabilities score as average or above on intelligence assessments, and their academic problems (primary among this group) are rooted in brain function rather than emotional, social, or cultural conditions (Silver 1998). Many teens with learning disabilities are described as having "eight-hour disabilities"—limitations that assert themselves primarily during the school day—and they are more likely than youth in most other disability categories to have educational experiences that mirror those of nondisabled youth (Silver 1998).

Almost one fourth of youth with learning disabilities had their disabilities first identified before they entered school; more than half were diagnosed with learning disabilities in their early elementary years (Wagner 2003b). In addition to their diversity of learning problems, some youth with this classification also exhibit a variety of other disabling conditions. Parents of high-school-age students classified with learning disabilities report that almost one third have ADHD, and 5 percent have emotional disturbances. More than one in five are reported to have some degree of difficulty communicating, and half have at least some trouble with functional cognitive skills, such as reading common signs, counting change, telling time, or looking up telephone numbers (Gresham 2002; Wagner, Blackorby, and Levine 2003).

Emotional disturbances and behavior disorders. This category of youth includes both those who have "internalizing" disabilities, such as depression or eating disorders, as well as those whose "externalizing" disabilities result in behavior and conduct disorders. (See chapters 10 and 11, which concern challenges and policy issues facing youth with serious mental disorders.) Emotional/behavioral challenges can affect children and youth across all the disability categories, as well as those without disabilities. But for young people in this category, their emotional/behavioral issues are chronic and incessant, impeding their ability to learn, to develop and maintain socially acceptable relationships, and to function successfully as adults (Furlong, Morrison, and Dear 1994; Edgar 1990).

Although youth with emotional disturbances are similar to youth with learning disabilities in the age at which their disabilities first were identified, they are less likely than youth in any other disability category to receive services for their disability before adolescence (Wagner 2003b). Because a learning disability is more often an academic impairment, children with learning disabilities tend to receive special education services earlier in their school careers than children with emotional disturbances whose distinctive behaviors and attributes tend to escalate during adolescence. Like youth with learning disabilities, those with emotional disturbances have a range of secondary disabilities, according to parents. More than 60 percent are reported to have ADHD, and 28 percent are reported to have learning disabilities (Wagner 2003b). The wide range of disabilities encompassed in this category is reflected in quite varied functional abilities in different domains[3] (Gresham and Elliot 1990). For example, although this category of disability often is associated with poor social adjustment, only 24 percent are reported by parents to have low social skills, whereas 15 percent have high social skills. This category is not generally associated with cognitive limitations, yet almost 40 percent of youth with emotional disturbances have at least some difficulty with functional cognitive skills, such as telling time and counting change (Gresham 2002).

Mental retardation. As noted above, children and youth with mental retardation comprise about 11 percent of secondary-school-age students receiving special education. The treatment, education, and integration of individuals with mental retardation has been debated and documented for over a century (e.g., Bicknell 1896; Johnson 1897; Barr 1899; Johnson 1900; Boehne 1912; Henninger 1912; Fernald 1919; Bronner 1933; Baller 1936; Talbot 1964; White and Wolfensberger 1969). Historically, the area of mental retardation has had the greatest influence on the evolution of special education policy and practice. "[A]s a policy focus . . . it is difficult to think of a major special education issue or procedure that has *not* emanated from the area of mental retardation" (Forness and Kavale 1984, 239).

Mental retardation is fundamentally a cognitive disorder, although some causes of mental retardation, such as Down syndrome, also manifest themselves in other forms of disability. In fact, parents of teens with mental retardation report that more than one fourth have been identified as having ADHD, approximately 10 percent have an orthopedic impairment, and the same percentage have a speech impairment. Mental retardation usually is apparent among young children—more than half of teens with mental retardation were diag-

---

3. The social skills—specifically assertion, self-control, and cooperation—of students with disabilities in SEELS and NLTS2 were assessed by asking parents eighteen questions drawn from the Social Skills Rating System, Parent Form (Gresham and Elliot 1990).

nosed by the age of four—although milder forms of mental retardation may not be apparent until children confront the higher-order thinking expectations in middle elementary school.

Cognitive limitations are quite pronounced for most students with mental retardation. Direct assessments of the reading abilities of a national sample of elementary and middle school students with disabilities reveal that 91 percent of students with mental retardation have letter-word recognition skills that are equivalent to those of the lowest 20 percent of students in the general population (Blackorby 2003). Among high-school-age students with mental retardation, 80 percent have at least some trouble with functional cognitive skills, such as reading signs or looking up telephone numbers.

Gender

Gender is a defining human characteristic and, during adolescence when young people are exploring their sexuality and gender roles, it can shape their experiences and choices in potent ways. Gender differences continue to influence the experiences of young people as they age in such domains as employment and family formation. Given the importance of gender in shaping experience in the transition and early adult years, the disproportionate representation of males among youth with disabilities must be kept clearly in mind.

Although the gender split for the general population is about fifty-fifty, almost two-thirds of youth with disabilities ages thirteen through seventeen are boys (Levine, Wagner, and Marder 2003). The reasons for male overrepresentation in special education have been addressed in the literature for decades. Investigators have claimed that parents and school staff are less tolerant of the learning disabilities, reading problems, or naughty behavior of boys than of girls and thus more readily refer boys for special education services (Miles 1986; Schlosser and Algozzine 1980; Gillespie and Fink 1974; Edgar 1990). More recent research has suggested that the higher share of boys among students receiving special education is due to inaccurate and biased identification and assessment practices, particularly among the largest category of youth with disabilities—those with learning disabilities (Shaywitz and Shaywitz 2001).

Despite these purported links between male overrepresentation and school practices, the National Early Intervention Longitudinal Study (NEILS) of a nationally representative sample of children ages birth to thirty months with developmental disabilities or delays found a similar proportion of boys (61 percent) among infants and toddlers as among school-age children (Hebbeler et al. 2001). This finding implies that the overabundance of boys among children with disabilities appears at very early ages, before school practice or assessment bias could occur. Research suggests that biological differences may account for gender variations in brain function (Gorman 1992; Perry 1992). Despite a lack of gender differences on tests of general intellectual ability (Hier 1979; Gould 1981), there are differences in brain function between boys and girls that may affect achievement variation, especially in academic subjects and learning styles (Gorman 1992; Perry 1992).

Findings from NLTS2 and the Special Elementary Education Longitudinal Study (SEELS, a study of more than 11,000 elementary and middle school students receiving special education) document gender differences by disability category, with about 75 percent of teens with emotional disturbances or other health impairments (often ADHD) and 85 percent of youth with autism being boys. In contrast, the proportions of boys and girls among youth with sensory impairments are much closer to the distribution in the general population.

Thus, both gender and type of disability may affect youth's transition experiences and postschool outcomes. For example, it has been suggested that sex role stereotyping in the high school curriculum, especially with regard to vocational education and transition planning, is a deterrent to positive outcomes for young women with disabilities (National Information Center for Children and Youth with Handicaps 1990, 1992; Rousso 1988; Williamson-Ige and McKitric 1985). A growing body of research also highlights gender differences in postschool outcomes—specifically engagement in postsecondary education and employment, due to the greater propensity for adolescent girls and young women with disabilities to bear and raise children during the early years of transition. These differences were significant for girls with disabilities, compared with their male peers, and compared with girls of the same age with no disabilities (Levine 1993; Levine and Edgar 1995; Wagner 1992).

Ethnicity and Race

The phenomenon of disproportionate representation of minorities in special education has become a focus of considerable policy attention (National Research Council 2002). Specifically African-American youth compose about 20 percent of high-school-age students with disabilities, compared with 16 percent of youth in the general population (Office of Special Education Programs 2002; U.S. Census Bureau 2002). A recent report on minority participation in special education reveals a wide range of personal, social, and environmental factors that are linked to a higher rate of disability among minority and low-income individuals and households, including poverty, parent's education, and social networks (National Research Council 2002). Although a variety of factors could account for this disproportionate representation, analyses of national data consistently find nonrandom rates of occurrence for illness, injury, and chronic health conditions across racial and ethnic boundaries (Center on Emergent Disability 2001; Bradsher 1995; Fujiura 1998; Fujiura, Yamaki, and Czechowicz 1998). In contrast to the overrepresentation of African-Americans among youth with disabilities, Hispanic students are somewhat underrepresented among youth with disabilities relative to the general population (13 vs. 16 percent). These differences in the distributions occur across the age range of children and youth with disabilities, from infancy through secondary school (Hebbeler et al. 2001).

However, the disproportionality of minorities among youth with disabilities appears in only a few categories. African-Americans are significantly overrepresented only among youth with mental retardation (35 percent are African-American) and with speech impairments (22 percent; Levine, Wagner, and Marder 2003). Similarly, Hispanic youth are underrepresented primarily among youth with mental retardation, other health impairments, and autism (6 to 9 percent are Hispanic in these three groups).

Poverty

A disproportionate share of children who grow up poor are identified as needing special education services (Wagner and Hebbeler 2000; Donovan and Cross 2002). In fact, 24 percent of school-age children with disabilities live in poverty, compared with 16 percent of students in the general population (Wagner, Marder, and Cardoso 2003; Levine et al. 2003). Being from a low-income household is linked to greater likelihood of poor health, poor academic performance, and poor outcomes in adolescence and young adulthood (Duncan and Brooks-Gunn 1997; Lewit, Terman, and Behrman 1997). Because they are more likely to be poor, children and youth with disabilities are more likely than their nondisabled peers to carry with them experiences of the family instability, high mobility, substance abuse, domestic violence, abuse and neglect, and criminal behavior that can be associated with poverty. These factors challenge youth with disabilities in establishing a solid social footing and succeeding as they move through school and into independent adult life (Coleman and Vaughn 2000; Osofsky 1995; Rylance 1997, 1998; Belsky and Vondra 1989; Tymchuk 1999). Added to the multidimensional challenges associated with disability, the detrimental effects of poverty can be devastating, reducing significantly the chances of success in adult life for youth with disabilities.

EARLY CHALLENGES TO TRANSITION SUCCESS: STUDENTS' HIGH SCHOOL EXPERIENCES

The seeds of a successful transition are planted well before college entrance examinations become realities and high school graduation looms. Experiences throughout high school help define the trajectory of students as they launch their postschool careers. This section summarizes aspects of the high school experiences of students with disabilities that are particularly powerful determinants of their early postschool experiences, focusing on the importance of high school completion and the factors that contribute to it as they are experienced by youth with learning disabilities, emotional disturbances, or mental retardation.

THE CRUCIAL ROLE OF HIGH SCHOOL COMPLETION IN POSTSCHOOL ADJUSTMENT

Dropout rates are markedly higher for youth with disabilities than youth in the general population. In the early 1990s more than one-third of students with disabilities who had been out of high school up to two years had left school by dropping out, compared with about one-fourth of students in the general population (Wagner 1991; Blackorby, Edgar, and Kortering 1991). Though it appears graduation rates have risen steadily for all youth in recent years, including youth with disabilities, as many as 29 percent of students receiving special education services leave school without the benefit of a diploma (U.S. Department of Education 2001b).

Compared to their peers with other disabilities, relatively high dropout rates occur among youth with learning disabilities (27 percent) and mental retardation (25 percent; U.S. Department of Education 2001b). However, the highest rate by far is among youth with emotional disturbances, more than half of whom (51 percent) drop out of high school (U.S. Department of Education 2001b). Once these students leave, they lack the social skills needed to develop positive relationships or connections or to secure and maintain employment (Bullis et al. 1993; Carson, Sitlington, and Frank 1995; Bullis and Gaylord-Ross 1991). These students tend to find low-paying, short-term jobs without benefits and earn less than students from most other categories (Frank and Sitlington 1997; Edgar 1990; Neel et al. 1988).

Large percentages of youth with disabilities experience the "bad news" associated with dropping out of school for all students, compounded by the limitations of disabilities (Kortering and Braziel 1999; Vitaro, Brendgen, and Tremblay 1999). For example, dropouts with disabilities are significantly less likely than graduates with disabilities to secure jobs with potential for promotion or career-oriented upward mobility, and few, if any, continue their education beyond obtaining a GED. More often, dropouts with disabilities have higher rates of involvement with juvenile corrections than do graduates with disabilities, or dropouts without disabilities (Razeghi 1998). These students who leave school are unable to benefit from provisions inherent in IDEA that could support their transition (e.g., remedial intervention, transition planning, therapeutic services; Walker, Colvin, and Ramsey 1995).

Academic Course Taking and Performance

Strong academic performance can give students feelings of success and self-efficacy as learners and often rewards them with positive feedback from adults at home and at school. On the other hand, academic deficits are among the most cogent predictors of dropping out (Coley 1995; Education Commission of the States 2003). At the high school level, failing courses means that students fail to earn credits toward high school graduation requirements, a failure that often leads to students being retained at grade level and, eventually, dropping out of school (Robertson 1997; Walters and Borgers 1995; Thompson and Cunningham 2000). According to NLTS, high school students served by special education have higher rates of course failure than do students in the general education population. Almost two-thirds of students with disabilities failed at least one course in high school (Wagner et al. 1993). Students with disabilities also are less likely than students without disabilities to complete courses in high school that prepare them to succeed in college. When they do attempt college preparatory curricula, the majority do poorly (Newman 1993b).

Grade retention also is common among students with disabilities. Studies of the general population report that 15 percent to 35 percent of students repeat at least one grade before entering high school (NELS 1997; NHES 1993, 1995; Thompson and Cunningham 2000). However, rates of grade retention are much higher for students with disabilities, although they have declined in recent years. In 1987, 67 percent of students with disabilities were older than the typical age for their grade level, a rate that had dropped to 47 percent by 2001 (Wagner, Cameto, and Newman 2003). Most studies reveal that students who repeat a grade typically do worse academically, and those who repeat two grades are almost certain to drop out of school (Robertson 1997; Shepard and Smith 1990). Retention, combined with being overage for grade, can contribute to low self-esteem, depressed student achievement, low motivation, and increased disengagement from school (Thompson and Cunningham 2000; Roderick 1995; Walters and Borgers 1995; Meisels and Liaw 1993).

Poor academic performance is particularly prevalent for youth in some disability categories. Although students with disabilities typically lag behind their peers in the language arts, especially in reading (Elbaum and Vaughn 1999; Gersten and Dimino 1989; Kavale 1994; Blackorby 2003), difficulties with specific language arts skills are particularly inherent in many forms of learning disabilities. NLTS reported that high school students with learning disabilities were three grade levels behind in reading ability, and 65 percent had failed at least one course in high school (Wagner, Hebbeler, and Blackorby 1993). Further, NLTS2 finds that 35 percent of students with learning disabilities have been retained at grade level at least once, according to parents (Wagner 2003d).

Not surprisingly, the cognitive limitations of mental retardation also show up in poor academic performance. Students with mental retardation are more likely than those in any other disability category to have been retained at grade level at least once (45 percent; Wagner et al. 2003). According to NLTS findings, high school students with mental retardation were more than five grade levels behind in both their reading and math skills (Wagner, Hebbeler, and Blackorby 1993).

Academic performance also is an issue for youth with emotional disturbances despite the fact that these youth have disabilities that are primarily social or emotional by nature. More than half have passage comprehension scores similar to the lowest 20 percent of the general population (Blackorby 2003), and students with emotional disturbances represented in NLTS were about two grade levels behind in both their reading and math skills. Although their academic skill ratings were higher than those for students with either learning disabilities or mental retardation, they were more likely than either group to have failed at least one course in high school—more than three-fourths had done so (Wagner, Blackorby, and Hebbeler 1993). Their higher failure rate may reflect the fact that student behavior, in addition to academic performance, can come into play in teachers' grading decisions. NLTS2 findings indicate that 38 percent of students with emotional disturbances had been retained at grade level at least once.

Engagement in School

Dropping out of school can be the culmination of a long process of students disengaging from school activities, which often shows up as high absenteeism. For students with disabilities, high absenteeism has been identified as the strongest predictor of academic failure and the decision to drop out of high school (Blackorby and Wagner 1996; Donahoe and Zigmond 1990; Thurlow, Sinclair, and Johnson 2002). On average, students with disabilities miss 2.6

days of school in one month; this comes to 23.4 days—over a full month—in a school year. About 14 percent of students with disabilities miss more than one week of classes in a one-month period (Newman and Davies 2003). School engagement differs markedly across disability categories, but students with emotional disturbances are less engaged than their peers with other kinds of disabilities. These students are the most likely to be absent from school, an average of 3.1 days per month, and 16 percent miss six or more days of school in a month (Newman and Davies 2003).

Disengagement from school can be demonstrated by the flaunting of school rules in ways that bring disciplinary action, including suspension and expulsion. Students with disabilities are overrepresented among students whose behaviors cause problems for themselves and often for others at school. NLTS2 findings show that one-third (33 percent) of youth with disabilities have been suspended or expelled at least once, according to parents, including 19 percent who had been suspended in their most recent school year and 4 percent who had been expelled that year. In contrast, 22 percent of same-age students in the general population are reported by parents to have been suspended or expelled (Wagner 2003a).[4]

Disengagement demonstrated by a propensity to rule violations continues to be experienced more commonly among students with some disabilities. More than one-fourth (27 percent) of high-school-age students with learning disabilities are reported by parents as having been suspended or expelled, as are one-third (33 percent) of those with mental retardation (Wagner 2003a). Not surprisingly, students with emotional disturbances are at highest risk for absenteeism and for being removed from instructional settings through suspensions and expulsions. Almost three-fourths (73 percent) are reported by parents to have been suspended or expelled at least once, including 44 percent who had been suspended and 18 percent who had been expelled in the most recent school year (Wagner 2003a). These data do not bode well for youth with emotional disturbances in transition to young adulthood.

Family Support for Education

Parent support for learning is an important contributor to students' success in school (Epstein 1987; Thorkildsen and Stein 1998) including better grades (Clark 1983), more consistent attendance (National Middle School Association 2000), homework completion, and more positive behavior (Epstein 1996).

4. Calculated for fourteen- to eighteen-year-olds from the National Household Education Survey of 1999.

Likewise, one of the greatest assets many youth with disabilities have in dealing with the challenges of fitting in, performing well in high school, and achieving a successful transition to adulthood is an active and supportive family. Families of youth with disabilities differ widely in the level of support they provide for their children at school and at home, and there is some evidence that their support exceeds that of families of youth in the general population. For example, 20 percent of parents of youth with disabilities provide help with homework compared to only 2 percent of parents of secondary school students in the general population (National Center for Education Statistics 1998; Wagner 2003c).

The greater challenges faced by students with disabilities often mean that families too are challenged to be even more involved and supportive of their adolescent children's education. By volunteering and participating in classroom and schoolwide activities, families send a powerful message to their children about the value of education. At the same time, family involvement fosters a shared commitment to learning by encouraging mutual support between families and teachers and strengthens links and communication between school and home. This also avails families the opportunity to create networks with other parents, offer mutual support, provide resources and experience, and develop social connections for their children and themselves.

Vocational Preparation

Students with disabilities who struggle academically may opt for employment after high school rather than pursuing further academic education. Many students with disabilities have access to a variety of programs and services that can help them prepare for employment, both while they are in high school and in the community after high school. Vocational education plays an important role in this preparation. During high school, NLTS2 found that 61 percent of students with disabilities take a vocational education course in a semester, but there is great variation in vocational course enrollment across disability categories. More than three-quarters of students with mental retardation (78 percent) are enrolled in vocational education compared to about 60 percent of students with emotional disturbances or learning disabilities (Cameto and Wagner 2003). About half of students with emotional disturbances or learning disabilities take occupationally specific vocational education, but only 30 percent take prevocational courses. This contrasts sharply with the pattern for students with mental retardation, who are about equally likely to take the two kinds of vocational courses (62 percent take courses for specific vocations, and 59 percent take prevocational classes) (Wagner 2003d).

NLTS2 findings also show that all students with disabilities are taking challenging academic courses, which constitute about 60 percent of their course work on average; the proportions are dramatically greater than was the case for students in the original NLTS (Wagner 2003d). In fact, since the mid-1980s, vocational education enrollment among students with disabilities has declined by 15 percentage points (Wagner, Cameto, and Newman 2003). While the increased emphasis on academic courses has been shown to increase the odds of attending college in the early years following high school (Wagner et al. 1993), this may not be beneficial for all students with disabilities, especially those with mental retardation.

NLTS reports optimistic findings on the contributions of vocational education in high school to positive outcomes in secondary school and early adulthood. Students with disabilities who took a concentration of courses in a special occupational area had a higher likelihood of competitive employment after high school and, for youth with learning disabilities, emotional disturbances, or mild mental retardation, it also contributed to higher earnings (Wagner et al. 1993). Achieving competitive employment is a stated transition goal of the majority of high school students with disabilities (Wagner 2003d). The conflicts between academic standards-based curricula and vocational education pose tremendous challenges for youth with disabilities preparing for the transition to adulthood, and their families and educators, as they strive to balance the current national push toward academic standards for all students with the practical need for many students to prepare for competitive employment after high school.

Self-determination and Transition Planning

Although students with disabilities face many challenges related to their academic performance, and school engagement and completion, their disabilities entitle them to the benefits of a transition planning process that is required by law to be in place in every high school.[5] Provisions for transition planning are explicit, but it is unclear how they translate into practice for schools and individuals. There are no uniform curricula or programs or specified standards to guide or evaluate the transition planning process. According to NLTS2 findings, transition planning has begun for three-fourths of high-school-age students with disabilities. However, the process receives mixed reviews from par-

---

5. See chapter 9 for details regarding federal legislation that mandate school, family, and student involvement in the transition process. The chapter reviews the evolution of transition planning while students are still in school and the policies relevant to providing streamlined support services for them once they leave secondary school programs.

ents who participate; about 36 percent report it to be very useful, whereas 46 percent report that it is somewhat useful, and 18 percent find it not useful (Newman and Wagner 2003).

There has been a notable change in recent years in the way young people with disabilities are viewed and treated by the adults in their lives. Increasingly and justifiably, youth with disabilities are viewed as capable of conceiving and shaping their own futures. Students receiving special education in secondary school are being encouraged to develop decision-making and self-determination skills to enhance their ability to express their views and advocate for their preferences and needs, and to make personal judgments that reflect competence, motivation, and personal ambition (Zhang 2001). Instead of having life choices made for them, the preferences and dreams of youth with disabilities are increasingly being expressed and taken into account in such areas as transition planning and service need determination. Knowing youth's expectations for their futures is an important context for setting trajectories into those futures (Johnson and Sharpe 2000).

A potential indicator of emerging independence for youth with disabilities is their level of participation in planning their own transition to adulthood through this formalized process. Recent research on self-directed transition planning characterizes self-determination as the "cornerstone for successful transitions." Students who are expected to take responsibility for planning their transition and engage in self-determination activities early in secondary school also take greater responsibility for their lives after school (Malian and Nevin 2002; Price, Wolensky, and Mulligan 2002). NLTS2 findings show that 70 percent of students with disabilities provide at least some direct input toward planning their transition goals, including 12 percent who take on a leadership role on their own behalf. The remaining 30 percent either do not attend or are present but do not contribute much to the process (Cameto, Levine, and Wagner 2004). As the self-determination movement grows, we can expect to see youth with disabilities become increasingly active in setting their own courses into young adulthood.

POSTSCHOOL OUTCOMES

This section describes the fruits born from the seeds of transition sown in secondary school—the postschool outcomes of youth with disabilities in the domains of postsecondary education, employment, independence, family formation, social adjustment, peer relationships, and criminal justice system involvement.

Postsecondary Education

Education has long been viewed as the means to advancement and opportunity in American society. Its importance has grown as our society has increasingly incorporated technology into the workplace, resulting in a large portion of available jobs requiring technologically advanced skills and knowledge. But few youth with disabilities who receive special education services as adolescents attend postsecondary education institutions (Levine and Edgar 1995; Blackorby and Wagner 1996; Fairweather and Shaver 1991; Vogel and Adelman 1992; Frank, Sitlington and Carson 1995; Levine and Nourse 1998). Research demonstrates that young adults with disabilities tend to enter the job market at an earlier age than their peers in the general population but without the benefit of postsecondary credentials. The college experience, with its multiple implications (e.g., future employment, independence from family, expanded social networks and relationships) differentiates long-term outcomes for youth with and without disabilities (Office of Special Education Programs 2002). By not pursuing postsecondary education and attaining postsecondary credentials, many youth with disabilities hinder their career and employment options. They also miss out on the social opportunities and activities associated with college life.

Studies differ in reporting the proportion of youth with disabilities who go to some form of postsecondary school. NLTS reported that 27 percent of youth with disabilities who had been out of high school three to five years had had some form of postsecondary education, compared with 68 percent of youth in the general population (Marder 1993). Youth with learning disabilities, emotional disturbances, or mental retardation had postsecondary school attendance rates of 30 percent, 26 percent, and 13 percent, respectively (Wagner and Blackorby 1996). Students with disabilities who do enroll in postsecondary education institutions do not often choose a four-year college or university. NLTS reports that only 4 percent of students who had received special education services in high school had ever been enrolled in a four-year college or university three to five years after high school. Rates of college attendance of students with learning disabilities or emotional disturbances mirror those of students with disabilities as a whole; no students with mental retardation had attended a four-year college (Marder 1993).

Not only do students with disabilities attend postsecondary institutions at lower rates than students in the general population, but their experiences there are different as well. Data from the Beginning Postsecondary Students Longitudinal Study (BPS) and from the National Postsecondary Student Aid Study (NPSAS) suggest that postsecondary education students who identify themselves as having disabilities are more likely than other students to delay a year before enrolling in postsecondary education, and generally are older (average age thirty) than students who do not report having a disability (average age twenty-six) (Horn and Berktold 1999). Many youth with disabilities who attend some form of postsecondary education either do not persist to credential attainment or take longer to do so than other students. Five years after entering college, only half of the students with disabilities had attained a degree or vocational certificate or were still enrolled compared with 64 percent of students without disabilities (Horn and Berktold 1999). Thus, low enrollment rates, coupled with low completion rates, mean that few youth with disabilities take with them into adulthood the economic and other advantages that a postsecondary education can provide.

Employment

Employment is the pathway to financial independence for the vast majority of adults, and persons with disabilities of all ages are at a disadvantage in the labor market. NLTS reported that three to five years after high school, 57 percent of youth with disabilities were competitively employed, a gain over the 46 percent competitive employment rate of those youth three years earlier (D'Amico and Blackorby 1993). However, at both points in time, their employment rates were markedly below those of youth in the general population (59 percent up to two years after high school, 69 percent three years later). But again, differences in the nature of youth's disabilities translated into different outcomes. Youth with learning disabilities were employed at virtually the same rate as youth in the general population (72 percent three to five years after high school), whereas the rates for youth with emotional disturbances or mental retardation were markedly lower (47 and 37 percent, respectively). NLTS findings for youth with mental retardation are consistent with those from the Decade Study, a ten-year follow-up study conducted in Washington State (Levine and Edgar 1995). It showed that employment rates for graduates with mild mental retardation ranged from 25 percent to 60 percent from one to seven years postschool, rates that were significantly lower than youth with learning disabilities, whose employment rates ranged from 60 percent to 91 percent, and from youth with no disabilities (52 percent to 87 percent) over the seven-year period.[6]

More recent findings from NLTS2 suggest that progress has been made in

6. That youth with no disabilities have lower employment rates than youth with learning disabilities is explained in part by the larger proportion of youth with no disabilities who attend postsecondary education during this period compared to their peers with learning disabilities.

closing the employment gap between youth with disabilities and the general population. According to parents, somewhat more than half of thirteen-through seventeen-year-olds with disabilities (54 percent) hold regular paid jobs during a one-year period, similar to the 50 percent of thirteen- to seventeen-year-olds in the general population who do so (Marder, Cardoso, and Wagner 2003). This progress could result from the strong economy in 2001. In the last years of the twentieth century and the first years of the twenty-first, this country was more prosperous than ever before. Rapid economic growth lowered unemployment to record levels, making employers aggressive in seeking workers for jobs at all levels. This period of prosperity, however, has taken an abrupt turn, and young people are already feeling the brunt of a depressed labor market. A recent study conducted by Northeastern University's Center for Labor Market Studies finds nearly 5.5 million sixteen- to twenty-four-year-olds who were out of school and jobless during 2002, a significant increase from the 4.9 million young adults who were reported out of school and jobless in 2000 (Sum et al. 2002). "Joblessness problems are especially acute among high school dropouts, youth from low income families, central city minorities with no postsecondary schooling, and residents of high poverty neighborhoods" (Sum et al. 2003, 2). Clearly, as we have demonstrated thus far, the majority of young adults with disabilities experience at least one of these high-risk factors and would be included among those out-of-school young adults who are "at substantial risk of being permanently left behind" (Sum et al. 2003, 2).

Independence

Most adolescents and young adults prepare for and enter this transitional period with the goal of becoming independently functioning adults. Over the past several decades, more people have come to realize that youth with disabilities can determine their own futures. Many factors come into play that affect the emerging independence for these youth, including skills that strengthen self-reliance (e.g., persistence, self-advocacy, self-care, functional cognition), responsibilities that accompany an independent lifestyle (e.g., employment, financial management, contributing to the care of the household), and activities or privileges associated with emerging independence (e.g., residence outside the family home, having a driver's license, autonomy regarding social choices).

Numerous factors challenge adolescents with disabilities in the transition to independent participation in the community, including the economic climate, employment options, access to the community (e.g., driver's license, automobile, public transportation), family support, personal resources, and functional ability (Borgen and Amundson 1995; Storey, Bates, and Hunter 2002). As youth mature, they often are expected to take on more responsibilities within the household (e.g., fixing meals, doing their laundry), as well as outside the home (e.g., shopping). Financial responsibility also is a key indicator of independence; young people traditionally encounter money management in the form of allowance and perhaps a savings account. But as they get older they are expected to acquire a checking account and credit card, indicative of another level of monetary responsibility, debt and debt payment, requiring a greater degree of independence.

NLTS2 findings show that most youth with disabilities have high self-care skills, and more than half have high functional cognitive skills, persistence (staying on task until finished), self-advocacy (asking for what one needs), and ability to perform household chores. About one-third of age-eligible youth have acquired a driver's license or permit, and more than half have been employed during a one-year period. Youth with learning disabilities are making progress toward achieving independence in greater degrees than youth with mental retardation on all factors. The same is true for youth with emotional disturbances, except that youth with mental retardation score higher than their peers with emotional disturbances in regard to persistence and self-advocacy (Cameto, Levine, and Wagner 2003).

For most youth, personal, educational, and career decisions are driven by the anticipation of leaving the family home and creating an independent, self-reliant lifestyle that includes choices regarding where and with whom to live (Borgen and Amundson 1995). Findings from NLTS reveal that in the first two years after leaving high school, 11 percent of youth with disabilities were living independently. Although this rate had increased to 37 percent three years later, it remained substantially behind the rate at which youth in the general population lived independently (60 percent; Newman 1993a). The Washington State Decade Study showed that seven years after high school graduation, the rates of residential independence were similar for the graduates with learning disabilities and no disabilities (60 and 78 percent for males and females with learning disabilities, and 68 and 73 percent for males and females with no disabilities). But this was not the case for youth with mild mental retardation, who were residing independently at the low rates of 30 percent for males and 44 percent for females (Levine and Edgar 1995).

Family Formation

Although studies of the postschool outcomes of youth with disabilities tend to focus on employment and postsecondary education, family formation—marriage and parenting—are personal and socially acceptable goals for many young adults with and without disabilities. Although getting married and having children generally are positive aspects of adult independence, marriage and parenting during adolescence and early adulthood can be problematic. Research demonstrates the detriments of teenage parenting and suggests that women who have children as teens are less well-educated as adults, have lower incomes and are more likely to live in poverty, are less likely to get married, and have children who lag in their early development (Alan Guttmacher Institute 1994; Hoffman 1998).

Studies conducted over the past fifteen years reveal that young women with disabilities raise children at a younger age and in greater proportions than their male peers or other young women without disabilities, and often without the advantages of a supportive partner (Levine and Edgar 1995; Levine and Nourse 1998). NLTS reported that young women with disabilities were less likely than their nondisabled peers to be married three to five years after high school (30% vs. 38%), but were more likely to be mothers (40 vs. 28 percent; Wagner 1992). Whereas the rate of parenting for young women with mental retardation (31 percent) was close to that of the nondisabled population, it was particularly high for young women with learning disabilities (50 percent) or emotional disturbances (48 percent). For teenagers and young adults with disabilities, parenting at a young age and often alone is a severe impediment to long-term independence.

Criminal Justice System Involvement

The overrepresentation of youth with disabilities in juvenile corrections facilities is a poignant illustration of the many overlaps and troubling disparities among the vulnerable populations described in this volume. As discussed further in chapters 3 and 5, the strong links between such involvement and marginal literacy skills, low academic performance, and poorly developed social skills are especially pertinent for young adults with learning disabilities, emotional disturbances, or mental retardation (Leone, Meisel, and Drakeford 2002; Burrell and Warboys 2000; Leone, Rutherford, and Nelson 1991). In addition, excessive proportions of incarcerated youth and adults exhibit low levels of basic functional skills needed to hold a job, manage a residence, or sustain meaningful relationships (Burrell and Warboys 2000).

As shown in NLTS2, many youth with disabilities begin their involvement with the criminal justice system early. According to parents, 12 percent of youth with disabilities had been arrested by their middle or high school years. Arrest rates are higher for older youth (16 percent for sixteen-year-olds and 17 percent for seventeen-year-olds), and boys are arrested more often than girls (15 vs. 7

percent). More than one-third of youth with emotional disturbances (34 percent) were arrested at least once during their adolescence, a significantly higher rate than their peers with learning disabilities (11 percent) or mental retardation (8 percent). An even higher percentage of youth with emotional disturbances (56 percent) had engaged in actions that led to their being stopped by police, and 25 percent are on probation or parole, indicating conviction for a crime (Cameto et al. 2003).

Students who exhibit problem behaviors at school also are likely to do so in their nonschool hours, and often in their postschool years. NLTS showed that the arrest rate of youth with disabilities who were no more than two years out of high school was significantly higher than youth in the general population (12 vs. 8 percent; Marder and D'Amico 1992), and climbed sharply in the ensuing three years, to 30 percent (Wagner 1992). The rate was similar for youth with learning disabilities (31 percent), and substantially lower for youth with mental retardation (18 percent). However, more than half of youth with emotional disturbances (57 percent) had been arrested three to five years after high school, but almost three-quarters (73 percent) of youth with emotional disturbances who had dropped out of school had been arrested within five years of leaving high school (Wagner 1992).

Once youth who exhibit problematic behavior in school, at home, or in the community interact with the juvenile corrections system and are incarcerated, the prognosis for rehabilitation is extraordinarily poor. (See chapters 3 and 4 for fuller discussions of youth in the juvenile justice system.) In other words, the challenges facing youth who receive special education and are incarcerated are exponentially greater than the challenges faced by youth with disabilities but no interactions with juvenile justice or who are incarcerated but not identified as having disabilities (Scott, Nelson, and Liaupsin 2001; Jolivette et al. 2000; Leone et al. 1995; Duncan, Forness, and Hartsough 1995; Wagner et al. 1993).

DISABILITY, TRANSITION, AND THE NEW MILLENNIUM

The first few years of the twenty-first century have witnessed the beginning of notable changes in American society that are likely to continue and have significant impacts on the challenges faced by youth receiving special education services as they transition to young adulthood. These involve the demographics of our society, economic fluctuations, the growing influence of technology, an increased attention to issues of risk and violence in our schools and communities, and important trends in the disability community, including the shifting prevalence of disabilities themselves and the inclusion and advocacy movements.

Some of these issues are discussed below, as well as in the following chapter with its focus on policy issues.

Economic Fluctuations

For youth with disabilities, the decreases in employment opportunities, in agency funding streams, and in adult support services, amid an overall national uncertainty, are likely to compound an already stressful transitional period. Because groups that have a more marginal foothold in the labor market in times of prosperity generally are the last to reap the benefits of economic recovery, many youth with disabilities are likely to face a daunting task finding solid footing in the labor market for some years to come.

Technology and Wide-Spread Internet Access

The accelerating dynamic state of technology is changing the nature of the workplace, postsecondary education, community access, recreational opportunities, and independence for people with disabilities. Computer use is common among high-school-age students with disabilities, with 70 percent having a computer at home and more than 90 percent of them knowing how to use it for homework and entertainment, according to their parents. More than two thirds of youth (71 percent) who have a home computer use e-mail or visit World Wide Web chat rooms (Cadwallader and Wagner 2003).

Computers, and the Internet in particular, are changing the way people with disabilities can gain access to their communities and the world—without leaving home. For example, in July 2000, the Social Security Administration launched a new high-tech Web site to promote employment for people with disabilities. A section is specifically devoted to youth, with information tailored to their needs. The Internet will contribute increasingly to easing isolation for some people who face barriers due to limited mobility, challenged communication, language differences, and remote geography (Levine et al. 2001). Although the World Wide Web cannot remedy the lack of wheelchair-accessible buses, it does provide for on-line shopping and similar conveniences. Growth in distance education and other Web-based instruction will expand opportunities for participation in postsecondary education by youth with disabilities. Support networks that were nonexistent or difficult to find or access are now created through chat rooms, discussion lists, Web-based journals, and e-mail. The Internet also serves as an outlet for expression and individuality that has been out of reach for many young people with disabilities. The anonymity that accompanies the "invisibility" associated with socializing through a television monitor gives young people with disabilities greater freedom of expression and control over how they present themselves. In some cases this virtual community expands communication among people who otherwise might never interact socially (e.g., conversations between hearing and deaf people, or with those who have speech impairments) or have the opportunity to develop relationships outside their own environment (e.g., teenagers with special chronic health care needs and confined to home, or with orthopedic impairments that inhibit mobility).

We will continue to see advances in other forms of technology that affect the educational experiences of all students, including those served through special education. Computers as instructional tools are now prevalent in schools, and it is becoming more common for youth with disabilities to use computers in their course work. NLTS2 reveals that essentially all students with disabilities attend schools with computers that connect to the Internet and are available for student use in the library, media center, or computer lab, and almost all students are in schools where there are computers in the classrooms (Wagner and Levine 2003). This is an important component of the larger concept of access to the general education curriculum for students with disabilities. There also appears to be an increase in the extent to which students receiving special education take courses that impart computer skills or prepare them for technology-related employment (Burgstahler 2002).

Further, young people with diverse disabilities will increasingly have better access to a variety of activities through assistive technologies, such as communication boards, lighter-weight and more compact wheelchairs, improved prosthetic and other mobility devices, dictation mechanisms, voice simulators, and improved transportation accessibility, to name a few. Advances in medical technologies, including pharmaceutical interventions, provide new supports for youth with the kinds of disabilities that act as a barrier to inclusion.

However, technology change can be a two-edged sword. The growing emphasis on technology in the workforce can have negative implications for youth with disabilities. Rapid technological advances have created a shift in labor force expectations. Historically, employment options for people with disabilities tended toward service and blue-collar industries. A growing share of jobs and careers now require workers with advanced analytical, abstract, and technical knowledge and skills and the ability to work independently. These types of competencies present immense challenges for many youth receiving special education services. Continuing growth in the demand for highly skilled workers for the technology-driven economy raises questions as to how young people with disabilities fit into future economic times.

Changes in the Prevalence of Disabilities

In addition to changes that will increasingly influence the population at large, some changes in our world have specific implications for the population of youth with disabilities, including the mix of disabilities they represent. The medical profession has discovered remarkable ways to save premature and medically vulnerable children from death, as well as increasing survival rates for children who suffer from the effects of accidents, serious illnesses, abuse or neglect, and alcohol and drug use by mothers during pregnancy. These medical advances have increased the numbers of children who have survived trauma but bear the long-term physical and developmental effects of that experience through their lifetimes. Many of them require special education in order to participate and benefit from public education. For some students, especially those with multiple or severe disabilities or functional limitations, the need for a continuum of supports continues throughout adulthood.

The medical profession also has made advances in the diagnosis of some conditions (e.g., Asperger's syndrome, ADHD) that have increased dramatically the number of children identified in certain categories. Enrollment for children ages three through twenty-one receiving special education has increased by nearly 70 percent since the 1970s, a period in which overall school enrollment has been relatively static. The current federal disability classification system now includes autism and traumatic brain injury (TBI), two categories that did not exist ten years ago.

The increasing diversity of the population of youth with disabilities will challenge the systems that serve them, both during the school years and in early adulthood, to increase the range and flexibility of services and supports available to help them succeed.

SUMMARY

The challenges facing youth who receive special education services as children and adolescents are numerous and diverse. This chapter describes the demographic and environmental characteristics peculiar to this population as a group and highlights the wide variability within the population, particularly among young people with learning disabilities, emotional disturbances, or mental retardation. Data from the child-based longitudinal studies sponsored by the U.S. Department of Education Office of Special Education Programs (OSEP) (especially the two National Longitudinal Transition Studies, NLTS and NLTS2), demonstrate the crucial role of school experiences, especially high school completion, academic performance, and social adjustment, on successful transition to adulthood. These data also show the influences of preparation and planning for transition, work experiences, skills training, and family involvement on transition outcomes.

The discrepancies between those who do and do not attend college or have jobs that provide competitive wages, adequate benefits, and opportunities for advancement have been well-documented for youth who have disabilities, who are from ethnic minorities, who come from poor families, or who grow up in the foster care system. A disproportionate share of youth with disabilities leave school without a diploma, are among incarcerated juveniles, or are in foster care. Youth with disabilities often have multiple risk factors, the detrimental effects of which are compounded. In many ways, the growing wealth of data from special education research may serve as the barometer for the varied and complex needs of all youth as they maneuver through the floundering period of early adulthood.

Despite these challenges, many changes have had an enormously positive and often profound effect on people with disabilities. The 1975 landmark Education of the Handicapped Act (EHA) and amendments in 1990 and 1997 reauthorizing the act as the Individuals with Disabilities Education Act (IDEA), changed the fundamental nature of special education, including the option of staying in school through age twenty-one and an expanded focus on transition and adult outcomes. The Americans with Disabilities Act (ADA) sets the stage for increased public awareness of the needs for people with disabilities and broadens access to the community and its resources. Youth with disabilities and their parents are empowered to be more active in the choices and decisions that govern their future. Young people with disabilities who may have been isolated in institutions just a few decades ago now have greater opportunities for independence, opportunities that are due in part to increased focus on secondary school engagement and completion, academic performance, vocational options, access to the Internet, technically advanced prosthetic, mobility, and communication tools, and a heightened focus on self-determination.

The transition from adolescence to adulthood for youth with disabilities can be daunting. This chapter stresses the importance of demographic shifts and societal changes as they help us understand the complicated lives of youth with disabilities, and the multiple deterrents they must circumnavigate as they enter their adult years. By viewing the needs of youth beyond single contextual risk factors, we gain a better understanding of the multidimensionality of challenges confronting high-risk youth, a first and critical step in determining how best to help them meet those challenges and succeed in school and beyond.

REFERENCES

Alan Guttmacher Institute. 1994. *Sex and America's teenagers.* New York: Alan Guttmacher Institute.

Baller, W. R. 1936. A study of the present social status of a group of adults who when they were in elementary schools were classified as mentally deficient. *Genetic Psychology Monographs* 18: 165–244.

Barr, M. J. 1899. The how, the why, and the wherefore of the training the feeble-minded child. *Journal of Psycho-asthenics* 4: 204–212.

Belsky, J., and J. Vondra. 1989. Lessons from child abuse: The determinants of parenting. Pp. 153–202 in *Child maltreatment: Theory and research on the causes and consequences of child abuse and neglect.* Edited by D. Cicchetti and V. Carlson. Cambridge: Cambridge University Press.

Bicknell, E. P. 1896. Custodial care of the adult feeble-minded. *Journal of Psycho-asthenics* 1: 51–63.

Blackorby, J. 2003. Variations in the academic performance of students with disabilities in different educational settings: A national perspective. Presentation at the annual meeting of the Part B data managers, Washington.

Blackorby, J., E. Edgar, and L. Kortering. 1991. A third of our youth? A look at the problem of high school dropout among students with mild handicaps. *Journal of Special Education* 25: 102–113.

Blackorby, J., and M. Wagner. 1996. Longitudinal postschool outcomes of youth with disabilities: Findings from the National Longitudinal Transition Study. *Exceptional Children* 62: 399–413.

Boehne, G. M. 1912. Regarding special classes for sub-normal children. *Journal of Psycho-asthenics* 17: 20–28.

Borgen, W., and N. Amundson. 1995. *Models of adolescent transition.* Greensboro, NC: ERIC Clearinghouse on Counseling and Student Services; Ottawa: Canadian Guidance and Counseling Foundation.

Bradsher, J. E. 1995. Disability among racial and ethnic groups. *Disability Statistics Abstracts* 10: 1–4.

Bronner, A. F. 1933. Follow-up studies of mental defectives. *Proceedings and Addresses of the American Association for the Study of the Feebleminded* 38: 258–264.

Bullis, M., and R. Gaylord-Ross. 1991. Transitions for youth with behavioral disorders. In *Working with behavioral disorders.* Edited by L. Bullock and R. B. Rutherford Jr. Reston, VA: Council for Exceptional Children.

Bullis, M., V. Nishioka-Evans, V., H. D. Fredricks, and C. Davis. 1993. Identifying and assessing the job-related social skills of adolescents and young adults with emotional and behavioral disorders. *Journal of Emotional and Behavioral Disorders* 1: 236–250.

Burgstahler, S. 2002. *The role of technology in preparing youth with disabilities for postsecondary education and employment.* http://www.rrtc.hawaii.edu/products/phases/phase3.asp (MS#074-H02).

Burrell, S., and L. M. Warboys. 2000. Special education and the juvenile justice system. *Juvenile Justice Bulletin,* July. Washington: Office of Juvenile Justice and Delinquency Prevention.

Cadwallader, T. W., and M. Wagner. 2003. Interactions with friends. In *Life outside the classroom for youth with disabilities: A report from the National Longitudinal Transition Study-2 (NLTS2).* Edited by M. Wagner, T. W. Cadwallader, L. Newman, and C. Marder, with P. Levine, N. Garza, and D. Cardoso. Menlo Park, CA: SRI International.

Cameto, R., P. Levine, and M. Wagner. 2004. *Transition planning for students with disabilities: A* special topic report of findings from the National Longitudinal Transition Study-2 (NLTS2). Menlo Park, CA: SRI International.

Cameto, R., C. Marder, T. Cadwallader, and M. Wagner. 2003. The daily living and social skills of youth with disabilities. In *The individual and household characteristics of youth with disabilities: A report from the National Longitudinal Transition Study-2 (NLTS2)*. Edited by M. Wagner, P. Levine, R. Cameto, T. Cadwallader, C. Marder and J. Blackorby. Menlo Park, CA: SRI International.

Cameto, R., and M. Wagner. 2003. Vocational education courses and services. In *Going to school: What it's like for youth with disabilities: A report from the National Longitudinal Transition Study-2 (NLTS2)*. Edited by M. Wagner, L. Newman, R. Cameto, P. Levine, and C. Marder. Menlo Park, CA: SRI International.

Carson, R. R., P. L. Sitlington, and A. R. Frank. 1995. Young adulthood for individuals with behavioral disorders: What does it hold? *Behavioral Disorders* 20: 127–135.

Center on Emergent Disability. 2001. *Report from the Center on Emergent Disability (part 2)*. Austin: Southwest Educational Development Laboratory.

Clark, R. 1983. *Family life and school achievement: Why poor black children succeed or fail.* Chicago: University of Chicago Press.

Coleman, M., and S. Vaughn. 2000. Reading interventions for students with emotional/behavioral disorders. *Behavioral Disorders* 25: 93–105.

Coley, R. J. 1995. *Dreams deferred: High school dropouts in the United States*. Princeton, NJ: Educational Testing Service, Policy Information Center.

D'Amico, R., and J. Blackorby. 1993. Trends in employment among out-of-school youth with disabilities. In *What happens next? Trends in postschool outcomes of youth with disabilities*. Edited by M. Wagner, R. D'Amico, C. Marder, L. Newman, and J. Blackorby. Menlo Park, CA: SRI International.

Donahoe, K., and N. Zigmond. 1990. Academic grades of ninth-grade urban learning-disabled students and low-achieving peers. *Exceptionality* 1: 17–28.

Donovan, M. S., and C. T. Cross, eds. 2002. *Minority students in special and gifted education*. Washington: National Academy Press.

Duncan, B., S. R. Forness, and C. Hartsough. 1995. Students identified as seriously emotionally disturbed in day treatment: Cognitive, psychiatric, and special education characteristics. *Behavioral Disorders* 20: 238–252.

Duncan, G. J., and J. Brooks-Gunn. 1997. *Consequences of growing up poor*. New York: Russell Sage Foundation.

Edgar, E. 1990. *System support and transition to adulthood for adolescents with seriously disordered behaviors: Orchestrating successful transitions*. Paper presented at the National Adolescent Conference V, Programming for the Developmental Needs of Adolescents with Behavior Disorders, Miami, October 4.

Edgar, E., and P. Levine. 1987. Special education students in transition: Washington State data 1976–1986. University of Washington, Experimental Education Unit.

Education Commission of the States. 2003. *At risk: Dropouts*. http://www.ecs.org/html/issue.asp?issueid=13&subIssueID=74.

Elbaum, B., and S. Vaughn. 1999. Grouping practices and reading outcomes for students with disabilities. *Exceptional Children* 65: 399–415.

Epstein, J. 1987. Involvement: What research says to administrators. *Education and Urban Society* 19: 119–136.

Epstein, J. 1996. Perspectives and previews on research and policy for school, family, and community partnerships. Pp. 209–246 in *Family-school links: How do they affect educational outcomes?* Edited by A. Booth and J. F. Dunn. Mahwah, NJ: Lawrence Erlbaum Associates.

Fairweather, J. S., and D. Shaver. 1991. Making transition to postsecondary education and training. *Exceptional Children* 57: 264–270.

Fernald, W. E. 1919. After-care of the patients discharged from Waverly for a period of 25 years. *Ungraded* 5: 25–31.

Forness, S. R., and K. A. Kavale. 1984. Education of the mentally retarded: A note on policy. *Education and Training of the Mentally Retarded* 19: 239–245.

Frank, A. R., and P. L. Sitlington. 1997. Young adults with behavioral disorders—before and after IDEA. *Behavioral Disorders* 23: 40–56.

Frank, A. R., P. L. Sitlington, and R. R. Carson. 1995. Young adults with behavioral disorders: A comparison with peers with mild disabilities. *Journal of Emotional and Behavioral Disorders* 3: 156–164.

Fujiura, G. T. 1998. *Trends in childhood disability prevalence: Poverty and family structure.* Chicago: Center on Emergent Disability, University of Illinois at Chicago.

Fujiura, G. T., K. Yamaki, and S. Czechowicz. 1998. Disability among ethnic and racial minorities in the United States. *Journal of Disability Policy Studies* 9: 111–130.

Furlong, M. J., G. M. Morrison, and J. D. Dear. 1994. Addressing school violence as part of schools' educational mission. *Preventing School Failure* 38: 10–17.

Gersten, R., and J. Dimino. 1989. Teaching literature to at-risk students. *Educational Leadership* 46: 53–57.

Gillespie, P., and Fink, A. 1974. The influence of sexism on the education of handicapped children. *Exceptional Children* 5: 155–162.

Gorman, C. 1992. Sizing up the sexes. *Time,* January 20: 42–51.

Gould, S. J. 1981. *The mismeasure of man.* New York: Norton.

Gresham, F. M. 2002. Response to treatment. Pp. 467–564 in *Identification of learning disabilities: Research to practice.* Edited by R. Bradley, L. Danielson, and D. Hallahan. Washington: Department of Education.

Gresham, F. M., and S. N. Elliot. 1990. *Social skills rating systems manual.* Circle Pines, MN: American Guidance Service.

Hasazi, S., L. R. Gordon, and C. A. Roe. 1985. Factors associated with the employment status of handicapped youth exiting high school from 1979 to 1983. *Exceptional Children* 51: 455–469.

Hebbeler, K., M. Wagner, D. Spiker, A. Scarborough, R. Simeonsson, and M. Collier. 2001. *A first look at the characteristics of children and families entering early intervention services.* Menlo Park, CA: SRI International.

Henninger, C. H. 1912. The feeble-minded outside the institution and their relation to society. *Journal of Psycho-asthenics* 16: 151–159.

Hier, D. B. 1979. Sex differences in hemisphere specialization: Hypothesis for the excess of dyslexia in boys. *Bulletin of the Orton Society* 29: 74–83.

Hoffman, S. D. 1998. Teenage childbearing is not so bad after all . . . or is it? A review of the new literature. *Family Planning Perspectives* 30: 236–239.

Horn, R., and J. Berktold. 1999. *Students with disabilities in postsecondary education: A profile of preparation, participation, and outcomes.* National Center on Education Statistics, U.S. Department of Education, Statistical Analysis Report no. 199–187. Washington: U.S. Government Printing Office.

Johnson, A. 1900. The self-supporting imbecile. *Journal of Psycho-asthenics* 4: 91–100.

Johnson, D. R., and M. N. Sharpe. 2000. Results of a national survey on the implementation of transition service requirements of IDEA. *Journal of Special Education Leadership* 13: 15–26.

Johnson, G. E. 1897. Contribution to the psychology and pedagogy of feeble-minded children. *Journal of Psycho-asthenics* 1: 90–107.

Jolivette, K., J. P. Stichter, C. M. Nelson, T. M. Scott, and C. J. Liaupsin. 2000. *Improving post-school outcomes for students with emotional and behavioral disorders.* ERIC Digest, ED447616. Arlington, VA: ERIC Clearinghouse on Disabilities and Gifted Education. Available at http://ericec.org/digests/e597.html.

Kavale, K. A. 1994. Setting the record straight on learning disability and low achievement: Implications for policymaking. *Learning Disabilities Research and Practice* 9: 70–77.

Kortering, L. J., and P. M. Braziel. 1999. School dropout from the perspective of former students: Implications for secondary special education programs. *Remedial and Special Education* 20: 78–83.

Leone, P. E., S. M. Meisel, and W. Drakeford. 2002. Special education programs for youth with disabilities in juvenile corrections. *Journal of Correctional Education* 53: 46–50.

Leone, P. E., R. B. Rutherford, Jr., and C. M. Nelson. 1991. Special education in juvenile corrections. *Council of Exceptional Children.*

Leone, P. E., B. A. Zaremba, M. S. Chapin, and C. Iseli. 1995. Understanding the overrepresentation of youths with disabilities in juvenile detention. *District of Columbia Law Review* 3: 389–401.

Levine, P. 1993. Do males and females with learning disabilities and no disabilities have different postschool experiences? Implications for special education teachers. *Issues in Teacher Education* 2: 36–49.

Levine, P., and E. Edgar. 1995. An analysis by gender of long-term post-school outcomes for youth with and without disabilities. *Exceptional Children* 61: 282–300.

Levine, P., C. Marder, M. Wagner, and D. Cardoso. 2003. Characteristics of students' households. In *The children we serve: The demographic characteristics of elementary and middle school students with disabilities and their households: A report from the National Longitudinal Transition Study-2 (NLTS2).* Edited by M. Wagner, C. Marder, and J. Blackorby. Menlo Park, CA: SRI International.

Levine, P., and S. Nourse. 1998. What follow-up studies say about postschool life for young men and women with learning disabilities: A critical look at the literature. *Journal of Learning Disabilities* 13: 212–233.

Levine, P., M. Richardson, D. Lishner, and A. Porter. 2001. Faces on the data: Access to health care for people with disabilities in rural America. Pp. 179–198 in *The hidden America: Social problems in rural America for the twenty-first century.* Edited by R. M. Moore. Selingrove, PA: Susquehanna Press.

Levine, P., Wagner, M., and Marder, C. 2003. Demographic characteristics of youth with disabilities. In *The children we serve: The demographic characteristics of elementary and middle school students with disabilities and their households: A report from the National Longitudinal Transi-*

tion Study-2 (NLTS2). Edited by M. Wagner, C. Marder, and J. Blackorby. Menlo Park, CA: SRI International.

Lewit, E. M., D. L. Terman, and R. E. Behrman. 1997. Children and poverty: Analysis and recommendations. *Future of Children* 7: 4–24.

Malian, I., and A. A. Nevin. 2002. Review of self-determination literature: implications for practitioners. *Remedial and Special Education* 23: 68–74.

Marder, C. 1993. Education after secondary school. In *What happens next? Trends in postschool outcomes of youth with disabilities*. Edited by M. Wagner, R. D'Amico, C. Marder, L. Newman, and J. Blackorby. Menlo Park, CA: SRI International.

Marder, C., D. Cardoso, and M. Wagner. 2003. Employment among youth with disabilities. In *Life outside the classroom for youth with disabilities: A report from the National Longitudinal Transition Study-2 (NLTS2)*. Edited by M. Wagner, T. W. Cadwallader, L. Newman, and C. Marder. Menlo Park, CA: SRI International.

Marder, C., and R. D'Amico. 1992. *How well are youth with disabilities really doing? A comparison of youth with disabilities and youth in general*. Menlo Park, CA: SRI International.

Meisels, S. J., and F. Liaw. 1993. Failure in grade: Do students catch up? *Journal of Educational Research* 50: 69–77.

Miles, D. 1986. Why do more boys than girls receive special education? *Contemporary Education* 57: 104–106.

Mithaug, D. E., C. Horiuchi, and P. Fanning. 1985. A report on the Colorado statewide follow-up survey of special education students. *Exceptional Children* 51: 397–404.

National Center for Education Statistics (NCES). 1998. Digest of education statistics, National Household Education Survey, 1996, unpublished data. http://nces.ed.gov/pubs99/digest98/d98t025.html.

National Center for Education Statistics (NCES). 2000. *A recommended approach to providing high school dropout and completion rates at the state level* (NCES 2000–305). Washington: U.S. Department of Education.

National Center for Health Statistics (NCHS). 2001. Disabilities and impairments. http://www.cdc.gov/nchs/fastats/disable.htm.

National Information Center for Children and Youth with Handicaps (NICHCY). 1990. Having a daughter with a disability: Is it different for girls? *News Digest* 14 (October): 1–15.

National Information Center for Children and Youth with Handicaps (NICHCY). 1992. Sexuality education for children and youth with disabilities. *News Digest* 1: 1–28.

National Middle School Association (NMSA). 2000. *NMSA Research Summary #18: Parent involvement and student achievement at the middle level*. http://www.nmsa.org/services/ressum18.htm.

National Organization on Disabilities. 2000. *2000 N.O.D./Harris survey of Americans with disabilities*. Washington: Louis Harris and Associates.

National Research Council. 2002. *Minority representation in special and gifted education*. Washington: National Research Council.

Neel, R. S., N. Meadows, P. Levine, and E. Edgar. 1988. What happens after special education: A statewide follow-up study of secondary students who have behavior disorders. *Behavioral Disorders* 13: 209–216.

NELS. 1997. Statistical analysis report: Profiles of students with disabilities as identified in

NELS:88. National Center for Education Statistics, April (NCES 97-254). http://nces.ed
.gov/pubs97/97254.html.

Newman, L. 1993a. A place to call home: Residential arrangements of out-of-school youth with disabilities. In *What happens next? Trends in postschool outcomes of youth with disabilities.* Edited by M. Wagner, R. D'Amico, C. Marder, L. Newman, and J. Blackorby. Menlo Park, CA: SRI International.

Newman, L. 1993b. Academic course-taking. In *The secondary school programs of students with disabilities.* Edited by M. Wagner. Menlo Park, CA: SRI International.

Newman, L., and E. Davies. 2003. School engagement of youth with disabilities. In *The achievements of youth with disabilities during secondary school: A report from the National Longitudinal Transition Study-2 (NLTS2).* Edited by M. Wagner, C. Marder, J. Blackorby, R. Cameto, L. Newman, and P. Levine. Menlo Park, CA: SRI International.

Newman, L., and M. Wagner. 2003. Family expectations for the future. In *The achievements of youth with disabilities during secondary school: A report from the National Longitudinal Transition Study-2 (NLTS2).* Edited by M. Wagner, C. Marder, J. Blackorby, R. Cameto, L. Newman, and P. Levine. Menlo Park, CA: SRI International.

NHES. 1993, 1995. *National Household Education Surveys Program.* http://nces.ed.gov/nhes/.

Office of Special Education Programs (OSEP). 2002. Office of Special Education Programs Mission. http://www.ed.gov/offices/OSERS/OSEP/About/aboutusmission.html.

Office of Special Education Programs (OSEP). 2003. Federal child count of students receiving special education services under IDEA. http://www.IDEAdata.org.

Osofsky, J. D. 1995. Children who witness domestic violence: The invisible victims. *Social Policy Reports: Society for Research in Child Development* 9, no. 3: 1–16.

Perry, N. J. 1992. Why it's so tough to be a girl. *Fortune,* August 10, 82–84.

Price, L. A., D. Wolensky, and R. Mulligan. 2002. Self-determination in action in the classroom. *Remedial and Special Education* 23: 109–115.

Razeghi, J. A. 1998. A first step toward solving the problem of special education dropouts: Infusing career education into the curriculum. *Intervention in School and Clinic* 33: 148–156.

Robertson, A. S. 1997. *If an adolescent begins to fail in school, what can parents and teachers do?* ERIC Digest, ED415001. Champaign, IL: ERIC Clearinghouse on Elementary and Early Childhood Education.

Roderick, M. 1995. Grade retention and school dropouts: Policy debate and research questions. *Phi Delta Kappan Research Bulletin* 15 (December): 1-6.

Rousso, H. 1988. Daughters with disabilities: Defective women or minority women? Pp. 139–171 in *Women with disabilities: Essays in psychology, culture, and politics.* Edited by M. Fine and A. Asch. Philadelphia: Temple University Press.

Rylance, B. J. 1997. Predictors of high school graduation or dropping out for youths with severe emotional disturbances. *Behavioral Disorders* 23: 5–17.

Rylance, B. J. 1998. Predictors of post-high school employment for youth identified as severely emotionally disturbed. *Journal of Special Education* 32: 184–92.

Schlosser, L., and B. Algozzine. 1980. Sex, behavior, and teacher expectancies. *Journal of Experimental Education* 48: 231–236.

Scott, T. M., C. M. Nelson, and C. J. Liaupsin. 2001. Effective instruction: The forgotten component in preventing school violence. *Education and Treatment of Children* 24: 309–322.

Shaywitz, S. E., and B. A. Shaywitz. 2001. *The neurobiology of reading and dyslexia.* Washington: National Academy Press.

Shepard, L. A., and M. L. Smith. 1990. Synthesis of research on grade retention. *Educational Leadership* 47: 84–88.

Siegel, S., M. Robert, M. Waxman, and R. Gaylord-Ross. 1992. A follow-along study of partici- pants in a longitudinal transition program for youths with mild disabilities. *Exceptional Chil- dren* 58: 346–356.

Silver, L. 1998. *The misunderstood child: Understanding and coping with your child's learning dis- abilities.* 3rd ed. New York: Times Books.

Sitlington, P. L., and A. R. Frank. 1989. *Iowa statewide follow-up study: Adult adjustment of indi- viduals with mental disabilities one year after leaving school.* Des Moines: Department of Edu- cation.

Storey, K., P. Bates, and D. Hunter, eds. 2002. *The road ahead: Transition to adult life for persons with disabilities.* Saint Augustine: Training Resource Network.

Sum, A., I. Khatiwada, N. Pond, M. Trubskyy, N. Fogg, and S. Palma. 2002. *Left behind in the la- bor market: Labor market problems of the nation's out-of-school young adult populations.* Center for Labor Market Studies, Northeastern University for Alternative Schools Network, Chi- cago. http://www.nupr.neu.edu/2-03/left_behind.pdf.

Talbot, M. E. 1964. *Edouard Seguin: A study of an educational approach to the treatment of mentally defective children.* New York: Bureau of Publications, Teachers College, Columbia University.

Thompson, C. L., and E. K. Cunningham. 2000. *Retention and social promotion: Research and im- plications for policy.* ERIC Digest Number 161/ED449241. New York: ERIC Clearinghouse on Urban Education.

Thorkildsen, R., and M. R. Stein. 1998. *Is parent involvement related to student achievement? Explor- ing the evidence.* Research Bulletins Online, 22. http://www.pdkintl.org/edres/resbull22.htm.

Thurlow, M. L., M. F. Sinclair, and D. R. Johnson. 2002. Students with disabilities who drop out of school: Implications for policy and practice. *Issue Brief: Examining Current Challenges in Secondary Education and Transition.* Minneapolis: National Center on Secondary Education and Transition.

Tymchuk, A. J. 1999. Moving towards integration of services for parents with intellectual disabil- ities. *Journal of Intellectual and Developmental Disability* 24: 59–74.

U.S. Census Bureau. 2002. *Current Population Survey.* Washington: U.S. Department of Com- merce.

U.S. Department of Education. 1999. *Twenty-first annual report to Congress on the implementation of the Individuals with Disabilities Education Act.* Washington: U.S. Department of Educa- tion.

U.S. Department of Education. 2000a. *Twenty-second annual report to Congress on the implemen- tation of the Individuals with Disabilities Education Act.* Washington: U.S. Department of Education.

U.S. Department of Education. 2000b. *U.S. Department of Education's 1999 performance report and 2001 annual plan.* Washington: U.S. Department of Education. http://www.ed.gov/ pubs/AnnualPlan2001/index.html.

U.S. Department of Education. 2001a. *State and local implementation of IDEA.* Washington: ABT Associates.

U.S. Department of Education. 2001b. *Twenty-third annual report to Congress on the implementa-tion of the Individuals with Disabilities Education Act.* Washington: U.S. Department of Education.

Vitaro, F., M. Brendgen, and R. E. Tremblay. 1999. Prevention of school dropout through the re-duction of disruptive behaviors and school failure in elementary school. *Journal of School Psy-chology* 37: 205–226.

Vogel, S. A., and P. B. Adelman. 1992. The success of college students with learning disabilities: Factors related to educational attainment. *Journal of Learning Disabilities* 25: 430–441.

Wagner, M. 1991. *Dropouts with disabilities: What do we know? What can we do?* Menlo Park, CA: SRI International.

Wagner, M. 1992. A little help from my friends: The social involvement of youth people with dis-abilities. In *What happens next? Trends in postschool outcomes of youth with disabilities.* Edited by M. Wagner, R. D'Amico, C. Marder, L. Newman, and J. Blackorby. Menlo Park, CA: SRI International.

Wagner, M. 2003a. The education-related histories of youth with disabilities. In *Going to school: What it's like for youth with disabilities: A report from the National Longitudinal Transition Study-2 (NLTS2).* Edited by M. Wagner, L. Newman, R. Cameto, P. Levine, and C. Marder. Menlo Park, CA: SRI International.

Wagner, M. 2003b. Disability profiles of secondary school students receiving special education. In *The children we serve: The demographic characteristics of elementary and middle school stu-dents with disabilities and their households: A report from the National Longitudinal Transition Study-2 (NLTS2).* Edited by M. Wagner, C. Marder, and J. Blackorby. Menlo Park, CA: SRI International.

Wagner, M. 2003c. Youth with disabilities, how are they doing? In *The achievements of youth with disabilities during secondary school: A report from the National Longitudinal Transition Study-2 (NLTS2).* Edited by M. Wagner, C. Marder, J. Blackorby, R. Cameto, L. Newman, and P. Levine. Menlo Park, CA: SRI International.

Wagner, M. 2003d. An overview of the school programs of secondary school students with dis-abilities. In *Going to school: What it's like for youth with disabilities: A report from the National Longitudinal Transition Study-2 (NLTS2).* Edited by M. Wagner, L. Newman, R. Cameto, P. Levine, and C. Marder. Menlo Park, CA: SRI International.

Wagner, M., and J. Blackorby. 1996. Transition from high school to work or college: How special education students fare. *Future of Children* 6: 103–120.

Wagner, M., J. Blackorby, R. Cameto, and L. Newman. 1993. *What makes a difference? Influences on postschool outcomes of youth with disabilities: The third comprehensive report from the Na-tional Longitudinal Transition Study of Special Education Students.* Menlo Park, CA: SRI In-ternational.

Wagner, M., J. Blackorby, and P. Levine. 2003. The functional abilities of youth. In *The children we serve: The demographic characteristics of elementary and middle school students with disabil-ities and their households: A report from the National Longitudinal Transition Study-2 (NLTS2).* Edited by M. Wagner, C. Marder, and J. Blackorby. Menlo Park, CA: SRI International.

Wagner, M., R. Cameto, and L. Newman. 2003. *Youth with disabilities: A changing population: A report of findings from the National Longitudinal Transition Study (NLTS) and the National Longitudinal Transition Study-2 (NLTS2).* Menlo Park, CA: SRI International.

Wagner, M., and K. Hebbeler. 2000. *Representation of minorities and children of poverty among those receiving early intervention and special education services: Findings from two national longitudinal studies.* Menlo Park, CA: SRI International.

Wagner, M., K. Hebbeler, and J. Blackorby. 1993. *Beyond the report card: The multiple dimensions of secondary school performance of students with disabilities.* Menlo Park, CA: SRI International.

Wagner, M., and Levine, P. 2003. The schools attended by youth with disabilities. In *Going to school: What it's like for youth with disabilities: A report from the National Longitudinal Transition Study-2 (NLTS2).* Edited by M. Wagner, L. Newman, R. Cameto, P. Levine, and C. Marder. Menlo Park, CA: SRI International.

Wagner, M., C. Marder, J. Blackorby, R. Cameto, L. Newman, and P. Levine. 2003. *The achievements of youth with disabilities during secondary school: A report from the National Longitudinal Transition Study-2 (NLTS2).* Menlo Park, CA: SRI International.

Wagner, M., C. Marder, and D. Cardoso. 2003. Characteristics of students' households. In *The children we serve: The demographic characteristics of elementary and middle school students with disabilities and their households: A report from the National Longitudinal Transition Study-2 (NLTS2).* Edited by M. Wagner, C. Marder, and J. Blackorby. Menlo Park, CA: SRI International.

Walker, H. M., G. Colvin, and E. Ramsey. 1995. *Antisocial behavior in school: Strategies and best practices.* Pacific Grove, CA: Brooks/Cole.

Walters, D. M., and S. B. Borgers. 1995. Student retention: Is it effective? *School Counselor* 42: 300–310.

White, W. D., and W. P. Wolfensberger. 1969. The evolution of dehumanization in our institutions. *Mental Retardation* 7: 5–9.

Will, M. 1984. Bridges from school to working life. *Programs for the Handicapped: Clearinghouse on the Handicapped,* March/April, 1–5.

Williamson-Ige, D. K., and E. J. McKitric. 1985. An analysis of sex differences in educating the handicapped. *Journal of Research and Development in Education* 18: 72–78.

Zhang, D. 2001. Self-determination and inclusion: are students with mild mental retardation more self-determined in regular classrooms? *Education and Training in Mental Retardation and Developmental Disabilities* 36: 357–362.

CHAPTER NINE

Transition Experiences of Young Adults Who Received Special Education Services as Adolescents: A Matter of Policy

PHYLLIS LEVINE AND MARY WAGNER

We gratefully acknowledge our colleagues Renee Cameto, Camille Marder, Lynn Newman, and Jose Blackorby, and the staff of SRI International Center for Education and Human Services. This project has been funded at least in part with Federal funds from the U.S. Department of Education under contract number ED-01-CO-0003. The content of this publication does not necessarily reflect the views or policies of the U.S. Department of Education nor does mention of trade names, commercial products, or organizations imply endorsement by the U.S. government.

When spider webs unite, they can tie up a lion.

African proverb

INTRODUCTION

Transition has been entrenched in the language of special educators and parents of children and youth with disabilities since the early 1980s, when, conceptualized as a "bridge" from school to adult life, transition became a serious issue of special education policy and practice (Will 1984). Until then, most students with disabilities had little or no preparation for life after school, net or no net. Over the past two decades, transition planning and postschool outcomes have received a lot of attention in special education research, with results influencing changes in classroom instruction, school policies, and legislation.

Referred to as the "floundering period" (Halpern 1992, 1990), transition became synonymous with the vague time interval starting right after high school until the former student got his or her act together and either went to college or found a decent job. In special education vernacular, the term has become more complex and less limited regarding age and time. It is now commonly recognized that development and growth are not linear, but instead are a path that is strewn with a variety of "transitional moments," with some being more jolting or noticeable than others. Some transitions are experienced by many of us (e.g., entering kindergarten, moving once or twice, losing the first tooth); others are less common (e.g., separation from parents or siblings through divorce, family death, frequent mobility, serious illness or accident). Some individuals may perceive transitions as difficult or confusing; others may see them as opportunities for change. Some people may venture through these periods in a relatively short amount of time, others may linger, taking years to adjust. And some transitions may have particularly potent effects on later life.

For special educators, the notion of transition generally refers to several distinct stages during which children and youth may enter or exit from special education services, as determined by age, disability assessment, and individual need. They are: early intervention (birth to age three), preschool, kindergarten, elementary school, middle school, high school, and young adulthood. These transitional stages present challenges for children and youth served by special education and provide focus for practitioners. In essence, what occurs during these stages also has become a matter of policy.

This chapter highlights the transitional period marked by the early years following exit from secondary school and addresses the legislative and policy decisions that have transformed how that period is experienced by youth with disabilities who received special education services as adolescents. The chapter describes the evolutionary nature of the laws and regulations that govern education practices for youth with disabilities while they are still in school and the policies specifically targeted to prepare them for the transition to adulthood. It follows with an overview of laws and policies that affect opportunities for these youth to work, live, and socialize in the community as young adults, especially as they face the many challenges to postschool independence described in the previous chapter.

The chapter illustrates some of the difficulties facing youth and their families as they straddle the school-based, child-oriented service delivery system and the community-based, adult-oriented systems, often with conflicting eligibility and administrative rules. Some of the strengths and weaknesses of current policy directions are mentioned briefly in the context of a fresh approach to transition policy that moves us toward system reform. We begin this policy overview with an emphasis on the importance of informing both transition policy and practice with ongoing methodologically sound research and data.

INFORMING POLICY AND PRACTICE

Although it has only recently come to dominate the education reform spotlight, accountability in education is not a new concept. Longitudinal survey research has been producing empirical data in support of improved service delivery in education since the turn of the twentieth century (e.g., Pinsent 1906; Boehne 1912; Fitts 1916). A hundred years later, we still recognize that improving policy and practice demands persuasive arguments using information that is comprehensive, broadly applicable, and amenable to methodological scrutiny (Levine and Nourse 1998; Halpern 1999; Dixon and Carnine 1993; Burstein 1980). In 1983, the U.S. Congress understood the value of conducting such an inquiry in the transition arena, and, through the U.S. Department of Education's Office of Special Education Programs (OSEP), commissioned the National Longitudinal Transition Study (NLTS).

NLTS influenced special education policy and practice in many ways, including by intensifying the focus on the transition from school to adulthood. The logic of informing policy and practice decisions with data continues, in part, through OSEP's investment in a series of large-scale, nationally representative child-based longitudinal studies and other policy studies. Included in this unique portfolio is the second generation of the National Longitudinal Transition Study (NLTS2),[1] which is generating a wealth of information in a world that has changed dramatically in recent years, and within a field of special education that is more sophisticated, intelligent, informed, and compassionate than in the past. In addition to documenting the characteristics, school experiences, and outcomes of secondary school students with disabilities,

---

1. NLTS2 is a ten-year study of a nationally representative sample of more than eleven thousand youth who were ages thirteen through sixteen and were receiving special education services in grade seven or above when the study began in 2001. Findings generalize to youth with disabilities nationally and to youth in each of the twelve federal special education disability categories in use for students in the NLTS2 age range. Additional information about NLTS2 is available at www.nlts2.org. Other studies sponsored by OSEP's National Assessment Program include: the Special Elementary Education Longitudinal Study (SEELS), which provides a comprehensive look at the experiences and outcomes of elementary and middle school students with disabilities; the National Early Intervention Longitudinal Study (NEILS), which is in its sixth year of following a national sample of children who received early intervention services at ages birth to three; the Pre-elementary Education Longitudinal Study (PEELS), which involves children with disabilities ages three to five; the Study of Personnel Needs in Special Education (SPeNSE); an evaluation of the State and Local Implementation and Impact of the Individuals with Disabilities Education Act (SLIIDEA); and the Special Education Expenditure Project (SEEP), which examines how federal, state, and local funds are used to support programs and services for students with disabilities.

NLTS2 also illuminates where transitional youth who are served by special education fit and function within the labyrinth of changing systems, resources, and demographic diversity. It explores the interactive and multidimensional relationships among social, political, economic, educational, cultural, and family factors that ultimately affect successful transition and long-term outcomes for youth with disabilities.

THE POLICY CONTEXT FOR SCHOOL-AGE STUDENTS WITH DISABILITIES

The lives of school-age children and youth with disabilities are affected in important ways by federal legislation that specifically addresses their unique circumstances and by broader education legislation that shapes the school experiences of all students.

Federal Special Education Legislation

The first federal legislative foray into the world of children and youth with disabilities grew out of a period of social upheaval and a growing tolerance for diversity and had both civil rights and education goals. But tolerance, let alone acceptance, of people with disabilities is a relatively new notion. Throughout the first half of the twentieth century, state-supported custodial institutionalization of people with disabilities in the United States was generally accepted. Most often individuals with a wide range of disabilities did not attend schools with their peers, employment took place primarily on farms or in segregated workshops, recreational opportunities were limited, and marriage and parenting were prohibited (Kuhlman 1917; Barrows 1913). In general, they were not expected to participate in the activities typical of other citizens of the community (Milburn 1909).

The civil rights of individuals became a focus in the political and social reform campaigns of the 1960s and 1970s (e.g., the women's movement, Society for Protection of Children), inspiring new attitudes toward human diversity, including disability. This fortuitous historical period fueled a growing unrest that brought dramatic changes during the latter part of the century; during those years, people with developmental disabilities or mental illness gradually moved out of institutions and into the community (Wolfensberger 1983; Meyer and Skrtic 1995).

By the early 1970s, people with disabilities and their families found a growing pocket of supporters and new avenues for self-advocacy. Recognizing that the American public education system in many ways acts as an entry point to the "American dream," they targeted their efforts toward opening that system to the full participation of children and youth with disabilities. In 1975, the landmark Education for All Handicapped Children Act (EHA; PL 94-142), opened doors to children and youth with disabilities and their families in unprecedented ways. EHA, which guaranteed protections under the rights of due process and access to a free and appropriate education in the least restrictive environment for all children and youth with disabilities, changed the fundamental nature of how children and youth with disabilities are treated not only in the classroom but in society. It was instrumental in advancing Child Find strategies[2] for identifying children in need; establishing clearer, assessment-based criteria for disability classification; forging "people first" language to describe disability categories that carried less stigma than previous labels; enhancing curricular and instructional methods; and providing a platform for inclusive principles and practices. The school-based legislation crossed over into adult policy by mandating the option for students with disabilities to stay in school to age twenty-one.

In the 1980s, educators and family members of students with disabilities began to draw attention to the issues involved in helping students make the transition from high school to young adulthood. Concerns about the multiple barriers facing these youth were reflected in policies that focused on transition planning, school-to-work programming, vocational training, and research at the federal, state, and local levels (Will 1984; Hasazi, Gordon, and Roe 1985; Heal et al. 1989; Affleck et al. 1990; Edgar 1990). During the subsequent two decades, a surge of disability and education research inspired scrutiny of the law, and EHA evolved into the Individuals with Disabilities Education Act (IDEA; PL 101-476). In its most recent incarnation, the Individuals with Disabilities Education Act Amendments of 1997 (IDEA'97; PL 105-17), this law governs such important aspects of special education services as funding streams, assessment and instructional practices, regulations, eligibility criteria, development of student individualized education programs (IEP), and due process.

Although IDEA plays a crucial role in shaping the school experiences of children and youth receiving special education, it is not the only federal legislation that focuses specifically on the needs of students with disabilities. Section 504 of the Rehabilitation Act of 1973 and the 1992 amendments specify accom-

---

2. Child Find is a screening and evaluation process designed to locate, identify, and refer as early as possible all young children with disabilities and their families who are in need of early intervention (part C) or preschool special education services (part B/619) under IDEA; http://www.childfindidea.org/overview.htm.

modations for students whose physical or mental disabilities substantially limit one or more major life activity, including access to school activities or services, but do not impede their academic ability enough to qualify for special education services. (For a discussion of policies concerning youth with special health care needs and physical disabilities, see chapter 13). For example, accommodations might include large-print or Braille texts or computers that magnify classroom board work for students with visual impairments. In some cases a Section 504 accommodation might require assignment to a new school, for example, for a student who uses a wheelchair and needs a school building that can accommodate his or her mobility needs.

IDEA'97 provides federal funding, administered through the states, to support special education services for children and youth who meet stringent eligibility criteria for services in one of the federally defined disability categories. It also requires and regulates specific evaluation procedures, parent participation guidelines, and extensive procedural safeguards, particularly in regard to due process and disciplinary practices. By contrast, Section 504 is a civil rights, not a programmatic, statute that governs all public and private programs or activities that receive federal financial assistance but conveys no specific funding. Compared with IDEA'97, Section 504 is much more limited in scope, but it also is more flexible, its eligibility criteria are less rigid, and the procedural safeguards are less rigorous, making it easier and more efficient for some youth with disabilities to receive the accommodations they need (Cohen 2003).

Federal Legislation Affecting All Students

The educational experiences of students with disabilities also are shaped by legislation and policies that define the larger educational context for all students. Currently, the most influential of these is the No Child Left Behind Act of 2002 (NCLB, PL 107-110). NCLB emphasizes the accountability of schools, school districts, and states for the academic performance of all students, with the intent of closing the achievement gap between disadvantaged and minority students and their peers. NCLB requires states to implement statewide accountability systems that are based on challenging academic standards in core areas, to test annually all students in grades three through eight, and to publish annually statewide progress objectives to ensure that all groups of students reach academic proficiency by the time they graduate from high school. Though improved academic performance is consistent with the goals of IDEA'97, it is not the only or ultimate outcome expected for children and youth with disabilities. The primary intention of the free appropriate public education guaranteed by

IDEA to children and youth with disabilities is to "prepare them for employment and independent living" [Sec. 601(d)(1)(A)].[3]

EARLY CHALLENGES TO TRANSITION SUCCESS: STUDENTS' HIGH SCHOOL EXPERIENCES

The legislation outlined above has both subtle and profound influences on the experiences of youth with disabilities in school and in the transition to young adulthood. Key examples pertain to IDEA's transition planning process for secondary school students with disabilities and NCLB's academic and accountability pressures.

Transition Planning and Services

When Congress reauthorized IDEA in 1990 and 1997, the law underwent significant revisions that redirected its focus from guaranteeing access to education programs and related services to improving student achievement and outcomes. The revised regulations include an emphasis on principles of "inclusion," access to the general education curriculum, increased academic performance standards, participation in assessments, and increased parental involvement. Requirements also were added to include transition planning in the Individualized Education Programs (IEP) of all secondary school students with disabilities in an effort to prepare them for the challenges of adulthood (U.S. Department of Education 1997 2001a).

Specifically, IDEA requires that school and postschool transition service needs of students with disabilities be met through a formal interagency process. A transition plan must be included in each student's IEP by age fourteen, and services must be in place and implemented by age sixteen (but preferably earlier). Studies conducted during the early years of these regulations indicated minimal levels of compliance regarding transition requirements in many states (Hasazi, Furney, and DeStefano 1997, 1999; Johnson and Sharpe 2000). But recent findings from NLTS2[4] indicate tremendous progress in the last decade. For example, in 1990, only 43 percent of twelfth-grade students with disabilities had a written transition plan (Cameto 1993). According to NLTS2, 89 percent of secondary school students with disabilities in 2001 had a completed

---

3. Challenges posed by NCLB for students with disabilities are mentioned in the next section

4. NLTS2 data and details regarding its design, sample, and analysis procedures are available at www.nlts2.org.

transition plan in place; this was true for three-quarters of fourteen-year-olds, and for almost all sixteen-year-olds (91 percent). About two-thirds of students with transition plans started the process by age fourteen, and approximately one in five started at age fifteen, but 14 percent did not start planning their transition until age sixteen or older. Two-thirds of students with transition plans received instruction specifically focused on teaching skills related to participating in this process.

Together with their parents, students with disabilities are expected to play a vital role in their own transition planning, particularly in regard to career decisions, residential options, recreational and social choices, and independent living (U.S. Department of Education 2001a). As noted in the previous chapter, almost three-quarters of students with disabilities contribute to their transition goals, including 12 percent who take on a leadership role. Whereas those participation data characterize students with learning disabilities or emotional disturbances, only about half of youth with mental retardation provide input into the planning process, and only 3 percent of these students take on a leadership role (Cameto, Levine, and Wagner 2004). As shown in table 9.1, about two-thirds of parents are satisfied with their level of involvement in the decisions

Table 9.1 Family involvement in transition planning

	Students receiving special education services Primary disability classification			
Percentage of students whose family:	Total	Learning disabilities	Mental retardation	Emotional disturbances
Reports that their involvement in transition planning is just about right	64.9 (1.7)	66.4 (2.6)	58.5 (2.7)	60.6 (2.8)
Wants to be more involved in transition planning	33.7 (1.7)	32.3 (2.6)	40.1 (2.7)	37.4 (2.7)
Reports that transition planning is very useful	35.9 (2.1)	34.8 (3.2)	43.1 (3.3)	34.1 (3.4)
Reports that transition planning was not very or not at all useful	17.9 (1.7)	18.0 (2.6)	8.7 (1.9)	25.3 (3.1)

Source: NLTS2 Wave 1 student school program survey; NLTS2 Wave 1 parent interviews.

Standard errors are in parentheses.

that determine their student's transition plan, and about one-third also report that the process is very useful for planning for life after high school. Even though 40 percent of youth with mental retardation have parents who express the desire for more involvement in the IEP and transition planning process, they are more likely than youth with learning disabilities or emotional disturbances to have parents report that the process has been "very useful" in preparing their sons or daughters for life after school (43 percent compared to 35 and 34 percent respectively). In contrast, the parents of about one-fifth of youth with learning disabilities and one-quarter of youth with emotional disturbances report transition planning has been "not very" or "not at all useful" compared to parents of only 9 percent of youth with mental retardation who report this low rating (Cameto, Levine, and Wagner 2004).

In the *Twenty-third Annual Report to Congress on the Implementation of the Individuals with Disabilities Education Act* (U.S. Department of Education 2001a), the National Center on Secondary Education and Transition (NCSET) cites several studies that report the failure of many states to achieve even minimal levels of compliance in regard to transition services. In fact, many of the requirements featured in IDEA'97 reportedly are being implemented inadequately, if at all (U.S. Department of Education 2001a; Hasazi, Furney, and DeStefano 1999; Johnson and Sharpe 2000; National Council on Disability 2000). The realities of transition planning in many schools show that even a strong legislative foundation for effective programming can be insufficient to ensure that policy meets the needs of young people with disabilities.

The success that youth with disabilities achieve in adulthood can be influenced by access to a range of services that support their education and transition goals while they still attend high school. (See chapter 8 for a discussion on the importance of transition planning for students with disabilities.) As part of its mandate, IDEA'97 requires the provision of educational assistance to students with disabilities, including related services. According to NLTS2 findings, nearly three-quarters of secondary school students with disabilities are reported by parents to receive some type of related services that typically support traditional academic activities (e.g., tutoring), personal development and growth (e.g., therapeutic interventions, counseling), or access to an inclusive school environment and to the community (e.g., mobility training, assistive technology), a 16 percentage point increase from 1987 (Wagner, Cameto, and Newman 2003).

Importantly, parents report that these services are most often provided from or through their children's school or school district—60 percent of students with disabilities receive one or more related services from school sources (table 9.2). (Outside agencies or individuals are more likely to provide services that require nonacademic professionals, such as psychiatrists or psychologists, med-

Table 9.2. Provision of related services and programs for youth with disabilities

| Percentage of students whose family: | Students receiving special education services primary disability classification | | | |
	Total	Learning disabilities	Mental retardation	Emotional disturbances
learns about services through the school*	81.0	85.7	78.1	69.0
	(1.3)	(1.7)	(2.2)	(2.4)
receives information from the school about services available after high school	56.7	53.8	61.6	61.5
	(2.5)	(3.8)	(3.6)	(4.9)
reports youth has a case manager	53.0	53.1	46.9	56.0
	(1.8)	(2.9)	(2.8)	(2.8)
reports case manager is someone at school	44.0	49.3	30.2	36.9
	(1.8)	(2.9)	(2.6)	(2.7)
reports barrier to obtaining services:**				
lack of information	23.7	21.0	23.4	34.1
	(7.7)	(2.0)	(2.2)	(2.5)
services not available	22.6	18.8	25.6	33.5
	(1.4)	(1.9)	(2.2)	(2.4)
poor quality	20.3	17.1	20.6	30.2
	(1.3)	(1.9)	(2.1)	(2.4)
costs of services	17.3	14.8	17.4	25.4
	(1.2)	(1.8)	(1.9)	(2.2)
youth ineligible for services	17.2	14.5	18.4	24.2
	(1.2)	(1.8)	(2.0)	(2.2)

Notes: *From 3 to 12 percent of families report learning about services from other sources such as the Internet, newsletters, physicians, professional consultants, conferences, family members, parent groups, and other sources.

**From 4 percent to 18 percent of parents also report scheduling conflicts, location of services, lack of time, transportation, language and other obstacles as barriers to access to services.

Source: NLTS2 Wave 1 student school program survey; NLTS2 Wave 1 parent interviews.

Standard errors are in parentheses.

ical diagnosticians, and some physical therapists and social workers.) In addition, schools overwhelmingly function as the primary source of information about related services for families; parents of 81 percent of youth with disabilities report learning about services from their children's school, compared with 3 to 12 percent who do so from other sources.

For youth with disabilities who receive services, particularly those who receive multiple services, case management can be an important support through which services are coordinated so they are most effective and least burdensome for youth and families and so that problems of duplication or gaps in service are avoided. Among youth with disabilities who receive any related services, about half have parents who report they also have a case manager to coordinate services. Schools also provide this case management for four to six times as many youth with disabilities as do other professionals or family members.

Thus, parents depend on the schools for information about services, service coordination, case management, and most of the services and supports for their sons and daughters with disabilities. Clearly, schools have accepted a responsibility for students with disabilities that extends well beyond the classroom and that requires the support of education resources and policies to be implemented effectively. Further, youth who drop out of school or experience long-term suspensions or expulsion miss out on these types of school connections, services, programs, and support at a time when they are most needed.

More than half of families also report that schools provide information about the various transition and support services that are available in the community for youth with disabilities after leaving school. However, the wide array of services students with disabilities access can involve multiple service systems, including education, health, child welfare, and vocational rehabilitation, for example. Parents and youth may not be aware of the services provided through these systems. Further, these multiple systems can have different, even incompatible, eligibility criteria and sometimes complex processes for establishing qualifications for services. Other barriers to service may also be encountered in attempting to obtain services, including high cost, inaccessibility, and services being inadequate to meet demand (table 9.2). There often is a serious lack of coordination among local service providers and schools, and the notion of a smooth "hand off" from school to community services or resources can be illusive (Hasazi, Furney, and DeStefano 1999; Johnson and Sharpe 2000; National Council on Disability 2000).

Programs Targeting Risk Behaviors

IDEA'97 requires teams that plan students' IEPs to address behaviors that impede students' learning or that of others. Youth with disabilities can participate in an array of programs that focus on preventing specific problematic behaviors through education or that serve youth who already engage in those behaviors. For example, programs to educate youth about the abuse of alcohol, recreational drugs, and other harmful substances provide instruction and information to help youth make informed choices and behave responsibly, whereas treatment programs support youth in freeing themselves of substance abuse. Helping youth make informed choices also provides the framework for repro-ductive health education. Preventing teenage parenting through reproductive health education and services is optimal; however, structured parenting educa-tion programs are essential for teenage parents and also can help youth who may plan to become parents as adults. Other programs teach students how to manage conflict and anger, skills that generalize to the exercise of self-control, the development of healthy relationships, and the taking on of the responsibil-ities and privileges of adulthood. Developing a mature recognition of the connections among high-risk behaviors, personal choice and responsibility, and the subsequent short- and long-term consequences are at the crux of these programs.

According to school staff, most youth with disabilities participate in at least one program aimed at teaching prevention or at amelioration of behaviors that place students at risk for poor outcomes (table 9.3). These programs and the percentages of youth with disabilities reported to participate are: reproductive health education or services (53 percent); substance abuse education or services (41%); anger management, conflict resolution, or violence prevention (28%); and teen parenting education or services (21%). School staff also perceive that approximately one-third of students with disabilities across these programs do not participate in them but would benefit from them. Students with learning disabilities or emotional disturbances are reported to participate in these pro-grams at higher rates than others, but these youth also are among the students reported to have relatively high levels of unmet needs. In fact, according to school staff, youth with emotional disturbances have the highest proportions of unmet needs for each of the four risk behavior programs. With the current focus on school violence and abstinence regarding teen sexual activity, it is noteworthy that the percentages of students reported to have unmet needs for programs involving conflict resolution/anger management/violence preven-tion or teen parenting are larger than the percentages of those participating in these programs.

Vocational Education and Preparation for Employment

"What do you want to be when you grow up?" is a question posed to most chil-dren in American society, and the expectation is that schooling will eventually lead to the end goal of this question—employment. Indeed, many youth be-gin to enter the workforce in early adolescence, and the majority of youth are reported to hold a job at some point during their high school years (National

Table 9.3. Participation of youth in school-based programs targeting risk behaviors, by disability category

	Students receiving special education services primary disability classification			
Percentage of youth participating in or who could benefit from:	*Total*	*Learning disabilities*	*Mental retardation*	*Emotional disturbances*
reproductive health education/services				
participating	53.1	54.0	43.2	51.0
	(2.1)	(3.1)	(3.2)	(4.0)
not participating, could benefit				
from program	29.6	28.1	33.7	34.1
	(1.9)	(2.9)	(3.1)	(3.9)
teen parenting education/services				
participating	21.3	21.6	17.3	17.0
	(1.1)	(2.6)	(2.5)	(3.0)
not participating, could benefit				
from program	37.0	36.9	39.3	44.0
	(2.0)	(3.2)	(3.2)	(4.1)
substance abuse education/services				
participating	40.9	41.5	34.7	47.1
	(2.1)	(3.2)	(3.2)	(4.1)
not participating, could benefit				
from program	30.9	31.6	30.3	35.5
	(2.0)	(3.0)	(3.1)	(3.9)
conflict resolution/anger management				
participating	28.3	23.1	29.1	43.4
	(1.9)	(2.7)	(3.0)	(4.0)
not participating, could benefit				
from program	35.9	36.1	33.9	44.2
	(2.0)	(3.1)	(3.1)	(4.0)

Source: NLTS2 Wave 1 student school program survey.

Standard errors in parentheses.

Research Council 1998; Rothstein and Herz 2000). NLTS2 data show that about six in ten youth with disabilities are reported by their parents to be employed in a regular paid job at least some time in a one-year period while they are in high school, and 22 percent are employed at any given time (Cameto and Wagner 2003). Regular paid employment during high school has been found to be an important foundation for finding employment in the postschool years (Blackorby and Wagner 1996; Rylance 1997; Phelps and Hanley-Maxwell 1997).

Workforce development for youth with disabilities is especially challenging at the beginning of the twenty-first century, a time of economic fluctuations and rapid technological change that increases the demand for highly skilled and trained workers. Legislation such as the Carl D. Perkins Vocational and Technical Education Act Amendment of 1998 and the Workforce Investment Act of 1998 has influenced school vocational training programs and interagency collaborations to promote youth workforce development. About 60 percent of secondary school youth participate in vocational education, including about half who take occupationally specific vocational education courses. In addition, school-sponsored on-the-job work experience is on the course schedules of one-fourth of youth with disabilities, with higher participation among high school juniors and seniors. Schools also provide a variety of vocational services that include youth with disabilities such as career skills assessment, counseling, job readiness training, job search instruction, job shadowing, placement support, and others.

Policy initiatives embedded in IDEA'97 include participation of students with disabilities in the kinds of classes and courses attended by the general student population. NLTS2 findings suggest that students with disabilities take challenging academic courses in greater proportions than they did a decade ago (Wagner, Newman, and Cameto 2004). The increase in academic coursework, often associated with postsecondary education preparation, demonstrates progress for some students with disabilities, but also corresponds with a marked decline in vocational course taking. Research has shown positive relationships between participation in occupation-specific vocational education courses and an increased likelihood of high school completion (Wagner 1991) and improved prospects for postschool employment and earnings for youth with disabilities (Wagner et al. 1993). A fine balance will be necessary within our policy environments to weigh carefully the benefits and value of academic inclusion and performance standards with those of vocational programs and job preparation.

Academic Performance and Assessment

NCLB is ratcheting up the pressure in schools to improve academic performance, with increased emphasis on assessing that performance as its cornerstone. This legislation poses a dilemma for students receiving special education, especially for those preparing for the transition to adulthood. NCLB requires schools to demonstrate annually increased proficiency in reading and math for the student population as a group by the end of their twelfth year in school, regardless of some students' disability status. Although increasing accountability may lead to better instruction and improved outcomes for many students, it can present insurmountable obstacles for students with cognitive disabilities that prohibit them from meeting grade-level standards.

Because students' participation in and performance on standardized tests help determine district and state compliance with NCLB accountability requirements, schools or districts may encourage linking special education IEP goals with the content standards of the general education curriculum to beef up test scores. Although that may function well for some students with disabilities, it may not adhere to the individualized objectives required by IDEA'97, which are based on specific student need rather than academic goals of the general student population. The conflicting intentions may affect how schools focus and allocate their resources for students with disabilities preparing for the transition from high school. It is possible that if school policies are entangled in accommodating the terms of NCLB to avoid sanctions, the more practical (and realistic) aspects of transition preparation for the majority of adolescent students receiving special education services will be left behind.

FEDERAL POLICIES AFFECTING YOUTH WITH DISABILITIES AFTER HIGH SCHOOL

When youth with disabilities leave school, they also leave behind the integrating features and supports of IDEA and other school-based legislation. IDEA provides a dedicated resource for school-age individuals with disabilities; once outside the school walls, young adults who need supports and services must cobble them together from a patchwork of adult-oriented policies, programs, and laws. If solid transition plans are developed and implemented while students are still in school, then prospects for positive postschool outcomes are heightened. Regardless, legislative strides have been made in the past few decades expanding community access and civil rights for all adults with disabilities, including young adults who received special education services. Most notable of these laws is the Americans with Disabilities Act (ADA).

Access and ADA: Employment, Postsecondary Education, and Independence

The Americans with Disabilities Act (ADA) was signed into law on July 26, 1990. Sweeping in its protection of individuals with disabilities, ADA prohibits discrimination in employment, postsecondary education, programs, and services provided by state and local governments, in goods and services provided by private companies, and in commercial facilities. It ensures that people with disabilities of all ages have equal access to employment, transportation, public spaces, and telecommunications. ADA requires that reasonable accommodations be made by businesses and public services to enable a person with a disability to use and enjoy the goods and services available to the rest of the public.

ADA embodies the fundamental principles of freedom and dignity in a democratic society. It serves as the foundation for a wide array of disability-related services and supports, including many that affect the emerging autonomy of young adults with disabilities. For example, Title II of ADA prohibits discrimination by public postsecondary education institutions and requires them to provide accommodations to qualified students to ensure their access to postsecondary programs and training opportunities. Specifically, ADA includes requirements for the provision of auxiliary aids and services (e.g., taped texts, interpreters, electronic readers, videotext displays, Braille equipment, assistive listening devises, and others) in higher education institutions that receive funding from the U.S. Department of Education.

ADA protections from discriminatory practices may affect young adults with disabilities during their transition years in such areas as obtaining adequate employment benefits and finding reasonable and, in some cases, accessible housing. Many of the ADA mandates target issues of access, including removing physical barriers so individuals with disabilities are able to enter buildings, use bathrooms, navigate store aisles, and get onto public transportation. But access also can mean inclusion policies such as the right to attend community events, participate in social or recreational activities, and find appropriate medical care. Access to the democratic process via voting also is a right protected by ADA and one that some young people with disabilities may otherwise miss.

ADA Title II regulations also coincide with nondiscrimination enforcement of Section 504 of the Rehabilitation Act of 1973. Section 504 can directly affect young people with disabilities across age-based settings, including while they are in secondary school (as described earlier), during transition, and as young adults. This legislation protects education and employment rights for people with disabilities and, in turn, influences vocational education and job preparation programs in secondary schools. It supports options during the transition years, such as vocational rehabilitation programs, independent living centers, and training projects for some youth whose disabilities substantially limit one or more major life activity and require reasonable accommodation to have access to public programs and services. One purpose of the act is to empower people with disabilities to prepare for and obtain postsecondary education and employment, with the long-term goal of economic self-sufficiency, independence, and community integration. The amendments adopted in 1992 require rehabilitation agencies to establish policies and procedures to facilitate the transition of youth with disabilities from school to the rehabilitation service system. In addition, the amendments to Section 508 of this act promote access to the Internet and information technology purchased by the federal government.[5]

Poverty and Public Assistance

Implementation of federal welfare reform through the Personal Responsibility and Work Opportunity Reconciliation Act of 1996 affects youth from families with incomes below the poverty level. Nearly a third of the nation's children live in families with incomes at or below 150 percent of the federal poverty line, and a disproportionate share of children and youth who grow up poor are identified as needing special education services (Wagner and Hebbeler 2000; Donovan and Cross 2002; Levine et al. 2003). Support services for these youth and their families have traditionally come from an assortment of policy environments such as health, education, and income assistance, including Temporary Assistance to Needy Families (TANF). Once these young adults turn age eighteen, and especially past their twenty-first birthdays, however, they are no longer protected under the policy umbrella that governs school and children. Taking on the responsibilities associated with public assistance eligibility mandates can add a particularly stressful demand during a time when young adults with disabilities already may be struggling with multiple issues of emerging independence.

Of particular relevance is the fact that TANF's reauthorization as the Personal Responsibility, Work and Family Promotion Act of 2003 requires that 70 percent of a state's welfare recipients work forty hours per week by the year 2008. A greater proportion of young people with disabilities than of nondisabled youth drop out of school and do not benefit from postsecondary education. Thus, they often are not well prepared to meet such work requirements. When they do find work, the jobs they obtain often are entry-level positions with low wages, no benefits, and few opportunities for advancement. In addition, young women with disabilities are more likely to become mothers during adolescence and early adulthood than their nondisabled peers, further challenging their ability to meet work requirements. Because youth with disabilities disproportionately experience the detrimental effects of poverty, they are much

5. The importance of technology and the Internet for youth with disabilities is described in detail in the previous chapter (and later in this chapter in the discussion of the New Freedom Initiative). The previous chapter also discusses the relationship between self-determination and adult independence. These features of the ADA are especially relevant for youth with disabilities in transition.

more susceptible to the repercussions of legislation and policies that link public assistance with work requirements.[6]

The Supplemental Security Income (SSI) program provides monthly cash benefits to people age sixty-five and older, and to people of any age if they have "a medically determinable physical or mental impairment which results in marked and severe functional limitations, and which can be expected to result in death or which has lasted or can be expected to last for a continuous period of not less than 12 months" (Social Security Administration 1997). Cash supplement programs, such as SSI, are essential for many families with children with disabilities, especially those with expensive medical, personal, or therapeutic care needs. But for many youth and young adults with disabilities, these types of cash programs can present a serious predicament as they seek employment. Young adults who receive SSI and Social Security Disability Insurance (SSDI) cash benefits are faced with the dilemma of losing their monthly stipends and their Medicare part A health care coverage if they get a job. This is especially troubling for youth with low cognitive or social functioning, because many entry-level and low-end, service-oriented jobs that would be appropriate and available to these youth often do not include benefits, nor pay enough to compensate for lost cash benefits. Further, these employment disincentives are contradictory to the mission of IDEA, ADA, and other legislation and policies aimed at increasing successful transitions for young adults with disabilities and reducing dependency on welfare and other entitlements (Wittenburg and Maag 2002).

Work Investment Polices: Effects on Employment and Independence

Several other federal policies affect young adults with disabilities as they maneuver their way through the transition years. The Ticket to Work and Work Incentives Improvement Act (TWWIIA) of 1999 included programmatic changes to vocational rehabilitation and SSI (among others) aimed at expanding rehabilitation and training opportunities and improving employment options and outcomes for youth and adults with disabilities (Livermore et al. 2000). Recent changes to this act expanded Medicare part A for SSDI recipients who are employed; it now addresses, in part, the employment disincentives associated with the loss of health care benefits (Commission on Excellence in Special Education 2002).

The Workforce Investment Act of 1998 (WIA) creates a comprehensive job training system that consolidates federally funded programs to streamline the

---

6. See previous chapter for details, data, and references regarding the many challenges facing youth with disabilities in transition, especially those related to poverty.

process of getting job training and employment services and help employers find skilled workers. Plans call for greater collaboration among the private sector, education and training institutions, social service agencies, and economic development systems to promote cooperative preparation strategies. Shared funding and resources by "one-stop" partner federal programs (e.g., Adult Education and Family Literacy, Vocational Rehabilitation, Unemployment Insurance) support local delivery systems aimed at eliminating barriers to service provision for at-risk or low-wage workers, including youth with disabilities (U.S. Department of Labor 2003).

Title I of WIA includes state and local workforce preparation requirements that specifically target the developmental needs of youth ages fourteen to twenty-one, regardless of whether they are in or out of school. Generally, WIA youth services are earmarked for any low-income youth who also qualifies as being a dropout, homeless, a runaway, in foster care, a teen parent, a juvenile offender, or deficient in basic skills. But there are exceptions to the income restrictions that are especially relevant to youth with disabilities in transition. For example, if family income disqualifies an individual, eligibility may be based on a youth's income instead. Moreover, up to 5 percent of youth served in a local area may be exempt from any income requirements if they have a disability or are at a grade level below the age-appropriate one. WIA also requires that at least 30 percent of its funds be used for youth who have dropped out of school, who have graduated or obtained a GED but are deficient in basic skills, or who are unemployed (National Collaborative on Workforce and Disability for Youth 2003). Clearly, the flexibility inherent in these eligibility rules is favorable to youth with disabilities as they transition to adulthood. The key is knowing the rules and how to use them.

Similar to IEPs used for individualizing special education programs, WIA services are determined by youth's individual needs and outlined in an "individual service strategy" document. WIA mandates that their services contain certain features that research has shown to be effective for at-risk youth. These include tutoring, dropout prevention strategies, occupational skills training, work experience (including summer employment, internships and job shadowing), adult mentoring, leadership development (including community service and peer-centered activities that encourage responsibility and decision-making skills), supportive services, and comprehensive guidance (including drug and alcohol abuse referral and counseling). In addition, follow-up is required for at least twelve months after program completion (National Collaborative on Workforce and Disability for Youth 2003). These types of services are ideal for youth with disabilities in transition as they face the various barriers to employment, postsecondary training, and independence.

Disability, Transition, and the New Millennium: The New Freedom Initiative

As the National Council on Disability puts it, "For Americans without disabilities, technology makes things easier. For Americans with disabilities, technology makes things possible." The New Freedom Initiative, announced by the Bush administration on February 1, 2001, is a comprehensive plan to facilitate independence and community living for people with disabilities through enactment of related legislation and policies. The initiative's wide-ranging proposals focus on increasing access to assistive technologies, educational opportunities, home ownership, workforce integration, and transportation options. The underlying purpose is to ensure that persons with disabilities have opportunities to develop skills and receive supports that will enable them to live independently within the community. Such opportunities are especially vital during the youths' transition years.

Technology. Through the New Freedom Initiative, federal dollars are available for research and marketing of assistive technologies, especially to small businesses that typically do not have the capital to compete. It provides opportunities to individuals with disabilities to acquire low-interest loans to offset the often prohibitive costs of adaptive technologies, such as specially outfitted computers, customized prosthetics and orthotics, and communication boards. The initiative also encourages workforce integration, including opportunities for telecommuting.[7] Employers may receive tax benefits by providing computers and Internet access to employees with disabilities so they have more flexibility to work from home. Particularly for people with mobility or health impairments or physical or sensory disabilities, and for individuals with disabilities living in rural or remote areas, this flexibility increases employment options and can avoid related barriers having to do with transportation or building access. The initiative also addresses controversial regulations by the U.S. Department of Labor's Occupational Safety and Health Administration (OSHA) that assert employer responsibility for upholding standards of home offices, a move some think would discourage employers from offering such options to their employees with disabilities for fear of liability. The initiative amends the Occupational Safety and Health Act of 1970 to disallow OSHA from regulating

---

7. Telecommuting, also known as teleworking, is working from home. The widespread availability of home computers, high-speed Internet access, and telephone conferencing (including video conferencing), along with other technological innovations, has inspired the proliferation of home offices and greater tolerance of telecommuting by employers. In some circumstances it is less expensive to have employees work from home than provide office space and associated supports.

home work sites of employees who commute to work through telecommunication, computers, and other electronic means.

Transportation. Getting to school, work, the supermarket, or a doctor's appointment can be a formidable task for young adults with disabilities who are dependent on others for transportation. The New Freedom Initiative provides federal funding to state and local programs that facilitate community-based alleviations to transportation barriers. Funds can be used by nonprofit organizations and businesses to outfit and operate specialty vans; assist individuals with costs of modifying a vehicle; support non–mass transit options, such as rideshare programs; and implement other projects that promote access to alternative transportation and increase employment options.

Residential independence. The New Freedom Initiative promotes residential independence by providing rental assistance vouchers for public housing to low-income Americans, including individuals with disabilities.[8] Vouchers also may be received as an annual lump sum that can be used to finance a down payment on a home mortgage.[9] In addition to enhancing independence and choice, this creates a base for building equity, which for youth just entering adulthood carries implications for greater future security.

Community participation. Matching funds also are available through the initiative for facility renovations that increase access for people with disabilities to places of worship, civic organizations, and private clubs that are exempt under the ADA Title III mandates. This proposal also supports improved access to polling places and assures voting privacy. For young adults with disabilities who may have experienced a greater level of dependency or lack of choice than the general population, voting can symbolize emerging autonomy and societal trust. These in turn can underscore the responsibilities of duty and encourage personal decisions and actions that accompany the privileges of civic participation.

Economic Shifts and Funding Constraints

Laws help shape policy, and policy guides practice. But the success of America's vast legal and social structures is dependent on the consistent commitment of sufficient resources and adequate financial support. As shown in chapter 8, a high unemployment rate does not bode well for young adults with disabilities, especially during the transition years. In fact, the events that shook American

---

8. This is one of the strategies to reform Section 8 of the 1937 Housing Act.

9. The American Homeownership and Economic Opportunity Act of 2000 (PL 106-569) expands rental allowances for people who qualify for Section 8.

social and economic stability during the first few years of the twenty-first century threaten to have an adverse effect on some of the advances experienced by people with disabilities during the previous two decades.[10] These include intensifying the employment gap between people with disabilities and the general population.[11]

The federal budget for fiscal year 2004, proposed by President Bush on February 3, 2003, reflects the depressed economic picture and heightened political tension of the time. Many of the domestic programs that were developed or thrived during the latter part of the twentieth century were earmarked for elimination, reduction, or replacement. The large majority of these programs are housed in the Departments of Labor, Health and Human Services, and Education, agencies that typically serve vulnerable populations. For example, reductions were proposed for almost every program in the Department of Labor, including adult and dislocated employee services, and several programs targeting youth. Although the Department of Education's budget included some increased funding for special education programs, these were countered, in part, by elimination or reduction of funding for more than sixty social service programs, many of which affect people with disabilities (Maloney and Browning 2003). These and other funding reductions and associated policy and programmatic changes across all these departments (and others) have potentially adverse effects on youth with disabilities, especially as they transition from special education programs to an adult world that currently is steeped in difficult economic times.

BEYOND POLICY AND LEGISLATION

We find that the overriding barrier preventing a smooth transition from high school to adult living is the fundamental failure of federal policies and programs to facilitate smooth movement for students from secondary school to competitive employment and higher education.

Commission on Excellence in Special Education 2002, 46

Starting an independent adult life can be confusing for many youth with disabilities, but for some, it is overwhelming. It is a process experienced by all

---

10. Many of the changes and consequences for youth with disabilities of events occurring in the new millennium are discussed in chapter 8.

11. Among eighteen- to twenty-nine-year olds with disabilities who reported being able to work, half are employed, compared to almost three-quarters of their peers without disabilities (National Organization on Disabilities 2000).

youth as they reach the age of majority, but, unlike many of their nondisabled peers, young adults with disabilities often must rely on a labyrinth of public supports and services to achieve a minimum level of independence. As shown earlier in this chapter, the bundle of supports needed by youth with disabilities varies dramatically by the type, duration, and intensity of a wide range of disabilities, functional attributes, and family backgrounds. For example, a young adult with cerebral palsy and mental retardation may need a wide range of services, such as accessible transportation, supported employment, a group home, or attendant care. On the other hand, a high school graduate with a visual or hearing impairment may continue to college and a career needing only technical or prosthetic devises that aid mobility or communication. Youth with emotional disturbances may need intensive mental health interventions; an individual with a learning disability may transition from school to employment without any of these services.

But for many young adults with disabilities and their families, the process of acquiring the needed supports, especially outside of secondary school, can require enormous effort to identify, locate, demonstrate eligibility for, and coordinate needed services within sometimes discordant and disjointed social service and education systems. Despite efforts at both the federal and state levels to create a cohesive transition for students with disabilities from secondary schools to adult life, youth who need services in their postschool years can face conflicting eligibility standards, extensive documentation requirements, confusing payment structures, inconsistent procedures, and inexperienced staff.

For ethnically, culturally, and linguistically diverse students with disabilities, and for those whose disabilities are severe, these barriers are compounded by multiple factors, such as language, culture, or social class differences, lack of awareness or information about resources, lack of contacts or connections, and overall systemic inadequacies. These youth generally receive fewer disability-related services than the majority of their peers with disabilities and have far fewer opportunities to experience postsecondary education, meaningful work, and community integration (Flowers and Edwards 1996; Whelley, Hart, and Zaft 2002).

Educators, adult service providers, rehabilitation providers, and employment agencies often lack knowledge about each other's systems, rules, and procedures and are hampered by bureaucratic constraints and resources that preclude interagency cooperation. Decisions regarding placement, service provision, and duration of support can be agency driven and dependent on availability, waiting lists, financial resources, or narrow eligibility criteria, rather than on individual need.

As noted earlier, schools generally are the source of services and supports for school-age children with disabilities. Special education laws govern the policy direction and financing of most of these school-based services, including transportation and nonacademic supports (e.g., durable medical equipment, therapies, after-school programs). Community-based resources are tapped only after exhausting school sources, with the exception of pediatric or adolescent health care and psychiatric or mental health care. The shift from child- or youth-oriented services to adult services often is abrupt and poorly aligned, potentially causing problems with treatment consistency, information exchange, trusting relationships, and overall access. For example, youth with special health care needs find widely variable practices and standards and a lack of communication when they transition from pediatric care to adult health care, which can cause risky disruptions (Patterson and Lanier 1999).

The lack of continuity among and across service agencies can be described as vertical (from child-based to adult-based services) or lateral (from one agency to another). Interagency cooperation at the state and local levels is more common than even ten years ago, but there remains a need for a local and national comprehensive mechanism to map resources, identify or address service gaps, or coordinate communication and information sharing across agencies (Hart, Zimbrich, and Whelley 2002). The need for such a system is particularly salient for youth with multiple or complex needs who find themselves having to contend with new, often conflicting rules and procedures across services and supports.

Maneuvering through the Services Maze

Research has identified a variety of general strategies to address some of these barriers, including teaming, collaborative partnerships, individual empowerment, shared decision-making, self-determination, taking responsibility for the consequences of one's own actions, consumer choice, family involvement, focus on strengths, and providing services locally (O'Brien and Lovett 1993; Everson and Guillory 1998; Stodden and Smith 1996; Mitchell 1999). Winnick (1999) suggests the use of a personal support broker to guide the process.[12]

Recommendations also include the development of a national Web-based registry of postsecondary education institutions that focuses on the type and level of education support services and accommodations provided by those institutions. This would allow users to do a regional search for support provisions by type and level of disability. Support services also would share data and information on evidence-based practices for supporting a wider variety of individuals in postsecondary education (Stodden and Jones 2002).

---

12. A personal support broker is a person who is trusted by the individual with a disability, cares about the person, and can provide the time and energy to help figure out what is needed and how to get it.

The need for collaboration among multiple players at the individual and interagency systems levels (e.g., districts, schools, adult service providers, students, families, community organizations, employers, postsecondary institutions), is consistently articulated in both IDEA'97 and in research on promising practices (Kohler 1998; Everson and Guillory 1998; National Information Center for Children and Youth with Disabilities 1999; Chadsey, Leach, and Shelden 2001). Collaboration among all the players is the key to eliminating service gaps, duplication, or discontinuation and ensuring greater efficiency with limited and decreasing resources (Hart, Zimbrich, and Whelley 2002).

Policy Innovation Most Needed

There is growing recognition among educators, social service providers, and policy makers, that it is not only detrimental to compartmentalize children and youth within the bureaucratic slots traditionally defined by agencies and services, but it also is financially irresponsible and wasteful of resources. This recognition has led to greater communication and collaboration among professionals and academics in a variety of arenas (social, educational, psychological, health care, and political), with a common concern for the well-being of troubled or disenfranchised youth. Clearly, youth come through the various social service doors for multiple reasons that often confound eligibility rules, and with far more overlap than has been adequately documented. For example, approximately 30 to 50 percent of youth in juvenile corrections are identified as having a disability and are eligible for special education services (Burrell and Warboys 2000; see also chapters 3 and 4, on the juvenile justice system). Similarly, it is estimated that half of youth in foster care receive special education services while in school (Seyfried et al. 2000; see also Courtney and Heuring's chapter 2, on foster care) A disproportionate share of children and youth served by special education are poor, members of ethnic minorities, or English language learners; experience mental illness or chronic health impairments; and are at risk of falling victim to child abuse and violence. Changes in services in one program can be felt elsewhere in the complex maze of agencies that may be encountered in efforts to meet these diverse needs, but they are difficult to measure and understand in the bigger context. When there are service gaps, mismanagement, poor communication, or an information vacuum in one or more agencies with overlapping populations or missions, there is something of a ripple effect across the policy environments. This can create client backlogs, confusion, resource depletion, and numerous other problems.

An alternative to the entangled and at times conflicting service delivery and policy systems is a fresh version of old ideas (Edgar and Maddox 1982), through which service provision is made available through a "single-portal" approach to eligibility, funding, and support. A single entry and delivery point can reduce red tape, paperwork, client confusion, and lengthy waiting lists and alleviate the tendency for individuals who don't fit neatly into any one service category to fall through the cracks of agency ineligibility. A single-portal system would view youth from a holistic perspective and provide services according to individual need rather than agency or institutional criteria.

In October 2003, the U.S. Department of Health and Human Services provided one-year planning grants to thirty-one agencies serving children and adults with developmental disabilities and their families to develop a plan for coordinating efforts among agencies serving the same populations. Targeted agencies provide a variety of services including health and mental health care, family support, food stamps, child care, housing, transportation, special education, job training, and employment. The long-term goal is for agencies to enter into partnerships with one another and establish "one-stop shopping centers" where families can go to obtain services that are coordinated, outcome-oriented, and family-centered (U.S. Department of Health and Human Services 2003). If these collaborative efforts are successful, the process may serve as the model for expansion to agencies serving a wider range of populations. The innovation that should follow is a more comprehensive model that incorporates a one-stop mechanism that attends to all the related needs of individuals who have more than one vulnerability (e.g., a young man with a disability who received special education services, lives in foster care, has substance abuse problems, and has dropped out of school).

System Reform

American social service systems have typically provided services when individuals become dysfunctional (Hart, Zimbrich, and Whelley 2002). Reforming the system involves moving from the culture of failure that underlies this approach to one of prevention, early and accurate identification of learning and behavior problems, and aggressive intervention based on state-of-the-art research. This paradigm extends to planning and providing services for transition. By setting up a proactive system that supports early identification and prevention of high-risk behaviors and habits that are associated with detrimental long-term outcomes, rather than waiting for the problems to happen, there would be less of a scramble to correct them. The reactive "wait and fix it" approach too often results in punitive responses, such as expulsion and adjudication.

The medical model of disability, with its focus on fixing the person to fit society, has slowly lost credibility, acquiescing to a broader social model focused on access and transforming our communities to accommodate all their citizens. In truth, the paradigm is complex, with education, training, preparation, and good citizenship on the part of the individual meeting access, accommodation, acceptance, and long-term support from society.

Laws such as ADA and IDEA have brought to the forefront a growing societal awareness of people with diverse disabilities as viable members of the workforce and contributing citizens in our communities. Decades of research have demonstrated that people with diverse disabilities can successfully perform meaningful work, take advantage of postsecondary education and life-long learning opportunities, enjoy residential, financial, and decision-making independence, and participate fully as friends and neighbors (e.g., Benz, Doren, and Yovanoff 1998; Horn and Berktold 1999; Blackorby and Wagner 1996; Wagner, Blackorby, Cameto, and Newman 1993). But laws and policies alone, even with ample funding and service collaboration, cannot prevent discrimination against people with disabilities, create opportunities, or welcome a person to an accessible community. The reality of policy implementation, especially at the local level, goes well beyond legislative mandates. System reform is a matter of societal reform, which requires changes in public attitudes that inspire changes in the way communities function.

The Commission on Excellence in Special Education was created in October 2001 to study America's special education system through a series of open forums and public hearings with families, teachers, organizations, community providers, and individuals with disabilities. A year later, the commission compiled the findings from these hearings along with hundreds of written comments and published a set of recommendations for system reform in a document entitled *A New Era: Revitalizing Special Education for Children and Their Families* (Commission on Excellence in Special Education 2002). The report calls for a fundamental shift in the system's priorities to more clearly emphasize the individual needs of children and youth with disabilities so as to support improved in-school and postschool outcomes. The report advocates for policy reforms that embrace accountability for improved outcomes. The commission argues that now that access to a free, appropriate, and individualized public education is guaranteed by law for all children and youth through IDEA'97, it is time for policy makers to transcend compliance and process, and attend to achieving results.

On the other hand, it is imperative that the results sought at the system level do not overshadow the results sought for individuals. Individualized goals are at the heart of special education practice and directly affect postschool outcomes for youth in transition. The challenge of current reform efforts will be to find the appropriate balance between establishing system-wide achievement requirements for all students and accommodating the wide range of practical skill requirements for youth receiving special education services. The litmus test for true accountability rests in long-term outcomes—how those who had received special education services as children and adolescents fare not just during transition and early adulthood, but into adulthood. For real accountability, those outcomes must be measured and monitored regularly.

THE EVOLUTION OF DISABILITY POLICY: SUMMING UP

The past century witnessed enormous growth and maturation in American society's treatment of its most vulnerable citizens; in this case, children, youth, and adults with disabilities. From segregated institutional care to guaranteed education and civil rights, the immense changes that occurred in special education and disability laws and services over the latter part of the twentieth century reflect a profound paradigm shift giving rise to a new way of thinking about individuals with diverse disabilities and their potential. This has resulted in increased access to community resources and a heightened focus on the transitions and long-term outcomes of youth with disabilities as they maneuver through the labyrinth of choices, barriers, and opportunities that lead to adulthood.

There have been immense strides in legislation on behalf of children and youth with disabilities. Nevertheless, implementation of the laws and policies at the national and state levels remains dependent on historical precedents, prominent political leadership, and current priorities of the administrations in power. The move from policy to practice at the local and individual levels is shaped by community demographics, economic health, and availability of resources and funding, factors that are susceptible to frequent fluctuation and instability (Hasazi, Furney, and DeStefano 1997; Singer et al. 1986).

The transition from school-based services to adult services presents numerous challenges to youth seeking support from the widely variable and often conflicting agencies, especially for young adults with more severe or complex disabilities. Recommendations for resolving some of these barriers include collaborative, coordinated efforts among agencies, schools, postsecondary institutions, employers, and individuals with disabilities and establishing a single-portal access to support whereby services are provided according to need rather than agency eligibility or criteria.

Chapter 8, highlighting the challenges for youth with disabilities who receive special education services as children and adolescents, and this chapter, discussing related legislation and policies, reflect on transition issues for this population as they occur across time and in the larger context of our rapidly changing world. Some of these changes include demographic shifts in the student population, the changing nature of the workplace and economic fluctuation, increased advocacy of and focus on self-determination, technology's rapidly changing stature, widespread Internet use, and increased attention to youth violence, risk, and resilience. Many of the changes are rooted in technological advances and environmental transformations that touch American society in general; other differences come from global circumstances and paradigm shifts within education and social policy and practice. All of these factors influence and have significant and powerful implications for the transition and long-term outcomes of youth with disabilities as they seek a quality of life as adults. We have entered an unpredictable and turbulent period in our history. Perhaps now, more than ever before, it is vital to understand how our education, social, and political systems will respond, how school and social policies will shift, and most important, how our most vulnerable children, youth, and young adults will cope as they transition from childhood to adulthood during the coming years.

REFERENCES

Affleck, J. Q., E. Edgar, P. Levine, and L. Kortering. 1990. Postschool status of students classified as mildly mentally retarded, learning disabled, or nonhandicapped: Does it get better with time? *Education and Training in Mental Retardation* 25: 315–324.

Barrows, I. 1913. George Henry Knight. *Journal of Psycho-asthenics* 18: 3–7.

Benz, M., B. Doren, and P. Yovanoff. 1998. Crossing the great divide: Predicting productive engagement for young women with disabilities. *Career Development for Exceptional Individuals* 62: 3–16.

Blackorby, J., and M. Wagner. 1996. Longitudinal post-school outcomes of youth with disabilities: Findings from the National Longitudinal Transition Study. *Exceptional Children* 6: 399–413.

Boehne, G. M. 1912. Regarding special classes for sub-normal children. *Journal of Psycho-asthenics* 17: 20–28.

Burrell, S., and L. Warboys. 2000. Special education and the juvenile justice system. U.S. Department of Justice, Office of Juvenile Justice and Delinquency Prevention. http://www.ncjrs.org/pdffiles1/ojjdp/179359.pdf.

Burstein, L. 1980. The role of levels of analysis in the specification of educational effects. Pp. 119–190 in *Analysis of educational productivity: Issues in microanalysis.* Edited by R. Dreeben and J. A. Thomas. Cambridge, MA: Ballinger.

Cameto, R. 1993. Support services provided by secondary schools. In *The secondary school programs of students with disabilities.* Edited by M. Wagner. Menlo Park, CA: SRI International.

Cameto, R., P. Levine, and M. Wagner. 2003. The emerging independence of youth with disabilities. In *The achievements of youth with disabilities during secondary school: A report from the National Longitudinal Transition Study-2 (NLTS2).* Edited by M. Wagner, C. Marder, J. Blackorby, R. Cameto, L. Newman, and P. Levine. Menlo Park, CA: SRI International.

Cameto, R., P. Levine, and M. Wagner. 2004. *Transition planning for students with disabilities: A special topic report of findings from the National Longitudinal Transition Study-2 (NLTS-2).* Menlo Park, CA: SRI International.

Cameto, R., and M. Wagner. 2003. Vocational education courses and services. In *Going to school: What it's like for youth with disabilities: A report from the National Longitudinal Transition Study-2 (NLTS2).* Edited by M. Wagner, L. Newman, R. Cameto, P. Levine, and C. Marder. Menlo Park, CA: SRI International.

Chadsey, J., Leach, L. and Shelden, D. 2001. *Including youth with disabilities in education reform: Lessons learned from school-to-work states.* Champaign: University of Illinois at Urbana-Champaign, Transition Research Institute.

Cohen, M. D. 2003. *Section 504 and IDEA: Limited vs. substantial protections for Children with AD/HD and other disabilities.* http://www.chadd.org/pdfs/Section_504_and_by_Matt_Cohen.pdf.

Commission on Excellence in Special Education. 2002. *A new era: Revitalizing special education for children and their families.* Washington: U.S. Department of Education Office of Special Education and Rehabilitative Services. http://www.ed.gov/inits/commissionsboards/whspecialeducation/reports/index.html.

Dixon, B., and D. Carnine. 1993. The hazards of poorly designed instructional tools. *Learning Disabilities Forum* 18: 18–22.

Donovan, M. S., and C. T. Cross, eds. 2002. *Minority students in special and gifted education.* Washington: National Academy Press.

Fitts, A. M. 1916. How to fill the gap between the special classes and the institution. *Journal of Psycho-asthenics* 20: 78–87.

Edgar, E. 1990. Education's role in improving our quality of life: Is it time to change our view of the world? *Beyond Behavior,* winter, 9–13.

Edgar, E., and M. Maddox. 1982. *The cookbook model: An approach to interagency collaboration.* Seattle: Experimental Education Unit, University of Washington.

Everson, J., and J. Guillory. 1998. Building statewide transition services through collaborative interagency teamwork. In *Beyond high school: Transition from school to work.* Edited by F. R. Rusch and J. G. Chadsey. Belmont, CA: Wadsworth Publishing.

Flowers, C. R., and D. Edwards. 1996. Rehabilitation cultural diversity initiative: A regional survey of cultural diversity with CILS. *Journal of Rehabilitation,* July–September: 22–27.

Halpern, A. S. 1990. A methodological review of follow-up and follow-along studies tracking school leavers from special education. *Career Development of Exceptional Individuals* 13: 13–27.

Halpern, A. S. 1992. Transition: Old wine in new bottles. *Exceptional Children* 58: 202–211.

Halpern, A. S. 1999. Transition: Is it time for another rebottling? Paper presented at the 1999 Annual OSEP Project Directors' Meeting, Washington.

Hart, D., K. Zimbrich, and T. Whelley. 2002. Challenges in coordinating and managing services and supports in secondary and postsecondary options. *ERIC Issue Brief* 1: 1–8. http://searchERIC.org/ericdc/ED475332.

Hasazi, S. B., K. S. Furney, and L. DeStefano. 1997. Transition policies, practices, and promises: Lessons from three states. *Exceptional Children* 63: 343–355.

Hasazi, S. B., K. S. Furney, and L. DeStefano. 1999. Implementing the IDEA transition mandates. *Exceptional Children* 65: 555–566.

Hasazi, S. B., R. Gordon, and C. A. Roe. 1985. Factors associated with the employment status of handicapped youth exiting high school from 1979 to 1983. *Exceptional Children* 51: 455–469.

Heal, L. W., J. I. Copher, L. DeStefano, and F. Rusch. 1999. A comparison of successful and unsuccessful placements of secondary students with mental handicaps into competitive employment. *Career Development of Exceptional Individuals* 12: 167–177.

Horn, R., and J. Berktold. 1999. *Students with disabilities in postsecondary education: A profile of preparation, participation, and outcomes.* National Center on Education Statistics, U.S. Department of Education, Statistical Analysis Report no. 199–187. Washington: U.S. Government Printing Office.

Johnson, D. R., and M. N. Sharpe. 2000. Results of a national survey on the implementation of transition service requirements of IDEA. *Journal of Special Education Leadership* 13: 15–26.

Kohler, P. 1998. Implementing a transition perspective on education: A comprehensive approach to planning and delivering secondary education and transition services. Pp. 179–203 in *Beyond high school: Transition from school to work.* Edited by F. R. Rusch and J. G. Chadsey. Belmont, CA: Wadsworth Publishing.

Kuhlman. 1917. Minutes. *Journal of Psycho-asthenics* 22: 20–59.

Levine, P., C. Marder, M. Wagner, and D. Cardoso. 2003. Characteristics of students' households. In *The children we serve: The demographic characteristics of elementary and middle school students with disabilities and their households: A report from the National Longitudinal Transition Study-2 (NLTS2).* Edited by M. Wagner, C. Marder, and J. Blackorby. Menlo Park, CA: SRI International.

Levine, P., and S. Nourse. 1998. What follow-up studies say about postschool life for young men and women with learning disabilities: A critical look at the literature. *Journal of Learning Disabilities* 13: 212–233.

Livermore, G., M. Nowak, D. Wittenburg, and E. Eiseman. 2000. *Policy brief: Policies and programs affecting the employment of people with disabilities.* Draft report submitted to the Department of Education, National Institute on Disability and Rehabilitation Research.

Maloney, J., and J. Browning. 2003. *LDA News from Washington,* March-April. Learning Disabilities Association of America.

Meyer, E., and T. Skrtic. 1995. *Special education and student disability: An introduction to traditional, emerging, and alternative perspectives.* Denver: Love Publishing.

Milburn, R. M. 1909. Problems of feeble-mindedness. *Journal of Psycho-asthenics* 13: 51–59.

Mitchell, D. 1999. *Managed care and developmental disabilities: Reconciling the realities of managed care with the individual needs of persons with disabilities.* Homewood, IL: High Tide Press.

National Collaborative on Workforce and Disability for Youth (NCWD). 2003. Serving youth with disabilities under the Workforce Investment Act of 1998: The basics. *Info Brief, 4,* September. NCWD/Youth All Publications. www.ncwd-youth.info.

National Council on Disability. 2000. *Back to school on civil rights.* Washington: National Council on Disability.

National Council on Disability. 2002. *The New Freedom Initiative.* www.whitehouse.gov/news/freedominitiative/text/freedominitiative.html

National Information Center for Children and Youth with Disabilities (NICHCY). 1999. Transition planning: A team effort. *National Information Center for Children and Youth with Disabilities,* vol. TS10 (January): 1–24.

National Organization on Disabilities. 2000. *2000 N.O.D./Harris survey of Americans with disabilities.* Washington: Louis Harris and Associates.

National Research Council. 1998. *Preventing reading difficulties in young children.* Washington: National Academy Press.

Newman, L., and M. Wagner. 2003. Family expectations for the future. In *The achievements of youth with disabilities during secondary school: A report from the National Longitudinal Transition Study-2 (NLTS2).* Edited by M. Wagner, C. Marder, J. Blackorby, R. Cameto, L. Newman, and P. Levine. Menlo Park, CA: SRI International.

O'Brien, J., and H. Lovett. 1993. *Finding a way toward everyday lives: The contribution of person-centered planning.* Harrisburg: Pennsylvania Office of Mental Retardation.

Patterson, D. L., and C. Lanier. 1999. Adolescent health transitions: Focus group study of teens and young adults with special health care needs. *Family and Community Health* 22: 43–58.

Phelps, L. A., and C. Hanley-Maxwell. 1997. School-to-work transitions for youth with disabilities: A review of outcomes and practices. *Review of Educational Research* 67: 197–226.

Pinsent, H. 1906. The employment of the feeble-minded. *Journal of Psycho-asthenics* 9: 184–190.

Rothstein, D., and D. Herz. 2000. *A detailed look at employment of youths aged 12 to 15.* Washington: U.S. Bureau of Labor Statistics.

Rylance, B. J. 1997. Predictors of high school graduation or dropping out for youths with severe emotional disturbances. *Behavioral Disorders* 23: 5–17.

Seyfried, S., P. J. Pecora, A. C. Downs, P. Levine, and J. Emerson. 2000. Assessing the educational outcomes of children in long-term foster care: First findings. *School Social Work Journal* 24: 68–88.

Singer, J. D., J. A. Butler, J. S. Palfrey, and D. K. Walther. 1986. Characteristics of special education placements: Findings from probability samples in five metropolitan school districts. *Journal of Special Education* 20: 319–337.

Social Security Administration (SSA). 1997. *Annual statistical supplement to the Social Security Bulletin, 1997.* Washington: Social Security Administration.

Social Security Administration. 1999. *Number of SSI recipients by category and age, December 1975 to September 1999.* http://www.ssa.gov/policy/programs/ssi2.html.

Social Security Administration. 2001. *Social Security online: Social Security Administration launches new program to help people with disabilities go to work.* www.ssa.gov/pressoffice.

Stodden, R. A., and M. Jones. 2002. Implication for policy, practice, and priorities in postsecondary education and employment: Report on proceedings from the National Policy Summit in Washington (teleconference).

Stodden, R. A., and G. J. Smith. 1996. *The nine principals of teaming.* Honolulu: Hawaii UAP Multimedia Productions.

U.S. Department of Education. 1998. *Auxiliary aids and services for postsecondary students with disabilities: Higher education's obligations under Section 504 and Title II of the ADA.* Washington: U.S. Department of Education, Office of Civil Rights.

U.S. Department of Education. 2001a. *Twenty-third annual report to Congress on the implementation of the Individuals with Disabilities Education Act.* Washington: U.S. Department of Education.

U.S. Department of Education. 2001b. *The IDEA Amendment Acts of 1997.* http://www.ed.gov/offices/OSERS/Policy/IDEA.

U.S. Department of Health and Human Services (HHS). 2003. New programs to support fami-

lies of and persons with developmental disabilities (press release), October 13. www.acf.dhhs
.gov/programs/add/hhsgrants.htm.

U.S. Department of Labor. 2003. *The Workforce Investment Act of 1998*. www.doleta.gov.

Wagner, M. 1991. *Dropouts with disabilities: What do we know? What can we do? A report from the National Longitudinal Transition Study of Special Education Students*. Menlo Park, CA: SRI International.

Wagner, M., J. Blackorby, R. Cameto, and L. Newman. 1993. *What makes a difference? Influences on postschool outcomes of youth with disabilities*. Menlo Park, CA: SRI International.

Wagner, M., R. Cameto, and L. Newman. 2003. *Youth with disabilities: A changing population*. Menlo Park, CA. SRI International.

Wagner, M., and K. Hebbeler. 2000. *Representation of minorities and children of poverty among those receiving early intervention and special education services: Findings from two national longitudinal studies*. Menlo Park, CA: SRI International.

Wagner, M., L. Newman, and R. Cameto. 2004. *Changes over time in the secondary school experiences of students with disabilities: A report of findings from the National Longitudinal Transition Study (NLTS) and the National Longitudinal Transition Study-2 (NLTS2)*. Menlo Park, CA: SRI International.

Whelley, T., D. Hart, and C. Zaft. 2002. *Coordination and management of services and supports for individuals with disabilities from secondary to postsecondary education and employment*. http://www.rrtc.hawaii.edu/products/phases/phase3.asp (MS#072-H02).

Will, M. 1984. Bridges from school to working life. *Programs for the Handicapped: Clearinghouse on the Handicapped,* March/April, 1–5.

Winnick, D., ed. 1999. *Implementing choice: A guide for understanding self-directed services*. Madison, WI: Dane County, Department of Human Services.

Wittenburg, D. C., and E. Maag. 2002. School to where? A literature review on economic outcomes of youth with disabilities. *Journal of Vocational Rehabilitation* 17: 265–280.

Wolfensberger, W. 1983. Social role valorization: a proposed new term for the principle of normalization. *Mental Retardation* 21: 234–239.

CHAPTER TEN

Risks along the Road to Adulthood: Challenges Faced by Youth with Serious Mental Disorders

J. HEIDI GRALINSKI-BAKKER, STUART T. HAUSER,
REBECCA L. BILLINGS, AND JOSEPH P. ALLEN

This review was supported by the MacArthur Foundation Research Network on the Transitions to Adulthood and a grant from the National Institute of Mental Health R01 MH44934-12, "Adolescent Paths to Successful Midlife Adjustment."

INTRODUCTION

Over the past twenty years, a series of national-level reports have focused attention on treatment and prevention of adolescent mental disorders (U.S. Public Health Service 1999, 2000). Broadly speaking, these reports raised public awareness about some of the issues and problems in the field of adolescent mental health. In this process, attention has been paid to describing the scope of mental disorders during adolescence and defining adolescent mental health needs. There also has been growing interest in understanding the effectiveness of treatments for helping adolescents who are struggling to cope with mental disorders. Of particular concern are questions about the benefits of treatment in everyday practice including the systemic contexts in which treatments are provided (Bickman 1996; Stroul and Friedman 1996; Weisz and Jensen 1999). A common theme has been the personal and social costs of mental disorders, including links with teens' capacities to develop age-appropriate skills needed to carry out their personal, educational, family, and social responsibilities. More recently, this theme has been extended to include longer-term consequences of adolescent mental disorders with a view toward understanding how they may affect psychological growth and functioning over time (National Advisory Mental Health Council Workgroup on Child and Adolescent Mental Health Intervention Development and Deployment 2001).

With this longitudinal interest in mind, this chapter summarizes what is known about the course and consequences of mental disorders during the period of *transition* from adolescence through the late teens and early twenties. In recent years, this age period has been conceptualized as *emerging adulthood*, reflecting an extended period of transition from adolescence to adult life in contemporary industrialized societies (Arnett 2000). This period of transition involves changing expectations and new demands. Emerging adulthood is characterized by explorations of ideas, opportunities, and lifestyles. It is a time when adult commitments and responsibilities are delayed as young people develop their own beliefs and values, explore multiple roles, and have varied life experiences. The major challenges facing emerging adults include developing a mature view of self; making choices about education or employment; leaving the parental home; establishing intimate romantic relationships; making independent decisions; and learning to accept responsibility for one's self (Eccles et al. 2001).

The transition to becoming an adult is a challenge for all young people in our society, but young people with serious mental disorders may travel an especially challenging road. In general, there is considerable variation in individual trajectory patterns over the emerging adult period (Cohen et al. 2003). School attendance is one area in which there is substantial diversity. About 50 percent of America's high school graduates pursue postsecondary education in the year following high school. However, only 32 percent complete their undergraduate college education in four to five years (U.S. Census Bureau 2000). Some combine college education with work, while others return to school after periods of nonattendance. Moreover, a substantial minority (40 percent) do not pursue higher education after high school. Depending on the path taken, differences in level of education and training are likely to affect people's incomes and occupational achievements for the remainder of their adult work lives (William T. Grant Foundation Commission on Work 1988). College students typically experience the transition to marriage and parenting at a later date than their noncollege peers (Sherrod, Haggerty, and Featherman 1993). For these young people, the delay in assuming adult roles may provide additional opportunities to prepare for the challenges they will face as adults, to focus on career development, and to explore the roles and behaviors they will ultimately integrate into their adult lives (Cohen et al. 2003).

Despite the possibility of such long-term effects, there is no single "normal" course that everyone must follow during emerging adulthood and there are no absolute criteria signaling completion. As a result, emerging adulthood may be relatively short for those who quickly take on adult roles and responsibilities compared with those who postpone such commitments. By the end of this

period, however, most young people have made life choices that have important implications for their adult lives. In other words, some may be on their way
to productive and satisfying adult lives, while others may be at risk for a range
of negative outcomes. The result may be a diminished quality of life and a limited sense of psychological well-being.

Within a developmental framework, we review what is known about emerging adulthood for adolescents from an especially vulnerable population—those
selected for out-of-home treatment in residential mental health settings. In
general, our review is influenced by social policy concerns about what happens
to these young people when they "age out" of the adolescent mental health care
system. Specifically, it is guided by questions about longer-term recovery and
functioning among young people who received the most expensive and most
restrictive care when they were adolescents. For example, do those who received
out-of-home treatment during adolescence suffer from recurrent symptoms of
mental disorders? Do serious adolescent-era mental disorders derail development in ways that compromise abilities to make a successful transition to becoming an adult? How do these emerging adults function in school, and then
as workers, partners, and parents? Are mental health services and supports
available?

To address these questions, we consider what is known from published research about the extent to which this vulnerable population struggles with the
transition to adulthood. We focus on patterns of continuity and change in signs
and symptoms of common mental disorders, including mood, anxiety, and disruptive behavior or conduct disorders. We also consider evidence describing
how those with adolescent-era mental disorders approach emergent adult roles,
including key areas of school, work, and love. Well-planned choices and emergent competencies are likely to increase the chances of a successful transition to
adult life (Clausen 1991). In contrast, those who lack direction or have problems in key social roles tend to be at high risk for continuing maladaptive outcomes over time.

Although there is growing awareness that many teens with mental disorders
continue to struggle with many challenges of everyday life, there is relatively
little recent research linking serious mental disorders and their correlates during adolescence to later adjustment during the transition to becoming an adult.
Despite the heuristic appeal of developmental transitions, the significance of
emerging adulthood as a transition to becoming an adult has only recently been
identified and examined (e.g., Cohen et al. 2003; Shiner, Masten, and Tellegen
2002). More specifically, there are few studies of the unique mental health
needs of emerging adults, leading to limited information about pathways from
adolescence through the late teens and early twenties among young people with

serious mental disorders. Because this is a complex topic requiring increasing conceptual and empirical efforts, our intent is to summarize key findings that may help to draw attention to a vulnerable population within an under-studied developmental transition. Within this context, we acknowledge that longitudinal and causal pathways are incompletely understood. There also is a high degree of variation among young people with serious mental disorders in terms of symptoms, causes, course of the disorder, response to treatment, mechanisms of change, and outcomes over time. Explication of such diversity is beyond the scope of this brief review. Instead, our focus is on the most common and debilitating disorders, including mood and disruptive behavior disorders. The most common mood disorder is depression, which is one of the leading causes of disability worldwide (Murray and Lopez 1996). In turn, disruptive behavior disorders involving persistent antisocial and aggressive behaviors are a form of psychopathology that is very costly for society and those who suffer from it (Moffitt et al. 2002; Robins 1966; Simons et al. 2002).[1] Our primary emphasis is on research that describes markers of adjustment to the transition to becoming an adult from psychological and psychiatric perspectives. Although recognized when germane, evidence from neuroscience, genetics, pharmacology, and other biological perspectives are beyond the scope of this review.

MENTAL HEALTH DISORDERS DURING ADOLESCENCE AND EMERGING ADULTHOOD

To understand the nature and significance of mental disorders among adolescents receiving residential mental health treatment, we begin with an overview of the magnitude and costs of mental disorders in the general population. For example, what are current estimates of the annual rate of new (incidence) and existing (prevalence) cases of mental disorders among adolescents? How many of these adolescents are characterized as having severe mental disorders? What is the likelihood that mental disorders may continue across the transition to adulthood? What are some of the costs associated with adolescent-era mental disorders? Answers to these questions can clarify the seriousness of mental disorders within the general population. They also can provide a framework for understanding the consequences of mental disorders among those who received the most costly and most restrictive treatment during adolescence.

Broadly speaking, mental disorders are relatively common in the general U.S. population. Adult mental disorders are of special concern because of their

---

1. This disruptive behavior also tends to bring youth into contact with the juvenile and criminal justice systems, which are the topics of chapters 3 through 6 of this volume.

prevalence, the disability they produce, and the costs of treatment (U.S. Public Health Service 1999). A recent report indicates that nearly fifty-four million (20 percent) adult Americans have a diagnosable mental disorder during a given year (Roper Starch Worldwide 2001). Moreover, 15 percent of those with a mental disorder suffer from more than one diagnosable mental disorder at a given time, placing them at increased risk for significant functional impairment as well as on a path to chronic or recurring disorder over time (Kessler et al. 1994). A recent evaluation of the personal and social costs of mental disorders indicates that they are among the leading causes of morbidity, premature mortality, and disability in the United States (Murray and Lopez 1996). In particular, mental disorders are associated with higher rates of unemployment and reliance on public assistance than the national average, as well as lost days of productivity and decreased effectiveness at work. In light of such adverse impacts, it is not surprising that economists estimate that during 2001 mental disorders cost American business, government, and families approximately $113 billion (National Mental Health Association 2001).

Prevalence of Mental Disorders during Adolescence

Mental disorders are also a common and growing source of disability during adolescence. Several large-scale studies conclude that approximately 20 percent of American adolescents experience a clinically significant diagnosable mental disorder within any given year (Costello et al. 1996). Within the traditional mental health paradigm, a diagnosis is made when the combination and intensity of signs and symptoms meet the criteria for a disorder listed in the standard manual for diagnosis of mental disorders in the United States, the *Diagnostic and Statistical Manual of Mental Disorders* (DSM), currently in its fourth edition (American Psychiatric Association 1994). Among adolescents, the most common conditions are diagnoses of mood, anxiety, and disruptive behavior or conduct disorders (U.S. Public Health Service 1999). Several studies suggest that 3 to 8 percent of all high school students experience a diagnosable depressive or mood disorder at some time during adolescence; approximately 4 percent experience anxiety disorders; and 2 percent are diagnosed as having disruptive behavior disorders (Lewinsohn et al. 1993). It also is common for adolescents to meet criteria for a diagnosis of more than one of these disorders at the same time. For teens with these comorbid conditions, the presence of symptoms associated with more than one disorder may indicate more severe impairments or a fundamentally different disorder than a single condition that occurs alone (Krueger et al. 1998; U.S. Public Health Service 1999, 2000).

By and large, mental disorders involve impairments in psychological or behavioral functioning. Depressive and anxiety disorders are characterized by the repeated experience of intense internal or emotional distress, including unreasonable fear or worry, ongoing sadness, low self-esteem, or feelings of worthlessness. Conduct disorders, on the other hand, are defined by a spectrum of troublesome behaviors that interfere with ongoing relationships and group activities. These behaviors include poorly controlled impulsive outbursts often involving aggression or violence toward peers, hostility toward authority figures, or defiance of social norms and laws.

Whether related to mood, anxiety, or conduct, all of these disorders are typically associated with impaired functioning in important domains of adolescent life, including home, school, peer, and community contexts (Costello et al. 1996). Among 2 percent of all adolescents, mental disorders are classified as *severe* because they are accompanied by marked functional impairment across a number of these areas. Moderately severe disorders affect approximately 8 percent of all adolescents, whereas the remaining 10 percent experience *milder forms* of disorder that nonetheless include impairment specific to their diagnoses.

PREVALENCE OF MENTAL DISORDERS IN THE TRANSITION LEADING TO ADULTHOOD

The experience of mental disorder during adolescence does not *necessarily* lead to psychopathology in adulthood. However, a growing body of research using retrospective reports suggests that mental disorders tend to be persistent and recurrent (U.S. Department of Health and Human Services 2000). In addition, emerging evidence from longitudinal studies of small samples of American youth suggests that adolescents with mental disorders are at an increased risk for a wide range of mental health problems during emergent adulthood (Davis and Vander Stoep 1997; Feehan et al. 1995). Additional support comes from a longitudinal study of the health and behavior of a complete birth cohort of children born between April 1, 1972, and March 31, 1973, in Dunedin, New Zealand (Silva and Stanton 1996). Although these findings are based on a single New Zealand cohort that includes few participants of color, previous research suggests that the prevalence and developmental course of mental disorders may be similar to findings from studies conducted in the United States (Kessler et al. 1994; Narrow et al. 2002; Newman et al. 1996). With respect to the transition to becoming an adult, results from the Dunedin study showed that 74 percent of the sample who met criteria for a diagnosable mental disorder during adolescence (ages fifteen and eighteen) experienced chronic or recurring disorders that may wax and wane but still persist to age twenty-one (Newman et al. 1996). The data also showed substantial continuity in psychopathology when participants were twenty-six years old, indicating that 77 percent of those with a diagnosable mental disorder at twenty-six had a first diagnosis before they were eighteen years old and approximately 50 percent had received a diagnosis before age fifteen (Kim-Cohen et al. 2002). To the degree that these findings are replicated in national samples in the United States, they underscore strong links between adolescent and adult disorders and a high risk of recurrence that extends from adolescence into adulthood. The findings also highlight the importance of targeting interventions before young people face the challenges of assuming adult roles.

MENTAL DISORDERS AND SOCIAL ADJUSTMENT
DURING THE TRANSITION TO ADULTHOOD

A number of studies conducted in the United States provide powerful evidence that many adolescents with mental health problems struggle during the transition to adult life. For example, in the National Comorbidity Study (NCS), Kessler and his colleagues (1995, 1997) found significant links between retrospectively reported information on age of onset of psychiatric disorders and the domains of education, parenting, and marriage. Compared to those without disorders, people with a history of early-onset mental disorders are at high risk for dropping out of high school, teenage parenthood, and marital instability during adulthood (Kessler et al. 1997; Kessler et al. 1995). In each of these domains, males with conduct disorders were at the highest risk of maladaptive outcomes. (See also chapters 3 and 5 concerning challenges facing youth involved in the juvenile and criminal justice systems.)

A number of longitudinal studies examining the developmental course of adolescents over time describe similar results. Comparing young people who met diagnostic criteria for a mental disorder during adolescence with those who did not, these studies report that young people with previous disorders have poorer outcomes across a range of broad social and socioeconomic domains. For example, Vander Stoep et al. (2000) found that emerging adults with a history of mental disorder are at high risk of failing to complete secondary school, being neither in school nor employed, engaging in criminal activity (such as stealing, property damage, and interpersonal aggression), abusing substances, and experiencing unplanned pregnancies. Proportions of youth experiencing each of these outcomes ranged from 24 to 39 percent among those who had a history of mental disorder, compared to 7 to 10 percent for those without disorder (Vander Stoep et al. 2000).

With respect to findings from longitudinal studies of samples with specific mood and conduct disorders, results show a range of poor outcomes in markers of a successful transition to becoming an adult. For example, emerging evidence suggests links between adolescent depression and later low academic achievement, reduced likelihood of entering a university, recurrent unemployment, and early parenthood (Fergusson and Woodward 2002). Some data show that young people who met criteria for depression during adolescence report limited satisfaction with their career development, a need for social support, and interpersonal problems such as difficulties communicating with others (Giaconia, Reinherz, Paradis, Carmola Huff, and Stashwick 2001). Indeed, those with earlier depressed mood tend to have difficulty establishing intimate interpersonal relationships (Kandel and Davies 1986). These difficulties include a limited sense of connectedness and intimacy with others. Young women with histories of depression, in particular, describe problems in intimate relationships, including a lack of closeness as well as reports that their partners use psychological or physical coercion to resolve conflict (Rao, Hammen, and Daley 1999).

Depression can have other profound consequences among emerging adults, including a range of other mental health problems, such as anxiety disorders and substance abuse or dependence. In addition, depression is often associated with an increased risk of suicidal thinking and behaviors (Lewinsohn et al. 2001). Although many suicidal behaviors are of low lethality, suicide is currently the third leading cause of death among fifteen- to twenty-four-year-olds (National Center for Health Statistics 2003).

Among those with a history of conduct disorder, a growing body of research suggests that almost 50 percent are chronically troubled with a number of problems that persist into adult life (e.g., Moffitt 1993; Robins 1966; Sampson and Laub 1993). Approximately 20 to 35 percent of those with earlier disorder are at high risk for antisocial outcomes, including high rates of arrest and drug addiction. Compared to their peers, they have high rates of school failure, poor work histories in low-status, unskilled jobs, and a trend toward early, albeit unstable, marriages and youthful childbearing. Many continue to be involved in interpersonal conflict over the life course (Moffitt et al. 2002; Pajer 1998). Such conflict is often reflected in problematic romantic relationships characterized by personal ambivalence about the relationship, poor conflict management, physical violence, and uncertainty about the future (Woodward, Fergusson, and Horwood 2002).

Among those who do not continue to exhibit antisocial behaviors, there is evidence of other forms of maladjustment as adults. According to Moffitt et al. (2002), a small minority of formerly antisocial adolescents develops into adults who are depressed, anxious, and socially isolated. By the time they are twenty-six, these young people have limited educational attainment, low-status occupations, difficulty making friends, and few commitments to intimate romantic relationships.

Summary

As described above, general community samples provide evidence of considerable continuity in mental disorders from adolescence across the transition to becoming an adult. Regardless of whether adult psychiatric disorders are predicted by earlier disorders of the same or of a different type (e g., adult depression predicted by adolescent depression or by adolescent conduct disorder), most emerging adults with psychiatric disorders had a first diagnosis before the age of eighteen. In addition to a range of mental health problems, a substantial minority of these young people is at high risk of failing to attain the status markers of becoming an adult. This risk may be heightened, in part, because adolescent-era mental disorders derail normal development in ways that seriously compromise a successful transition to adulthood. Adolescents with mental disorders may have difficulty catching up with age-appropriate social and emotional development; consequently, there is a heightened risk that mature adult role functioning will be compromised. The risk might even be greater for adolescents and emerging adults who face barriers to receiving appropriate mental health care (U.S. Department of Health and Human Services 2001; U.S. Public Health Service 1999, 2000).

TREATMENT FOR MENTAL DISORDERS

In general, the mental health care system in the United States includes a complex and fragmented array of services (New Freedom Commission on Mental Health 2003; U.S. Public Health Service 1999). Within this system, individuals may receive care from a variety of providers and in multiple public and private service sectors, including primary care, specialty mental health, welfare, and other human service systems, such as school-based counseling, criminal-justice-based services, or social services (Grisso 2004). Those who receive care include people who differ in the severity of their symptoms and functional disability as well as their social and medical service needs (U.S. Public Health Service 1999). A guiding philosophy within the mental health care system is to deliver care at the most local level possible and within an organized continuum. The importance of community care is based on the assumption that the community will provide social and tangible support to increase the likelihood of desired outcomes. Within the specialty mental health sector, in particular, services are provided in a variety of settings typically reflecting degrees of therapeutic intensity and oriented toward averting more costly and restrictive treatments in hospitals or other residential settings (U.S. Public Health Service 1999). This array of services includes outpatient psychotherapy or medication management in office-based practices or public or private clinics; intensive case management; day treatment or partial hospitalization; and intensive out-of-home care in residential treatment centers or hospitalization in inpatient psychiatric facilities.

Among adolescents between the ages of twelve and seventeen, an estimated 18 percent received treatment for mental health problems during 2001 (Kataoka, Zhang, and Wells 2002). This represents about 4.3 million adolescents, including an estimated 2 million who received school-based mental health services—the most common source of care—and an estimated 1.9 million, or approximately 8 percent of all adolescents, who used specialty mental health services. Based on the most recently available data, an estimated 332,000 adolescents, approximately 7.8 percent of those in specialty mental health care, received the most restrictive and costly care in residential or inpatient settings (Sturm et al. 2000). As described later in this chapter, these adolescents are commonly viewed as the most troubled of all youngsters receiving specialty mental health care. They also include a number of "system kids" who shuttle in and out of the mental health, child welfare, and juvenile justice systems— separated from families and community schools and services (Grisso 2004).

Specialty Mental Health Treatment for Adolescents and Emerging Adults

Comparisons of adolescents and emerging adults receiving specialty mental health care show several significant differences. Nationwide data gathered in the 1997 Client/Patient Sample Survey show that teenagers comprise a relatively large group within the population receiving mental health care, especially when compared with emerging adults between the ages of eighteen and twenty-four. According to *Mental Health, United States, 2000*, 13 percent of the population receiving outpatient care is between the ages of 12 and 17, while 10 percent are emerging adults (U.S. Department of Health and Human Services 2000). Among those receiving inpatient and residential treatment, about 38 percent are teens whereas 18 percent are emerging adults. Principal diagnoses of persons receiving inpatient and residential care also vary. Almost 50 percent of the total populations receiving inpatient treatment carry diagnoses of affective disorders; in contrast, less than 25 percent of the youngsters in residential treatment are classified as having affective disorders, whereas slightly more than 33 percent are diagnosed as having disruptive behavior disorders.

Taken together, these findings highlight the relatively low rates of specialty mental health service use by emerging adults. In addition to showing that many teens in residential treatment suffer from mood and disruptive behavior disorders, the data also raise important questions about what happens within the adult mental health system to young people with disruptive behavior disorders, including those who transition to adult antisocial personality disorder.

From a different perspective, a growing body of evidence suggests that many adolescents with a need for mental health services do not receive professional help or appropriate services (Burns et al. 1995; U.S. Public Health Service 2000; Weisz and Hawley 2002). Only 30 to 35 percent of those with diagnosable mental disorders receive mental health treatment (Kataoka, Zhang, and Wells 2002). Moreover, this gap between rates of mental health need and service use varies across race-ethnic groups. In particular, estimated rates of untreated mental health problems range from 86 percent among Hispanics to 78 percent for African-Americans and 69 percent for white European Americans (Sturm et al. 2000). Ethnic minority teens with mental health problems are also more likely than nonminority adolescents with similar problems to enter the juvenile justice system (see also chapter 3). For example, research examining factors that differentiate those who enter the juvenile justice system from those receiving mental health care suggest that male gender, ethnic minority membership, low socioeconomic status, and public health insurance increase the likelihood of a juvenile justice placement (Scott, Snowden, and Libby 2002). Consequently, some teens with serious mental disorders may end up in the juvenile justice system where poor and minority youths are disproportionately represented (Sheppard and Benjamin-Coleman 2001). In a similar vein, Grisso (2004) recently argued that limited public mental health services have contributed to "a functional diversion of mentally disordered youths into juvenile justice facilities" (5).

Residential Treatment for Adolescents

In the current health care system, residential treatment tends to be viewed as less intensive and less restrictive than inpatient psychiatric hospitalization (Bickman, Foster, and Lambert 1996). Psychiatric hospitalization is used primarily to manage serious, acute risk. Such risk is typically defined as a realistic potential to seriously harm oneself or another person (American Academy of Child and Adolescent Psychiatry and American Psychiatric Association 1997). In this context, treatment focuses on acute management of symptoms and crisis stabilization; as a result, inpatient treatment is often short-term (e.g., one week or less) and offered in locked facilities with services provided mostly by nursing staff and psychiatrists.

In contrast, residential treatment tends to be justified by mental health treatment providers as necessary for those who need continuous, intensive services for serious mental disorders that may include suicidal or homicidal thoughts, plans, or attempts (Barker 1998; Lyons et al. 1998). These services are generally provided in an out-of-home group environment in unlocked facilities by trained staff. The facilities are often geographically removed from the community. Most residential treatment programs emphasize a structured, supervised therapeutic environment. According to one guiding philosophy, the entire milieu is important in treating youngsters; therefore, an extended length of stay (usually six to eighteen months) may be required (Lyman and Campbell 1996). Treatment typically includes an array of services, involving both individual and group counseling, social skills training, on-site schooling, and, in some cases, initiation and management of a stabilizing medication regimen (Bates, English, and Kouidou-Giles 1997; Lyman and Campbell 1996).

Characteristics of Adolescents in Residential Treatment

Adolescents in residential treatment typically exhibit multiple chronic emotional or behavioral problems that impair their functioning in everyday life or represent a potential danger to themselves or other people (American Academy of Child and Adolescent Psychiatry and American Psychiatric Association 1997; Strauss, Chassin, and Lock 1995; Wells and Whittington 1993). As mentioned earlier, a recent national survey suggests that diagnoses of disruptive behavior and depressive disorders are common (U.S. Department of Health and Human Services 2000). Some of these teens also exhibit symptoms of posttraumatic stress disorders and have histories of prior physical or sexual abuse (Frensch and Cameron 2002). A substantial proportion meet criteria for more than a single diagnosis, highlighting the breadth and severity of their mental health problems (National Advisory Mental Health Council Workgroup on Child and Adolescent Mental Health Intervention Development and Deployment 2001; U.S. Public Health Service 1999, 2000). In addition, they tend to exhibit impaired functioning in school, at home, and in the community. These impairments are reflected in poor academic performance; poor control of emotions and behaviors; suicide risk; violence toward others; impulsive or chaotic behaviors; high levels of self-derogation; low social competency; and troubled relationships with family and peers (Lyman and Campbell 1996; Wells and Whittington 1993). In particular, difficult relations with parents, from acute states of parent-child conflict to rejection by parents, are common. Many of these teens describe their parents as having ineffective parenting styles and being emotionally distant and unsupportive (Jewell and Stark 2003; Prange et al. 1992). The complex and long-standing nature of the difficulties facing these teens is underscored further by evidence suggesting that many receive treatment in mental health, education, child welfare, and juvenile justice systems prior to their admission to residential treatment but do not respond adequately to such less intensive interventions (Frensch and Cameron 2002).

Family Environments of Adolescents in Residential Treatment

In addition to difficult family relations, the lives of adolescents in residential treatment are often characterized by chronic residential instability (Quinn and Epstein 1998). They are likely to come from low-income families and to have previously lived outside the home. Many also come from single-parent or blended families facing multiple psychosocial adversities. A significant proportion of these families have histories of alcohol and drug abuse, family violence, mental illness, and criminality (Quinton and Rutter 1984a,b). In addition, these families tend to be characterized by relatively high rates of marital instability, interparental conflict, serious acting out by family members, and very poor communication (Lyons et al. 1998). Often parents describe themselves as experiencing high levels of stress, being unable to control children in their home, having strained relationships with close relatives, and generally lacking sources of support in the community (Jenson and Whittaker 1989; Quinton and Rutter 1984b). Many also report relatively high levels of negative feelings associated with caring for a teen with mental health problems, including feelings of worry, guilt, sadness, and fatigue (Brannan, Heflinger, and Foster 2003). Overall, families with adolescents in residential treatment may lack sufficiently strong bonds to link them together after the teen's discharge from residential care (Embry et al. 2000).

DEVELOPMENTAL CONTEXT OF ADOLESCENTS IN RESIDENTIAL TREATMENT

Placed within a developmental perspective, the symptoms expressed by adolescents in residential treatment reflect the multiple and complex challenges they face. These challenges are likely to compromise their abilities to successfully negotiate the major social developmental tasks of adolescence. Benchmarks for these tasks typically include developing a sense of psychological autonomy, revising relationships with parents, developing and sustaining increasingly close relationships with friends, and learning an array of skills necessary to cope emotionally, socially, and financially as an independent emerging adult (Feldman and Elliott 1990). By failing to master such tasks, these teens may then lack the competencies or "bridging mechanisms" that could provide the foundation for positive outcomes over time (Ramey and Ramey 1998).

For many teens, developing a sense of autonomy is a critical constituent of overall positive adaptation. A sense of autonomy allows adolescents to explore new areas, master new personal competencies, and make choices based on their emerging values and beliefs. Without meaningful practice in adolescence, exploring and making important life decisions during emerging adulthood becomes virtually impossible (Allen, Moore, and Kuperminc 1997). Whether such practice can occur within the context of a structured residential treatment environment is not completely known. Further attention to this process is important because educational and occupational decisions facing emerging adults can be considered extensions of becoming an autonomous individual (Bell et al. 1996; O'Connor et al. 1996). Moreover, those who develop a sense of autonomy and clear identity during adolescence may be better equipped to cope with the multiple challenges of finding their place in adult worlds of work and family life (Maggs et al. 1997).

In addition, some teens in residential treatment may not develop the competencies needed to meet the challenges of higher education, entering adult work roles, or developing intimate relationships with others. These include teens who show evidence of academic difficulties, limited abilities to regulate their emotions and behaviors, or poor social competencies. Without the skills needed, some may experience severe difficulties in decision making, self-control, and conflict resolution as well as in understanding and cooperating with others (Allen et al. 2002). Such difficulties may place them at high risk for drawing upon established patterns of maladaptive or dangerous behavior, such as withdrawal, moodiness, or aggression; they may also set the stage for a problematic transition to becoming an adult (Cicchetti and Cohen 1995). Although these difficulties may be revisited and resolved later, they may also place some adolescents at considerable risk for failing to negotiate many, or most, of the challenges inherent in their postadolescent years.

At the same time, separating adolescents from their families may alter the role of key mechanisms typically associated with optimal adolescent mental health (Powers, Hauser, and Kilner 1989). Although no single ingredient is consistently important for all teens in all contexts, a number of studies underscore the role of providing a structure that encourages adolescent autonomy within the context of an underlying positive relationship with parents (Allen et al. 1994; Allen, Moore, and Kuperminc 1997). A key element within this process involves opportunities for adolescents to establish their autonomy through negotiation and cooperation rather than coercion or neglect. In practical terms, adolescents typically need to question adults' authority while also responding to thoughtful comments adults make in return (Allen et al. 1994). Whether such opportunities are present in residential treatment centers, however, has received scant empirical attention.

A second critical component involves the role of a relationship with a caregiving adult whom the adolescent perceives as psychologically available (Allen, Hauser, and Borman-Spurrell 1996; Allen and Land 1999; Allen et al. 1998). The expectation of a psychologically available adult can provide an emotional base from which to launch into adult roles (Allen, Hauser, and Borman-Spurrell 1996). Such a relationship can provide adolescents the flexibility to explore emotionally the possibility of living independently, in part because they know they can return to the supportive adult in cases of real need (Allen et al. 1994). Without such exploration, adolescents may experience difficulties in developing a sense of themselves as capable of taking on new challenges or coping with the emotions engendered in learning to live independently (Kobak and Sceery 1988). It may also be difficult to develop peer relationships where one both receives and offers care and support (Allen and Land 1999). Such difficulties may contribute to ongoing problems in social functioning, including negative expectations about others, hostility, and poor social skills; they may also undermine the ability to establish satisfying friendships and long-term intimate relationships (Allen et al. 1998). With these important links in mind, it is essential to understand better how separating teens from their families—or providing alternatives in residential care—might alter outcomes over time.

General Outcomes Associated with Residential Treatment during Adolescence

Despite the questions we have raised about the developmental context of residential treatment, this setting is potentially a significant force in the lives of these adolescents. Unfortunately, systematic efforts aimed at understanding its possible effects have varied considerably in scope and methodological rigor. In some instances, presentations of case studies and general anecdotal accounts have been used to determine whether treatment reduced or eliminated emotional distress or behavioral problems in a given adolescent. Although such work is likely to be clinically interesting, revealing the richness and diversity of therapeutic experiences, these findings are often limited to the specific treatment processes and/or the people described. Perhaps partly in reaction to the case study approach, other follow-up research has focused almost exclusively on the evaluation of treatment success rates, with little description of the treatment process. For the most part, this research consists of studies that lack a comparison group or use idiosyncratic measures (Allen and Pfeiffer 1991; Pfeiffer and

Strzlecki 1990). As a result, it is unclear whether the findings reflect the natural course of a disorder, developmental maturation, effects of treatment, or potentially confounding factors that could account for the results (U.S. Public Health Service 1999).

Strong caveats about the quality of studies that do not include a comparison group notwithstanding, several consistent findings have emerged. In general, three outcome groups of adolescents experienced problems sufficiently severe to require residential care: those who get better; those who remain troubled with problems that look the same; and those who remain troubled but in whom the problems change over time (Mattanah et al. 1995). Among those who improve, the findings also describe factors likely to predict positive change during treatment as well as later adaptation to the community. Broadly speaking, these factors fall into three categories: characteristics of the adolescents, of their families, and of the treatment they received. In terms of adolescent characteristics, residential treatment appears to be somewhat more effective with adolescents who have mood or anxiety disorders than with those who have conduct disorders (Lyons et al. 2001). In particular, adolescents with serious aggressive or destructive behaviors show the poorest outcomes. Some recent studies also point to individual strengths that can influence how adolescents respond to residential care. These include a sense of humor, the ability to enjoy positive life experiences, and a strong relationship with a sibling (Lyons et al. 2000).

Among those with positive outcomes, parental involvement in the therapeutic process plays an important role. In addition to facilitating gains during treatment, parental involvement and family support are related to adolescents' abilities to adapt to the community following discharge (Frensch and Cameron 2002). Finally, with respect to treatment, those adolescents who receive treatment in a program oriented specifically to adolescents and continue in therapy after discharge adjust better in returning to their community than those who discontinue treatment or receive age-inappropriate care (Frensch and Cameron 2002).

THE TRANSITION TO BECOMING AN ADULT

In general, there are limited findings regarding the health and functioning of emerging adults who were in residential treatment during adolescence. Studies drawing their samples from settings in which both children and adolescents were treated do not typically differentiate outcomes by age group. In studies focused solely on adolescents, some have relatively brief (e.g., six-month to two-year) follow-up periods, thereby yielding no findings about the continuity of symptoms or level of functioning in the transition to becoming an adult. Other studies include observations separated by a relatively long period between discharge and follow-up. Consequently, little can be said specifically about the transition period itself.

The latter set of studies can imply—though without substantiation—that if mental disorder or functional impairment is present both in adolescence and later adulthood, its traces are also present in the intervening period of emerging adulthood. Moreover, much of this research is based on samples from the Scandinavian countries, where birth registries facilitate long-term follow-up of relatively large samples. These large-scale studies contrast with research conducted within the United States. Most American studies rely on relatively small samples selected from individual residential treatment sites. This selection bias raises questions about how the findings from small samples can generalize to teenagers who received treatment in varied American treatment settings. A potential problem with relying on research based on samples from the Scandinavian countries concerns the population studied. This research has followed adolescents who received treatment in inpatient psychiatric facilities. Since the nature of hospitalization and residential treatment in America has changed substantially in the past twenty years, it is likely that, at the very least, these Scandinavian adolescents received different treatment than American adolescents in residential treatment today. On the other hand, irrespective of national origin, these adolescents are likely to represent those with the most persistent and serious mental disorders. Previous research also suggests that general findings about the course of mental disorders among people in advanced Western industrialized societies are likely to be of some relevance to nonminority American samples (Gibson-Cline 2000). Therefore, our goal is to summarize basic findings that may point to possible long-term outcomes for adolescents with problems sufficiently severe to require residential care.

We also include relevant outcomes from our own twenty-five-year longitudinal study of adolescents who received inpatient psychiatric treatment and a comparison group of high school students. In this study, original participants in the psychiatrically hospitalized group consisted of successive fourteen- to fifteen-year-old admissions to a private hospital's children's unit ($n = 70$). Most carried diagnoses related to conduct problems or symptoms of depressive or anxiety disorders; those diagnosed as having a thought disorder or organic brain damage were excluded. High school students ($n = 76$) were drawn from freshman volunteers attending a suburban high school and matched to the clinic group as closely as possible for age, gender, and social class. Families in both groups were predominantly middle- and upper middle-class and European American, although social class was moderately higher in the high school sample (Hauser et al. 1983).

For four years during adolescence, teens responded to a number of personality and developmental measures, such as ego development, self-image, and self-esteem. Each year, teens also participated in a semistructured clinical interview and a family interaction procedure (Hauser et al. 1983; Hauser et al. 1984). Approximately eleven years after their initial interviews, original participants were reinterviewed when they were twenty-five years old. The young adult assessments included measures of psychological maturity, close relationships, attachment representations, social competence, and psychological distress, as well as educational attainment and occupational prestige (Allen and Hauser 1996; Allen, Hauser, and Borman-Spurrell 1996; Hauser 1999)

Because adolescence is an important period for the development of vocational and interpersonal skills as well as social relationships, deficits observed during this time may persist into the transition to adulthood—even among those who recover from symptoms. Therefore, it is important to consider the question of adaptation over time in relation to both psychiatric symptoms as well as outcomes representing autonomous functioning in developmentally salient domains. Among emerging adults, these nonclinical outcomes include school performance, work success, personal well-being, and quality of family and peer relationships, as well as marital and family status.

Difficulties in Social and Personal Domains

Studies that have examined the adjustment of emerging adults who previously received residential care report findings suggesting that many (30 to 40 percent) continue to experience significant problems in everyday life. Often these problems are reflected in low levels of success in assuming adult roles. These include low occupational achievement as well as high rates of unemployment, reliance on public assistance, and residential instability or homelessness (Davis and Vander Stoep 1997). They may also be evident in high rates of criminality, poor relationships with family and friends, or volatile relationships with intimate partners (Lyman and Campbell 1996).

A significant number of emerging adults who received residential care are also likely to have at least one substance use disorder (Substance Abuse and Mental Health Services Administration 2002). The combination of mental disorders and substance disorders can increase the risk for unemployment, poor family relationships, and homelessness. For example, substance abuse may interfere with young people's abilities to hold a job or maintain a stable residence; it may also play a critical role in isolating them from their families. Indeed, young people with histories of drug and alcohol use tend to be at high risk for homelessness within five years after discharge from residential treatment (Embry et al. 2000). The risk for becoming homeless is also relatively high among young people who experienced pretreatment physical abuse within their families of origin. (Chapter 7 discusses these issues for the general population of homeless youth.)

Findings from our longitudinal study suggest similar patterns of maladaptive outcomes across the transition to adulthood (Allen, Hauser, and Borman-Spurrell 1996; Bell et al. 1996; O'Connor et al. 1996). In terms of educational attainment, just over 50 percent of the former patients earned high school diplomas by age twenty-five, while fewer than 10 percent had completed college; high school and college completion rates for the matched sample, in contrast, were 98 percent and 70 percent, respectively (Best et al. 2004). Compared to the matched sample of former high school students, former patients also were significantly more likely to be married or living with a romantic partner and to have become parents at a relatively early age. Despite involvement in such intimate family relationships, former patients, on average, reported relatively high levels of loneliness and low levels of self-worth, both on an overall basis and in specific domains regarding job competence, sociability, and capacities to have and sustain intimate relationships. Difficulties in interpersonal relationships may be explained, in part, by friends' descriptions about ways in which our participants deal with new and challenging situations. In general, peer assessments of former patients described them as more hostile, and less well-adjusted and interpersonally effective than did those provided by the former students' friends.

Additional evidence of the difficulties facing adolescents who received residential care comes from research conducted in the Scandinavian countries. In a relatively rare long-term follow-up study of adolescent psychiatric inpatients, Kjelsberg and her colleagues examined links between mental disorders and aspects of functioning defined by criminality, suicidality, and premature mortality. The sample for this study included a relatively large number of people who received treatment in the only inpatient facility for adolescent psychiatric patients in Norway during the years 1963–1981. The study population was monitored by record linkage to a national registry where relevant information is recorded using a unique personal identification code assigned to all Norwegian citizens.

In one report, the data showed that 44 percent of the sample had committed crimes during a fifteen- to thirty-three-year follow-up period (Kjelsberg and Dahl 1999). Most of the crimes were serious, with crimes against property being most common, followed by violent crimes and drug offenses, all showing considerable overlap. Among males, a diagnosis of disruptive behavior disorder or substance abuse was the strongest predictor of later criminal behavior. Verbal abuse in the home, disciplinary problems in school, and violation of rules during hospitalization also differentiated those who went on to commit crimes from those who did not. With the exception of rule violation, these predictors also differentiated females at high risk for criminal development from those at relatively low risk. Moreover, 44 percent of those with a criminal record at follow-up had committed violent crimes (Kjelsberg 2002). Males with violent crime convictions committed crimes earlier, peaked later, and had a longer criminal career than their nonviolent counterparts. Moreover, substance abuse at admission and poor impulse control predicted later violent criminality for both men and women.

Substance abuse at admission and poor impulse control also predicted premature death, particularly among males from families with low socioeconomic status and serious marital conflict (Kjelsberg, Sandvik, and Dahl 1999). In the group of males who showed evidence of these characteristics, approximately 41 percent died during the course of the follow-up period of fifteen to thirty-three years. The authors suggest that this increased mortality may be explained by increased risk of death by drug overdose. In contrast, approximately 2 percent of the entire sample of adolescent inpatients completed suicide during a fifteen-year follow-up period (Kjelsberg, Neegaard, and Dahl 1994). Because this is a low base-rate phenomenon, it is important to note that these findings reflect suicide rates six times the community norm for males and nineteen times the norm for females. Moreover, those who completed suicide had more difficulty with depressive symptoms, lower self-esteem, and a greater tendency to reject help during their hospitalization than a matched group of living former patients.

In general, these long-term findings are consistent with results from short-term follow-up studies, described earlier. The data show that differences in treatment outcome are explained in part by differences that exist when adolescents present for treatment. By and large, the continuities of dysregulated anger, hostility, and aggression are of substantial social and clinical importance. Adolescents with conduct or disruptive behavior disorders tend to experience considerable difficulty after discharge from treatment; those with the highest risk for social dysfunction include adolescents with diagnoses of disruptive behavior disorders that co-occur with substance abuse disorders and poor impulse control. At the same time, residential treatment may be somewhat more effective with adolescents who have mood or anxiety disorders rather than conduct disorders.

These findings underscore the need to understand why residential treatment appears to work better for some adolescents than others. One explanation might be factors endogenous to the disorders themselves. For example, residential treatment may appear to be less effective for youth with conduct disorders, but only because these tend to be more severe than disorders of mood or anxiety. As a result, teens in treatment may have better outcomes than those they would experience without treatment—even though they still have significant problems. A second explanation might relate to the types of treatment being offered. Only in the last ten years has research on Henggeler's Multisystemic Therapy (MST) suggested that there may really be effective treatments for those with serious conduct disorders (Borduin et al. 1995; Henggeler et al. 1998; Henggeler, Schoenwald, and Pickrel 1995; Huey et al. 2000). Using strategies derived from family and behavior therapy, MST is an intensive highly individualized family- and home-based therapy designed to address problems at the individual, family, peer, school, and neighborhood levels. It focuses on processes known to be related to disruptive behavior disorders, such as family conflict, poor affective relations, deviant peer association, and poor school performance. MST offers treatment guidelines rather than specific intervention strategies; its overarching goal is to alter key aspects of the social context in ways that promote prosocial behavior rather than antisocial behavior. At the family level, it is designed to increase family structure and cohesion and provide parents with skills and resources to monitor and discipline their children effectively. At the peer level, it focuses on ways that parents can help engage the teen in mainstream activities with prosocial peers and disengage the teen from associations with delinquent peers. By facilitating change in family and peer contexts, MST reduces the frequency and severity of problem behaviors in teens. A recent study suggests further that it is important for therapists to help family members become actively involved in treatment and to view treatment as a collaborative process (Huey et al. 2000). Indeed, teens and family members who rated their therapist as controlling had unsuccessful or negative family and peer outcomes. These findings suggest that understanding the course of mental disorders and their treatments may involve an examination of the nature of treatment provided as well as the quality of individual and family involvement rather than the setting in which treatment is offered.

Difficulties in the Community

Although few studies have examined the role of social and community structures in the transition to becoming an adult, research about the experiences of adults with a variety of disabilities offers some insight. These studies indicate that emerging adults who previously received residential care for mental disorders may encounter barriers to employment (Schwean 1999). Often these barriers are reflected in negative reactions from potential employers as well as coworkers. For example, some potential employers form negative impressions because they believe that people with mental disorders are personally responsible for their problems. Other potential employers question the employability of people with mental disorders, often without a basis for such concern (Rutman 1994).

An additional barrier is the weak link between the adolescent mental health system and adult services, such as vocational rehabilitation and mental health programs (Davis and Vander Stoep 1997). All too often, young people and their families do not have the support that they need to make a successful transition. With respect to employability, in particular, some emerging adults who previously received residential care may have deficits that limit their ability to acquire or sustain meaningful employment (Schwean 1999). The transition may be especially stressful for those who dropped out of high school (Graber and Brooks-Gunn 1996). These young people may enter the transition to the workforce with fewer marketable skills as well as less opportunity for additional training (William T. Grant Foundation Commission on Work 1988).

Moreover, success in the work environment typically depends on abilities to exercise self-control as well as organize, plan, follow directions, accept criticism, seek assistance, and get along with coworkers. To avoid a negative transition, those who show evidence of limited abilities to regulate their emotions and behaviors, a diminished sense of autonomy, or poor social competencies require a community-based system of support offering age-appropriate services. Without the support needed, some may lack the skills needed to secure gainful employment; others may be vulnerable to termination from their jobs.

In addition to being a critical marker of a successful transition to adulthood, gainful employment may have other personal and social benefits. For example, meaningful employment is typically associated with the capacity to become self-supporting as well as a sense of personal well-being. Work environments often become contexts of development as well. Frequently, they provide emerging adults with opportunities to interact with others and to develop new interpersonal relationships. These relationships may become sources of support in dealing with everyday stressors and strains; some may also become intimate partnerships. Thus, in a very complex interactive system, meaningful employment provides resources to facilitate independent living. Such employment can enhance personal well-being and provide a context to form healthy interpersonal relationships. Conversely, failure to succeed in the work environment may diminish opportunities to lead a fulfilling adult life. These potential benefits and risks highlight the importance of designing interventions to facilitate a successful transition into the workplace.

RESILIENCE AS AN OUTCOME

Resilience is a theme stressed throughout this volume because it is essential to balance consideration of the difficulties vulnerable populations face with attention to their successes. As described earlier, the reports by Kjelsberg and her colleagues each focus on one aspect of maladaptive adult functioning and seek adolescent-era correlates of the outcomes. Each provides some perspective on the adolescent attributes and behaviors that are associated with subsequent difficulty. However, Kjelsberg (1999) took her studies one step further—this time by seeing what could be learned from the histories of those former patients who, at follow-up, had thus far *avoided* being recorded in all three of the death, disability, and crime registries (Kjelsberg 1999). This examination showed that 23 percent of the former inpatients had avoided entry into all three registers. Among males, the likelihood of this nonnegative outcome was highest among those who scored relatively well on an intelligence test, had few disciplinary problems in school, and showed no evidence of disruptive behavior or substance abuse disorders. For females, intelligence, lack of disruptive behavior or substance use disorders, and limited functional impairment at admission were shown to be strong favorable predictors.

Data from our longitudinal study also show striking instances of individuals who have overcome the adversities they faced in adolescence to live normal and, by and large, successful lives in young adulthood (Hauser 1999; Hauser and Allen forthcoming). While some of the earliest contributions to the growing literature about resilience were stimulated by the puzzle of how a subgroup of patients with serious mental disorders (schizophrenia) had favorable long-term outcomes (Garmezy 1971; Rutter 2000), there is a notable paucity of research examining resilience within the context of the developmental course of adolescents who were previously hospitalized. As a result, we know little about what individual and contextual strengths enable some former patients in their adult years to rejoin their communities, find meaningful employment, sustain close relationships, and live fulfilling adult lives. In our longitudinal study, we discovered that ten years after a sample of seventy adolescents had been psychiatrically hospitalized for treatment of serious nonpsychotic disorders, a small group of them were performing at high levels across several domains of competence when they were twenty-five (Hauser 1999; Hauser and Allen forthcoming). Based on theoretical and empirical literature, we constructed an empirical profile defining "resilience," which led to our identifying nine emerging adults (including both men and women) who fit our stringent multidimensional definition. To be labeled as "resilient," these people had to be in the top half of *all* the emerging adults (including those seventy-six within our sample who had no history of psychiatric hospitalization) along the lines of each of seven key competencies. The emerging adult competencies were based on evidence of psychological maturity, close relationships, attachment coherence, and social adjustment (as reflected in the relative absence of criminality, substance abuse, and psychological distress; see Hauser 1999, and Hauser and Allen under review). For comparison with this group of nine, we then identified a second group of former patients who, only within the group of former patients, represented *average* outcomes on the same measures of competence. In other words, we chose a comparison group who were functioning neither poorly (at the bottom of the patient group) nor superbly (at the top of it) on *any* of our seven measures defining resilience.

To understand more deeply how the perceptions and perspectives of our group of nine could have contributed to their later successful adaptation, we examined their discourse during annual adolescent open-ended clinical research interviews, looking closely at what they had to say about their own experiences. Their narratives represent a special kind of data—what Cowan has called "naturally occurring accounts of life experiences, organized, stored, and recounted in personally meaningful ways" (Cowan 1999, 163). We hoped that these narratives would offer a new kind of window on how adolescents cope with difficult experiences: how *these* adolescents, for example, saw their lives before treatment, how they made the best of things while in the hospital, how they had made (or failed to make) sense of their turbulent adolescent years. We hoped that we might find the first hints of strengths previously unnoticed— their own interpretations, or special sensitivities or insights or gifts—that could explain (and that would have shaped) such unexpectedly successful emerging adulthoods.

Based on these interview analyses, nine central features were identified, reflecting two sets of dimensions. Along the lines of individual-oriented dimensions, those who had resilient outcomes revealed features characterized by stepping back to consider their own actions as well as their motives, thoughts, and feelings; taking responsibility for their actions in contrast to claiming to be consistently shaped by the behaviors of others and adverse conditions they did not influence; understanding themselves in complex ways; setting goals and persisting in attaining them; adjusting their own perceptions of self-esteem and confidence with an overall increase over time; and, within their interviews, telling their stories coherently, in contrast to the more diffuse and disjointed narratives of the average outcome group. In terms of relationship-oriented dimensions, the resilient adolescents expressed many instances of reflection about others' motives and feelings. They saw friendships and other close relationships as being key resources in their lives; and they acknowledged many and varied intersections among their self-representations, their relationships, and their actions with others.

While clearly preliminary, this new way of looking at our data has the promise of shedding light on how these former patients adapted to trying circumstances during adolescence. Tracing the flow of meanings constructed by adolescents and emerging adults can lead to our locating new individual and relational protective factors. These thematic and structural (e.g., coherence) characteristics of the teenage narratives are among the special features that distinguish the resilient emerging adults from other former patients. Through such developing strengths represented in their evolving narratives, these adolescents may have compensated for serious psychopathology as well as capitalized on available resources—psychotherapy, special teachers, friends, and schools.

CONCLUSIONS

This review suggests a complex matrix of difficulties faced by emerging adults with serious mental health problems. The preponderance of negative outcomes underscores the need to understand better the processes that place adolescents at risk for continuing problems during the transition to becoming adults. This will make it possible to better target scarce resources to help those in greatest need. So too, since not all adolescents with serious mental health problems are beset by difficulties in emerging adulthood, future research needs to consider determinants of unexpectedly successful adaptation (resilience)—overall and in specific domains (e.g., work, relationship, academic).

In terms of dysfunction in emerging adulthood, where we have the most studies and most data, it is arguably important for future analyses to rigorously consider the compounding of negative outcomes over time. For example, minimal education will likely prevent some young people from attaining reasonable and well-paying jobs and contribute to a downward socioeconomic spiral. Limited economic resources may contribute to increased family stress, particularly among those who marry at an early age. In turn, family stress in combination with a physically violent relationship may exacerbate marital instability, play a role in inappropriate parenting, and contribute to feelings of uncertainty about the future. Clearly, this compounding of socioeconomic, psychological, and social outcomes underscores the many levels of impairments that may be associated with mental health problems during the transition to emerging adulthood. These results point to the importance of targeting such young people for interventions to ease the transition to community settings and becoming an adult. They also highlight the need to design and facilitate access to developmentally appropriate community-based intervention programs.

REFERENCES

Allen, J. P., and S. T. Hauser. 1996. Autonomy and relatedness in adolescent-family interactions as predictors of young adults' states of mind regarding attachment. *Development and Psychopathology* 3: 793–809.

Allen, J. P., S. T. Hauser, K. L. Bell, and T. G. O'Connor. 1994. Longitudinal assessment of autonomy and relatedness in adolescent family interactions as predictors of adolescent ego development and self-esteem. *Child Development* 65: 179–194.

Allen, J. P., S. T. Hauser, and E. Borman-Spurrell. 1996. Attachment theory as a framework for understanding sequelae of severe adolescent psychopathology: An 11-year follow-up study. *Journal of Consulting and Clinical Psychology* 64: 254–263.

Allen, J. P., S. T. Hauser, T. G. O'Connor, and K. L. Bell. 2002. Prediction of peer-rated adult hostility from autonomy struggles in adolescent-family interactions. *Development and Psychopathology* 14: 123–127.

Allen, J. P., and D. Land. 1999. Attachment in adolescence. Pp. 319–335 in *Handbook of attachment: Theory, research, and clinical applications.* Edited by J. Cassidy and P. R. Shaver. New York: Guilford Press.

Allen, J. P., C. M. Moore, and G. P. Kuperminc. 1997. Developmental approaches to understanding adolescent deviance. Pp. 548–567 in *Developmental psychopathology: Perspectives on adjustment, risk, and disorder.* Edited by S. S. Luthar, J. A. Burack, D. Cicchetti, and J. R. Weisz. Cambridge: Cambridge University Press.

Allen, J. P., C. M. Moore, G. P. Kuperminc, and K. L. Bell. 1998. Attachment and adolescent psychosocial functioning. *Child Development* 69: 1406–1419.

Allen, J. P., and S. I. Pfeiffer. 1991. Residential psychiatric treatment of adolescents who do not return to their families. *Comprehensive Mental Health Care* 1: 209–222.

American Academy of Child and Adolescent Psychiatry and American Psychiatric Association. 1997. *Criteria for short-term treatment of acute psychiatric illness.* Washington: American Academy of Child and Adolescent Psychiatry and American Psychiatric Association.

American Psychiatric Association. 1994. *Diagnostic and statistical manual of mental disorders.* 4th ed. Washington: American Psychiatric Association.

Arnett, J. J. 2000. Emerging adulthood: A theory of development from the late teens through the twenties. *American Psychologist* 55: 469–480.

Barker, P. 1998. The future of residential treatment for children. Pp. 1–16 in *Children in residential care: Critical issues in treatment.* Edited by C. Schaefer and A. Swanson. New York: Van Nostrand Reinhold.

Bates, B. C., D. J. English, and S. Kouidou-Giles. 1997. Residential treatment and its alternatives: A review of the literature. *Child and Youth Care Forum* 26: 7–51.

Bell, K. L., J. P. Allen, S. T. Hauser, and T. G. O'Connor. 1996. Family factors and young adult transitions: Educational attainment and occupational prestige. Pp. 345–366 in *Transitions through adolescence.* Edited by J. Graber, J. Brooks-Gunn, and A. C. Petersen. Hillsdale, NJ: Erlbaum.

Best, K. M., S. T. Hauser, J. H. Gralinski-Bakker, J. P. Allen, and J. A. Crowell. 2004. Eleven and twenty years after adolescent psychiatric hospitalization: Higher mortality, greater distress, and less education than a matched cohort. *Archives of Pediatrics and Adolescent Medicine* 158: 749–752.

Bickman, L. 1996. A continuum of care: More is not always better. *American Psychologist* 51: 689–701.

Bickman, L., E. M. Foster, and E. W. Lambert. 1996. Who gets hospitalized in a continuum of care? *Journal of the American Academy of Child and Adolescent Psychiatry* 35: 74–80.

Borduin, C. M., B. J. Mann, L. T. Cone, S. W. Henggeler, B. R. Fucci, D. M. Blaske, and R. A. Williams. 1995. Multisystemic treatment of serious juvenile offenders: Long-term prevention of criminality and violence. *Journal of Consulting and Clinical Psychology* 63: 569–578.

Brannan, A. M., C. A. Heflinger, and E. M. Foster. 2003. The role of caregiver strain and other family variables in determining children's use of mental health services. *Journal of Emotional and Behavioral Disorders* 11: 77–91.

Burns, B. J., E. J. Costello, A. Angold, D. Tweed, D. Stangl, E. M. Z. Farmer, and A. Erkanli. 1995. Datawatch: Children's mental health service use across service sectors. *Health Affair* 14: 147–159.

Cicchetti, D., and D. J. Cohen, eds. 1995. *Developmental psychopathology.* New York: Wiley.

Clausen, J. S. 1991. Adolescent competence and the shaping of the life course. *American Journal of Sociology* 96: 805–842.

Cohen, P., S. Kasen, H. Chen, C. Hartmark, and K. Gordon. 2003. Variations in patterns of developmental transitions in the emerging adulthood period. *Developmental Psychology* 39: 657–669.

Costello, E. J., A. Angold, B. J. Burns, A. Erkanli, D. Stangl, and D. Tweed. 1996. The Great Smoky Mountains study of youth: Functional impairment and serious emotional disturbance. *Archives of General Psychiatry* 53: 1137–1143.

Cowan, P. A. 1999. Commentary: What we talk about when we talk about families. Pp. 163–176 in *The stories that families tell: Narrative coherence, narrative interaction, and relationship beliefs,* by B. H. Fiese, A. J. Sameroff, H. Grotevant, F. S. Wamboldt, S. Dickstein, and D. L. Fravel. Maldon, MA: Blackwell.

Davis, M., and A. Vander Stoep. 1997. The transition to adulthood for youth who have serious emotional disturbance: Developmental transition and young adult outcomes. *Journal of Mental Health Administration* 24: 400–427.

Eccles, J. S., B. L. Barber, M. Stone, and J. Templeton. 2001. Adolescence and emerging adulthood: The critical passage ways to adulthood. Pp. 383–406 in *Well-being: Positive development across the life-span.* Edited by M. H. Bornstein, L. Davidson, and C. L. M. Keyes. Mahwah, NJ: Erlbaum.

Embry, L. E., A. Vander Stoep, C. Evens, K. D. Ryan, and A. Pollack. 2000. Risk factors for homelessness in adolescents released from psychiatric residential treatment. *Journal of the American Academy of Child and Adolescent Psychiatry* 39: 1293–1299.

Feehan, M., R. McGee, S. M. Williams, and S. Nada-Raja. 1995. Models of adolescent psychopathology: Childhood risk and the transition to adulthood. *Journal of the American Academy of Child and Adolescent Psychiatry* 34: 670–679.

Feldman, S. S., and G. R. Elliott, eds. 1990. *At the threshold: The developing adolescent.* Cambridge: Harvard University Press.

Fergusson, D. M., and L. J. Woodward. 2002. Mental health, educational, and social role outcomes of adolescents with depression. *Archives of General Psychiatry* 59: 225–231.

Frensch, K. M., and G. Cameron. 2002. Treatment of choice or a last resort? A review of residential mental health placements for children and youth. *Child and Youth Care Forum* 31: 307–339.

Garmezy, N. 1971. Vulnerability research and the issue of primary prevention. *American Journal of Orthopsychiatry* 41: 101–116.

Giaconia, R. M., H. Z. Reinherz, A. D. Paradis, A. M. Carmola Huff, and C. K. Stashwick. 2001. Major depression and drug disorders in adolescence: General and specific impairments in early adulthood. *Journal of the American Academy of Child and Adolescent Psychiatry* 40: 1426–1433.

Gibson-Cline, J., ed. 2000. *Youth and coping in twelve nations: Surveys of 18–20-year-old young people.* London: Routledge.

Graber, J. A., and J. Brooks-Gunn. 1996. Adolescent transitions in context. Pp. 369–383 in *Transitions through adolescence.* Edited by J. Graber, J. Brooks-Gunn, and A. C. Petersen. Hillsdale, NJ: Erlbaum.

Grisso, T. 2004. *Double jeopardy.* Chicago: University of Chicago Press.

Hauser, S. T. 1999. Understanding resilient outcomes: Adolescent lives across time and generations. *Journal of Research on Adolescence* 9: 1–24.

Hauser, S. T., and J. P. Allen. under review. *Climbing back: Narratives of resilient adolescents.*

Hauser, S. T., A. M. Jacobson, G. G. Noam, and S. I. Powers. 1983. Ego development and self-image complexity in early adolescence. *Archives of General Psychiatry* 40: 325–331.

Hauser, S. T., S. I. Powers, G. G. Noam, A. M. Jacobson, B. Weiss, and D. J. Folansbee. 1984. Familial contexts of adolescent ego development. *Child Development* 55: 195–213.

Henggeler, S. W., S. K. Schoenwald, C. M. Borduin, M. D. Rowland, and P. B. Cunningham. 1998. *Multisystemic treatment of antisocial behavior in children and adolescents.* New York: Guilford.

Henggeler, S. W., S. K. Schoenwald, and S. G. Pickrel. 1995. Multisystemic therapy: Bridging the gap between university- and community-based treatment. *Journal of Consulting and Clinical Psychology* 63: 709–717.

Huey, S. J., S. W. Henggeler, M. J. Brondino, and S. G. Pickrel. 2000. Mechanisms of change in multisystemic therapy: Reducing delinquent behavior through therapist adherence and improved family and peer functioning. *Journal of Consulting and Clinical Psychology* 68: 451–467.

Jenson, J. M., and J. K. Whittaker. 1989. Partners in care: Involving parents in children's residential treatment. Pp. 207–227 in *Residential and inpatient treatment of children and adolescents.* Edited by R. D. Lyman, S. Prentice-Gunn, and S. Gabel. New York: Plenum Press.

Jewell, J. D., and K. D. Stark. 2003. Comparing the family environments of adolescents with conduct disorder or depression. *Journal of Child and Family Studies* 12: 77–89.

Kandel, D. B., and M. Davies. 1986. Adult sequelae of adolescent depressive symptoms. *Archives of General Psychiatry* 43: 255–262.

Kataoka, S. H., L. Zhang, and K. B. Wells. 2002. Unmet need for mental health care among U.S. children: Variation by ethnicity and insurance status. *American Journal of Psychiatry* 159: 1548–1555.

Kessler, R. C., P. A. Berglund, C. L. Foster, W. B. Saunders, P. E. Stang, and E. E. Walters. 1997. The social consequences of psychiatric disorders. 2. Teenage parenthood. *American Journal of Psychiatry* 154: 1405–1411.

Kessler, R. C., C. L. Foster, W. B. Saunders, and P. E. Stang. 1995. The social consequences of psychiatric disorder. 1. Educational attainment. *American Journal of Psychiatry* 152: 1026–1032.

Kessler, R. C., K. A. McGonagle, S. Zhao, C. B. Nelson, M. Hughes, S. Eshleman, H. Wittchen, and K. S. Kendler. 1994. Lifetime and 12-month prevalence of DSM-III-R psychiatric disorders in the united states: Results from the national comorbidity study. *Archives of General Psychiatry* 51: 8–18.

Kim-Cohen, J., A. Caspi, T. E. Moffitt, H. Harrington, B. J. Milne, and R. Poulton. 2002. Prior juvenile diagnoses in adults with mental disorder. *Archives of General Psychiatry* 60: 709–717.

Kjelsberg, E. 1999. A long-term follow-up study of adolescent psychiatric inpatients. 4. Predictors of a non-negative outcome. *Acta Psychiatrica Scandinavica* 99: 247–251.

Kjelsberg, E. 2002. Pathways to violent and non-violent criminality in an adolescent psychiatric population. *Child Psychiatry and Human Development* 33: 29–42.

Kjelsberg, E., and A. A. Dahl. 1999. A long-term follow-up study of adolescent psychiatric inpatients. 2. Predictors of delinquency. *Acta Psychiatrica Scandinavica* 99: 237–242.

Kjelsberg, E., E. Neegaard, and A. A. Dahl. 1994. Suicide in adolescent psychiatric patients: Incidence and predictive factors. *Acta Psychiatrica Scandinavica* 89: 235–241.

Kjelsberg, E., L. Sandvik, and A. A. Dahl. 1999. A long term follow-up of adolescent psychiatric inpatients. 1. Predictors of early death. *Acta Psychiatrica Scandinavica* 99: 231–236.

Kobak, R. R., and A. Sceery. 1988. Attachment in late adolescence: Working models, affect regulation, and representations of self and others. *Child Development* 59: 135–146.

Krueger, R. F., A. Caspi, T. E. Moffitt, and P. A. Silva. 1998. The structure and stability of common mental disorders (DSM-III-R): A longitudinal-epidemiological study. *Journal of Abnormal Psychology* 107: 216–227.

Lewinsohn, P. M., H. Hops, R. E. Roberts, J. R. Seeley, and J. A. Andrews. 1993. Adolescent psychopathology. 1. Prevalence and incidence of depression and other DSM-III-R disorders in high school students. *Journal of Abnormal Psychology* 102: 133–144.

Lewinsohn, P. M., P. Rohde, J. R. Seeley, and C. L. Baldwin. 2001. Gender differences in suicide attempts from adolescence to young adulthood. *Journal of the American Academy of Child and Adolescent Psychiatry* 40: 427–434.

Lyman, R. D., and N. R. Campbell. 1996. *Treating children and adolescents in residential settings.* Thousand Oaks, CA: Sage Publications.

Lyons, J. S., L. N. Libman-Mintzer, C. L. Kisiel, and H. Shallcross. 1998. Understanding the mental health needs of children and adolescents in residential treatment. *Professional Psychology: Research and Practice* 29: 582–587.

Lyons, J. S., P. Terry, Z. Martinovich, J. Peterson, and B. Bouska. 2001. Outcome trajectories for adolescents in residential treatment: A statewide evaluation. *Journal of Child and Family Studies* 10: 333–345.

Lyons, J. S., N. D. Uziel-Miller, F. A. A. Reyes, and P. T. Sokol. 2000. Strengths of children and adolescents in residential settings: Prevalence and associations with psychopathology and discharge placement. *Journal of the American Academy of Child and Adolescent Psychiatry* 39: 176–181.

Maggs, J. L., P. M. Frome, J. S. Eccles, and B. L. Barber. 1997. Psychosocial resources, adolescent risk behavior, and young adult adjustment: Is risk taking more dangerous for some than others? *Journal of Adolescence* 20: 103–119.

Mattanah, J. J. F., D. F. Becker, K. N. Levy, W. S. Edell, and T. H. McGlashan. 1995. Diagnostic stability in adolescents followed up 2 years after hospitalization. *American Journal of Psychiatry* 152: 889–894.

Moffitt, T. E. 1993. Adolescence-limited and life-course persistent antisocial behavior: A developmental taxonomy. *Psychological Review* 100: 674–701.

Moffitt, T. E., A. Caspi, H. Harrington, and B. J. Milne. 2002. Males on the life-course persistent and adolescent-limited antisocial pathways: Follow-up at age 26 years. *Development and Psychopathology* 14: 179–207.

Murray, C. J. L., and A. D. Lopez, eds. 1996. *The global burden of disease and injury series: A comprehensive assessment of mortality and disability from diseases, injuries, and risk factors in 1990 and projected to 2020*. Cambridge: Harvard University Press.

Narrow, W. E., D. S. Rae, L. N. Robins, and D. A. Regier. 2002. Revised prevalence estimates of mental disorders in the united states. *Archives of General Psychiatry* 59: 115–130.

National Advisory Mental Health Council Workgroup on Child and Adolescent Mental Health Intervention Development and Deployment. 2001. *Blueprint for change: Research on child and adolescent mental health*. Washington: 20001.

National Center for Health Statistics. 2003. *Health, United States, 2003*. Hyattsville, MD: Public Health Service.

National Mental Health Association. 2001. *Labor Day 2001 report: A message to American business and government leadership*. Alexandria, VA: National Mental Health Association.

New Freedom Commission on Mental Health. 2003. *Achieving the promise: Transforming mental health care in America*. Rockville, MD.

Newman, D. L., T. E. Moffitt, A. Caspi, L. Magdol, P. A. Silva, and W. R. Stanton. 1996. Psychiatric disorder in a birth cohort of young adults: Prevalence, comorbidity, clinical significance, and new case incidence from ages 11 to 21. *Journal of Consulting and Clinical Psychology* 64: 552–562.

O'Connor, T. G., J. P. Allen, K. L. Bell, and S. T. Hauser. 1996. Adolescent-parent relationships and leaving home in young adulthood. *New Directions in Child Development* 71: 39–52.

Pajer, K. A. 1998. What happens to "bad" girls? A review of the adult outcomes of antisocial adolescent girls. *American Journal of Psychiatry* 155: 862–870.

Pfeiffer, S. I., and B. A. Strzlecki. 1990. Inpatient psychiatric therapy of children and adolescents: A review of outcome studies. *Journal of the American Academy of Child and Adolescent Psychiatry* 29: 847–853.

Powers, S. I., S. T. Hauser, and L. A. Kilner. 1989. Adolescent mental health. *American Psychologist* 44: 200–208.

Prange, M. E., P. E. Greenbaum, S. E. Silver, R. M. Friedman, K. Kutash, and A. J. Duchnowski. 1992. Family functioning and psychopathology among adolescents with severe emotional disturbances. *Journal of Abnormal Child Psychology* 20: 83–102.

Quinn, K., and M. H. Epstein. 1998. Characteristics of children, youth, and families served by local interagency systems of care. Pp. 81–114 in *Outcomes for children and youth with emotional and behavioral disorders and their families*. Edited by M. H. Epstein, K. Kutash, and A. J. Duchnowski. Austin: Pro-Ed.

Quinton, D., and M. Rutter. 1984a. Parents of children in care. 2. Intergenerational continuities. *Journal of Child Psychology and Psychiatry and Allied Disciplines* 25: 231–250.

Quinton, D., and M. Rutter. 1984b. Parents with children in care. 1. Current circumstances and parenting. *Journal of Child Psychology and Psychiatry and Allied Disciplines* 25: 211–229.

Ramey, C. T., and S. L. Ramey. 1998. Early intervention and early experience. *American Psychologist* 53: 109–130.

Rao, U., C. Hammen, and S. Daley. 1999. Continuity of depression during the transition to adulthood: A five year longitudinal study of young women. *Journal of the American Academy of Child and Adolescent Psychiatry* 38: 908–915.

Robins, L. N. 1966. *Deviant children grown-up: A sociological and psychiatric study of sociopathic personalities.* Baltimore: Williams and Wilkins.

Roper Starch Worldwide. 2001. America's mental health survey 2001. Roper no. CNT505. Report prepared for the National Mental Health Association. Alexandria, VA: Roper Starch Worldwide.

Rutman, I. D. 1994. How psychiatric disability expresses itself as a barrier to employment. *Psychosocial Rehabilitation Journal* 17: 15–35.

Rutter, M. 2000. Resilience reconsidered: Conceptual considerations, empirical findings, and policy implications. Pp. 651–682 in *Handbook of early childhood intervention.* Edited by J. P. Shonkoff and S. J. Meisels. Cambridge: Cambridge University Press.

Sampson, R. J., and J. H. Laub. 1993. *Crime in the making: Pathways and turning points.* Cambridge: Harvard University Press.

Schwean, V. L. 1999. Looking ahead: The adjustment of adults with disabilities. Pp. 587–609 in *Handbook of psychosocial characteristics of exceptional children.* Edited by D. H. Saklofske. New York: Plenum.

Scott, M. A., L. Snowden, and A. M. Libby. 2002. From mental health to juvenile justice: What factors predict this transition? *Journal of Child and Family Studies* 11: 299–311.

Sheppard, V. B., and R. Benjamin-Coleman. 2001. Determinants of service placements for youth with serious emotional and behavioral disturbances. *Community Mental Health Journal* 37: 53–65.

Sherrod, L. R., R. J. Haggerty, and D. L. Featherman. 1993. Introduction: Late adolescence and the transition to adulthood. *Journal of Research on Adolescence* 3: 217–226.

Shiner, R. L., A. S. Masten, and A. Tellegen. 2002. A developmental perspective on personality in emerging adulthood: Childhood antecedents and concurrent adaptation. *Journal of Personality and Social Psychology* 83: 1165–1177.

Silva, P. A., and W. R. Stanton, eds. 1996. *From child to adult: The Dunedin multidisciplinary health and development study.* New York: Oxford University Press.

Simons, R. L., E. Stewart, L. C. Gordon, R. D. Conger, and G. H. Elder. 2002. A test of life-course explanations for stability and change in antisocial behavior from adolescence to young adulthood. *Criminology* 40: 401–434.

Strauss, G. S., M. Chassin, and J. Lock. 1995. Can experts agree when to hospitalize adolescents? *Journal of the American Academy of Child and Adolescent Psychiatry* 34: 418–424.

Stroul, B. A., and R. M. Friedman. 1996. The system of care concept and philosophy. in *Systems of care for children's mental health.* Edited by B. A. Stroul and R. M. Friedman. Baltimore: Brookes.

Sturm, R., J. Ringel, C. Bao, B. Stein, K. Kapur, W. Zhang, and F. Zeng. 2000. *National estimates of mental health utilization and expenditures for children in 1998.* Los Angeles: Research Center on Managed Care for Psychiatric Disorders: A joint program of the UCLA Neuropsychiatric Institute and Rand.

Substance Abuse and Mental Health Services Administration. 2002. *Report to Congress on the prevention and treatment of co-occurring substance abuse disorders and mental disorders.* Rockville, MD: Substance Abuse and Mental Health Services Administration.

U.S. Census Bureau. 2000. *United States census 2000: Educational attainment.* Washington: U.S. Census Bureau.

U.S. Department of Health and Human Services. 2000. *Mental health, United States, 2000.*

Rockville, MD: U.S. Department of Health and Human Services, Substance Abuse and Mental Health Services Administration.

U.S. Department of Health and Human Services. 2001. *Mental health: Culture, race, and ethnicity—a supplement to Mental health: A report of the surgeon general.* Rockville, MD: U.S. Department of Health and Human Services, Substance Abuse and Mental Health Services Administration, Center for Mental Health Services.

U.S. Public Health Service. 1999. *Mental health: A report of the surgeon general.* Rockville, MD: U.S. Department of Health and Human Services, Substance Abuse and Mental Health Services Administration, Center for Mental Health Services, National Institute of Health, National Institute of Mental Health.

U.S. Public Health Service. 2000. *Report of the surgeon general's conference on children's mental health: A national action agenda.* Washington: Department of Health and Human Services.

Vander Stoep, A., S. A. A. Beresford, N. S. Weiss, B. McKnight, A. M. Cause, and P. Cohen. 2000. Community-based study of the transition to adulthood for adolescents with psychiatric disorder. *American Journal of Epidemiology* 152: 352–362.

Weisz, J. R., and K. M. Hawley. 2002. Developmental factors in the treatment of adolescents. *Journal of Consulting and Clinical Psychology* 70: 21–43.

Weisz, J. R., and P. S. Jensen. 1999. Efficacy and effectiveness of child and adolescent psychotherapy and pharmacotherapy. *Mental Health Services Research* 1: 125–157.

Wells, K., and D. Whittington. 1993. Characteristics of youths referred to residential treatment: Implications for program design. *Child and Youth Services Review* 15: 195–217.

William T. Grant Foundation Commission on Work, Family, and Citizenship. 1988. *The forgotten half: Non–college bound youth in America.* Washington: William T. Grant Foundation.

Woodward, L. J., D. M. Fergusson, and L. J. Horwood. 2002. Romantic relationships of young people with childhood and adolescent onset antisocial behavior problems. *Journal of Abnormal Child Psychology* 30: 231–243.

CHAPTER ELEVEN

Coping with Mental Health Problems in Young Adulthood: Diversity of Need and Uniformity of Programs

PHILLIP M. LYONS, JR., AND GARY B. MELTON

We gratefully acknowledge the valuable library research assistance of Karen Kalmbach.

Young people with mental health problems who are in transition into adulthood move from one fragmented and disorganized patchwork of agencies and funding streams into another. Mental health services should be delivered seamlessly, without the need to move from one agency or program to another or to maneuver through a gigantic but tattered web of rules for eligibility, whether based on diagnosis, age, or some other criterion. However, conventional policies and practices differ enormously from the vision of an integrated, uncomplicated, consumer-responsive system.

Nurcombe's (1995) description of the relationships among the major mental health service providers and brokers is bleak but unfortunately accurate:

> In large cities, private hospitals, public hospitals, state mental hospitals, community mental health centers, private practitioners, child welfare agencies, juvenile correctional agencies, the courts, and the educational system act independently, guarding their territories against those they perceive as rivals. . . . Private hospitals compete with each other on the basis of cost, efficiency, perceived quality and publicity. Residential treatment centers and alternatives to hospital such as home-based intensive care compete with hospitals rather than complementing them. . . . The contemporary mode of mental health care financing promotes fragmentation, competition, and waste, and has recently introduced an adversarial form of managed care that attempts to curb the growing expense of the disjunctive system. (113–114)

Even when systems are supposed to be unitary, the formal transition to adulthood closes the service door for some as it opens the door for others. As we will explain later, Medicaid eligibility, for example, ends at eighteen for some young people, while it begins at that age for others. Analogously, the criteria for admission into independent living programs and vocational rehabilitation programs may be both narrower and broader than the eligibility for foster care and special education.

Many might assume, however, that the absolute cessation of services that accompanies the formal transition to adulthood in special education or foster care is not a concern in the mental health system. After all, the same agency is typically responsible for providing mental health services to children, adolescents, and adults. Unfortunately, however, the termination of mental health services for youth in transition to adulthood often occurs just as precipitously as it does in other systems (Barry 2003). Despite the lifespan coverage of most public mental health agencies, services are often rigidly bifurcated in age-based programs with separate administration, philosophy, modalities, financing, and location. Simply put, adolescent mental health services work differently from adult services, even within the same agency. Thus the transition from child and adolescent mental health services to adult mental health services can be as problematic as that from agencies that serve only children and adolescents.

In this chapter, we first briefly describe the nature of mental health problems confronting youth in transition to adulthood as separable into three broad categories. We then argue that a differentiated approach is necessary to address these different types of problems effectively, even if it is also useful to embed these services in a context of universal support. Building from that premise, we describe a model of mental health services for youth in transition that is grounded in policy-relevant empirical research and normative principles. We conclude with recommendations.

THE NATURE OF MENTAL HEALTH PROBLEMS IN ADOLESCENCE AND YOUNG ADULTHOOD

The transition to adulthood, like all transitions, is likely to be challenging even for those who do not have mental disorders and are not likely to develop them. For those who *do* experience problems, a clearer understanding of the nature of those problems helps inform policy. In broad perspective, mental health problems affecting those transitioning to adulthood are similar to those of people in other phases of the lifespan. The problems are generally ones of behavior (e.g., conduct disorders), thought (e.g., psychotic disorders), mood (e.g., depression), or a combination of these types. These three categories are distinct from one another in terms of (a) referral sources, (b) signs and symptoms, (c) levels of associated subjective distress, (d) degree of impairment, (e) prognosis, and (f) treatment. Consequently, a differentiated approach is needed if these categorically distinct types of problems are to be addressed effectively.

The first type of problem is behavioral; many young people enter mental health treatment because of conduct problems. Indeed, the primary reason for referral is not that young people are troubled but rather that their conduct is troubling to others (Hobbs 1982; Silver et al. 1992; for a discussion, see Melton et al. 1998, chap. 1). Although troublesome conduct is the problem that captures the attention of others, subjective distress associated with other problems is often present (Fombonne et al. 2001a,b; Knapp et al. 2002; Simic and Fombonne 2001). These conduct problems are marked by the same behavior that brings young people into contact with the juvenile justice system during adolescence and with the criminal justice system in later years. Thus, the issues discussed in chapters 3 through 6 of this volume often apply to this group as well.

Second, many young people experience reactive, transient, or situational disorders that are likely to improve with relatively little intervention (Angold, Costello, and Worthman 1998; Blinder et al. 1978; Bloom and Hopewell 1982; Brooks-Gunn and Attie 1996; Jackson-Beeck, Schwartz, and Rutherford 1987). These disorders typically consist of mildly disturbed thought or mood. Because they are common in adolescence and young adulthood (U.S. Department of Health and Human Services 1999), such problems are sometimes viewed as inconsequential. Such a perception is shortsighted. Treatments have been developed that reduce the severity of the distress that many young people experience and shorten depressive episodes (Compton et al. 2002; Dickinson, Coggan, and Bennett 2003; Waslick, Schoenholz, and Pizarro 2003); a humane policy demands making such services widely available. Moreover, youthful depression, although often transitory, is a major precipitant of suicide attempts (Birmaher, Arbelaez, and Brent 2002; O'Carroll et al. 2001).

The third group is relatively small but important to recognize. Adults with chronic severely disabling conditions often first experience symptoms of their disorders during the transition to adulthood (e.g., Walker, Walder, and Reynolds 2001). Such individuals and their families need to acquire the social and economic support and the personal skills that enable coping with a serious and often debilitating chronic illness.

THE NEED FOR A DIFFERENTIATED APPROACH

Given how different these three groups are, notwithstanding that individuals often belong to more than one (Fombonne et al. 2001a,b, Knapp et al. 2002;

Simic and Fombonne 2001), it is unsurprising that they typically enter the mental health system by different means, if at all. This point can be illustrated by considering who uses mental health services in senior high schools. In schools with health centers, a large proportion of the students who seek services come with complaints related to mental health or substance abuse (Kramer et al. 2003). Most commonly, these students are bothered by situational depression (e.g., Youth Health Services 2002). On the other hand, when school-based *mental* health services are present as a freestanding program (rather than a component of school-based health centers), the young people who receive services most often have conduct problems, and they are referred by school personnel, not by themselves (Kiesner 2002; Weist et al. 2003). Identification of students with emerging chronic adult thought disorders is haphazard in both types of programs, and there rarely are programs specifically designed to assist them in making the transition to adulthood (Phillips et al. 2002).

By contrast, after leaving high school and achieving the legal status of adults, young people with schizophrenia and other major chronic disorders may find a variety of specialized vocational, social, and housing programs in mental health centers to enable them to have some success in semi-independence (for examples, see Henggeler and Santos 1997). On the other hand, mental health centers rarely have specialized programs for young adults with other kinds of problems. (Clinics in settings that themselves are specialized in serving young adults—notably colleges and universities—are obvious exceptions.)

Regardless of the specific set of services that is available, it is well-suited to only one of the three broad diagnostic groups. We know of nowhere that a systematic differentiated effort has been made to respond to the needs of each as they try to manage the transition to adulthood, despite their obviously different circumstances and developmental outlooks.

Of course, in many—probably most—communities, neither health nor mental health services are available in the senior high schools. Not only is this fact indicative of the relative scarcity of mental health services for young people (see Kataoka, Zhang, and Wells 2002; Pumariega and Winters 2003), but it also illustrates a more general problem in the American service system. Services that vary from established residential treatment and center-based outpatient psychotherapy models commonly are treated as demonstration projects and thus are available only to a small fraction of young people who might benefit from them, even when the models have been systematically tested and have key political support (Melton 1997). "Going to scale" is not a strong point in American human services (Melton and Sullivan 1993).

It is thus unlikely but perhaps optimal that an approach would be adopted that truly served each of the three diagnostic groups and that also had preventive effects by making services universal. Given that the transition to adulthood is challenging for most young people, it may be most useful—and certainly least stigmatizing—to consider ways that support could be built into the institutions of everyday life (cf. Melton 2002). A stronger sense of community that includes young people would probably modulate problems of transition for those with special problems. Even within such an approach, however, a humane response would be individualized.

SYSTEMIC ISSUES AFFECTING SERVICE MODELS

The overlap between systems. Further, as important as the nature of the *problems* is, the nature of the *systems* serving young people and their families also influences service models, perhaps even more so. In confronting the mental health needs of young people in transition, one is immediately struck by the daunting complexity of the issues. Having been built and sustained in part to fulfill the interest of particular professional constituencies, numerous systems operate to achieve multiple goals that may change over time and even operate at cross-purposes.

Over and above the system-specific goals (e.g., incapacitation of offenders, increase in vocational skills), the relevant systems also share a therapeutic purpose (i.e., reduction of deviant behavior and, perhaps to a lesser degree, subjective distress). Therapeutic goals can be found not only in the specialty mental health system but also the juvenile justice system (see chapters 3 and 4), special education system (see chapters 8 and 9), child welfare system (see chapter 2), and substance abuse service system.

As we have noted elsewhere, "The children's service systems interlock to such a degree that consideration of them as separate systems is an artificial (even if legally recognized) categorization that invites incomplete policy analysis" (Melton et al. 1998, 11). For example, the overlap in function means that regulation of one system aimed at reduced use of institutional settings may simply create incentives for gatekeepers to follow a path of less resistance (Farmer et al. 2003; Garland et al. 2001). It also means that seemingly extraneous considerations (e.g., race) can operate to route young people in need of treatment into systems that vary in their consumer-friendliness and their focus on control (Baker and Bell 1999; Hough et al. 2002; U.S. Department of Health and Human Services 2001).

Of course, the complexity of the overall service system also reflects the wide range of needs of young people with conduct disorders, thought disorders, or a combination of disorders. The causes and correlates of conduct problems, for example, are perhaps noteworthy for their diversity. Such behavior disorders are typically accompanied by socioeconomic, educational, family, and psychological problems (for reviews, see Henggeler 1989; Howell 2003). Incipient chronic mental disorders also carry diverse problems of family life, peer relations, job stability, etc. (see, e.g., Bryson et al. 1998; Patterson et al. 2001; Velligan et al. 2000, and citations therein). Such pervasiveness of poor adjustment almost inevitably invites actual or possible intervention by multiple agencies.

Successful navigation among these service sectors is made even more difficult by the common ambiguity of their goals. Agencies often have mixed motives when it comes to "serving" youth. Policy issues and problems in design of systems to serve young people with mental health problems often reflect long-standing conceptual contradictions.

Some scholars (e.g., Platt 1977) have argued that Progressive Era innovations that appeared to be exclusively intended to promote the well-being of young people—"in the best interest of the child"—in fact often had deeper purpose of social control. Indeed, the case has been made that the very notion of adolescence was invented in order to regulate conduct (Kett 1977). The confusion surrounding the real purpose of these institutions continues today and contributes to the complexity surrounding the systemic response to the needs of teenagers and young adults. Further complicating matters is the fact that the level of control orientation—as opposed to treatment orientation—tends to change over time as society alternatively embraces and then retreats from "get tough" approaches to crime and social disorder (Gray 2003; Grisso 2000).

Concerns associated with formal transitions into and from systems. As if having to deal with multiple service systems were not difficult enough, those in transition to adulthood also must contend with the fact that the transition itself may close the gates to some systems and necessitate opening the gates to others. For those young people who have mental health problems and remain in school long enough to complete it (such youths are at substantially higher risk for dropping out, see, e.g., Cullinan, Epstein, and Sabornie 1992), graduation from high school for mainstream students and reaching the age of twenty-one for special education students represents the end of involvement with the public education system. (See chapter 9 for a detailed discussion of special education policies during the transition to adulthood.) Because the public education system is a major provider and broker of therapeutic services (see, e.g., Melton et al. 1998), ouster from the public education system often also constitutes termination of mental health services.

Like the public education system, the juvenile justice system also has a rigid, statutorily specified age beyond which prospective service recipients are excluded (to the extent the system is really about services, see discussion above). Unlike the schools, though, each state has its own rules for minimum and maximum ages for eligibility because in most cases juvenile justice is a state, rather than federal, function. At first blush, it seems as though the loss of juvenile justice "services" should not be much of a problem. After all, as chapters 2 and 3 make clear, the juvenile justice system is the child and family service system that conceptually seems least oriented toward providing help with mental health problems. Unfortunately, however, juvenile justice is the only system available to many; it is often the end-of-the-line system for youths who cannot receive services through other means (Farmer et al. 2003; Compton et al. 2003; Fergusson et al. 2003; MacKinnon-Lewis, Kaufman, and Frabutt 2002; Marmorstein and Iacono 2003; Pear 2004; Redding 2000). Even more troubling is the apparent trend toward ever-increasing rates of mental disorder among institutionalized youth (Grisso 2004) (see chapter 4 for an extensive review of juvenile justice policy and the transition to adulthood).

Eligibility requirements for services in the health care system. The underlying problems that make matters complex for potential consumers of services that we have discussed thus far are largely conceptual. Sometimes, however, the issues are relatively narrow and technical. Perhaps the best example is the difficulty—or the opportunity—that many young people with mental disabilities have in moving from "child" to "adult" status in the Social Security system. (See chapter 13 for a general discussion of eligibility for health care services during the transition to adulthood.)

For seven decades, the federal government has provided financial support for persons unable to secure gainful employment as a result of disability, including mental disability. This support is provided chiefly through two programs, Social Security Disability Insurance and the Supplemental Security Income Program. The former program, as the name implies, operates in a manner similar to insurance. People are eligible for the benefits if they have paid their premiums by working (and paying into the Social Security Trust Fund) for half of the preceding ten years. SSI provides benefits to persons based on disability level, regardless of employment history. According to the statute:

> The term "disability" means inability to engage in any substantial gainful activity by reason of any medically determinable physical or mental impairment which can be expected to result in death or which has lasted or can be expected to last for a continuous period of not less than 12 months. (42 U.S.C. § 432(d)(1)(A) (2003))

In making the foregoing determination of disability for adults, the Social Security Administration has established a five-step process that begins with establishing (a) whether the person has been impermissibly gainfully employed and, if not, (b) whether she or he has a severe impairment that is (c) listed in the statute (i.e., organic, psychotic, affective, developmental, anxiety, somatoform, personality, and substance dependence disorders). If so, the person is eligible for benefits. The person also may be eligible for benefits without a listed disorder if (d) the impairment precludes engaging in the kind of work previously undertaken and (e) the person does not have functional abilities that would allow some other type of employment.

Because this volume concerns those in transition from adolescence to adulthood, it is important to consider eligibility of minors as well. For children, the eligibility determination is somewhat different. The first two steps in determining Supplemental Security Income eligibility are roughly the same as for adults. However, the third step involves a determination as to whether the child's impairment is equivalent to a listed impairment. The impairments listed for children differ from those listed for adults and include (a) organic mental disorders, (b) psychotic disorders, (c) mood disorders, (d) developmental disorders, (e) somatoform and related disorders, (f) substance dependence disorders, (g) attention-deficit/hyperactivity disorder, and (h) various disorders in infancy.

The differentiation of eligibility criteria for children vis-à-vis adults is a gate that swings both ways. On the one hand, many children who had been eligible for benefits tied to developmentally gauged criteria may suddenly be ineligible once they reach adulthood and the criteria become more absolute. A youth eligible for services because of attention deficit disorder, for example, will be ineligible for those services upon reaching adulthood because the disorder is not covered by the statute governing adults. On the other hand, the expectation of self-sufficiency (more specifically, the discontinuation of taking account of parental income to determine eligibility) that accompanies adulthood may open the gates of eligibility for young adults who had previously been ineligible for benefits. Thus a young person with a serious mental disorder who was unable to obtain services through SSI because parental income was too high would suddenly become eligible for SSI upon reaching adulthood unless he or she was able to obtain and hold a job.

Although the side of the gate on which a young adult finds himself or herself may seem arbitrary, its consequences can be enormous. Most obviously, the disability examiner's opinion will determine whether a basic livelihood is guaranteed for an individual who is not in the workforce. It also will determine whether the young adult will be eligible for Medicaid services, including mental health services, regardless of his or her parents' income. For a young adult who may not be easily insurable because of a prior chronic condition, this point may be critical. It may be doubly so for a young adult who has a mental disorder, because case management, home-based services, and other important means of meeting the young person's social needs may be covered by Medicaid, but such services rarely are within the scope of private health insurance.

In that regard, the image of the gate that swings two ways applies to the private as well as the public health care system. Like public systems, private systems also may have precipitous cessation of services as, say, when a minor achieves the age of majority and is no longer eligible for coverage through her or his parents' insurance policy. Also as is true with public services, however, where doors close for some, they open for others. For example, the loss of access to private services may facilitate access to public ones.

Special education. As is discussed in the chapters of this volume devoted to special education (chapter 8 and 9), the Individuals with Disabilities Education Act (IDEA) and related statutes require schools to bear much of the responsibility for meeting the needs of youth with mental disorders. The law compels public schools to provide "free appropriate public education" (§ 1401(8)) that emphasizes special education and related services to meet the "unique needs" of children with mental disorders (§ 1401(25)). Psychological services are included among these "related services" (§ 1401(3)(A)(ii)). Although the courts have construed the mandates of IDEA fairly narrowly (see, e.g., Cunningham 2000, and citations therein), it remains an important source through which services may be made available to young people in transition to adulthood, particularly given that eligibility can continue through age twenty-one.

RESEARCH-BASED PRINCIPLES TO GUIDE MENTAL HEALTH SERVICES FOR YOUNG PEOPLE IN TRANSITION

As Gralinski-Bakker and her colleagues make clear in the preceding chapter, the problems confronting young people with mental health problems as they transition to adulthood are difficult and complex. Further, successfully navigating the maze of eligibility requirements does not mean that appropriate services will necessarily be available. In developing a model for mental health services for this population we believe the sensible approach is to build on what we know works (i.e., approaches supported by empirical evidence) and how people ought to be treated (i.e., normative principles).

Transitions are difficult. The transition to adulthood—like most major transitions in life—is a difficult one for many people. This is so regardless of presence or severity of mental health problems. Consequently, policies should be oriented not only toward addressing the needs of those who have mental health problems (tertiary prevention), but also the needs of those who are at high risk for developing disorders (secondary prevention) as well as people making the transition who are not at heightened risk (primary prevention).

Transitions should be predictable. Knowing who will transition successfully and who will not may be a difficult task; knowing when the transition will occur is not. Prevention efforts are stymied by our inability to identify precisely who is at highest risk for developing mental health problems as they transition into adulthood. This difficulty, however, is offset somewhat by the fact that we do know precisely when the transition will occur. We can and should plan accordingly.

Planning based on predictable transitions is not new. Special education service providers, for example, are required to plan for transitions from services, often years in advance of the cessation of those services. This can be accomplished because everyone transitions out of those services at the same age and service providers can plan accordingly. Where transitions vary from person to person, as in the context of transitions from prison, plans can be made in advance of one's release. As aftercare planning in advance of release from hospitals demonstrates, such efforts are possible even where there is considerable uncertainty as to when the transition will occur.

Efforts should be community based. In order to address the needs of people at this critical transition point, families, social support networks, and the broader community should be fortified so as to be in a position to provide support. Communities should be strengthened in ways that render support both close and easily accessible. As Burns (2003) notes, community-based treatments work. However, they can be effective only if they are accessible. Attention to the ecological context of service delivery is important.

In this regard, "closeness" refers to both geographic proximity (i.e., services should be available where people live and work) and interpersonal proximity (i.e., support should be made available through the people to whom one is closest, such as families). Community-based approaches should be the treatments of choice for a variety of reasons, not the least of which is that they have been shown to be relatively highly effective (for a review, see Burns 2003, and citations therein).

The strengthening of relationships should occur not only at the family and immediate support network levels, but also at the neighborhood and community levels. Moreover, efforts should involve strengthening the connections between and among the individual and each of these institutions and groups (e.g., by increasing opportunities for community involvement).

To provide an analogy, such a blueprint already has been sketched out in the context of community building to enhance child protection efforts:

> We hope to strengthen community institutions—the . . . [places where] children and their families "naturally" go—to make help easily available where they

are when they need it without having to become "clients" or "patients." In short, we want to make the Golden Rule not only the prevailing norm but also a standard that the community makes easy to practice. (Melton 2002, 2)

In the context under discussion in this volume, the implementation of the Golden Rule necessarily differs from that of the child protection context, in part because young adults do not necessarily go to the same places as young children. Although school-based services, for example, may not fit the needs of young adults to the same extent as for adolescents, ecologically appropriate services can still be offered in the community through neighborhood centers, houses of worship, and the like. Adults other than staff members are not necessarily found in primary and secondary schools naturally, but going to schools should not be an unnatural experience. This premise is particularly true for *young* adults, for whom the school experience is not so far removed in time (but see, e.g., Cullinan, Epstein, and Sabornie 1992, on youth with mental health problems dropping out of school earlier and at higher rates than their peers).

Effort should be multisystemic. Just as we know with confidence that community-based approaches are generally preferable to institutional ones, we also know that multisystemic approaches are better than those that address a single domain. The comorbidity of disorders (having more than one disorder at a time) suggests that a singular focus is likely to overlook much. So does the complexity of causes and correlates of mental health problems in adolescence and young adulthood. In addition to comorbid disorders, many of these transitional youth and their families must also cope with (a) abuse and neglect, (b) undereducation, (c) underemployment, (d) poverty, and (e) involvement with the juvenile justice and criminal justice systems. These stressors tax and may even overwhelm personal coping strategies.

Family involvement is key. When personal resources are not sufficient, social support becomes particularly important. A recurrent theme throughout this volume is that, overwhelmingly, strong family connections are associated with much better outcomes than are weak family connections. Treatment approaches work better when families are involved. This is true whether the identified problem is conduct related and is being addressed through multisystemic treatment (e.g., Henggeler et al. 1998; see also Henggeler et al. 2002) or is chronic and disabling schizophrenia and is being addressed through vocational habilitation and assisted living efforts (e.g., Hogarty et al. 1991; North et al. 1998).

Families serve an important role by operating in the background of people's lives as sources of varying levels of support throughout the lifespan. Families likely can do more, though. With training and assistance they can help bridge the support gap at critical transition points, for example, as school-based services move to community-based services.

Involving families meaningfully likely will require overcoming barriers in the form of negative attitudes held by mental health professionals about family involvement in treatment of adults with mental illnesses. Many such professionals work only with adults. Therefore, the family-oriented models for treating children and adolescents may be unfamiliar. Although professionals regard many family members as supportive caregivers, they regard many others as making negative contributions to mental health. This skepticism is part of an overall pattern of tending to view them as "good families" or "bad families" (Riebschleger 2001).

GUIDING NORMATIVE PRINCIPLES

In discussions of mental health services for children (Melton 1991; Melton and Lyons in press), we have noted that the principles embedded in the Convention on the Rights of the Child (1989) usefully frame the normative context within which such treatment occurs. In a similar vein, we believe that the Principles for the Protection of Persons with Mental Illness and the Improvement of Mental Health Care (1991), a resolution adopted by the United Nations General Assembly, provides a clear blueprint for the ethical treatment of people with mental illness. These principles also support the theme of social inclusion, which appears throughout the present volume. (See chapter 14.)

The first principle is especially germane to the present discussion:

Principle 1: Fundamental Freedoms and Basic Rights

§ 1.   All persons have the right to the best available mental health care, which shall be part of the health and social care system.

§ 2.   All persons with a mental illness, or who are being treated as such persons, shall be treated with humanity and respect for the inherent dignity of the human person.

§ 3.   All persons with a mental illness, or who are being treated as such persons, have the right to protection from economic, sexual and other forms of exploitation, physical or other abuse and degrading treatment.

§ 4.   There shall be no discrimination on the grounds of mental illness. "Discrimination" means any distinction, exclusion or preference that has the effect of nullifying or impairing equal enjoyment of rights. . . .

§ 5.   Every person with a mental illness shall have the right to exercise all civil, political, economic, social and cultural rights.

These foundational principles thus articulate the rights of people with mental illness to (a) treatment as persons, (b) protection from exploitation, (c) quality treatment, and (d) equal protection of the law. They may have special meaning to people at a stage of life typified by initial expression of the privileges of citizenship and assertion of independence.

It is worth underscoring that the first section of the first principle refers to quality mental health care. We believe that this provision parallels our assertion that sound policy ought to build on what we know works. Also worth noting is that the prohibition on discrimination (§ 4) presumably addresses stigma, given the reciprocal causal relation between the two phenomena.

The stigma associated with mental health problems is one of the reasons that nearly two-thirds of all people with mental health problems do not seek treatment (Bush 2002; Mechanic 2002; U.S. Department of Health and Human Services 1999; World Health Organization 2002). Stigma is particularly problematic for those transitioning to adulthood because of its profound effect on capacity to fulfill the developmental tasks associated with that period. In addition to the problems associated with mental illness itself, the stigma of mental illness has been shown to diminish choices in the fundamental domains of life. Stigmatized persons may have difficulty in succeeding in education, employment, and the formation of relationships (Corrigan and Penn 1999; Perlick 2001; Weiden, Scheifler, and Diamond 1998). Consumers of mental health services experience discrimination in multiple contexts, including their own families, churches, and even mental health services themselves (Corrigan 2002; Farina et al. 1974; Schulze and Angermeyer 2003; Wahl 1999).

The personal experience of stigma is a deeply troubling and persistent problem. It is so robust that it can survive even when there is improvement clinically (Link et al. 1997). Although the effect is quite pronounced for the person directly stigmatized, the impact is much broader. Stigma implicates a wide range of stakeholders (i.e., the individual, family, community, mental health care providers, government agencies, employers) with potentially differing agendas. As the body of research on stigma grows (see Penn and Wykes 2003; U.S. Department of Health and Human Services 1999), it becomes increasingly apparent just how pervasive and detrimental its effects are. Discriminatory attitudes, beliefs, and practices deeply affect individuals, families, and communities.

In seeking to combat stigma, international human rights law parallels relatively recent initiatives of the federal government. In 1999, the U.S. surgeon general launched a groundbreaking initiative that identified stigma as "the most formidable obstacle to future progress in the arena of mental illness and health" (U.S. Department of Health and Human Services 1999, 3). The report concluded that stigma should no longer be tolerated.

More recently, President Bush (2002) expressed his desire to combat the stigma of mental illness. He noted that "Americans with mental illness deserve our understanding, and they deserve excellent care. They deserve a health care system that treats their illness with the same urgency as a physical illness." In announcing the creation of the President's New Freedom Commission on Mental Health, President Bush said he had created the commission to shore up the cracks in the system through which vulnerable Americans may slip.

The second principle for protection calls for "special care" in the context of treatment of minors with mental illness to protect their rights. Although young people in transition to adulthood obviously are moving from their status as minors, legally and socially vulnerable youth are especially deserving of protection. Changes in legal status carry with them increased obligations of self-determination where treatment decisions are concerned, regardless of whether youth are prepared for that level of autonomy.

Principle 3, aptly entitled "Life in the Community," ties together many of the issues we have presented. In positing that "[e]very person with a mental illness shall have the right to live and work, as far as possible, in the community," the provision not only calls for reliance on community-based treatments, but it also facilitates the preservation of family and other relationships essential to personhood.

CONCLUSION: WHAT NEEDS TO HAPPEN

Transitions are nearly always difficult. For young people with mental health problems moving into adulthood, the transition is made more difficult by the complexity of both the problems themselves and the systemic responses that they engender. We have suggested three general directions for reform.

First and foremost, efforts should be undertaken to strengthen communities so that they can serve as caring communities—spontaneously providing support when, where, and how it is needed. These supportive networks should be able (a) to ease the transition for those who are struggling through it with difficulties at subclinical levels, (b) to adapt to the changing need levels for people whose problems will ebb and flow, and (c) to serve as the foundation on which to build permanent habilitative and other assistance for people whose problems are chronic, severe, and disabling.

Second, where caring communities will lead to services that are more intensive than background support, those services should be based in the communities wherever possible. Moreover, they should be multisystemic and involve families. Because of the importance of families, they should be supported well and early so that they can assume and maintain a central role in meeting ongoing needs. Where families have become fragmented, efforts should be undertaken to rebuild them to serve this function. Where this is impossible, familylike structures should be developed as alternatives.

Third, in all of our efforts to address the needs of transitional youth and their families, we should maintain fidelity to normative principles guiding how people deserve to be treated. At a minimum, this means treating youth in transition and their families as persons and, in so doing, protecting them from exploitation and discrimination and promoting their social inclusion.

REFERENCES

Angold, A., E. J. Costello, and C. M Worthman. 1998. Puberty and depression: The roles of age, pubertal status, and pubertal timing. *Psychological Medicine* 28: 51–61.

Baker, F. M., and C. C. Bell. 1999. Issues in the psychiatric treatment of African Americans. *Psychiatric Services* 50: 362–368.

Barry, E. 2003. At 18, mental patients face perilous change. *Boston Globe,* February 3, A1.

Birmaher, B., C. Arbelaez, and D. Brent. 2002. Course and outcome of child and adolescent major depressive disorder. *Child and Adolescent Psychiatric Clinics of North America* 11: 619–638.

Blinder, B. J., W. M. Young, K. R. Fineman, and S. J. Miller. 1978. The children's psychiatric hospital unit in the community. 1. Concept and development. *American Journal of Psychiatry* 135: 847–851.

Bloom, R. B., and L. R. Hopewell. 1982. Psychiatric hospitalization of adolescents and successful mainstream reentry. *Exceptional Children* 48: 352–357.

Brooks-Gunn, J., and I. Attie. 1996. Developmental psychopathology in the context of adolescence. Pp. 148–149 in *Frontiers of developmental psychopathology.* Edited by Mark F. Lenzenweger. London: Oxford University Press.

Bryson, G., M. D. Bell, E. Kaplan, and T. Greig. 1998. The functional consequences of memory impairments on initial work performance in people with schizophrenia. *Journal of Nervous and Mental Disease* 186: 610–615.

Burns, B. 2003. Children and evidence-based practice. *Psychiatric Clinics of North America* 26: 955–970.

Bush, G. W. 2002. President's New Freedom Commission on Mental Health. Speech given at the University of New Mexico, Albuquerque, April 29. http://www.whitehouse.gov/news/releases/2002/04/print/20020429-1.html.

Compton, K., J. Snyder, L. Schrepferman, L. Bank, and J. W. Shortt. 2003. The contribution of parents and siblings to antisocial and depressive behavior in adolescents: A double jeopardy coercion model. *Development and Psychopathology* 15: 163–182.

Compton, S. N., B. J. Burns, H. L. Egger, and E. Robertson. 2002. Review of the evidence base for treatment of childhood psychopathology: Internalizing disorders. *Journal of Consulting and Clinical Psychology* 70: 1240–1266.

Convention on the Rights of the Child. 1989. U.N. Doc. GA/Res/44/25 1989.

Corrigan, P. W. 2002. Empowerment and serious mental illness: Treatment partnerships and community opportunities. *Psychiatric Quarterly* 73: 217–228.

Corrigan, P. W., and D. L. Penn. 1999. Lessons from social psychology on discrediting psychiatric stigma. *American Psychologist* 54: 765–776.

Cullinan, D., M. Epstein, and E. Sabornie. 1992. Selected characteristics of a national sample of seriously emotionally disturbed adolescents. *Behavioral Disorders* 17: 273–280.

Cunningham, M. 2000. Playing doctor: Discerning what medical services school districts must provide to disabled children under *Cedar Rapids Community School District v. Garret F. Baylor Law Review* 52: 171–189.

Dickinson, P., C. Coggan, and S. Bennett. 2003. TRAVELLERS: A school-based early intervention programme helping young people manage and process change, loss, and transition. Pilot phase findings. *Australian and New Zealand Journal of Psychiatry* 37: 299–306.

Farina, A., J. Thaw, J. D. Lovern, and D. Mangone. 1974. People's reactions to a former mental patient moving into their neighborhood. *Journal of Community Psychology* 2: 108–112.

Farmer, E. M. Z., B. J. Burns, S. D. Phillips, A. Angold, and E. J. Costello. 2003. Pathways into and through mental health services for children and adolescents. *Psychiatric Services* 54: 60–66.

Fergusson, D. M., B. Wanner, F. Vitaro, L. J. Horwood, and N. Swain-Campbell. 2003. Deviant peer affiliations and depression: Confounding or causation? *Journal of Abnormal Child Psychology* 31: 605–618.

Fombonne, E., G. Wostear, V. Cooper, R. Harrington, and M. Rutter. 2001a. The Maudsley long-term follow-up of child and adolescent depression. 1. Psychiatric outcomes in adulthood. *British Journal of Psychiatry* 179: 210–217.

Fombonne, E., G. Wostear, V. Cooper, R. Harrington, and M. Rutter. 2001b. The Maudsley long-term follow-up of child and adolescent depression. 2. Suicidality, criminality, and social dysfunction in adulthood. *British Journal of Psychiatry* 179: 218–223.

Garland, A. F., R. L. Hough, K. M. McCabe, M. Yeh, P. A. Wood, and G. A. Aarons. 2001. Prevalence of psychiatric disorders in youths across five sectors of care. *Journal of the American Academy of Child and Adolescent Psychiatry* 40: 409–418.

Gray, E. S. 2003. Children, crime, and consequences: Juvenile justice in America: The media—don't believe the hype. *Stanford Law and Policy Review* 14: 45–56.

Grisso, T. 2000. The changing face of juvenile justice. *Law and Psychiatry* 51: 425–426, 438.

Grisso, T. 2004. *Double jeopardy: Adolescent offenders with mental disorders.* Chicago: University of Chicago Press.

Henggeler, S. W. 1989. *Delinquency in adolescence.* Newbury Park, CA: Sage.

Henggeler, S. W., and C. M. Bourduin. 1995. Multisystemic treatment of serious juvenile offenders and their families. Pp. 113–130 in *Home-based services for troubled children.* Edited by I. M. Schwartz and P. AuClaire. Lincoln: University of Nebraska Press.

Henggeler, S. W., and A. B. Santos, eds. 1997. *Innovative approaches for difficult-to-treat populations.* Washington: American Psychiatric Press.

Henggeler, S. W., S. K. Schoenwald, C. M. Borduin, M. D. Rowland, and P. B. Cunningham. 1998. *Multisystemic treatment of antisocial behavior in children and adolescents.* New York: Guilford.

Henggeler, S. W., S. K. Schoenwald, M. D. Rowland, and P. B. Cunningham. 2002. *Serious emotional disturbance in children and adolescents: Multisystemic therapy.* New York: Guilford.

Hobbs, N. 1982. *The troubled and troubling child: Reeducation in mental health, education, and human services programs for children and youth.* San Francisco: Jossey-Bass.

Hogarty, G. E., C. M. Anderson, D. J. Reiss, S. J. Kornblith, D. P. Greenwald, R. F. Ulrich, and

M. Carter. 1991. Family psychoeducation, social skills training, and maintenance of chemotherapy in the aftercare treatment of schizophrenia. 2. Two-year effects of a controlled study on relapse and adjustment. *Archives of General Psychiatry* 48: 340–347.

Hough, R. L., A. L. Hazen, F. I. Soriano, P. Wood, K. McCabe, and M. Yeh. 2002. Mental health services for Latino adolescents with psychiatric disorders. *Psychiatric Services* 53: 1556–1562.

Howell, J. C. 2003. *Preventing and reducing juvenile delinquency.* Thousand Oaks, CA: Sage.

Individuals with Disabilities Education Act. 1990. Pub. L. No. 101-476 1990, 20 U.S.C. §§1400–1485 2004. [Originally enacted as the Education of the Handicapped Act and subsequently known as the Education for all Handicapped Children Act, first enacted in 1975. Name change to IDEA was enacted by Pub. L. No. 101-476 and required no change in text.]

Jackson-Beeck, M., I. M. Schwartz, and A. Rutherford. 1987. *Trends and issues in juvenile confinement for psychiatric and chemical dependency treatment in the U.S., England, and Wales.* Minneapolis: University of Minnesota, Center for the Study of Youth Policy.

Kataoka, S. H., L. Zhang, and K. B. Wells. 2002. Unmet need for mental health care among U.S. children: Variation by ethnicity and insurance status. *American Journal of Psychiatry* 159: 1548–1555.

Kett, J. F. 1977. *Rites of passage: Adolescence in America, 1790 to the present.* New York: Basic Books.

Kiesner, J. 2002. Depressive symptoms in early adolescence: Their relations with classroom problem behavior and peer status. *Journal of Research on Adolescence* 12: 463–478.

Knapp, M., P. McCrone, E. Fombonne, J. Beecham, and G. Wostear. 2002. The Maudsley long-term follow-up of child and adolescent depression. 3. Impact of comorbid conduct disorder on service use and costs in adulthood. *British Journal of Psychiatry* 180: 19–23.

Kramer, T. L., J. M. Robbins, S. D. Phillips, and T. L. Miller. 2003. Detection and outcomes of substance use disorders in adolescents seeking mental health treatment. *Journal of the American Academy of Child and Adolescent Psychiatry* 42: 1318–1326.

Link, B. G., E. L. Struening, M. Rahav, J. C. Phelan, and L. Nuttbrock. 1997. On stigma and its consequences: Evidence from a longitudinal study of men with dual diagnosis of mental illness and substance abuse. *Journal of Health and Social Behavior* 38: 177–190.

MacKinnon-Lewis, C., M. C. Kaufman, and J. M. Frabutt. 2002. Juvenile justice and mental health: Youth and families in the middle. *Aggression and Violent Behavior* 7: 353–363.

Marmorstein, N. R., and W. G. Iacono. 2003. Major depression and conduct disorder in a twin sample: Gender, functioning, and risk for future psychopathology. *Journal of the American Academy of Child and Adolescent Psychiatry* 42: 225–233.

Mechanic, D. 2002. Removing barriers to care among persons with psychiatric symptoms: A well-functioning managed care approach can provide an acceptable level of care and cost. *Health Affairs* 21: 137–147.

Melton, G. B. 1991. Socialization in the global community: Respect for the dignity of children. *American Psychologist* 46: 66–71.

Melton, G. B. 1997. Why don't the knuckleheads use common sense? Pp. 351–370 in *Innovative approaches for difficult-to-treat populations.* Edited by S. W. Henggeler and A. B. Santos. Washington: American Psychiatric Press.

Melton, G. B. 2002. Strong communities for children in the Golden Strip. Retrieved April 11, 2003 from http://www.clemson.edu/strongcommunities/pdfs/melton_remarks.pdf.

Melton, G. B., and P. M. Lyons, Jr. In press. *Mental health services for children and families: Building a system that works.* New York: Guilford.

Melton, G. B., P. M. Lyons, Jr., and W. J. Spaulding. 1998. *No place to go: The civil commitment of minors.* Lincoln: University of Nebraska Press.

Melton, G. B., and M. Sullivan. 1993. The concept of entitlement and its incompatibility with American legal culture. Pp. 47–58 in *Visions of entitlement: The care and education of America's children.* Edited by M. A. Jensen and S. G. Goffin. Albany: SUNY Press.

North, C. S., D. E. Pollio, B. Sachar, B. Hong, K. Isenberg, and B. Bufe. 1998. The family as caregiver: A group psychoeducation model for schizophrenia. *American Journal of Orthopsychiatry* 68: 39–46.

Nurcombe, B. 1995. The future of psychiatric hospitalization for children and adolescents. Pp. 101–116 in *Children's mental health services: Research, policy, and evaluation.* Edited by L. L. Bickman and D. J. Rog. Thousand Oaks, CA: Sage.

O'Carroll, P. W., A. Crosby, J. A. Mercy, R. K. Lee, and T. R. Simon. 2001. Interviewing suicide "decedents": A fourth strategy for risk factor assessment. *Suicide and Life Threatening Behavior* 32 (supp.): 3–6.

Patterson, T. L., S. Goldman, C. L. McKibbin, T. Hughs, and D. V. Jeste. 2001. The USCD performance-based skills assessment: Development of a new measure of everyday functioning for severely mentally ill adults. *Schizophrenia Bulletin* 27: 235–245.

Pear, R. 2004. Many youths reported held awaiting mental help. *New York Times,* July 8, A18.

Penn, D. L., and T. Wykes. 2003. Stigma, discrimination, and mental illness. *Journal of Mental Health* 12: 203–208.

Perlick, D. A. 2001. Special section on stigma as a barrier to recovery: Introduction. *Psychiatric Services* 52: 1613–1614.

Phillips, L. J., S. B. Leicester, L. E. O'Dwyer, S. M. Francey, J. Koutsogiannis, A. Abdel-Baki, D. Kelly, S. Jones, C. Vay, A. R. Yung, and P. D. McGorry. 2002. The PACE Clinic: Identification and management of young people at "ultra" high risk of psychosis. *Journal of Psychiatric Practice* 8: 255–269.

Platt, A. M. 1977. *The child savers: The invention of delinquency.* 2nd ed. Chicago: University of Chicago Press.

Principles for the Protection of Persons with Mental Illness and the Improvement of Mental Health Care. 1991. U. N. Doc. GA/Res/119 1991.

Pumariega, A. J., and N. C. Winters. 2003. Trends and shifting ecologies. 2. *Child and Adolescent Psychiatric Clinics of North America* 12: 779–793.

Redding, R. E. 2000. *Barriers to meeting the mental health needs of offenders in the juvenile justice system.* Juvenile Justice Fact Sheet. Charlottesville: Institute of Law, Psychiatry, and Public Policy, University of Virginia.

Riebschleger, J. 2001. What do mental health professionals really think of family members of mental health patients? *American Journal of Orthopsychiatry* 71: 466–472.

Schulze, B., and M. C. Angermeyer. 2003. Subjective experiences of stigma: A focus group study of schizophrenic patients, their relatives, and mental health professionals. *Social Science and Medicine* 56: 299–312.

Silver, S. E., A. J. Duchnowski, K. Kutash, R. M. Friedman, M. Eisen, M. E. Prange, N. A. Brandenburg, and P. E. Greenbaum. 1992. A comparison of children with serious emotional disturbance served in residential and school settings. *Journal of Child and Family Studies* 1: 43–59.

Simic, M., and E. Fombonne. 2001. Depressive conduct disorder: Symptom patterns and correlates in referred children and adolescents. *Journal of Affective Disorders* 62: 175–185.

U.S. Department of Health and Human Services. 1999. *Mental health: A report of the Surgeon General.* Rockville, MD: Center for Mental Health Services and National Institute of Mental Health.

U.S. Department of Health and Human Services. 2000. *Report of the Surgeon General's Conference on Children's Mental Health: A national action agenda.* Washington: U.S. Department of Health and Human Services.

U.S. Department of Health and Human Services. 2001. *Mental health: Culture, race, and ethnicity: A supplement to Mental health: A report of the surgeon general.* Rockville, MD: Center for Mental Health Services and National Institute of Mental Health.

Velligan, D. I., C. C. Bow-Thomas, R. K. Mahurin, A. L. Miller, and L. C. Halgunseth. 2000. Do specific neurocognitive deficits predict specific domains of community function in schizophrenia? *Journal of Nervous and Mental Disease* 188: 518–524.

Wahl, O. F. 1999. Mental health consumers' experience of stigma. *Schizophrenia Bulletin* 25: 467–478.

Walker, E. F., D. J. Walder, and F. Reynolds. 2001. Developmental changes in cortisol secretion in normal and at-risk youth. *Development and Psychopathology* 13: 721–732.

Waslick, B., D. Schoenholz, and R. Pizarro. 2003. Diagnosis and treatment of chronic depression in children and adolescents. *Journal of Psychiatric Practice* 9: 354–366.

Weiden, P. J., P. L. Scheifler, and R. J. Diamond. 1998. The road back: Working with those with severe mental illness: My patient is better: Now what? 2. Dealing with interpersonal relationships. *Journal of Practical Psychiatry and Behavioral Health* 4: 309–315.

Weist, M. D., A. Goldstein, L. Morris, and T. Bryant. 2003. Integrating expanded school mental health programs and school-based health centers. *Psychology in the Schools* 40: 297–308.

World Health Organization. 2002. Mental health: Responding to the call for action: Report by the Secretariat. 55th WHO Assembly, Provisional agenda item 13.13. A55/18.

Youth Health Services. 2002. *Youth Health Services annual report 2001–2002: Building community partnerships for youth.* Seattle: Public Health Seattle and King County.

CHAPTER TWELVE

Adolescents with Disabilities in Transition to Adulthood

ROBERT WM. BLUM

The author acknowledges Peter Scal for his assistance with valuable data analyses from the National Health Information Survey 1994–95 disability supplement, and Linda Boche for her work on manuscript preparation. This paper is a product of the KDWB University Pediatrics Family Center, Department of Pediatrics, University of Minnesota.

INTRODUCTION

A generation ago most young people with chronic and disabling conditions died before they reached their teenage years. Today, well over 90 percent of children born with these same conditions survive into adulthood and beyond. Fetal surgery, neonatal interventions, and childhood chemotherapies have created life-sustaining possibilities where none existed previously. But many young adults living with previously fatal conditions are like the first astronauts to explore space—going where none has gone before without any hint of what they may anticipate along the journey. This chapter reviews what is known about adolescents with chronic physical conditions as they make the transitions to adulthood, what they may encounter, and what those of us who develop programs and influence policy for them should know. We start with definitions of terms and concepts. Subsequently, prevalence, survival to adulthood, and outcomes of adults with disabilities will be discussed. Finally, factors that influence outcomes will be reviewed.

DEFINITIONS

In discussing the transition to adulthood for adolescents with physical disabilities, the definition of disability greatly influences both prevalence rates and the research on the impact of a chronic condition.

As a start, it is worth distinguishing "disability" from the related concepts of "impairment" and "handicap." The term *impairment* refers to an individual's physical condition. An inward-turning eye or severe scoliosis is an impairment. *Disability* is the consequence of having impairment. Thus, an individual with a high-level spina bifida may not be ambulatory; the inability to walk is a disability. *Handicap* refers to the social limitations that result from a disability. Thus, the inability of young adults who are not ambulatory to participate in certain activities that may not be accessible is a handicap. Impairments are physiological; disabilities are functional; and handicaps are socially constructed.

Disability tends to be operationalized in one of three ways: functional limitations, compensatory mechanisms, or service utilization (Westbrook, Silver, and Stein 1998). Definition determines not only prevalence rates but also service eligibility, public policies, and programs. For example, the functional limitation of lagging behind peers more than two years in reading qualifies a student for special education services. A change in this definition of learning disability would alter both the prevalence of learning disabilities and individual eligibility for services. This chapter will explore issues related to young adults having not only impairments (physical limitations) but disabilities (functional limitations) and handicaps (social limitations). Each term will be used when referring to the specific concept.

The National Center for Health Statistics (NCHS) considers a condition chronic if it is present for more than three months or if it is expected to last more than three months. Thus, under this definition, duration determines chronicity. Instead of duration, Newacheck (1999) uses a functional definition of disability based on social role limitations, where adolescents are defined as having a disability if they are limited in or unable to conduct "age-appropriate school activities" due to chronic conditions. Disability Statistics Abstract (Scal et al. 2003) operationalizes a similar definition by looking at limitations within age groupings. For those ages five through seventeen, those who attend special schools, have other school limitations, or have limitations other than school are considered to have disabilities. For adults, the definition focuses on those who have limitations related to employment or housework.

The Maternal and Child Health Bureau (MCHB) focuses less on the chronicity of illness and more on the concept "special health care needs"; "those who have or are at increased risk for a chronic physical, developmental, behavioral, or emotional condition and who also require health and related services of a type or amount beyond that required by children generally" are considered to have such needs (McPherson et al. 1998, 138). Thus, this definition focuses on service utilization. An individual who has mild asthma, for example, may have a chronic condition by the NCHS definition, but would not necessarily have special health care needs according to the MCHB. Other federal agencies focus on the interaction between individual characteristics and characteristics in the environment, with disability at the end of a continuum that begins with enablement. This, for example, is the perspective of the National Institute on Disability and Rehabilitation Research (NIDRR); it is also the framework used by the World Health Organization.

DEMOGRAPHICS

Prevalence

Using a functional limitation definition of disability, Newacheck, Stoddard, et al. (1998) concluded from the National Health Interview Survey (NHIS) that 18 percent of youth under the age of eighteen have disabilities and need special health care services (table 12.1).

Survival to Adulthood

While the data are limited, there is clear evidence that the vast majority of children born with both chronic illnesses (as measured by duration) and disabling conditions (as measured by functional impairments) will survive to adulthood.

Table 12.1. Prevalence of leading chronic conditions of adolescence*

Conditions	Percentage
Asthma	4.3
Congenital heart disease	1.5
Epilepsy	0.24
Cerebral palsy	0.18
Diabetes	0.10
Cancer	0.04
Spina bifida	0.02

*Based upon a definition of functional impairment.

Source: Newacheck, Stoddard, et al. 1998.

Specifically, for the entire cohort of those children, Blum (1992) estimated that more than 90 percent will become adults (table 12.2).

Over the past thirty years there have been dramatic changes in survival rates for most chronic and disabling conditions. For example, survival rates to age twenty with cystic fibrosis have increased more than 700 percent; today, the average survival among those with cystic fibrosis cared for in major medical centers is approximately thirty years of age. Where a generation ago the majority of children with spina bifida died during the first decade of life, today the majority will reach their twentieth birthday and beyond (Blum 1992). So too, survival with childhood leukemia has increased more than 200 percent since the mid-1960s (Blum 1992).

Technological Supports

In the United States, 1,214,000 youth and young adults under twenty-four years of age use assistive technologies (table 12.3). Assistive technologies have had a vast impact on reducing barriers, allowing those with disabilities to enter the mainstream. As these individuals become older many of these technologies increase in importance. But accessing them is not the only problem some young adults have to face. Reliance on such technologies at times may also represent an acknowledgment of having a more severe impairment than one (or one's family) heretofore would choose to acknowledge. Let's look, for example, at a young adult who decides to use a wheelchair. Not uncommonly, children who have mobility impairments spend endless hours in physical therapy learning to ambulate on their own or with crutches or with a walker. Ambulation is heralded as "normalcy"; however, as the child gets older the slow pace of such ambulation further separates him from his peers—in the time it takes him to cross the room peers or coworkers will be out the door. A wheelchair allows one to keep up but not infrequently it is also seen as a defeat, a statement that "I will never walk again." It serves as one more reminder of the individual's difference from peers even as it allows more access to the mainstream.

Disability Patterns

While exact prevalence rates may depend on the definition used, there is general agreement regarding a number of patterns: (1) using NHIS data, prevalence rates of disabilities among young people, including those with special health care needs, have increased more than 250 percent since 1975; (2) prevalence rates increase with age (Wenger, Kaye, and LaPlante 1996); (3) ethnic minorities and

Table 12.2. Estimated survival to age 20 with select chronic conditions*

Conditions	Estimated proportion surviving (%)
Asthma (moderate and severe)	98
Congenital heart disease	71†
Diabetes mellitus	95
Cleft lip/palate	92
Spina bifida	>50
Sickle cell anemia	90
Cystic fibrosis	75
Hemophilia	90
Acute lymphocytic leukemia	71‡
End-stage renal disease	90§
Muscular dystrophy	>50

*Data from S.L. Gortmaker and W. Sappenfield (1984), "Chronic Childhood Disorders: Prevalence and Impact." *Pediatr. Clin. North Am.* 31(1):#3, with revisions as noted.

†J. Moller and R. Anderson (1991), "1000 Consecutive Children with a Cardiac Malformation: 26–37 Year Follow-Up." Unpublished data.

‡Birth through 14 years of age. *Cancer Statistical Review,* NIH Publ. no. 89-2789. National Cancer Institute, May 1989.

§Actuarial 2-year survival data for patients ages 10–19 with end-stage renal disease begun on treatment (transplant or dialysis). U.S. Renal Data System, *USRDS 1989 Annual Report* (Bethesda, MD: NIH, National Institute of Diabetes and Digestive Kidney Disease, 1989).

Originally published in Blum 1992 with subsequent revisions.

Table 12.3. Assistive technologies by device

Assistive technologies	N
Any anatomical device (e.g., artificial limb, brace)	646,000
Any mobility technology device (e.g., wheelchair, walker)	240,000
Any hearing technology (e.g., TDD/TTY, hearing aid)	152,000
Vision technology devices (e.g., Braille, white cane)	12,000
Speech technology devices (e.g., communication board, computer)	8,000
Other types of technology device	156,000
Total	1,214,000

Source: U.S. Department of Education, 2001.

young people of color sustain more disability with more limitations than their European-American peers (Newacheck, Strickland, et al. 1998) and are less likely to access services (Mueller and Askenazi 1999; Mueller, Patil, and Boilesen 1998); (4) families who are poor with less educated parents or single-parent families are more likely to have children with disabling conditions (Newacheck, Strickland, et al. 1998; Aron, Loprest, and Steverle 1996); (5) more than 90 percent of children with disabilities are living longer than ever before and are reaching adulthood (Blum 1992).

According to the U.S. Department of Education (1993), students with disabilities are twice as likely to be African-American as European-American. Indeed, African-Americans are overrepresented in all disability categories, particularly in mental retardation and serious emotional disorders. Latino students and Asian/Pacific Island students are underrepresented when accounting for disabilities (U.S. Department of Education 1993). Although American Indian children make up only 1 percent of the nation's public school population, they account for nearly 11 percent of the special education population (Joe 1997). (See chapter 8 for further discussion of ethnicity and special education.)

HOW YOUNG ADULTS WITH PHYSICAL DISABILITIES FARE

There is growing awareness that despite a generation of legislation aimed at creating equal opportunities for people with disabilities—in education, health services, and the workplace—the reality does not fully match the promise. A 1998 Harris poll reported several functional indicators of adult life that show major discrepancies in what those with disabilities have been able to achieve in education/school, employment/income earned, and social relationships. In addition, discrepancies have been seen in emotional well-being.

Education/School

Research suggests three critical junctures for young people with chronic and disabling conditions: diagnosis, puberty, and school completion. The latter transition is often associated with the greatest social disruption—the end of formal education, the end of a structured schedule provided by school, and rising expectations for work and independent living—one or both of which may not be achieved.

As can be seen in figure 12.1, young people with intellectual and physical im-

Figure 12.1. School completion status of students with disabilities
who attended regular high schools.

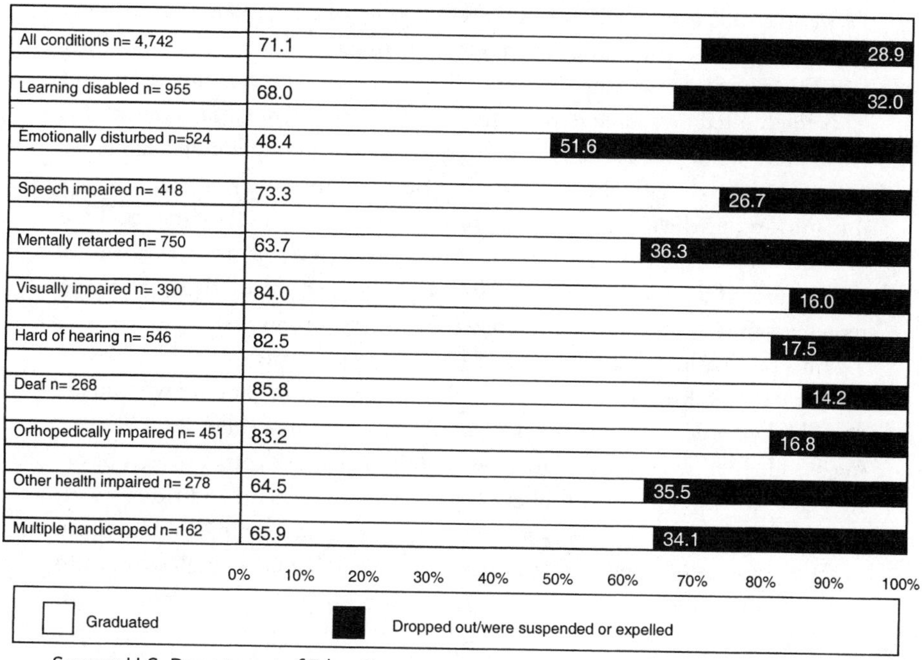

	Graduated	Dropped out/were suspended or expelled
All conditions n= 4,742	71.1	28.9
Learning disabled n= 955	68.0	32.0
Emotionally disturbed n=524	48.4	51.6
Speech impaired n= 418	73.3	26.7
Mentally retarded n= 750	63.7	36.3
Visually impaired n= 390	84.0	16.0
Hard of hearing n= 546	82.5	17.5
Deaf n= 268	85.8	14.2
Orthopedically impaired n= 451	83.2	16.8
Other health impaired n= 278	64.5	35.5
Multiple handicapped n=162	65.9	34.1

0%   10%   20%   30%   40%   50%   60%   70%   80%   90%   100%

☐ Graduated   ■ Dropped out/were suspended or expelled

Source: U.S. Department of Education, 2001.

pairments are significantly educationally disadvantaged.[1] Specifically, about 27 percent of those with speech impairments (e.g., dysarticulations, mutism) will not graduate from high school; the same is true of more than 36 percent of those with mental retardation. More than one in six young people who are deaf or hard of hearing will not complete twelfth grade; nearly the same is true for those with orthopedic impairments. A young person with multiple impairments has only a 66 percent chance of graduating from high school.

In looking at high school graduation as a measure of disability, based upon data from the National Health Interview Study on Disabilities (also known as NHIS-D 1994-95), Scal et al. (2003) found that graduation rates declined based on severity of condition: among the general population of adults aged eighteen to thirty years, 82.6 percent graduated from high school. However, for those with disabilities, graduation rates were as follows, based on the severity of the condition: mild, 79.5 percent; moderate, 76.1 percent; and severe, 61.4 percent.

1. Many students with disabilities qualify for special education services, especially those with learning disabilities and mental retardation. The transition to adulthood for these young people is also addressed by chapters 8 and 9 of this volume.

For these analyses, terms were defined based on one or more of the following five functional domains: (1) activities of daily living (ADL) such as bathing, showering, or dressing; (2) instrumental activities of daily living (IADL) such as preparing meals or managing money; (3) functional areas such as lifting something heavy or walking up stairs; (4) cognitive/intellectual functions; and (5) being limited or unable to participate in one's expected major activity. Onset in childhood was defined as the onset of any of the qualifying disability categories prior to age eighteen. A severity-of-disability score was established as the sum, among the five domains, of the highest reported level of impact of the disability. That is, the severity represents both the level of impact as well as the number of domains impacted. Three equally sized groups were created to represent mild, moderate, and severely impacted young adults.

An examination of attainment of higher education reveals similar trends (table 12.4). While nearly 85 percent of all young people in America will pursue some higher education, only 60 percent of those who are deaf or hard of hearing are likely to seek postsecondary schooling. For those with a speech or orthopedic impairment, the number falls to below 50 percent. Individuals with multiple disabilities have a one in twelve chance of gaining a higher education.

What these data suggest is that many who could complete high school and pursue higher education do not have the resources (e.g., family supports, assis-

Table 12.4. Postsecondary school enrollment of youth with disabilities out of school three to five years

Primary disability category	Percentage of youth who, since high school, had enrolled in:			
	Any postsecondary school	Postsecondary vocational school	2-year college	4-year college
All conditions	26.7	15.9	11.3	4.2
Learning disability	30.5	19.0	13.7	4.4
Emotional disturbance	25.6	15.4	10.1	4.2
Speech impairment	48.8	16.4	25.4	13.3
Mental retardation	12.8	9.6	3.6	.0
Visual impairment	57.0	15.6	27.5	33.4
Hard of hearing	60.4	16.0	40.4	15.7
Deafness	60.0	22.5	33.2	22.1
Orthopedic impairment	46.3	12.6	32.3	12.9
Other health impairment	56.0	33.9	28.4	21.9
Multiple disabilities	8.6	.7	7.9	2.2

Source: Scal et al. 2003.

tive technologies, educational assistance, financial resources) to achieve their maximal potential. For example, there is no inherent reason why young people who are deaf or hard of hearing have only a 60 percent chance of higher education. The same is true for both speech and orthopedic impairments. Those who have such conditions are about half as likely to attain a postsecondary education as their peers without disabilities. As will be discussed later, there is tremendous heterogeneity among those with any given impairment. The *severity* of that impairment, which is the extent that it limits one functionally, involves an interaction among the impairment itself, the task to be undertaken, one's perception of the impairment, and available resources.

Employment

As is true with educational limitations, young adults with disabilities are less likely than peers to receive work-related training and are less likely to be employed. Given the paucity of relevant domestic data, it may be instructive to look at the experience of young adults with disabilities in countries where the employment structure is different from that of the United States. Pless, Power, and Peckham (1993) found that in a British sample adult males with disabilities were more likely than their peers to report greater leisure time, more unemployment, and poor educational qualifications. The same was not found for females. In a Finnish longitudinal cohort, 23 percent of those with disabilities had received no vocational training—more than twice the number of young adults aged nineteen to twenty-five years in the comparison group. Those with disabilities were also less likely to be permanently employed (44 vs. 50 percent) (Kokkonen 1995). At the age of thirty-six, unemployment differences among women with and without disabilities seem to have been eliminated. For men with and without chronic conditions, it remained dramatically different (14 vs. 59 percent). Likewise, in the same study, at age thirty-six both males and females with chronic conditions were more likely to have remained single than age-matched peers: 30.6 vs. 9.8 percent for men; 19.1 vs. 4.7 percent for women.

Among U.S. adults with disabilities, Scal et al. (2003) found significant employment differences by age and disability status when analyzing the National Health Information Survey (NHIS) disability supplement from 1994–95. Again, when Scal et al. looked at employment by severity they saw an even more powerful trend. While 78.8 percent of those aged eighteen through thirty were in the labor force, 72.4 percent of those with mild disabilities were working, falling to 38.7 percent for those with severe disabilities (Scal et al. 2003). Similar differences in vocational outcomes have been seen in other populations of young adults with chronic conditions. For example, among American adults

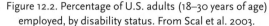

Figure 12.2. Percentage of U.S. adults (18–30 years of age) employed, by disability status. From Scal et al. 2003.

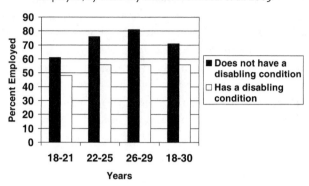

with renal disease, 53 percent were working full-time compared with 75 percent of peers (Reynolds et al. 1993).

What becomes evident, whether in the United States, Britain, or Finland, is that those young adults with disabilities are less likely to be employed independent of how disability may have been operationalized (see figure 12.2; for a more detailed discussion of cross-national comparisons of disability data, see Suris and Blum 1993). Again, as with educational disadvantages the social barriers to employment far exceed the barriers that might be created by the impairment. For example, employers not uncommonly believe that those with disabilities have a higher number of absences than nondisabled peers. The truth is the opposite. There is also the bias that making accommodations for employees with disabilities consistent with the Americans with Disabilities Act (ADA) will be resented by nondisabled coworkers. This too is not sustained by data. Given that employment is a primary source of self-esteem as well as income, the cost of employment disadvantage is high.

Social Relationships

Another consequence of having a disability in the United States is social isolation. Those with disabilities have fewer friends, more friends who are three or more years older or younger than they, and fewer marital relationships (Blum 1992). Reynolds et al. (1993) found that those with disabilities were more than twice as likely to be living with their parents as adults (68 vs. 29 percent), and more likely to be single (76 vs. 65 percent) than nondisabled peers. Marital status was dramatically different for male and female dialysis patients: nearly 50 percent of all females were married, while none of the males was married.

There are similar findings for adults with cystic fibrosis (Walters, Britton, and Hudson 1993) and congenital heart disease (Utens et al. 1994) and among adult survivors of childhood tumors (Mackie et al. 2000). In the NHIS 1994–95 disability supplement, 34.0 percent of eighteen- to thirty-year-olds without a disability had been married compared with 28.2 percent of those with a disability. The differences increase as the population gets older. However, such discrepancy is not consistently found among young adults who are cancer survivors, or have diabetes or juvenile rheumatoid arthritis. In these groups the differences with other adults in work, marriage, and living arrangements appear to be minimal (Gledhill, Rangel, and Garralda 2000).

Emotional Well-Being

According to several epidemiological studies, young adults with chronic illnesses and disabilities have an increased risk of developing psychological and behavioral problems (Gortmaker et al. 1990; Pless, Power, and Peckham 1993; Zill 1985). In a meta-analysis of eighty-seven studies comparing the adjustment of young people who had chronic physical disorders with those who did not, Lavigne and Faier-Routman (1992) reported a mean effect size of approximately 0.5 SD, suggesting that those with chronic disabilities were considerably more likely than peers to show psychosocial symptoms.

Whether these problems persist into adulthood is unclear. In a study of a birth cohort of individuals in Great Britain who were followed for twenty-three years, Pless, Power, and Peckham (1993) examined long-term psychosocial sequelae of chronic physical disorders that began during childhood. They found no great psychosocial problems for adult females with chronic physical disorders compared with those without such disorders. These findings are consistent with those of Huurre and Aro (2002) in the long-term follow-up study of Finnish adults with and without limiting conditions. An increasing number of studies report that many youth with chronic illnesses and disabilities adapt to the added demands of the condition, show no symptomatic behavior, and make the transition to adulthood quite well (Drotar 1981; Gortmaker et al. 1990).

The difference between the youth who successfully adapt and those who do not is believed to be related to their ability to develop coping behaviors and to acquire and maintain needed resources for managing the added demands of a chronic illness or disability—what can be called protective factors (Patterson and Blum 1996). Meijer et al. (2002) found that young adults with disabilities who had coping styles characterized as "seeking social support" and "confrontational" had better social adjustment than those who appeared depressed or anxious or who projected low self-esteem.

A MODEL OF CONDITION-PERSON-
FAMILY-ENVIRONMENT FIT

The level of independence a young adult with a disability is capable of achieving is ultimately determined by a combination of factors. These include the individual, his or her condition, the family, and the environments in which they live, and the fit between the four (see figure 12.3). The interaction among these four factors will dramatically impact the functioning of young adults with disabilities.

OUTCOME FACTORS FOR
YOUNG ADULTS WITH DISABILITIES

Individual Factors

Condition-specific factors. The work of Wells, Sandefur, and Hogan (forthcoming) suggests that the nature of one's condition directly influences the *way* one transitions to adulthood and not just one's relative success in the transition *process.* Specifically, they found that young women with sensory and orthopedic impairments were more likely than peers with learning disabilities to be pursuing higher education while those with learning disabilities were more likely to be working while living at home or starting their own families. Those who had significant mental retardation and/or multiple physical impairments were more likely to remain fully dependent than adult peers who have other disabilities. Wells, Sandefur, and Hogan (forthcoming) concluded that the type of disability one has and its effects overshadow race/ethnicity, family structure, and number of siblings as factors that impact the transition to adulthood for young adults with diabetes. Likewise, family economic resources had a smaller impact on transitions to adulthood for those with disabilities than for those without such limitations.

Brain involvement. While diagnosis (e.g., the disease or condition itself) may not be the primary factor affecting psychosocial outcomes, there is some evidence that certain characteristics of chronic conditions, which often cut across diagnostic labels, may have differential impacts on adolescent and young adult outcomes. For example, conditions where there is brain involvement (e.g., seizure disorders or mental retardation) appear to increase the negative impact (Breslau 1993; Reiss, Steinglass, and Howe 1993). However, much less is known about the differential impact of other types of impairment (e.g., sensory or motor impairment).

Degree and type of incapacity. Those with medically assessed *mild* involvement

Figure 12.3. A model of person-condition-family-environment fit.

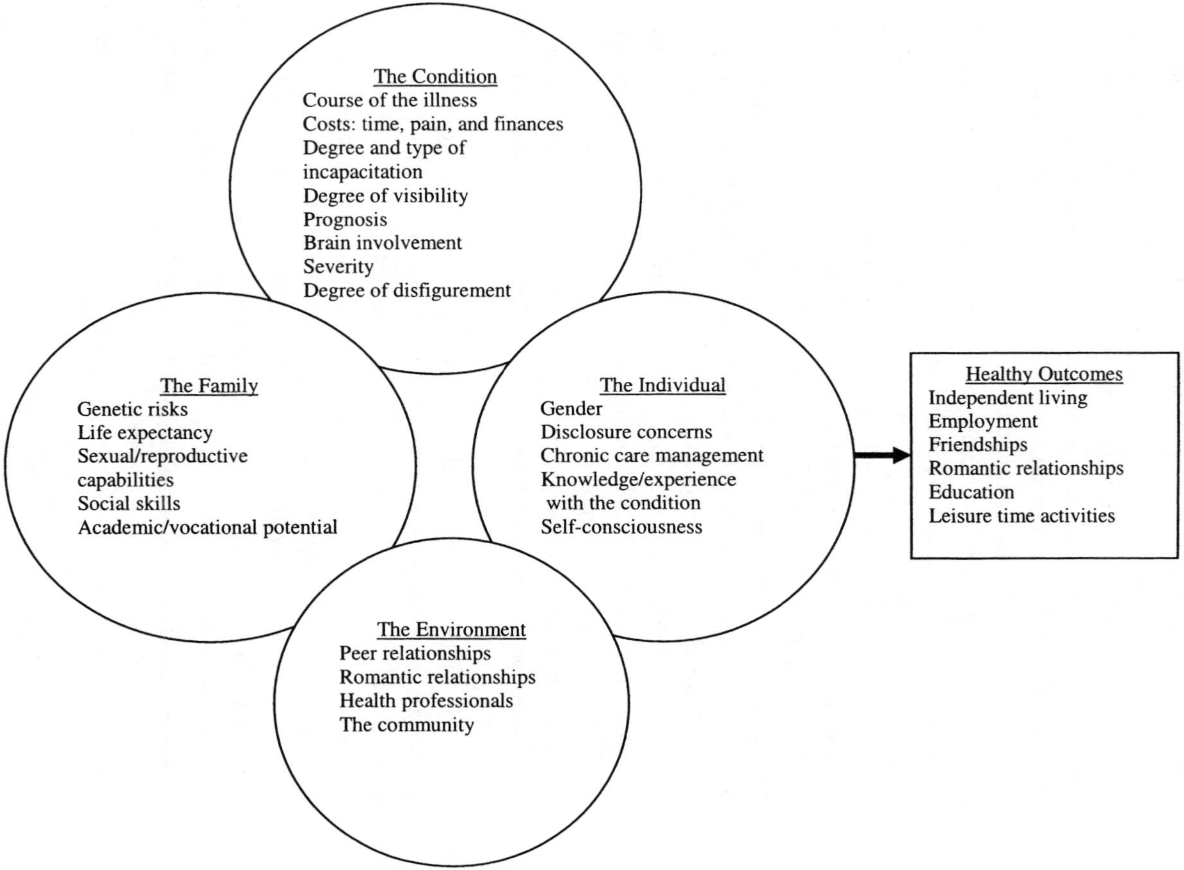

The Condition
Course of the illness
Costs: time, pain, and finances
Degree and type of
incapacitation
Degree of visibility
Prognosis
Brain involvement
Severity
Degree of disfigurement

The Individual
Gender
Disclosure concerns
Chronic care management
Knowledge/experience
with the condition
Self-consciousness

The Family
Genetic risks
Life expectancy
Sexual/reproductive
capabilities
Social skills
Academic/vocational potential

The Environment
Peer relationships
Romantic relationships
Health professionals
The community

Healthy Outcomes
Independent living
Employment
Friendships
Romantic relationships
Education
Leisure time activities

(e.g., a limp) seem to have more emotional difficulties than those with more severe impairments (e.g., wheelchair dependency). This issue was highlighted by a twenty-year-old woman with spina bifida whom I followed clinically since early adolescence. She was in her second year of college, studying to be a social worker and had only a mild gait disturbance. One would assume Laura would easily fit into the college scene. But nothing could have been further from the truth. During a clinic visit, after what she heard as a particularly insightless comment I made, she turned to me and snapped, "You don't get it, do you? I am rejected by those with spina bifida and cerebral palsy, and I am rejected by those who are able-bodied. I live in no man's land!"

Degree of visibility. Contrary to common belief, those who have *invisible* conditions have consistently been found to have more emotional problems than those with more visible limitations or deformities (Kellerman et al. 1980; Blum 1992). Think, for example, of an elevator where someone enters at the third floor and presses the second-floor button. You think to yourself, "Why doesn't he walk?" If someone looks healthy we assume they are healthy; and if they can't meet our expectations the psychological price they pay is failure.

Prognosis. The stress of *uncertainty* is greater than that when the course is known, even when the clinical trajectory leads to death. We see this most dramatically in young adults who have conditions where once the course was certain death, but today the long-term prognosis is simply unknown. What will such young people tell prospective partners? Potential employers? Insurance companies?

Course of illness. Rather than chronic persistent conditions, those that are remitting and relenting are most emotionally burdensome. Such is the case, for example, with many cancers or epilepsy, which can recur at any moment. When does one see herself as cancer free? When does one become comfortable driving or handling heavy equipment if he has a seizure disorder?

Medically assessed condition severity. If the presence of chronic conditions is associated with some risk for negative outcomes, it might be expected that more severe conditions (as defined by health professionals) would increase this risk. Interestingly, there is little evidence to support the conclusion that severity of the condition, per se, is associated with more negative outcomes (Perrin et al. 1993; Stein et al. 1993). However, there is little empirical evidence either within specific disease or across conditions that severity itself is not significantly associated with poorer psychosocial outcomes.

Additionally, there is little evidence for differences in psychosocial impact on either the individual or the family based on medically assessed severity of the condition (Perrin et al. 1993). This reinforces the perception that it is the fit among the condition, the individual, the family, and the environment that most significantly influences the condition's impact.

The Individual

Beyond the condition characteristics, individual factors influence adaptation and independent functioning. What are his or her past experiences or knowledge of the condition? Have there been other family members who have had it? What happened to them? Does the individual have friends or neighbors with the condition? When there is familiarity with a condition it tends to be demystified.

Perceived responses from others. Another factor affecting one's perception is the response that knowledge of the condition elicits in others. A classic example is cancer. While many tumors today are associated with high recovery rates, public response to the diagnosis may be one of viewing the individual as having a terminal illness, which in turn affects one's sense of self.

Additionally, the condition itself may elicit a response in others, especially if the condition is disfiguring. Gliedman and Roth (1980) have described a hierarchy of acceptability in which mobility impairments are more acceptable than intellectual impairments, and they in turn are more acceptable than facial disfigurements. This was measured by asking adults to identify whom they would rather live next door to. These data were dramatically highlighted in a clinical encounter with a twenty-three-year-old male who had recently completed college. The young man had an uncommon condition, dermatomyositis, that left him with significant facial disfigurement. On speaking with him about what he planned to do after college he began to cry. After composing himself he said that he had hoped to go to law school and had the grades to do so but "no one would accept me because I'm so ugly." I had the feeling that he was correct.

Gender. Contrary to the general population of young adults, for those with chronic and disabling conditions it appears that males have more somatic concerns, especially when the condition is associated with short stature or low weight. These differences persist at least until the midtwenties and they most likely result from sex-role stereotypes, under which it is more unacceptable in our society for men to be dependent on others than for females. Additionally, many chronic conditions have as a consequence appearing years younger than one's chronologic age or developmental stage; such is the case, for example, with cystic fibrosis and chronic renal failure. As a consequence, young adults with these conditions may be treated as much younger children—a response less socially tolerable for males than females.

Costs. As one would anticipate, those conditions and treatments that are the most costly in terms of pain, home care, time, as well as money are also the ones that have the highest emotional costs.

Disclosure. Regarding one's condition, with whom to disclose and when are major concerns of young adults, especially those with invisible, potentially severe conditions. Conditioned over their years, many young adults with chronic and disabling conditions have learned that premature disclosure can cost them friends and future possibilities. For example, the invisibility of a chronic condition can challenge a young adult in an emerging relationship when to tell a partner. For some, withholding disclosure may have negative health consequences (e.g., those with cystic fibrosis who suppress their cough so as to avoid continually explaining their condition to others). On the other hand, early disclosure runs significant risks for rejection and social isolation.

Chronic care management. For many young adults with chronic conditions, work, school, and social settings pose added complications for managing the myriad elements of their condition. For example, the interface of the condition and a social situation may require the young adult with diabetes to adjust his evening insulin dose to account for an anticipated evening of drinking; or it may be that a young adult female with bladder incontinence secondary to spina bifida needs to periodically excuse herself from social and work appointments to avoid urine leakage, odor, and the resulting social isolation. The greater the complexity of condition management the greater the need for preplanning for social encounters.

A time-consuming, complicated treatment regimen required for some conditions (e.g., cystic fibrosis) can increase risk because if it is adhered to, the treatment regimen reduces time for normal activities and meeting of obligations. On the other hand, avoiding the regimen may lead to poorer health status and associated psychosocial problems. Highlighting the issue is the finding among youth with diabetes that young people with the best metabolic control (as well as the best adherence to diet, glucose testing, and a treatment regimen) experienced more psychological problems than those in moderate control (Evans and Hughes 1987; Smith et al. 1991). These findings suggest that balancing illness-related demands with other needs may be adaptive in the long run. The very act of complying with a treatment regimen is a constant reminder of having less than normal health status that may affect one's sense of himself or herself (Blum 1992).

Family Concerns

For families who have young adults with disabling conditions, the end of high school coincides with a number of transitions for which many are unprepared:

from school to work, home to independent living, pediatric to adult health care are but a few. For many families, lingering questions remain.

Genetic risks. While some may have received genetic counseling when their child was young, at that time questions focused primarily on themselves and their reproductive future as parents. Now there are questions that pertain to their young adult children having children.

Life expectancy. With improved survival, many young adults with previously fatal diseases of childhood are pioneers on an uncharted course. We may not be able to provide much information, but we can acknowledge the isolation they and their parents experience.

Sexual capabilities. Few young adults have had accurate physical assessments to ascertain their biophysiologic reproductive capacities; and fewer still have received accurate information about their reproductive potential or the sexual options available to them given their physical limitations. Sexual needs and desires tend to be denied and ignored by health care professionals and other service providers. As a consequence, some young adults with physical conditions will consider themselves sterile and fail to contracept when in fact their reproductive capacity may be no different from that of their peers.

Social skills. The isolation often experienced by those with disabilities results in a failure to develop the social skills critical to successful adult functioning. The development and enhancement of the skills are a critical concern of families. Social skills training requires young adults to have access to others with and without physical conditions. It requires that when behavior is inappropriate, they receive appropriate feedback both from peers and caretakers. All too often there is a functional acceptance where those without chronic conditions ignore socially aversive behaviors of peers with disabilities or excuse those behaviors (e.g., drooling, foul odor, inappropriate sexual behaviors) while peers with similar behaviors receive direct and immediate critical feedback (Resnick 1984). The consequence is social isolation and persistence of those behaviors.

Academic and vocational potential. Families need to begin the future planning of their young adult children with special needs long before the completion of high school. What resources are available and how can families obtain the assessment and services they need to assure an optimal transition to adulthood for their teenagers? With the vast majority of adults with disabilities unemployed and underemployed, these are critical concerns (Magill-Evans et al. 2001).

When exploring the family factors that influence the type of transition to adulthood a young person with a disability may experience, such as family formation, full-time schooling, working/living at home, and persistent dependence, Wells, Sandefur, and Hogan (forthcoming) found that only family income had a significant impact. Specifically, the higher the family income, the greater the likelihood of being a full-time student. In fact, these researchers found that disability type and family income were the *only* factors that were significant determinants of youth's transitions to adulthood: race and ethnicity, family structure, number of siblings, geographic residence, and socioeconomic status were weakly associated with transitions for youth with disabilities. This is important since a number of these factors influence transition for nonimpaired peers.

The Environment

Peer Factors

Social isolation. Young adults with disabilities have a more limited social network, have fewer friends, participate in fewer social events, and as a consequence are more socially isolated than their nonimpaired peers. Social isolation is the foundation for depression. Without the social skills to meet people, the likelihood that one will develop ongoing relationships with either same-sex or opposite-sex peers diminishes. Too often the focus of well-meaning adults is on risk avoidance; however, without the social skills to meet others, young adults will never be exposed to the risks that we educate them to avoid.

Sexual relationships. Issues of peer relationships become more pronounced as interest in sexual relations increases. With it comes a host of complex questions that challenge our values as parents and professionals. Is sex for procreation alone? If so, what about young people for whom procreation is ill-advised or not possible? Is sex for pleasure? How explicit do we become for those who are quadriplegic? We harbor the myth that those with chronic illness are asexual, yet the available data indicate that sexual activity among those with and without disabilities is comparable (Suris et al. 1996; Blum, Kelly, and Ireland 2001).

Sex education for people with disabilities needs to include the following topics: personal hygiene, menstruation, sexually transmitted diseases, birth control, social skills development, masturbation, sexual and social relationships (same sex and heterosexual), and sexual exploitation. Because of their cognitive and social deficits, and because they tend to be very sensitive to affirmation and approval by others, young adults who are intellectually impaired are especially vulnerable to sexual exploitation (Greydanus, Rimsza, and Newhouse 2002).

Sexual behavior is learned. Social isolation and lack of opportunity appear to be the primary limiting factors. Having the social skills to locate a partner is key to developing sexual relationships. Thus, social skills are critical not solely or even primarily to develop sexual relationships, but much more importantly to develop social relationships.

Additionally, the complexities of the sex act are not uncommon barriers to normal sexual relationships for many young adults with physical impairments. Consider, for example, the story told by the late Irvin Zola, the brilliant sociologist from Brandeis University, who had had polio as a child. He describes in detail a sexual encounter with a young woman who was quadriplegic:

> She parallel parked her wheelchair next to the bed, grinned, and pointed to the side arm. . . . The board had to be placed with the wider part on the bed and the narrower section slipped under her. . . . I lay down on the mattress and shoved the transfer board under her. . . . I was huffing but she sat in a sort of bemused silence. Then came the scary part. Planting myself as firmly as I could behind her, I leaned forward, slipped my arms under hers and around her chest and then with one heave hefted her onto the bed. She landed safely with her head on the pillow and I joined her wearily for a moment's rest. For this I should have gone into training.
>
> . . . She turned her head toward me and looked down as I lay stretched out momentarily. . . . "Now the real fun part," she teased, "You have to undress me. . . ." I was sweating as much from anxiety as exertion. . . . Slacks, underpants, corset all came off in not so rapid succession.
>
> . . . She was not the first woman with a disability I'd ever slept with but she was, as she had said earlier, "more physically dependent than I look." And she was. . . . In recent years, I often find myself asking where and how they like to be touched. To my questions she replied, "my neck . . . my face . . . especially my ears. . . ."
>
> "Tell me . . . tell me," she said again as she pulled me tighter. With a deep breath, I meekly answered, "Tell you what?" "Tell me what you're doing," she said softly, "so I can visualize it." (Zola 1993, 153–155)

Health Professionals

In 1987 Blum reported that fully 50 percent of physicians nationally indicated that they were deficient in the management of chronic conditions for their adolescent patients. Likewise, Blum and Bearinger (1990) reported that more than 33 percent of nurses and 66 percent of psychologists and social workers felt ill-prepared to work with young adults who have chronic conditions. In addition, health professionals often lack the skills needed to facilitate transition to adulthood for young people with chronic conditions with their families (Evans et al. in press; Blum 1987).

Recently, Blum and his colleagues (Evans et al. in press) surveyed a national sample of health care providers to see what changes had occurred in the care of young adults with chronic conditions over the previous decade. The good news is that there was an overall higher self-assessed skill level among health professionals; however, major deficits persist. For pediatricians, both awareness of community resources for young adults with disabilities and planning for transition to adult health care professionals remains problematic (see White and Gallay, chapter 13 in this volume). For nurses, particular deficiencies emerge in sexuality education for youth with disabilities, planning for transition services, and meeting the emotional needs of these young adults and their families. The same deficiencies (awareness of community resources and planning for transition to adult care providers) were reported by psychologists. Data show that self-perceived skills in these areas are higher among recent graduates than among their older peers.

In 1993 a panel of health experts identified "chronic illness and its complex health care" as the most important aspect of pediatrics and adolescent health for the future (American Academy of Pediatrics 1993); a decade later a joint statement of the American Academy of Pediatrics and the American Academy of Family Practice and the American College of Physicians focused attention on the specific needs of young adults transitioning to adult health care services (American Academy of Pediatrics 2002). To achieve a model of health services for young adults with disabilities that meet their comprehensive needs, we must first pay greater attention to the emotional as well as functional needs of these young people and their parents than currently exists.

Second, if we are to meet the comprehensive needs of young adults with disabilities, health professionals and social service providers will need to pay greater attention to the sexual health needs of youth with disabilities. While most health professionals assess their knowledge/skills related to sexual health issues of youth with disabilities as moderate, myths abound; and there is reason to believe that many of the issues and concerns of young people are rarely addressed (Blum 1997; Cromer et al. 1990). We know that young adults with disabilities have less information regarding sexual issues than their peers (Suris and Blum 1993), yet they are no less likely than others to be sexually active; and they are more vulnerable to sexual abuse (Suris et al. 1996; Svetaz, Ireland, and Blum 2000; Blum 1997). Evidence from both parents and those with disabilities themselves suggests that many sexual and reproductive health questions remain unanswered.

Third, racial and ethnic differences can have a profound impact on partnerships between families and providers. DiCaprio et al. (1999) analyzed providers' and minority families' perceptions about the role of cultural beliefs and prejudice in accessing health services. By and large, providers were unaware of cultural barriers and denied that discrimination (either de facto or de jure) played a role in limiting health care for young adults of color who have a disability. In fact, many European-American providers did not see themselves as having a distinct culture or set of cultural assumptions that influenced interactions with families. In DiCaprio et al.'s study (1999) family perceptions and experiences were quite different.

The Community

The community is the social context for growth and development. It can be a source of both risk and protection. While in the protective environment of school, a young person's world is structured; however, with the end of schooling comes the expectation that, if one does not pursue higher education, one will transition to the workplace and to independent living. How their environments respond, the physical impediments they encounter, and the attitudinal barriers they face in their community will determine to a great extent the outcomes young adults will have. As Robertson (1993) noted, the attitudes and behavior of people in the community are often greater sources of strain than the condition itself. On the other hand, when the community provides support, the transitions to adulthood for the young adult with a chronic condition or physical disability are immeasurably easier.

Specifically, informal support systems appear to be a critical community factor. *Informal* refers to the voluntary connections that a young adult has with friends, people in the neighborhood, peers, and work associates. It is the social capital a young person has, and it can be viewed as providing a range of critical supports: (1) *emotional support,* which is a sense of being liked, cared about, and valued; (2) *informational support,* which includes ideas, resources, facts, advice, and helpful hints that contribute to problem solving and decision making; and (3) *tangible aid,* which occurs when someone does something for another, such as helping out or running an errand.

While the community can be a source of social capital, investigators also have reported that persons with disabilities often experience increased social isolation because of the stigma of being different. Time demands associated with care management also contribute to less social contact. Just keeping up with everything that must be done with regard to the condition frequently takes overwhelming energy. Limited time availability, real or perceived stigma, and the complexity that may be involved in planning social engagements all contribute to social isolation.

Making matters worse, the world of the young adult with a chronic condition may be filled with directives from well-meaning but often overly controlling nonparental adults that leave the young person with few means of positively demonstrating control over his or her environment. Nonadherence to the therapeutic regime may be one of the few available options, however self-injurious, of asserting control. In a study of adolescents, Blum et al. (1991) found "overprotection," as young people defined it, to be associated with less happiness, lower self-esteem, more anxiety, lower perceived popularity, and greater self-consciousness. There is no evidence that these issues diminish in young adulthood. Rather, young adults who have been reared in sheltered environments due to their disabilities are less likely to take responsibility for their own behavior and more likely to see the disability at the center of their identity than others in whom more independence was fostered in childhood (Blum 1992).

CONCLUSION

Over the past twenty-five years we have made dramatic strides in improving the survival of children with chronic and disabling conditions that previously were fatal. Today, most children born with disabilities will transition into adulthood. What is evident is that our ability to normalize the social environments in which these young adults live has been less successful than our medical advances. While little evidence supports the notion that these young adults have inherent social or emotional deficits (e.g., psychopathology), there is substantial evidence that young adults with disabilities are less likely than their peers to realize their future. They are less likely to marry—though their marital aspirations are no different from their peers—and they are less likely to be employed. They are less likely to achieve higher education and independent living.

These facts reflect the social creation of handicaps and are not the consequence of the inherent physical limitations of the disability itself. On Martha's Vineyard at the turn of the twentieth century there were two towns with a very high prevalence of deafness (Groce 1985). At this time, Martha's Vineyard was a collection of small fishing villages and not the playground of the rich and famous. To accommodate the hearing impaired in those two communities, everyone, hearing and deaf, learned to sign. Years later, town elders reported that they could not distinguish between those who were hearing and those who were not. In those communities deafness was a disability, not a handicap. Isn't that the goal for all our children—that they grow into adults who may have physical impairments, and that the societies in which they live enable and not handicap them?

REFERENCES

American Academy of Pediatrics, Committee on Children with Disabilities. 2002. Improving transition for adolescents with special health care needs from pediatrics to adult-centered health care. *Pediatrics* 110: 54–61.

American Academy of Pediatrics, Committee on Psychosocial Aspects of Child and Family Health. 1993. The pediatrician and the "new morbidity." *Pediatrics* 92: 731–733.

Aron, L. Y., P. J. Loprest, and C. E. Steverle. 1996. *Serving children with disabilities: A systematic look at programs.* Washington: Urban Institute.

Blum, R. W. 1987. Physicians' assessment of deficiencies and desire for training in adolescent health care. *Journal of Medical Education* 62: 401–407.

Blum, R. W. 1992. Chronic illness and disability in adolescence. *Journal of Adolescent Health* 13: 364–368.

Blum, R. W., ed. 1995. Conference proceedings: Moving on: Transition from pediatric to adult health care. *Journal of Adolescent Health* 17: 3–9.

Blum, R. W. 1997. Sexual health and contraceptive needs of adolescents with chronic conditions. *Archives of Pediatrics and Adolescent Medicine* 151: 289–297.

Blum, R. W., and L. H. Bearinger. 1990. Knowledge and attitudes of health professionals toward adolescent health care. *Journal of Adolescent Health Care* 11: 289–294.

Blum, R. W., and G. Geber. 1992. Chronically ill youth. Pp. 223–228 in *Textbook of adolescent medicine.* Edited by E. McAnarney, et al. Philadelphia: Saunders.

Blum, R. W., A. Kelly, and M. Ireland. 2001. Health risk behaviors and protective factors among adolescents with mobility impairments, learning and emotional disabilities. *Journal of Adolescent Health* 28: 481–490.

Blum, R. W., M. D. Resnick, R. Nelson, and A. St. Germaine. 1991. Family and peer issues among adolescents with spina bifida and cerebral palsy. *Pediatrics* 88: 280–285.

Breslau, N. 1993. Siblings of disabled children. Pp. 57–70 in *How do families cope with chronic illness?* Edited by R. Cole and D. Reiss. Hillsdale, NJ: L. Erlbaum Associates.

Cromer, B. A., E. Benedicta, K. McCoy, M. J. Gerhardstein, M. Fitzpatrick, and J. Judis. 1990. Knowledge, attitudes, and behavior related to sexuality in adolescents with chronic disability. *Developmental Medicine and Child Neurology* 32: 602–610.

DiCaprio, J., A. W. Garwick, C. Kohrman, and R. W. Blum. 1999. Culture and the care of children with chronic conditions: Their physicians' views. *Archives of Pediatric and Adolescent Medicine* 153: 1030–1035.

Drotar, D. 1981. Psychological perspectives in chronic childhood illness. *Journal of Pediatric Psychology* 6: 211–228.

Evans, C., and I. Hughes. 1987. The relationships between diabetic control and individual and family characteristics. *Journal of Psychosomatic Research* 31: 367–374.

Evans, T. A, M. D. Resnick, M. Ireland, D. Goetz, M. Shew, L. H. Bearinger, D. Neumark-Sztainer, M. Story, and R. W. Blum. In press. Multidisciplinary self-report of competencies in adolescent health practice: A comparative study of adolescent health professionals. *Journal of Adolescent Health.*

Gledhill, J., L. Rangel, and E. Garralda. 2000. Surviving chronic physical illness: Psychosocial outcomes in adult life. *Archives of Disease in Childhood* 83: 104–110.

Gliedman, J., and W. Roth. 1980. *The unexpected minority: Handicapped children in America.* New York: Harcourt Brace Jovanovich.

Gortmaker, S. L., D. K. Walker, M. Weitzman, and A. M. Sobol. 1990. Chronic conditions, socioeconomic risks, and behavioral problems in children and adolescents. *Pediatrics* 85: 267–276.

Greydanus, D. E., M. E. Rimsza, and P. A. Newhouse. 2002. Adolescent sexuality and disability. *Adolescent Medicine: State of the Art Reviews* 13: 223–247.

Groce, N. E. 1985. *Everyone here spoke sign language: Hereditary deafness on Martha's Vineyard.* Cambridge: Harvard University Press.

Huurre, T. M., and H. M. Aro. 2002. Long-term psychosocial effects of persistent chronic illness: A follow-up study of Finnish adolescents aged 16 to 32 years. *European Child and Adolescent Psychiatry* 11: 85–91.

Joe, J. R. 1997. American Indian children with disabilities: The impact of culture on health and education services. *Families, Systems, and Health* 15: 251–262.

Kellerman, J., L. Zeltzer, L. Ellenberg, J. Dash, and D. Rigler. 1980. Psychological effects of illness in adolescence: anxiety, self-esteem, and perception control. *Journal of Pediatrics* 9: 126–131.

Kokkonen, J. 1995. The social effects in adult life of chronic physical illness since childhood. *European Journal of Pediatrics* 154: 676–681.

Lavigne, J. V., and J. Faier-Routman. 1992. Psychological adjustment to pediatric physical disorders: a meta-analytic review. *Journal of Pediatric Psychology* 17: 133–157.

Mackie, E., J. Hill, H. Kondryn, and R. McNally. 2000. Adult psychosocial outcomes in long-term survivors of acute lymphoblastic leukaemia and Wilms' tumour: A controlled study. *Lancet* 355: 1310–1314.

Magill-Evans, J., J. Darrah, K. Pain, R. Adkins, and M. Kratochvil. 2001. Are families with adolescents and young adults with cerebral palsy the same as other families? *Developmental Medicine and Child Neurology* 43: 466–472.

McPherson, M., P. Arango, H. Fox, C. Lauver, M. McManus, P. W. Newacheck, et al. 1998. A new definition of children with special health care needs. *Pediatrics* 102: 137–140.

Meijer, S. A., G. Sinnema, J. O. Bijstra, G. J. Mellenbergh, and W. H. Wolters. 2002. Coping styles and locus of control as predictors for psychological adjustment of adolescents with a chronic illness. *Social Science and Medicine* 54: 1453–1461.

Mueller, K. J., and A. Askenazi. 1999. Health status and access to care among rural minorities. *Journal of Health Care for the Poor and Underserved* 10: 230–249.

Mueller, K. J., K. Patil, and E. Boilesen. 1998. The role of uninsurance and race in health care utilization by rural minorities. *Health Services Research* 33: 597–610.

Newacheck, P. W. 1999. Children with disabilities under the state children's health insurance program. February 23. http://www.mchpolicy.org/fact1.html.

Newacheck, P. W., J. J. Stoddard, D. C. Hughes, and M. Pearl. 1998. Health insurance and access to primary care for children. *New England Journal of Medicine* 338: 513–519.

Newacheck, P. W., B. Strickland, J. P. Shonkoff, J. M. Perrin, M. McPherson, M. McManus, C. Lauver, H. Fox, and P. Arango. 1998. An epidemiological profile of children with special health care needs. *Pediatrics* 102: 117–121.

Patterson, J. M., and R. W. Blum. 1996. Risk and resilience among children and youth with disabilities. *Archives of Pediatrics and Adolescent Medicine.* 150: 692–698.

Perrin, E. C., P. Newacheck, I. B. Pless, D. Drotar, S. L. Gortmaker, J. Leventhal, J. M. Perrin,

R. E. Stein, D. K. Walker, and M. Weitzman. 1993. Issues involved in the definition and classification of chronic health conditions. *Pediatrics* 91: 787–793.

Pless, I. B., C. Power, and C. S. Peckham. 1993. Long-term psychosocial sequelae of chronic physical disorders in childhood. *Pediatrics* 91: 1131–1136.

Reiss, D., P. Steinglass, and G. Howe. 1993. The family's organization around the illness. Pp. 173–213 in *How do families cope with chronic illness?* Edited by R. Cole and D. Reiss. Hillsdale, NJ: L. Erlbaum Associates.

Resnick, M. 1984. The social construction of disability. Pp. 29–46 in *Chronic illness and disability in childhood and adolescence.* Edited by R. W. Blum. New York: Grune & Stratton.

Reynolds, J. M., M. J. Morton, M. E. Garralda, R. J. Postlethwaite, and D. Goh. 1993. Psychosocial adjustment of adult survivors of a pediatric dialysis and transplant program. *Archives of Disease in Childhood* 68: 104–110.

Robertson, L. W. 1993. The world of parents of children with disabilities. Pp. 59–65 in *Families, disability, and empowerment: Active coping skills and strategies for family intervention.* Edited by G. H. S. Singer and L. E. Powers. Baltimore: Paul H. Brookes.

Scal, P., S. Larson, M. Ireland, and R. W. Blum. 2003. Young adults with childhood onset disability making their way into adulthood (abstract). *Pediatric Research* 53: 1287.

Smith, M. S., R. Maauseth, J. P. Palmer, R. Pecoraro, and G. Wenet. 1991. Glycosylated hemoglobin and psychological adjustment in adolescents with diabetes. *Adolescence* 26: 31–40.

Stein, R. F. K., L. J. Bauman, L. E. Westbrook, S. M. Coupey, and H. T. Ireys. 1993. Framework for identifying children who have chronic conditions: the case for a new definition. *Journal of Pediatrics* 122: 342–347.

Suris, J. C., and R. W. Blum. 1993. Disability rates among adolescents: An international comparison. *Journal of Adolescent Health* 14: 548–552.

Suris, J. C., and R. W. Blum. 2001. Adolescent health in Europe: An overview. *International Journal of Adolescent Medicine* 13: 91–99.

Suris, J. C., M. D. Resnick, N. Cassuto, and R. W. Blum. 1996. Sexual behavior of adolescents with chronic disease and disability. *Journal of Adolescent Health* 19: 124–131.

Svetaz, M. V., M. Ireland, and R. W. Blum. 2000. Adolescents with learning disabilities: risk and protective factors associated with emotional well-being. Findings from the National Longitudinal Study of Adolescent Health. *Journal of Adolescent Health* 27: 340–348.

U.S. Department of Education. 1993. *To assure the free and appropriate public education of all children with disabilities: 15th annual report to Congress on the implementation of the Individuals with Disabilities Education Act.* Washington: U.S. Government Printing Office.

U.S. Department of Education. 2001. *High school and beyond.* Washington: U.S. Government Printing Office.

Utens, E. M., F. C. Verhulst, R. A. Erdman, et al. 1994. Psychosocial functioning of a young adult after surgical correction for congenital heart disease in childhood: A follow-up study. *Journal of Psychosomatic Research* 38: 745–758.

Walters, S., J. Britton, and M. E. Hudson. 1993. Demographic and social characteristics of adults with cystic fibrosis in the United Kingdom. *British Medical Journal* 306: 549–552.

Wells, T., G. Sandefur, and D. Hogan. Forthcoming. What happens after the high school years among young persons with disabilities? *Social Forces.*

Wenger, B. L., H. S. Kaye, and M. P. LaPlante. 1996. Disabilities among children. *Disability Sta-*

tistics Abstract, March, no. 15. Disability Statistics Rehabilitation Research and Training Center, University of California, San Francisco.

Westbrook, L. E., E. J. Silver, and R. E. K. Stein. 1998. Implications for estimates of disability in children: A comparison of definitional components. *Pediatrics* 101: 1025–1030.

Zill, N. 1985. *The school-aged handicapped.* Washington: Child Trends Inc.

Zola, I. 1993. Tell me . . . tell me. Pp. 97–102 in *Reproductive issues for persons with physical disabilities.* Edited by F. Haseltine, R. Cole, and D. B. Gray. Baltimore: L. Paul H. Brookes.

CHAPTER THIRTEEN

Youth with Special Health Care Needs and Disabilities in Transition to Adulthood

PATIENCE HAYDOCK WHITE AND LESLIE GALLAY

In conjunction with the development of the Bureau of Maternal and Child Health's Healthy and Ready to Work ten-year plan in 2000, a group of youth with special health care needs and disabilities (SHCN/D) from around the United States was brought together. They outlined the following goals for their transition to adulthood: (1) being valued as a human being and treated with dignity, (2) having opportunities for social experiences, dating, community involvement, recreation, and worship, (3) obtaining education and/or job training, (4) becoming independent, and (5) finding meaningful work for reasonable pay (Blum 2002). To achieve these goals for a successful transition to adulthood, youth with SHCN/D have to attend to many issues. First and foremost they have to attend to their health, including the careful management of their condition and attention to preventive care issues.

Members of this vulnerable population include persons with disabilities or chronic conditions. As outlined in Perrin's (2002) definitions, disability is the inability to carry out age appropriate daily activities because of a health condition or impairment. A chronic condition is a health problem such as asthma or diabetes that at the time of diagnosis is predicted to be present for more than three months. Youth with SHCN/D include those with chronic illnesses such as asthma or cystic fibrosis as well as those with disabilities such as spina bifida, groups who often depend on daily medication or preventive precautions for their very survival. Youth with these special needs are a growing population. For example, the incidence of activity-limiting chronic illnesses and disabilities has grown from 2 to 4 percent over the past ten years and today 18 percent of all teenagers have a chronic illness or disability (Newacheck, Strickland, et al. 1998). This is in part due to the fact that, compared to a decade ago, over 90 percent of children with disabilities now survive into adulthood (Blum 1995). Maintaining health is especially critical for this population, and thus having affordable health insurance coverage and access to appropriate health care are essential if they are to survive, let alone make a successful transition to adulthood.

Unfortunately, the vision of full and equal participation outlined by the youth mentioned at the beginning of this chapter is far from the reality with which they live. Today, young adults with SHCN/D are more likely to be uninsured or underinsured than adults with disabilities who are over sixty-five years of age. In addition, young adults with disabilities are more likely to be unemployed, to have poorer health status, to live in households with an annual income less than $15,000, and to be isolated, without a network of friends and without available transportation, than those without disabilities (National Organization on Disability 1998). Furthermore, even those professionals who might be advocates for this group often contribute to the self-fulfilling prophecies that these youth will fail. Studies have shown that professionals, including health care providers, have low expectations for youth with SHCN/D in the areas of independence, social skills, and employment (Ospinow 1976).

This chapter will focus on the following issues of relevance to the transition to adulthood for youth with SHCN/D: (1) the definition and general concept of medical transition, as well as principles and policies developed by medical professional groups, (2) the availability of health insurance and its effects on youth with SHCN/D, (3) what youth with SHCN/D expect from their transition experience, and (4) available transition programs and their effectiveness. The chapter closes with suggestions for policy changes that would improve the medical transition process for youth with SHCN/D.

THE DEFINITION AND GENERAL PRINCIPLES OF MEDICAL TRANSITION

An awareness of the transition to adulthood is implied in the change in systems of care young people experience as they move from child-centered to adult-oriented health care systems. The goal of moving into adult-oriented health care systems is to maximize the young person's potential in adulthood by providing services that are patient centered, flexible, responsive, uninterrupted, coordinated, developmentally and age appropriate, psychologically sound, and comprehensive. This process includes four major components: (1) early preparation for a transition to an adult system and "letting go" of dependencies associated with child-oriented care; (2) skill building for the young adult in communication, decision making, assertiveness, and self-care and an awareness of funding issues associated with health care; (3) graduation from school to work and planning for independent living including financial planning and an awareness of community supports; and (4) self-determination/interdependence (Blum 1995).

No matter how the model of transition care is organized, there are certain general principles that apply.

First: The transition for youth with disabilities should be a process, not an event, and should involve the entire family as a support system. This process must be planned and take into account not only the young person's chronological age, but also his/her developmental stage and level of maturity as well as the type, activity, and severity of the medical illness or condition.

Second: The transition process should begin at diagnosis and include long-term sequential planning toward goals of independence and self-management. Late adolescence and early adulthood are a time when society expects individuals to be able to make decisions concerning their lives, work, and medical care. Thus, by this period in life, the young person with SHCN/D should be prepared to assume more responsibility for his/her life including his/her medical condition. Self-management of medications is a good example. Well before the age of majority, children with chronic illnesses should be accustomed to managing their medications, although family members would likely monitor the process. Nonetheless, the move to independence at young adulthood adds an additional responsibility to even this mundane task. There are, of course, individual differences in a young person's physical and psychological capacities as well as differences in his/her support systems. Thus, the planning process should be flexible but attentive and responsive to the youth's growing independence and increasing capacity to make choices.

Third: pediatricians, other health care providers, and the family must appreciate the young person's change in status as s/he moves from adolescence into adulthood. Those who care about him/her have to understand that letting go is in the best interests of their patient/child and that it is a change in the nature of support rather than the loss of support from caring adults that is needed at this stage. Some of the major barriers to this process result from fears about the unknown and increasing levels of environmental and family stress. For example, parents may worry about their son or daughter moving out of the house and how they will manage on their own. In many cases, a strategy of "why change if there is not a problem?" becomes the operating mode. As a result, the process of transition often occurs in crisis, when the young adult is forced by age, insurance restrictions, or life plans to move to another facility or provider. Making these changes when the youth is comparatively healthy and involved in the choice usually has better psychological and medical outcomes than change imposed during a time of illness or crisis.

The fourth principle of transition care is a logical extension of the third.

Respect for the young person's autonomy implies a changing role for the family and for health care providers. With respect to the latter, the young person is likely to find very different treatment modalities in the adult health care system than in the pediatric system. Pediatric health providers are oriented to team approaches to care, child development, and communicating with family members more than with the child. Not surprisingly, since their orientation is towards children, they are less focused on independence and adult issues such as employment and adult relationships. In contrast, the health care provider in the adult system is more oriented toward aging and slow physical decline.

At the brink of adulthood, the young person with SHCN/D is faced with two starkly contrasting systems of health care. Given that s/he is accustomed to the orientation of the pediatric system, it would not be surprising that s/he would prefer some of the elements of that system. At the same time, as an emerging adult, s/he should be encouraged to be independent and take charge of his/her own health. Thus, the adolescent patient who sometimes wants to be treated as an adult and at other times feels like a child is faced with different approaches to care and needs guidance to navigate these conflicting systems (Rosen 1995; Viner 1999). The different possibilities for moving into adult-oriented systems should be discussed with the adolescent so that s/he can be integral to the decision-making process. Above all, youth with SHCN/D must feel competent and confident that they have some control of their future and are free to ask for or reject help as they see the need. Since the current system of adult health care is not oriented to be responsive to the needs of these incipient adults, the youth themselves will have to be prepared to advocate for their own health care needs. The young person with SHCN/D must develop the skills to negotiate the gap between the pediatric and adult health care systems.

Although patient autonomy is respected in the adult system, the family, who can help to bridge the youth's movement toward independence, may be excluded from consultation in the adult health care system. In most cases this would be a mistake, since the family continues to be an important source of support during the transition to adulthood. However, the parents' role changes at this juncture, in part because adults enjoy protections to privacy that children do not. Once an individual with SHCN/D reaches adulthood, health care providers should communicate directly with the young adult rather than with his/her parent. In fact, to the extent that providers begin this practice when the young person is an adolescent, they would be helping the family accommodate to the confidential nature of patient-provider relationships and the privacy protections common in health care practices for adults. Confidentiality is particularly important in the arena of reproductive health care services (see chapter 12 by Blum). Although many laws protect the confidentiality of adolescents, few states or pediatric practices report guaranteeing confidentiality (Akinbami, Gandhi, and Cheng 2003; Lewit, Bennett, and Behrman 2003).

Health care providers in the adult system may have little or no training in adolescent developmental issues or in diseases that, until recently, did not present to adult physicians. An American survey of 3,066 physicians and other health professionals showed major deficits in their knowledge of and skills in adolescent health care, including care for youth with SHCN/D (Blum and Bearinger 1990). The demands of treating young adults with SHCN/D may outweigh the benefits, especially if the young adult with disabilities is noncompliant, confused, or demanding. In addition, systems of care (availability of case managers, social workers, and mental health services) and financial reimbursement practices have not caught up with the numbers of young adults with SHCN/D.

Fifth: Attitudes about physical disability or chronic illness (in society generally and among health care providers specifically) affect the young person's self-image and his/her ability to successfully transition to adulthood. Unfortunately, several studies have shown that the attitudes of health professionals themselves pose a problem in this regard. Because physicians and other providers are trained in a medical model, their tendency is to want to cure a disability or "fix" an individual. Yet there is also evidence that young people with a disability may not want to be "fixed." One study reported that the longer that a young person had lived with a disability, the less likely s/he was to opt for a surgical "cure" (Hallum 1995).

In fact, people with disabilities are likely to be uncomfortable with the medical model, in which most health professionals are trained and work. In the medical model, disability is framed as a deficiency or abnormality in the individual. The remedy is to cure or normalize the individual; the professional health care provider is viewed as the agent for this task. An interactional model, by contrast, frames disability in neutral terms; the disability is just one of many attributes that might describe a person. The "problem" of disability in this model derives from a mismatch between the needs of individuals and the attitudes of society. Thus, the solution is not in fixing individuals but in repairing relationships, institutions, and policies, goals that can be accomplished only with many agents, including people with disabilities and those who advocate for them (Gill 1996). A psychiatrist with a disability, who is chair of a large rehabilitation department, explains the need to change from a medical model to an interactive model: "Most of the negative consequences of having a disability are not the result of the disabling condition but rather by the way those without disabilities related to their disabled peers" (Strax 1991, 509) (see chapter 11 for Lyons and Melton's discussion of how stigma affects young people coping with mental health problems).

Sixth: Coordination between health care, educational, vocational, and social service systems is essential. For example, attention to the medical needs of young people with SHCN/D as they move into postsecondary schooling requires coordination between the education and health care systems. Many youth with SHCN/D drop out of postsecondary education for health reasons. Since education is necessary to obtain the best jobs, keeping youth engaged in education and school is essential. The concept of care coordination is so essential to quality outcomes that it has been identified as one of the twenty most important areas for quality improvement by the Institute of Medicine (Adams and Corrigan 2003).

In elementary and secondary schools, the educational system assumes responsibility for planning for the educational needs of children with SHCN/D. While the young person is in school, the family can ask for an individual education plan (IEP) under PL 94-142 or a 504 plan under Section 504 of the Rehabilitation Act of 1973 if a disability interferes with the child's education. The IEP contains a plan to assist the child with accommodations in special education classes; a 504 plan is a legal document designed specifically for an individual student who has special needs and is in a traditional educational setting. Both are methods to maximize the child's educational experience. Similarly, in all states an individual transition plan (ITP) is required for all youth with an IEP (see chapter 9 for a discussion of special education policies). After high school, youth with SHCN/D must rely on their own resources and those of their family to plan and make choices about further education and training. Table 13.1 offers a set of questions to consider as the young person with SHCN/D prepares to go on to further schooling without the protection of the IEP they had in high school.

Physicians and other health care providers play a key role in facilitating a successful transition for this vulnerable population of young adults, and professional medical societies have long recognized the importance of a transition plan for youth with SHCN/D. Over the past several years the American Academy of Pediatrics (American Academy of Pediatrics 1996, 2000), the Society of Adolescent Medicine (Blum et al. 1993), and the American Medical Association (Hamburg, Nightingale, and Takanishi 1987) have developed statements of support for certain principles of medical transition. A consensus document has been approved by the American Academy of Pediatrics, the American Academy of Family Physicians, and the American College of Physicians-American Society

Table 13.1. Possible impacts of SHCN/D on a student

Educational
- Has the illness necessitated any special accommodations at school?
- Was class missed at certain times of day to perform a health care routine?
- Did the illness affect attendance?
- Did medication affect ability to concentrate or participate in school? (Was the student more alert at certain times of the day? Were frequent breaks from class required to take medications or rest?)
- Was extra time necessary to complete class work, tests, or homework?
- Was technology, such as computers, used in the classroom or at home to fulfill academic requirements?
- Was in-class assistance required such as a person to take notes?

Medical
- Are any activities restricted?
- Does the student require specialized medical care (for example, dialysis)?
- Does the student require the coordinated care of many health care providers?
- Does the student have a care routine that must be performed at a specific time of day?
- Does the student have a care routine that can be done only by a specially trained individual, such as a physical therapist, respiratory therapist, or nurse?
- Is there a medication schedule that must be strictly adhered to?
- Are required drugs difficult to find?
- Is the care of a medical specialist required? How frequently?

Environmental
- Do certain environmental factors such as heat, cold, molds, dust, odors, and humidity affect the student's health and well-being?
- Does the student need to limit exposure to noise and distractions?
- Does the student require a special living environment?
- Are certain activities such as walking long distances or climbing stairs difficult?

With respect to activities of daily living
- Is assistance getting out of bed required?
- Is assistance with food preparation/eating needed?
- Does the student require a special diet?
- Does the student need assistance bathing or using the bathroom?
- Is assistance with dressing necessary?
- Is assistance with mobility required?

Source: Edelman, Schuyler, and White 1998.

of Internal Medicine (2002). This statement lists the six critical requirements for a successful transition:

1. Ensure that all young people with SHCN/D have an identified health care professional who attends to the unique challenges of transition and assumes the responsibility for current health care, care coordination, and future health care planning.
2. Identify the core knowledge and skills required to provide developmentally appropriate health care transition services to youth with SHCN/D and make them part of training and certification requirements for primary care residents and physicians in practice.
3. Prepare and maintain an up-to-date medical summary that is portable and accessible.
4. Create a written health care transition plan by age 14 together with the young person and family. At a minimum, this plan should include what services need to be provided, who will provide them, and how they will be financed. This plan should be reviewed, updated, and available when transfer of care occurs.
5. Apply the same guidelines for primary and preventive care for all adolescents and young adults with and without SHCN/D recognizing that youth with SHCN/D may require more resources and services than those without SHCN/D to optimize their health. (See Rosenbaum, Shaw, and Sonosky 2001; Schulzinger 2000; and the Social Security Administration website for examples of guidelines.)
6. Ensure affordable, continuous health insurance coverage for all youth with SHCN/D throughout adolescence and adulthood. This insurance should cover appropriate compensation for 1) healthcare transition planning and 2) care coordination for those who have complex medical conditions.

HEALTH CARE ACCESS AND NEEDS

The barriers to access faced by young people with SHCN/D are often multifaceted. They can be financial (lack of medical insurance or lack of coverage for special services such as specialized therapies and primary or subspecialty care); physical (inaccessible facilities, lack of transportation); social (communication challenges); and systemic (lack of coordinated care, lack of subspecialists within a reasonable distance).

American medical societies all recognize that affordable continuous health care coverage is essential and the lack of adequate health insurance is a major problem for young adults with SHCN/D today (see chapters 10 and 11 for discussions of health insurance gaps for youth with mental health problems). Access to health insurance is a problem that this vulnerable population shares with other young adults. One in seven Americans aged ten to eighteen has no form of health insurance, public or private (Newacheck, Brindis, and Cart 1999) and that percentage increases during the transition to adulthood. Young people aged nineteen to twenty-nine are the largest and fastest growing segment of the U.S. population without health insurance (Collins, Schoen, and Tenny 2003). By the age of nineteen or on graduation from high school or college, most Americans must find health insurance on their own. In addition, most of the jobs available to young adults with special health needs are low wage or temporary and do not offer health insurance benefits. A young person enrolled full-time in college can continue on their parent's health insurance policy until graduation (assuming that their parents have such a policy). However, many youth do not go to college and many with SHCN/D are unable to carry a full-time course load. The Commonwealth Fund recently concluded that "two of five college graduates and one half of high school graduates who do not go to college will endure a time without health insurance in the first year after graduation. Moreover if the pattern continues, two thirds of all young adults age 19 to 23 today are likely to lack health insurance at some point over the next four years" (American Academy of Pediatrics 1996, 1204).

Uninsured young adults accounted for twelve million of the forty-one million people without health insurance, according to the most recent U.S. census. Over the past decade the number has grown by two million from 22 percent in 1987 to 28 percent in 2001, almost twice the rate among adults aged thirty to sixty-four in 2001 (Collins et al. 2003). Low economic status increases the chance that a youth will be without health insurance. Two-thirds of the twelve million young adults who are uninsured live in households with incomes below the federal poverty level. Young people with SHCN/D are also more likely to come from poor households (Collins et al. 2003).

It is not surprising that children with chronic illness or disabilities would need more health care than their less vulnerable peers. In fact, preliminary data from the first nationwide survey of children with SHCN/D shows that, although they represent 15 to 18 percent of all American children, this group accounts for 50 percent of all health care expenditures for children (Newacheck 2002). In part this is due to the fact that many in this group have multiple health care needs. One in five adolescents with SHCN/D have at least one other serious health problem (U.S. Congress, Office of Technology Assessment 1991)

Young adults with SHCN/D can be especially vulnerable to not having health insurance. They often lose Medicaid coverage by aging out of it or by losing SSI. They can lose their parents' health care coverage due to age limitations and have less opportunity and ability to obtain jobs that offer health insurance. Like younger children without coverage, uninsured adolescents with SHCN/D use fewer health services, receive care less frequently, return for fewer follow-up appointments and are likely to seek care in an emergency room with less continuity of care (Lieu, Newacheck, and McManus 1993; Newacheck, Hughes, and Cisternas 1995). Continuity of care is crucial for this group. An interruption in access to care can have serious consequences for a youth, for example, with cystic fibrosis who is dependent on daily medications. Finally, those without health insurance often have to pay higher prices for services and drugs than those with health insurance, creating another barrier to seeking care.

Like all adolescents, those with SHCN/D take risks with their health. One in four is at risk for unprotected sexual intercourse or substance abuse (U.S. Congress, Office of Technology Assessment 1991). Adolescence is a period when engaging in health-damaging, risky behaviors can have life-long consequences. Thus, health care programs for adolescents with SHCN/D need to emphasize prevention, early intervention, and education. Notably, youth with SHCN/D often do not have the same opportunities for health maintenance or prevention as their less vulnerable peers. For example, someone with limitations in mobility or congenital heart disease may not be able to exercise. Furthermore, although preventive care can improve adolescent physical and mental health and establish health habits that last a lifetime (Newacheck et al. 1999), many private and public health insurance plans do not include preventive care (Collins et al. 2003).

Youth with SHCN/D often require access to both primary and subspecialty care to maintain and improve their functioning. Many with SHCN/D require prolonged drug treatment. For some (e.g., those with HIV/AIDS), the availability of drugs may be the reason they survived into adulthood. Other youth with SHCN/D may need durable medical equipment, assistive technologies, and long-term services such as personal assistance and continuous medical supervision (DeJong et al. 2002)

Because youth with SHCN/D may already have a chronic illness, secondary and other health conditions, including additional chronic ones, that would have a minor effect on a youth without SHCN/D can result in major functional impairments. For example, a young person with asthma takes drugs that might impair his/her immune system. Steroid treatment for asthma may lead to severe osteoporosis or diabetes. For that young person a routine infection such as mononucleosis could result in hospitalization and loss of days at work or school. Similarly, for a youth with arthritis, healing from a sports injury could be a long process insofar as his/her joints would require a lengthy period to regain function.

HEALTH INSURANCE OPTIONS FOR
ADOLESCENTS WITH SHCN/D

Why do young adults with SHCN/D face a gap in their health care coverage after the age of eighteen? A survey of the health insurance available to different age groups reveals a complex maze of state, federal, and private plans with eligibility criteria that change as the youth age from eighteen to twenty-one. In the next section we discuss issues and problems of health care coverage available to youths with SHCN/D as they move toward adulthood (White 2002).

Public insurance. The Medicaid program (Title XIX of the Social Security Act of 1965) is the major provider of medical assistance for low-income youth and families and for people with disabilities. Program funding comes from a combination of federal and state sources. Individual states determine levels of coverage and the federal government provides a match for the state expenditure. According to the U.S. General Accounting Office (GAO) 80 percent of adults under age sixty-five with severe disabilities reported using Medicaid. Individuals with disabilities insured by Medicaid are substantially more impaired than similar individuals with private health coverage (United States General Accounting Office 1999).

Although Medicaid is a national program, the rules for determining financial eligibility (income and resources) and nonfinancial requirements (categories of individuals such as welfare and SSI recipients) vary from state to state. Within the federal guidelines there is considerable flexibility for each state to determine who is eligible, for what type, amount, and duration of services. The reimbursement rates for those services also are determined independently by each state. Under federal law some Medicaid benefits are mandatory. These include the Early and Periodic Screening, Diagnosis and Treatment (EPSDT) program, basic hospital and physician care, laboratory and X-ray services, nursing facilities, home health services, and prescription drug coverage.

There are several ways that a youth with a disability could obtain Medicaid coverage. These include Supplemental Security Income (SSI) with constraints applied in 209(b) states; medically needy, home, and community based waivers; foster care Title IV-E and non–Title IV-E (see Schulzinger 2000 for a full description of these programs).

SSI. SSI is a means-tested program designed to supplement other income sources, including other public benefits. Children with SHCN/D who meet the disability criteria of the Social Security Administration (SSA) and whose parents meet the SSI income criteria can be covered. When those youth reach eighteen, their eligibility depends on several factors including the state in which they reside.

Starting in 1998 many states that received funds under section 209(b) elected to apply more restrictive income and resource standards than those under SSI. For example, many required eighteen-year-olds on SSI to be redetermined for SSA eligibility under the adult criteria. Since the adult criteria stipulate that the individual must be unable to work, which is often *not* the case for young adults with SHCN/D, the SSA estimated in 2001 that 30 percent of those who had SSI as a child would lose it at age eighteen. Many of these youth would also lose health coverage because they would no longer be eligible for Medicaid. Young adults with SHCN/D can continue on Medicaid if they are not redetermined off of SSI (Schulzinger 2000).

Redetermination can also result in groups of young people with SHCN/D remaining or becoming eligible for SSI. For example, those young people who were covered under their parents' eligibility and who get jobs but do not earn more than $700 per month (after taking into account income and asset limits) would remain eligible. Others, whose family income and assets were too high for them to qualify for SSI as children, may meet the means test of low income when they turn eighteen. Regardless of when individuals enter the SSI program, they are required to apply for and accept any other benefits for which they may be eligible before collecting SSI benefits.

Individuals receiving SSI benefits can also take advantage of work incentive programs that will let them work and still qualify for Medicaid insurance. To receive SSI and Medicaid, the young adult must be unemployed or, if working, earn below what is called substantial gainful activity (SGA). As earnings increase, SSI payments decrease. Under section 4733 of the Balanced Budget Act of 1997, states have the option to create and provide medical coverage to a "categorically needy" group, e.g., workers with disabilities who, because of earnings, would not qualify for Medicaid. Under this law, if the individual meets SSI disability criteria and has a net income below 250 percent of the federal poverty level, they can buy into Medicaid. However, these programs are in jeopardy due to state budget shortfalls.

The Ticket to Work Act, passed by Congress in 2000, also allows states to offer medical insurance to individuals who have a disability but do not qualify for SSI. In addition, states can offer Medicaid to people who have improved and are no longer totally disabled. However, the standards for defining disability are unclear and under this program most states have only enrolled people from SSI rolls without addressing disability. Thus, the legislation has had limited effects on uninsured young adults with SHCN/D.

SCHIP. In 1997 eligibility for public health insurance was expanded with the creation of the State Children's Health Insurance Program (SCHIP). Those eligible for SCHIP included those under age nineteen in families with incomes less than or equal to 200 percent of the federal poverty level. The federal match for SCHIP is more generous than the match for Medicaid. This financial incentive was built into the SCHIP program to encourage states to cover more adolescents in poverty. States have either placed their SCHIP program within their existing Medicaid Program or developed a separate SCHIP program, usually in conjunction with private insurance. Generally, the breadth of services offered by the Medicaid-related programs is greater than that offered through the private insurance programs. In particular, separate SCHIP programs contracting with managed care for prevention and chronic care services offer benefits that are narrower than those under Medicaid (Rosenbaum, Shaw, and Sonosky 2001). This is a serious consideration for those with SHCN/D because the comprehensive nature of the benefits offered by Medicaid is often essential to maintain the function and independence of those with disabilities.

OASDI/Medicare. People with SHCN/D are often also eligible for benefits under Title II of the Social Security program, known as the Old Age, Survivors, and Disability Insurance (OASDI) program. Title II benefits are not needs based and have no income or asset test. They trigger eligibility for Medicare after a two-year waiting period. Young people with disabilities may be eligible for OASDI benefits based on their own work history or they may be eligible based on the work history of their parents who are receiving Social Security benefits.

Monthly cash benefits paid by each of the Social Security programs is based on the amount of time worked and the amount of earnings in "covered" work. Most work is now covered, although some state government employees are not. For OASDI, an individual must work a minimum amount of time, calculated as work credits. Work credits are earned for work exceeding a threshold amount ($830 in 2002) and individuals may earn up to four work credits per year. In most cases, the individual must have earned twenty work credits in the last ten years before they can claim SSDI when they become disabled. In contrast, a young person with a severe disability that developed in childhood may earn eligibility for OASDI with only six work credits. Thus, a youth with disability can qualify for SSDI cash payments long before adults who developed their disability after childhood.

General Medicaid. Children can qualify for Medicaid in a variety of ways not related to disability. In most states Medicaid covers children until eighteen to twenty-one years of age as long as the family meets income eligibility criteria, which vary from state to state. If a child does not meet the SSI disability criteria, families often have to "spend down" their income to meet the Medicaid eligibility criteria, as is the case for families with children who have chronic illnesses such as cystic fibrosis, diabetes, or sickle cell anemia. Of children on Medicaid with a severe medical condition, 74 percent do not receive SSI, and an equal number of youth on SSI do not have a severe medical condition (Burwell, Crown, and Drabek 1997; Schneider, Victoria, and Ellberger 1999).

Many chronic medical conditions require expensive treatment but, if well-controlled, are not necessarily disabling. These include conditions such as severe asthma, HIV, cancer, and cystic fibrosis. When a youth with these conditions turns nineteen to twenty-one years of age, their high medical expenses continue but they may lose Medicaid coverage because they no longer meet state eligibility requirements.

A young adult with SHCN/D would typically not be eligible for Medicaid unless s/he had children of his/her own or met the SSI eligibility criteria for a disability. Only a few states to date have chosen to expand their Medicaid eligibility to adults without children. Thus, in most states, a low-income child with a disability that did not meet SSI criteria could receive Medicaid coverage. However, s/he would lose that coverage when s/he crossed the threshold into adulthood. Fishman estimated that 400,000 of the 20 million children in Medicaid have serious chronic health conditions, do not have SSI, and are at risk of losing their coverage at the age of nineteen (Fishman 2001).

Large state and federal budget deficits pose an additional problem for youth with SHCN/D. In an effort to free up money to cover unemployed families applying for Medicaid benefits due to a poor economy, the Center for Medical Services (CMS) is allowing states to use Medicaid waivers to decrease benefit packages for those with disabilities. At the same time, states are being compelled to take action to decrease their budget shortfalls. With the exception of Vermont, all states are required to balance their budgets every year (Iglehart 2003). The Kaiser Family Foundation in January 2003 found that forty-nine states planned to impose new controls on health care costs to meet budget constraints. Most have focused their efforts on constraining the costs of prescription drugs (forty-five states); reducing or freezing the payment rates for providers (thirty-seven states); reducing or restricting program eligibility (twenty-seven states); reducing benefits (twenty-five states) and increasing the copayments of beneficiaries (seventeen states) (Smith, Gilford, Ramesh, and Wachino 2003). This trend will continue into the foreseeable future as long as the states' budgets are running a deficit (Holahan, Bovbjerg, Coughlin, Hill, Ormond, and Zuckerman 2004).

DAC. One of the few ways a youth with SHCN/D can be eligible for medical coverage as an adult is through the Adult Disabled Child benefit (DAC). The intent of this program is to benefit children when their parent becomes disabled, retires, or dies. A child who was disabled before age twenty-two and is unable to work is eligible for a DAC benefit if his/her parent contributed enough to social security before the parent became disabled, retired, or died. The amount of support a child receives is based on a percentage of the parent's benefit amount. Often the DAC benefit is greater than the maximum allowable SSI benefit. Thus, if a disabled child gets DAC, s/he would lose whatever SSI benefit s/he had been receiving and the automatic Medicaid eligibility that goes with it. Some states have adopted options in Medicaid that allow workers with disabilities to buy into Medicaid as long as the young adult meets the disability criteria for SSI.

General Medicare. For some young adults with disabilities who lose Medicaid, Medicare may provide an alternative. A disabled adult dependent who has received Medicaid benefits for at least twenty-four months but then becomes ineligible for Medicaid could become eligible for some Medicare benefits. However, the benefit package in Medicare lacks the coverage for long-term care and prescription drugs provided in Medicaid.

Private insurance coverage. As mentioned previously, two-thirds of children with disabilities have private health insurance coverage through their parents' insurance plans. However, this does not mean their needs are adequately met. Due to limitations in the scope of most private health insurance, problems of underinsurance are common for children with SHCN/D. According to a recent study, 40 percent of children with SHCN/D also needed secondary health plan coverage, usually Medicaid (Hill and Lutzy 2001). A study conducted by the National Center for Health Statistics found that 16 to 20 percent of children with SHCN had insurance coverage that did not always meet their needs. Uninsured patients with chronic conditions had higher expenses and were five times less likely to see a health care provider than those with insurance (Hwang, Weller, Ireys, and Anderson 2001). Similarly, Newacheck found that adolescents without health insurance living in families with incomes below the poverty level were charged more for medical services than those in families with incomes above the poverty line with health insurance (Newacheck and McManus 1990). Insurance companies can often bargain for services or drugs because they control a large part of the market. In contrast, an individual without insurance has to pay full price as they have no bargaining power in the marketplace.

Of course, as young people transition to adulthood they typically lose eligibility for private group health insurance as their parents' dependents. Private health plans have an upper age limit after which children can no longer be covered under their parents' plan. Young adults with disabilities can continue coverage under their parents' health insurance plan under two conditions.

First, they may remain eligible if they do not work. This option is mandated under the Health Insurance Portability and Accountability Act of 1996 (HIPAA) for non–Employee Retirement Income Security Act (ERISA) plans and is available in forty-four states. However, a youth with SHCN/D can jeopardize health coverage under the parents' insurance plan by going to work and earning an income. This presents a catch-22 for the young adult. Either s/he can remain dependent on his/her parents and maintain the security of health care coverage or s/he can achieve one of the markers of adult status by getting a job but risk the loss of health coverage in the process. Under HIPAA, individuals with disabilities who have been working for the prior eighteen months in a company that offers equivalent workers' health insurance must be offered health insurance even when they have past or current problems. Often the cost of these plans is prohibitive and they have minimal benefit packages. Furthermore, many young adults are employed in part-time jobs that offer no health insurance benefits. Thus, this law does not apply to them.

A second way that a young adult with SHCN can maintain coverage on their parents' private health insurance is by being a full-time student. However, many young adults with disabilities are unable to take a full course load, and as a consequence they lose this option.

Youth with SHCN/D are unlikely to get their own private health insurance coverage policy. Not only are such policies prohibitively expensive to pay for on one's own, but restrictions on coverage are also typical. While a young adult with a SHCN/D can try to obtain health insurance from the market, individuals with conditions such as asthma, HIV, and cancer can face denial of coverage, limits on benefits, and premium surcharges (Pollitz and Sorian 2001).

Insurance regulation comes under state jurisdiction and many states have enacted high-risk pools in response to these problems. For example, the state can offer to pool young adults with SHCN/D who require expensive therapies together and negotiate a reduced cost. However, many states restrict covered benefits or cap enrollment to hold down costs in these high-risk pools. As a result, nationwide only about one million individuals are currently enrolled in state high-risk pools. This low number suggests that, as they are currently structured, these pools are an unlikely mechanism for meeting the needs of uninsured young adults with disabilities (Achman and Chollet 2001). A few states such as New York have tried to make coverage in the individual market more widely available, but this has increased costs for young healthy consumers to compensate for a reduction in cost for those with chronic conditions.

In twenty-one states, programs in Title V of the Social Security Act offer condition-specific health coverage. That is, states may provide coverage for one or more genetic diseases such as cystic fibrosis, hemophilia, and sickle cell disease. However, not only are these programs limited to a few genetic diseases, eligibility for a young adult requires that s/he was enrolled as a child.

In 1985, Congress passed a law to provide temporary access to health insurance for qualified individuals who lose their coverage due to a change in the individual's work or family status. Under Title X of the Consolidated Omnibus Budget Reconciliation Act (COBRA), an employer with twenty or more employees must provide employees and their families the option of continuing their coverage under the employer's group insurance plan under certain circumstances. The coverage generally lasts up to eighteen months—in some instances thirty-six months—and the beneficiary can be required to pay up to 102 percent of the premium (Yaker 2001). Thus, coverage under COBRA is expensive and short-lived.

In summary, problems are posed by many private plans because they are too expensive, have limited benefits, require that the young adult with SHCN/D not participate in the work force, and are typically offered for a limited time. Thus, neither the private market, as it is today, nor public health care programs with their eligibility problems, is a likely source of affordable or comprehensive health insurance for young adults with SHCN/D (Cooper 2001; Quinn, Schoen, and Buatti 2000).

POLICY OPTIONS AND RESEARCH RECOMMENDATIONS

Radical changes in health care coverage in general would be needed to help to address the insurance needs of people with SHCN/D. For example, the Institute of Medicine report focuses on the need to move from short-term episodic financing toward a reimbursement system that takes a life-long perspective on people's medical needs. The authors of this report argue that the most effective policy would be to implement systemwide changes that help to expand access to and stabilize coverage for the general population including those with SHCN/D (Committee on Quality of Health Care in America 2001).

Austin and Burnet recommend that Congress create individual tax incentives to encourage people to buy health insurance either as individuals or employers, mandate universal catastrophic coverage, and charter an independent Federal Health Insurance Reserve System to encourage efficient utilization of resources, improve individual choice options, and stimulate innovative and fair competition, thus expanding access and increasing coverage (Austin and Burnett 2003).

Short of a massive overhaul of the health insurance system, the following policy changes could have a significant impact on scaffolding the transition to adulthood for large numbers of youth with SHCN/D:

- First, with respect to private insurance, states should require private insurers and employers to extend coverage to all unmarried dependents through age twenty-five. Some states, such as Utah, already offer coverage to age twenty-six for unmarried dependents regardless of disability status. This benefit could be written as a rider or added to all policies. This would assist in covering an estimated 500,000 to 800,000 unmarried dependent youth under age twenty-two (Collins et al. 2004).

- Second, with respect to Medicaid, Congress should allow or require states to extend coverage to age twenty-three to young adults in Medicaid and SCHIP. Such a policy change could assist the 2.7 million uninsured young adults ages nineteen to twenty-three with incomes under 100 percent of the federal poverty level (Collins et al. 2004).

- Third, state legislatures should mandate that all colleges and universities require full- and part-time students to maintain minimum health insurance coverage and that health insurance be made available to students at a reasonable cost if they do not have coverage. State legislatures could offer premium support to offset costs. This would help cover the over two million part- and full-time students currently without coverage (Collins et al. 2004).

- Fourth, states should offer an expanded benefit package in state-designed SCHIP programs for youth with SHCN/D.

- Fifth, Congress should require the Social Security Administration to increase the redetermination age from eighteen to twenty-three years to allow youth the chance to obtain enough skills to garner a job with health care benefits. Alternatively, Congress could change SSI's "unemployability" standard for Medicaid eligibility for young adults. This would assist those young adults with functional disabilities where their disability status keeps them from participating in employer sponsored insurance (Fishman 2001).

- Sixth, new models need to be constructed to incorporate those with serious chronic illnesses so that they can participate in large insurance pools that could make the cost of health insurance affordable.

- Finally, states should make sure that their Medicaid and SCHIP programs cover appropriate preventive services for adolescents with SHCN/D in accordance with the most current guidelines. States should update their EPSDT periodicity schedules and ensure that all health plans and providers are using updated schedules.

Of course, policies should be informed by good data and understanding the health care issues faced by young adults with SHCN/D requires more comprehensive information. Large-scale longitudinal studies should focus on those who leave the child health insurance system with a spotlight on those who age out or otherwise leave when they are at the threshold of adulthood. These studies should identify both the numbers affected and the cost of providing appropriate care. In conjunction with longitudinal studies, case studies illustrating the problems young adults with SHCN/D face would be helpful so that legislators could understand the persons behind the medical categories.

Clarity about the health care needs of different groups could also be enhanced if the federal government and states would collect, analyze, and report program quality and performance data in a consistent way. For example, much could be learned if states used a consistent system of reporting program data by participant's gender, race, ethnicity, or age. Finally, working with consumers, purchasers, health plans, and health care professionals with expertise in caring for adolescents with and without SHCN/D, states should adopt adolescent-specific performance measures designed to monitor clinical effectiveness, use of services, access, and satisfaction with care (Alcalde 2000; American Medical Association 2000; Green and Palfrey 2000).

WHAT YOUNG PEOPLE WITH SHCN/D WANT FROM TRANSITION SERVICES/PROVIDERS

Youth with SHCN/D have ideas about what they are looking for when they think of transition services; their aspirations are typical of those at the transition. For example, many youth say they want jobs. More in-depth information is provided in one large comprehensive survey of young people with SHCN/D, conducted in 1995 by the PACER Center in Minneapolis. Over 11,000 households where young adults with disabilities lived were mailed a survey asking what these young people wanted in transition services. Over 1,300 youth (range fourteen to twenty-five years) with a variety of disabilities (learning disabilities, chronic illness, mental health problems, physical disabilities, arthritis, and sensory impairments) responded. All of them identified job training as the most important desire, with independent living skills and college or vocational guidance close behind (Wright 1996). Other noteworthy findings from this study include the fact that only 45 percent of the respondents said that they had received any guidance about making medical decisions and less than half had ever been asked about their work plans. Most of the respondents indicated that they were concerned about finding and paying for medical care, and 50 percent had heard of transition planning.

In another study of youth with sickle cell disease, the main concern raised by these young people was that they wanted their adult health care provider to feel comfortable with people with disabilities. Other concerns they had about planning for their transition to the adult medical system included: (1) not beginning transition planning soon enough, (2) lack of availability of a summary of their medical history, (3) difficulty finding an adult provider, (4) excessive use of medical jargon, (5) the difficulty of paying for medical care, and (6) concerns as to whether adult providers would understand how their illness/condition affects them as individuals (Telfair, Myers, and Drezner 1994).

In another study, a focus group of teenagers with disabilities was asked what the barriers to their transition into adulthood, and the solutions, would be. They commented that pediatric caregivers are more caring than adult medical providers and that their parents do not want to "let go." In particular, they said that they were burned out on health care in pediatric settings, wanted to be more involved in decisions related to their own health care, and felt that no one seemed to be planning for their transition to adulthood (Patterson and Lanier 1999). Youth with SHCN/D in this study suggested the following ideas as helpful approaches for a successful transition: (1) having an attentive health care provider who listens; (2) being allowed to make decisions related to health care; (3) having providers communicate about the transition process; (4) having the health care provider's gender match the young person's; (5) being introduced to a provider of adult care at age fifteen; and (6) being given options of care with a rationale for each option.

Needs assessment studies conducted in several states by transition service providers from the Healthy and Ready to Work program revealed that young people want education and employment and that coordination is lacking between professionals and between systems serving these young people (Healthy and Ready to Work National Center 2004). In addition, these needs assessments revealed that, although transition services may exist, young people often do not know about them or how to access them.

EFFECTIVE SHCN/D TRANSITION PROGRAMS

A 1999 national survey completed by the Minnesota Transition Center identified 126 programs that offered transition services for those with SHCN/D. The center identified these transition services by sending questionnaires to state rehabilitation and education offices, medical and other health providers, and parent groups (Scal, Evans, Blozis, Okinow, and Blum 1999). Of the programs, 62 percent were condition specific (e.g., spina bifida or cystic fibrosis) or specialty specific (e.g., pulmonary or rheumatological) and 38 percent were adolescent health centered (e.g., the program was located in an adolescent health clinic). A major barrier found in the survey was the lack of providers of adult care willing to take on the care of these young people with SHCN. Consumer involvement was rare and most programs focused on disease management rather than functional outcome. In other words, most of the programs focused on management of the medical illness and did not address other issues relevant to functioning as a young adult such as independence, postsecondary education, or prevocational readiness. Only 20 percent of the programs included vocational services. This disease management framework is at odds with the kinds of transition services young adults with SHCN/D say they need.

Viner (1999) points to three elements that would make transition programs more effective: (1) a policy concerning when the young person would be required to move to adult medical care; (2) a period of preparation and deliberate education prior to transfer to the adult clinic (such preparation would include understanding of the disease, the treatment rationale, the source of symptoms, signs of deterioration and appropriate responses, and how to seek and get help); (3) creation of a coordinated transfer process including a detailed written plan, pretransfer visits to the adult clinic, and meeting with the adult provider and with a designated coordinator such as a clinic nurse. He further argues for the importance of oversight of the transition from child to adult systems and recommends nurse specialists as ideal for this role. The tasks of these professionals would be to develop links between the systems, oversee financial and contracting issues, and evaluate transition arrangements.

White (1999) has summarized lessons for transitional planning based on the literature and on her decade of professional work in a generic transition-to-work program in a children's hospital. She argues for starting early, listening to what young people say they need, and including them in the decision-making process. Because getting a job with health insurance is a high priority, it is important that programs deal with prevocational issues. Support systems are also essential, and including a broad and deep net of such supports can help in the transition process. These support systems could include family members, mentors, and role models, peer supports, and community providers such as recreation providers and employers. Members of the support system should be included in training so that they understand their role in the process. Since the young person is at the brink of adulthood, it is important that adults who have been part of the child's support system learn how to let go and that peers and other mentors take over some of the support roles that families may have provided in the past.

Comprehensive services should be developmentally appropriate for the age and disease stage of the young person with SHCN/D. These services should be responsive not only to the medical condition but also to the vocational, emotional, social, sexual, and general health concerns of the young person. Finally, it is important to evaluate the outcome and quality of care in order to document who benefits from what services. Few studies have documented the efficacy of medical transition programs. However, the benefits of co-coordinated transitional care programs have been documented for several chronic illnesses. Improved disease control (Salmi, Huuponen, Oksa, Okala, Koivula, and Raita

1986), improved follow-up in a U.S. tertiary referral hospital-based population (Rettig and Athreya 1991), and improved quality of life (Nasr, Campbell, and Howatt 1992; Sawyer 1998) have been reported.

Research is also needed about the population of young people with SHCN/D and how their functioning has been affected over time. Epidemiological studies would supply a better description of the numbers as well as the needs of this population. These studies could also answer questions such as: How can one minimize the effects of a disability on the young person's ability to participate in age-appropriate activities? What characterizes a successful transition to adulthood by youth with SHCN/D, and what services promote a successful transition? Future research agendas should address many of the specialized therapies, their usefulness for different disabilities, and their cost-benefit ratios as well as optimal arrangements between primary and specialty care and ways to promote and study coordinated care.

Because medical care is both essential and costly, comprehensive studies of expenditures and utilization factoring in the sources of payment would assist in designing a payment system that maximized access and optimal outcomes. There is great need for research on optimal benefit packages and research on how to determine the appropriate cost using risk adjustment strategies. Finally, a clear gap in the transition from child to adult systems of health care is the lack of training of health professionals in the medical and developmental needs of youth with SHCN/D. More adult health care providers need to learn how to care for young adults who are surviving into adulthood with illnesses that in the past were seen only in childhood. Mandating by the appropriate accrediting bodies of training for health care providers in the special needs of this vulnerable population could go a long way toward providing a safety net that would ease this group's transition to adulthood.

REFERENCES

Achman, L., and D. Chollet. 2001. *Insuring the uninsurable: An overview of state high risk health insurance pools.* New York: Commonwealth Fund.

Adams, K., and J. M. Corrigan. 2003. *Priority areas for national action: Transforming health care quality.* Washington: National Academy Press.

Akinbami, L. J., H. Gandhi, and T. L. Cheng. 2003. Availability of adolescent health services and confidentiality in primary care offices. *Pediatrics* 111: 394–401.

Alcalde, G. 2000. *Providing reproductive health services for adolescents: State options.* Washington: National Conference of State Legislatures.

American Academy of Pediatrics, American Academy of Family Physicians, and American College of Physicians-American Society of Internal Medicine. 2002. A consensus statement on health care transitions for young adults with special health care needs. *Pediatrics* 110: 1304–1306.

American Academy of Pediatrics Committee on Children with Disabilities. 2000. The role of the pediatrician in transitioning children and adolescents with developmental disabilities and chronic illnesses from school to work or college. *Pediatrics* 106: 854–856.

American Academy of Pediatrics, Council on Children with Disabilities and Committee on Adolescents. 1996. Transition care provided for adolescents with special health care needs. *Pediatrics* 98: 1203–1206.

American Medical Association, Department of Adolescent Health. 2000. *Guidelines for adolescent health services(GAPS): Clinical evaluation and management handbook.* Chicago: American Medical Association.

Austin, G. E., and R. D. Burnett. 2003. An innovative proposal for the health care financing system of the U.S. *Pediatrics* 111:1093–1097.

Blum, R. W., ed. 1995a. Conference proceedings: Moving on: Transition from pediatric to adult health care. *Journal of Adolescent Health* 17: 3–36.

Blum, R. W. 1995b. Transition to adult health care: Setting the stage. *Journal of Adolescent Health* 17: 3–5.

Blum, R. W., ed. 2002. Improving transition for adolescents with special health care needs from pediatric to adult-centered health care. *Pediatrics* 110: 1301–1335.

Blum, R. W., and L. H. Bearinger. 1990. Knowledge and attitudes of health professionals towards adolescent health care. *Journal of Adolescent Health Care* 11: 289–294.

Blum, R. W., D. Garell, C. H. Hodgman, T. W. Jorissen, N. A. Okinow, D. P. Orr, and G. B. Slap. 1993. Transition from child centered to adult health care-systems for adolescents with chronic conditions. *Journal of Adolescent Health* 14: 570–576.

Burwell, B., W. Crown, and J. Drabek. 1997. *Children with severe chronic conditions on Medicaid.* Washington: U.S. Department of Health and Human Services, Office of the Assistant Secretary for Planning and Evaluation.

Collins, S. R., C. Schoen, K. Tenny, M. M. Doty, and A. Ho. 2004. *Rite of passage? Why young adults become uninsured and how new policies can help.* New York: Commonwealth Fund.

Committee on Quality of Health Care in America. 2001. *Crossing the quality chasm: A new health system for the 21st century.* Washington: National Academy Press.

Cooper, B. 2001. *Young adults with disability: Between a rock and a hard place.* Washington: National Health Policy Forum.

DeJong, G., S. E. Palsbo, P. W. Beatty, G. Jones, T. Kroll, and M. Neri. 2002. The organization and financing of health services for persons with disabilities. *Milbank Quarterly* 80: 261–301.

Edelman, A., V. E. Schuyler, and P. H. White. 1998. *Maximizing success for young adults with chronic health-related illnesses: Transition planning for education after high school.* Washington: HEATH Resource Center, American Council on Education.

Fishman, E. 2001. Aging out of coverage: Young adults with special health needs. *Health Affairs* 20: 254–266.

Fox, H., M. McManus, and M. Reichman. In press. Private health insurance for adolescents: Is it adequate? *Journal of Adolescent Health.*

Gill, C. 1996. *Vocational development.* Chicago: Institute of Disability Research, Rehabilitation and Training Research Center.

Green, M., and J. S. Palfrey, eds. *Bright futures: Guidelines for health supervision of infants, children, and adolescents.* 2nd ed. Arlington, VA: National Center for Education in Maternal and Child Health.

Hallum, A. 1995. Disability and the transition to adulthood: Issues for the disabled child, the family, and the pediatrician. *Current Problems in Pediatrics* 25: 12–50.

Hamburg, D. A., E. O. Nightingale, and R. Takanishi. 1987. Facilitating the transition of adolescence: Council on Adolescent Development. *Journal of the American Medical Association* 257: 3405–3406.

Healthy and Ready to Work National Center. 2004. www.hrtw.org/about_us/projects.html (visited January 2004).

Hill, I., and A. W. Lutzy. 2001. *Are we responding to their needs? States' early experiences serving children with special health care needs under SCHIP.* Washington: Urban Institute.

Holahan, J., R. R. Bovbjerg, T. Coughlin, I. Hill, B. H. Ormond, and S. Zuckerman. 2004. *State response to the budget crisis in 2004: Overview of 10 states: overview and case studies.* Washington: Kaiser Foundation.

Hwang, W., W. Weller, H. Ireys, and G. Anderson. 2001. Out-of-pocket medical spending for care of chronic conditions. *Health Affairs* 20: 267–278.

Iglehart, J. K. 2003. The dilemma of Medicaid. *New England Journal of Medicine* 348: 2140–2148.

Lewit, E. M., C. Bennett, and R. E. Behrman. 2003. Health insurance for children: Analysis and recommendations. *Future of Children* 13: 5–29.

Lieu, T., P. Newacheck, and M. McManus. 1993. Race, ethnicity, and access to ambulatory care among U.S. adolescents. *American Journal of Public Health* 83: 960–965.

Nasr, S. Z., C. Campbell, and W. Howatt. 1992. Transition program from paediatric to adult care for cystic fibrosis patients. *Journal of Adolescent Health* 13: 682–685.

National Organization on Disability. 1998. *NOD/Harris survey of people with disabilities, study no. 942003.* Washington: Louis Harris Association.

Newacheck, P. 2002. *Building community-based systems of care for children with special health care needs: A national perspective.* Presented at the Dr. Richard E. Behrman Lecture Series in Pediatrics, Palo Alto, November 15.

Newacheck, P., C. Brindis, C. Cart, K. Marchi, and C. E. Irwin. 1999. Adolescent health insurance coverage: Recent changes and access to care. *Pediatrics* 104: 195–202.

Newacheck, P., D. Hughes, and M. Cisternas. 1995 Children and health insurance: An overview with recent trends. *Health Affairs* 14: 244–254.

Newacheck, P. W., and M. A. McManus. 1990. Health care expenditure patterns for adolescents. *Journal of Adolescent Health Care* 11: 133–140.

Newacheck, P. W., B. Strickland, J. P. Shonkoff, J. M. Perrin, M. McPherson, M. McManus, C. Lauver, H. Fox, and P. Arango. 1998. An epidemiological profile of children with special health care needs. *Pediatrics* 102: 117–121.

Newacheck, P., and W. R. Taylor. 1992. Childhood chronic illness: Prevalence, severity, and impact. *American Journal of Public Health* 82: 364–371.

Ospinow, S. H. 1976. Vocational development problems of the handicapped. Pp. 49–61 in *Contemporary Vocational Rehabilitation.* Edited by H. Rusalen and O. Malikin. New York: New York University Press.

Park, M. J., T. M. MacDonald, E. M. Ozer, S. J. Burg, S. G. Millstein, C. D. Brindis, and C. E. Irwin, Jr. 2001. *Investing in clinical preventive health services for adolescents.* San Francisco:

University of California, San Francisco, Policy Information and Analysis Center for Middle Childhood and Adolescence and National Adolescent Health Information Center.

Patterson, D., and C. Lanier. 1999. Adolescent health transitions: Focus group study of teens and young adults with special health care needs. *Family Community Health* 22: 42–58.

Perrin, J. M. 2002. Health services research for children with disabilities. *Milbank Quarterly* 80: 303–324.

Pollitz, K., and R. Sorian. 2001. *How successful is individual health insurance for consumers in less-than-perfect health?* Washington: Kaiser Foundation.

Quinn, K., C. Schoen, and L. Buatti. 2000. *On their own: Young adults living without health insurance.* New York: Commonwealth Fund.

Rettig, P., and B. H. Athreya. 1991. Adolescents with chronic disease: Transition to adult health care. *Arthritis Care Research* 4: 174–180.

Rosen, D. 1995. Between two worlds: Bridging the cultures of child health and adult medicine. *Journal of Adolescent Health* 17: 10–16.

Rosenbaum, S., K. Shaw, and C. Sonosky. 2001. *Policy brief no. 3: Managed care purchasing under SCHIP: A nationwide analysis of free-standing SCHIP contracts.* Washington: Center for Health Services Research and Policy, George Washington University.

Salmi, J., T. Huuponen, H. Oksa, H. Oksala, T. Koivula, and P. Raita. 1986. Metabolic control in adolescent insulin-dependent diabetics referred from pediatric to adult clinic. *Annals of Clinical Research* 18: 84–87.

Sawyer, S. M. 1998. The process of transition to adult health care services. Pp. 255–268 in *Diabetes and the adolescent.* Edited by G. Werther and J. Court. Melbourne: Blackwell.

Scal, P., T. Evans, S. Blozis, N. Okinow, and R. Blum. 1999. Trends in transition from pediatric to adult health care services for young adults with chronic conditions. *Journal of Adolescent Health* 24: 259–264.

Schneider, A., S. Victoria, and R. Ellberger. 1999. *Medicaid eligibility for individuals with disabilities.* Washington: Kaiser Foundation.

Schulzinger, R. 2000. *Youth with disabilities in transition: Health insurance options and obstacles.* Healthy and Ready to Work Policy Paper, BMCH, HHS, June. Rockville, MD: Health Resources and Services Administration, U.S. Department of Health and Human Services.

Smith, V., K. Gilford, R. Ramesh, and V. Wachino. 2003. Medicaid spending growth: A 50 state update for fiscal year 2003. Menlo Park, CA: Kaiser Foundation.

Strax, T. E. 1991. Psychological issues faced by adolescents and young adults with disabilities. *Pediatric Annals* 20: 507–511.

Telfair, J., J. Myers, and S. Drezner. Transfer as a component of transition of adolescents with sickle cell disease to adult care: adolescent, adult, and parent perspectives. *Journal of Adolescent Health* 15: 558–565.

United States General Accounting Office. 1999. *Adults with severe disability: Federal and state approaches for personal care and other services.* Washington: United States General Accounting Office.

U.S. Congress, Office of Technology Assessment. 1991. *Adolescent health.* Vol. 1. *Summary and policy options.* Washington: Government Printing Office.

Viner, R. M. 1999. Transition from paediatric to adult care. Bridging the gaps or passing the buck? *Archives of Disease in Childhood* 81: 271–275.

White, P. H. 1999. Transition to adulthood. *Current Opinion in Rheumatology* 11: 408–411.

CHAPTER FOURTEEN

The Transition to Adulthood for Vulnerable Youth and Families: Common Themes and Future Directions

E. MICHAEL FOSTER, CONSTANCE FLANAGAN, D. WAYNE OSGOOD, AND GRETCHEN R. RUTH

This volume is intended to spur policy makers, opinion leaders, and scholars to devote greater attention to the issues facing vulnerable populations during the transition to adulthood. As chapter 1 indicates, young people have a great deal to accomplish during the years from the end of high school to age thirty. During this period the majority will finish their educations, leave the homes in which they were raised, establish themselves in the world of work, and begin raising their own families. Chapters 2 through 13 have both articulated the challenges that seven vulnerable populations face in undertaking these tasks and reviewed relevant issues of public policy.

This book is founded on assumptions that grew from prior work by the organizers of this volume, the Research Network on Transitions to Adulthood and Public Policy sponsored by the John D. and Catherine T. MacArthur Foundation. An earlier volume sponsored by the network (Settersten, Furstenberg, and Rumbaut 2005) established that (1) the transition to adulthood has become more difficult for most American youth in recent decades, and, as that has occurred, (2) American youth have become increasingly dependent on their families for assistance during the young adult years. We reasoned that, if an extended period of dependence has become more normative for most young adults, the situation must be considerably more problematic for youth who deal with challenges such as limited skills, physical, behavioral, or emotional problems, or neglectful or abusive families. We selected the seven vulnerable populations discussed in this volume because the state provides programs to address the needs of these groups in childhood and adolescence.

The policy chapters of this volume reveal that these programs are far less responsive to the needs of these populations after the age of eighteen. As we have seen, the loss of support programs raises important issues of public policy. Social policy is out of sync with contemporary social and economic realities that have increased the challenges of attaining adulthood and delayed the time at which younger generations can assume the responsibilities of adulthood. Furthermore, as Blum (chapter 12) and White and Gallay (chapter 13) point out, social policy does not reflect the medical advances that have changed the very populations of vulnerable groups who now make the transition to adulthood.

The chapters on the challenges clearly point to the disproportionate risks individuals in these vulnerable groups face in the major domains of the transition, such as education, employment, independent living, and family formation. Though the particular profile varies, each group struggles in many areas.

Furthermore, their experiences raise difficult and unresolved policy issues, primarily concerning the need for greater investment in effective services for these vulnerable populations during this critical period of their lives. These issues often involve eligibility, with services that had been available for adolescents being restricted or unavailable during early adulthood. Also, in many cases the services that are available are not well-suited to the needs of young adults. Indeed, in some instances, one fears that government involvement may even make their situation worse.

This concluding chapter draws together the threads spanning the chapters on the separate vulnerable populations. This volume considers multiple governmental systems and the youth and families involved in them. There are key differences among these populations and the systems that serve them, but shared themes emerge as one moves through the volume. We begin our conclusions by identifying recurrent themes, each raised by several authors, first in the challenges chapters and then in the policy chapters. Next we offer additional observations on broader themes as well as future directions. In addition to the general need for investment in these groups during the transition, these include the need for future research and possible means by which services might be improved. Finally, we argue that focusing on the deficits and problems of these groups is too narrow a framework and contend that a paradigm shift towards a social inclusion policy agenda would reveal the contributions these populations could make to society.

SHARED THEMES: CHALLENGES

The populations and policies considered in this volume differ in important ways, but several themes recur. For the chapters concerning the challenges posed by the transition to adulthood, these common threads include (1) the consistent overrepresentation of certain groups; (2) the diversity among those in each population; (3) the overlap among the various populations; (4) the poor outcomes across a variety of domains; and (5) the factors that promote a successful transition.

The first of the shared themes involves the overrepresentation of certain groups—namely boys, the poor, and youth of color.[1] Throughout this volume, the authors report that during childhood these groups are at risk for entering and remaining in the public systems that define our vulnerable populations. In the case of boys, this involvement may reflect specific biological factors or gender differences in behavior that bring youth into contact with these systems. For example, some specific disabilities, such as autism, are more common among boys, which leads to an overrepresentation of boys in special education (see chapter 8). That boys engage in more delinquency is well-established (Moffitt et al. 2001), and this behavior brings them into contact with juvenile justice more often than girls (Whitehead and Lab 1996). System-level factors matter, too. Whereas schools may not tolerate the disruptive behavior more common in boys, they may ignore depressive symptoms because these do not interrupt classroom activities. These factors interact as well. The reaction of teachers and counselors to boys with emotional and behavioral problems may reflect gender differences in which types of problems are most common (e.g., internalizing problems like depression for girls versus externalizing problems like delinquency for boys).

Youth of color also are overrepresented among the groups examined. As Blum notes (chapter 12), for example, students with disabilities are twice as likely to be African-American. Uggen and Wakefield (chapter 5) report similar findings for involvement in the criminal justice system: African-American men about six times more likely than white men to enter prison at some point during their lifetimes. In part, this racial imbalance reflects policies such as harsh sentences for the sale of crack cocaine. In part this imbalance also reflects the fact that the needs of different racial groups are often addressed through different institutions or systems of care. As Gralinski-Bakker et al. (chapter 10) point out, ethnic minority adolescents with mental health problems are more likely than their nonminority peers to end up in the juvenile justice system.

To some extent, the racial imbalance in vulnerability also reflects the overrepresentation of the poor among these vulnerable populations. In some instances, poverty is an eligibility criterion for the systems considered (e.g., federal funding for foster care). In other cases, poverty is a risk factor for the behaviors that bring youth into contact with the system. For example, poverty

---

1. Note that this discussion focuses on "youth" rather than young adults, reflecting the fact that it is often in childhood that the systems identify these vulnerable populations.

is associated with parental substance abuse, which may lead to neglect and a child's placement in the foster care system. In other cases, family income and resources may influence whether and how individuals move through these systems. For example, whether a youth picked up by the police is returned to his or her parents or formally processed may depend on family resources or standing in the community more generally.

That is not to say that all youth in these systems are poor. The relationship between family income or resources and system involvement can be quite complex. In the case of special education, families with more resources may be better able to have their child's condition diagnosed and to obtain needed services. Nonetheless, disabled youth are 50 percent more likely to live in poverty than are other youth (see chapter 8).

Community-level poverty matters, too, and in complex ways. Low-income neighborhoods may lack the organization and informal social control necessary to maintain low crime rates (Sampson, Raudenbush, and Earls 1997) and protect youth from becoming involved with the justice systems. Resource-rich neighborhoods may offer opportunities that help children learn, and these opportunities may influence how youth move through special education (e.g., whether they are placed out of the classroom). At the same time, the standard for learning may be higher in high-income communities, making it more likely that a struggling student lands in special education. Youth in low-income communities also are less likely to benefit from the nonformal learning opportunities, civic incorporation, and informal social control that community-based organizations offer because of their community's lower financial resources and higher child-to-adult ratios (Hart and Atkins 2002).

The relationship between family income and special education does highlight a second theme spanning the chapters—that of diversity within the groups studied. While youth in these groups differ from the population as a whole, they are far from homogeneous. Those in special education include youth with mental retardation as well as youth with emotional and behavioral problems. Violent offenders and those with extensive criminal justice contact experience greater childhood disadvantage and display less success in education and employment than nonviolent and first-time offenders (see chapter 5). Among youth with physical disabilities, those who are blind have quite different needs than do those with an orthopedic impairment. Of youth with emotional and behavioral problems, those suffering from depression and those with conduct problems differ in many ways (see chapter 11). These youth have different needs and require different resources, both before and after the transition. For example, aggressive boys are much more likely to encounter the juvenile justice system than are depressed young women.

As many of the chapter authors point out, the research base on these groups during the transition to adulthood is quite limited. Thus the authors often extrapolated from the larger body of research on children and adolescents. It is encouraging to note that a similar dearth once existed for adolescence, but our knowledge has grown as researchers have attended to the challenges facing adolescence. Similarly, the unique challenges of middle childhood are increasingly the focus of research.

The diversity within each vulnerable population highlights a third theme spanning the chapters—that of overlap among the populations studied. Indeed, the organization of this volume, which addresses the different populations separately, is somewhat misleading. We have followed the organization of the public systems that define the populations, but as discussed below, treating the groups separately is a failing of those systems.

We are sorely lacking epidemiological data on how many youth are involved in more than one system, thus falling into multiple vulnerable populations. Yet available data do provide information on the involvement of youth in some pairs of single systems. For example, Levine and Wagner (chapter 8) report that 34 percent of emotionally disturbed youth in special education were arrested at least once during their adolescence. To some extent, this overlap reflects the fact that the youth in different systems often share common problems, such as substance abuse, learning problems, family deficits, and community-level risk factors. For example, Chung, Little, and Steinberg (chapter 3) cite data suggesting that incarcerated adolescents suffer from significant academic deficits and perform well below others their age regardless of their intellectual abilities (Foley 2001). (See also chapter 6 for a discussion of the mental health needs of incarcerated young adults.)

As Uggen and Wakefield (chapter 5) note for the juvenile justice system, the most vulnerable youth often cycle in and out of these systems. Likewise, youth exit and return to the mental health system; Gralinski-Bakker et al. (chapter 10) aptly refer to them as "system kids."

But having common problems only partially explains the overlap in populations. To some extent the systems are linked administratively. In some cases, each system refers youth to the other systems. In the case of special education, for example, problems at school may lead the child to visit a mental health specialist as part of the assessment process. Problems at school also may bring the youth to the attention of the juvenile justice authorities or child welfare. In some instances, this reflects one system's attempt to find resources for the youth; in others (such as child welfare), the referral is legally required.

In some instances, the systems themselves may contribute to the problems that bring youth into contact with other systems. For example, youth in the juvenile justice system suffer from high rates of both internalizing and externalizing mental health problems (see chapter 3). The externalizing or acting-out problems may result in spending time in a youth detention facility, however, which could foster or exacerbate internalizing problems, such as anxiety and depression. Similarly, movement into and out of residential treatment facilities or foster care homes could not help but disrupt the process of learning, raising further barriers to success in school. Removal from the home and multiple placements, as noted by Courtney and Heuring (chapter 2), is also associated with increased criminal activity.

A fourth theme spanning the chapters involves the poor outcomes many of these youth experience across a variety of domains that mark the transition to adulthood. If achievements in education, employment, and residential stability mark a successful transition, youth from these vulnerable populations fall considerably short. Five years after leaving school, 30 percent of the youth in special education had been arrested (see chapter 8). The disabled are less likely to be employed, as are several of the other groups. These groups are plagued by residential instability, especially homeless youth and those leaving foster care. Early childbearing is common among several of the vulnerable populations as well. On the whole, most members of the groups examined in this volume fared poorly in at least one if not several of the domains considered.

Furthermore, youth facing multiple risks fare especially poorly. For instance, Chung, Little, and Steinberg (chapter 3) report that youth in the juvenile justice system who have educational disabilities face many difficulties, both in terms of their school achievement and in subsequent involvement with the courts.

The fifth shared theme involves the factors that foster a successful transition. Reflecting the diversity highlighted above, many youth in all of the populations achieve a basic level of self-sufficiency, and an even smaller group goes on to experience substantial success. Although overall the groups fare poorly across domains that mark the transition to adulthood, failure is not inevitable, and certain factors promote success. First among these is success in school. Courtney and Heuring (chapter 2) report that the majority of youth finish high school or earn a GED within twelve to nineteen months of leaving foster care. Obviously, completing high school is an indicator of educational progress and the failure to do so precludes higher levels of education. However, early school failure often precedes failure across a range of domains, including unemployment, involvement in crime and substance use, and unsatisfactory personal relationships. Policy interventions that interrupt this downward trajectory are key. Sometimes they turn, as Hagan and McCarthy (chapter 7) point out, on whether a community adds insult to injury by treating a vulnerable group like homeless youth as a criminal element.

A second protective factor is support from family and friends. In examining those factors that distinguish the most successful youth leaving residential treatment facilities, Gralinski-Bakker et al. (chapter 10) highlight the importance of healthy interpersonal relationships. Their work also identifies personality traits—persistence and confidence—as a third set of protective factors. Likewise, Chung, Little, and Steinberg (chapter 3) note that healthy interpersonal relationships are key if juvenile offenders are going to desist from crime in the future.

SHARED THEMES: POLICIES

Like the populations themselves, the goals and functioning of the programs and policies considered vary a great deal. However, key themes remain that span the chapters, all of which involve larger and more effective investments in these populations. These themes include (1) the exclusion of youth who might benefit from support during the transition; (2) the low levels of funding for transition services; (3) substantial barriers to youth-focused service delivery; and (4) lack of training of professionals who work with these groups in developmental issues associated with the transition to adulthood.

Though eligibility criteria differ, a key feature of all programs and policies considered is that they exclude many youth who might benefit from transition support. For example, youth who are involved in foster care but leave before aging out are not eligible for transition services (see chapter 2). Similarly, youth who are involved in the juvenile justice system but who are not placed in residential settings will not receive aftercare and the support it might offer during the transition to adulthood (see chapter 4). These systems are using past involvement as a proxy for severity and need, but as discussed throughout the volume, system involvement reflects a range of factors. As a result, key subgroups may not receive the services they need.

This theme points toward a second issue. While the resources dedicated to these populations are sometimes large in aggregate terms, their magnitude largely reflects the sizes of the populations involved rather than the amount of assistance offered. On a per-person basis, the amount of money can be rather small. Courtney and Heuring (chapter 2) best illustrate these low levels of funding. They find that new funds available to support the housing needs of youth leaving foster care are less than $700 per youth *per year*. In light of the challenges they face, funding levels are far exceeded by the needs of these youth.

A third theme involves barriers to effective service delivery. The lack of system integration is a problem that emerges repeatedly. Many of the systems involved function nearly independently, rarely communicating with the others.

Their main form of contact involves the children and youth who move between these systems. In many communities, there is no avenue for bringing youth in the criminal justice system to the attention of mental health providers should that become necessary (see chapter 11).

A second dimension of service fragmentation involves the barriers between the child- and adult-serving systems. As youth enter adulthood, they encounter still other systems, such as vocational rehabilitation. These systems have different eligibility requirements and often function quite separately from the systems with which youth have been involved.

These system-level barriers are complemented by barriers in the attitudes and training of service providers. Even if a youth lived in a community where the relevant agencies and departments worked well together, he or she still might face difficulties finding providers who are sensitive to the unique needs of youth transitioning to adulthood. Blum (chapter 12), for example, highlights how ill-prepared (or even unwilling) medical providers are to discuss issues of sexuality with disabled adolescents. White and Gallay (chapter 13) raise similar developmental issues. Noting the increased autonomy and privacy appropriate to services for young adults, the authors report that professionals often do not know how to explore new ways that families might provide support.

BROADER THEMES

Several broader themes emerge from these chapters as a group. These involve (1) the state of research on vulnerable populations during the transition to adulthood; (2) possible means for improving the transition; and (3) the value of a social inclusion perspective on these issues.

The Need for Better Research

Though there are notable exceptions (e.g., the National Longitudinal Transition Studies in special education), research on these populations at any age is very limited, and that is especially true for the transition to adulthood (Foster and Gifford 2005). Available research neither provides comprehensive, representative descriptions of the youths making these transitions nor identifies effective means for improving policies to most effectively invest in their future success. Lacking a strong empirical base, many of the policy recommendations made in the chapters reflect common sense or a sense of fairness and justice. Lyons and Melton (chapter 11), for example, refer to the Convention on the Rights of the Child as supporting many of their recommendations. The literature they are able to cite, however, is largely limited to model programs, such as multisystemic therapy, rather than programs that have been tested rigorously in widespread implementation. Furthermore, reforms that seem self-evident may in fact be ineffectual. As discussed below, one means for improving services involves creating integrated systems of care, and such integration seems to be a necessary condition for improving outcomes. However, in one system with such integrated services (children's mental health services), it is not clear that—by itself—system integration can improve child outcomes (Salzer and Bickman 1997). Common sense and ethical considerations should inform policy decisions, but they must be accompanied by sound research.

What would an appropriate research agenda look like? First and foremost, that research needs to be epidemiological in conceptualization and execution. It would produce a representative picture of the needs and challenges facing these youth (Foster and Gifford 2005). Research of this type requires scientific rather than convenience samples. In light of the diversity among these populations, unscientific samples can produce a misleading picture, as some subgroups are overrepresented while others are not included at all. Furthermore, data need to be collected from a range of communities. Many of the relevant systems are quite localized, and service delivery and community resources may vary considerably.

That is not to say that the sampling on which these studies are based has to be a simple random sample. Some subgroups or types of communities might be oversampled in order to understand the particular challenges they face. As long as researchers understand the process by which these samples are drawn, the resulting data could be used both to represent the populations as a whole as well as to explore variability both within and across subgroups.

A great deal might also be learned by the natural policy experiments to which many of the authors alluded. Hagan and McCarthy (chapter 7), for example, contrast Toronto's social welfare approach to homeless youth with Vancouver's law enforcement model. Whereas in Vancouver, youth under the age of nineteen can neither qualify for social welfare nor seek out shelter without parental permission, in Toronto the safety and security of homeless youth is ensured by provincial policy that defines sixteen as the legal age of majority. Courtney and Heuring's description (chapter 2) of the flexibility states enjoy in interpreting the independent living provisions of the Foster Care Independence Act is another example of a policy experiment. Since states can use these funds to extend supports for housing, Medicaid, or education and training to eighteen- to twenty-one-year-olds who leave foster care (and since some funding in the legislation is designated for program evaluation), comparing how youth with different sets of supports fare in the transition to independence could be illuminating.

A more fundamental issue is that the populations of interest are not only the youth who are involved in these public systems but also *those who are at risk of becoming involved.* To date, most studies have focused on the youth who are in these systems as they enter early adulthood. It is very difficult, however, to understand whether and how these systems address the needs of the youth they serve without also understanding how and why youth enter them. This link is particularly true with comparisons across communities; without such information, distinguishing differences in how communities serve youth from differences in which youth they serve is difficult.

A sample of youth at risk of becoming involved in these systems would provide a more accurate picture of how youth move between systems. A sample of youth who are in a system at a point in time will overrepresent the experiences of youth who have been in that system for a long time. On the other hand, a community-based sample will provide a more accurate understanding of the dynamics of system participation; it will, for example, provide data on the number of youth who will become involved in the system for short periods of time. Furthermore, such studies might even include at-risk youth who do not become involved in these systems. The experiences of these youth can provide added insight into resilience as well as serving as a comparison group that constitutes a standard against which the achievement and failures of the vulnerable group might be assessed.

An essential component of research on these populations also needs to be administrative data (Foster and Gifford 2005), by which we mean the records kept by the service systems themselves. While such data pose special challenges, they are needed for several reasons. First, eligibility for the programs and services may depend on technical distinctions that are difficult for individuals or parents to make. For example, special education services may resemble other school services (such as those funded by Title I or section 501 of the Rehabilitation Act of 1973), yet the distinction is critical in terms of eligibility for further services during the transition to adulthood (see chapter 9). Furthermore, for some relevant outcomes (such as cash assistance or Medicaid), program eligibility may change over time in ways that are difficult for respondents to report or even remember. It is especially dangerous to rely too heavily on respondents' reports when substance abuse or mental illness is involved. Administrative data also provide information that even the best-informed respondent would not know, such as the amounts of payments for services by sources like Medicaid or block grants.

A key goal of this research would be to improve services; a long list of questions might be considered. Such research might involve demonstration programs in which key program characteristics are altered. For example, the period of eligibility for transition services might be lengthened. This extension could involve starting those services earlier and/or allowing youth to participate at later ages. Eligibility might be oriented less to the youth's age and more to the youth's developmental needs.

Whether descriptive or evaluative, research on these populations also needs to involve the providers and agencies serving the vulnerable population. In the case of the disabled, for example, it seems essential to understand the perspective of the youth's provider and to account for his or her training. This research should involve not just providers from model programs but also the real world of providers in standing, full-scale programs working with the heterogeneous populations in actual treatment settings. The involvement of such professionals seems essential for linking research to means of improving the training of professionals.

Such a research agenda would be ambitious and would pose a variety of methodological challenges. Clearly, longitudinal studies of these vulnerable populations (such as the homeless) would involve tracking them over time. For some of the questions of interest, randomization may be difficult or undesirable, necessitating careful and sophisticated analyses that attempt to compare noncomparable groups. Furthermore, the involvement of study participants in institutional settings creates a variety of other challenges (e.g., human subjects issues related to the participation of prisoners). Even so, this research is essential if we are to improve the success of vulnerable youth in making the transition to adulthood.

Possible Means for Improving the Transition

How can our society most effectively invest to improve the chances of successful transition to adulthood for these vulnerable populations? There are several potential avenues for improving their prospects. The first is through programs and policy changes to benefit *all* youth during this period, as discussed by Settersten (2005). Reducing the challenges of the transition for all youth will, of course, reduce them for vulnerable youth as well. Indeed, these vulnerable populations likely would be among the groups that would benefit most from changes affecting all young adults, such as raising the minimum wage, improved curriculum and support services at community colleges, and universal health care.

A second general strategy for improving the transition to adulthood for the vulnerable populations is increasing access to programs and services during the transition. A dominant theme of the policy discussions in this volume is that access to programs and services decreases or ends during the transition to adulthood. Given the abundant evidence of continuing difficulties among these populations and the heavy dependence of most American young adults on their families, the need for public investment in these groups clearly does not end at age eighteen.

A simple response to this situation would be to remove all age restrictions and make the programs and services of childhood and adolescence available across the lifespan. Of course, this would not be practical or even desirable. Not only would the cost be prohibitive, but the life circumstances and developmental needs of early adulthood require specific approaches. But how much investment is our society willing to make in vulnerable populations during the transition to adulthood and what would be the most effective use of such an investment? We hope that the information provided in the present volume will spark (1) a broad discussion among policy makers and concerned citizens about the need for new investments in these vulnerable populations during the transition and (2) work by researchers and service professionals to determine what programs and policies will be most effective for these groups over this age span.

The next strategy is to improve services during the transition. During both the adolescence and the transition to adulthood, many of the vulnerable populations discussed in this volume would benefit from an integration of systems and from moving away from multiple systems to a singular system focused on the needs of young people. Such integration would mean adopting some of the philosophy and practices of the more child-oriented system (e.g., an emphasis on natural family and nonfamilial adults' support, on rehabilitation and restoration to the community rather than on retribution, punishment, and exclusion from the community) as well as the more mature treatment afforded in the adult systems (e.g., an emphasis on respect for the individual's autonomy, responsibility, and accountability). The integration of child and adult systems would occur on several levels. For example, at an administrative level, it would involve better integrating the eligibility requirements and eliminating any disjunctures. This integration also would affect the delivery of services and would pose more challenges. First among these is funding. Clearly, the public systems in many communities face recurrent financial problems and are overwhelmed. However, the barriers are not strictly financial. Some changes in the cultures of the systems involved will be needed as well.

As research in children's mental health services suggests, these vulnerable populations will not benefit from system-level change if the type or quality of services received is not improved. For the latter to occur, providers of all types need better training in dealing with transitioning youth. As Blum (chapter 12) indicates, physicians receive little or no training in dealing with the issues of sexuality and other developmental matters that young people face. Better training should include cultural competence as well. Such training seems essential given the overrepresentation of persons of color in these systems.

The fourth avenue for improving the transition to adulthood for vulnerable populations would be improving the systems in which they are involved during childhood and adolescence. The preceding discussions of the challenges facing these youth and the failures of the systems that serve them highlight possible means for improving those systems. First and foremost, the systems involved should minimize any damage done to the well-being of the children and youth they serve. As the chapters on the juvenile justice and criminal justice systems point out, these systems may not only fail to address some problems but may actually worsen them. Similarly, for youth in the foster care system, moving from one foster home to another can erode already tenuous emotional attachments to family as well as disrupt schooling.

Although improving these systems may seem daunting, the chapters continually promote three principles that would facilitate the transition to adulthood. The first is the degree to which systems enable young people to practice the normative tasks associated with transitioning to adult independence and responsibility. As Chung, Little, and Steinberg (chapter 3) argue, youth whose psychological development is arrested by years spent in detention are ill-prepared to take on the psychosocial tasks of early adulthood. Yet the lives of many of the youth in these vulnerable groups are not so strictly constrained, and specific skills training can be built into the systems that deal with those youth. For example, as Blum (chapter 12), Gralinski-Bakker et al. (chapter 10), and Courtney and Heuring (chapter 2) contend, life skills and management skills are essential for handling adult independence and responsibilities. Similarly, Uggen and Wakefield (chapter 5) note that job training and placement can help juvenile offenders to chart a new path away from crime.

The second principle that systems could incorporate is transition planning. This principle figures prominently in White and Gallay's discussion (chapter 13) of youth with special health care needs and disabilities. But aging out of systems is a fact for all of these vulnerable groups. Planning for that day and considering what it takes to make a successful transition to adulthood could shape program priorities and sequencing. Planning for individual needs is more integral to some systems (e.g., individualized educational plans are mandated in special education) and would seem to be a superior strategy to crisis management in any system. Unfortunately, changes in philosophy and shifts in policy can erode the transition planning that is embedded in a system. As Travis and Visher (chapter 6) point out, "tough on crime" policy shifts, and the fixed sentences and mandatory release practices that go with them, have replaced the transition planning that was part of the parole system.

A third means for improving these systems involves shifting to a child and family focus. Such a focus would recognize the diversity of the children and youth served and would increase the involvement by and address the needs of the families of these youth. It seems clear that—like all youth—these vulnerable populations are tied to their families, even in instances when those families are dysfunctional. Courtney and Heuring (chapter 2) cite data indicating that many youth leaving the foster care system continue to have contact with their families of origin. Relatedly, improved services should be community based. Many of the groups in this volume spend significant amounts of time in institutions or away from their parents. Since they will eventually return, it seems clear that the services involved should leave the youth in their homes, except in dire circumstances (e.g., when the youth's safety is in question). As many authors in this volume emphasize, services at the local level that build on natural support systems and keep young people connected in positive ways to their communities are the most logical choices.

Social Inclusion

The improvements in relevant policies and programs discussed above largely involve programmatic and administrative changes that likely would improve the lives of youth transitioning to adulthood. While important, these matters are largely technical. At a more fundamental level, however, what is needed is a transformation of the underlying philosophy on which these programs rest. Such a change is necessary if these youth are to fully take their place as members of our society. Such a change might be organized around the notion of *social inclusion*. This theme is posed in the introductory chapter and emphasized throughout the volume. In concluding, we return to this theme and describe it more completely.

The notion of social inclusion begins with the understanding that better policies would benefit not only the youth involved but society as a whole. At a minimum, attending to youths' needs during the transition to adulthood should reduce later problems, such as crime. Such a reduction reduces related governmental expenditures (e.g., on incarceration) as well as broader costs (e.g., costs to victims). With more thoughtful policy we have the potential of gaining not only the economic contributions of these youth as productive workers, but also their contributions to families, friends, and communities as supportive and engaged citizens.

The loss of these contributions can be indirect or direct. Former prisoners, for example, may lose their voting rights (see chapters 5 and 6). This form of social exclusion is one of several experienced by these groups. Others include stigma, separation from community social settings, and the loss of the opportunities that those contexts afford to practice normative developmental tasks. Exclusionary policies make what are already challenging tasks of adulthood impossible. As Uggen and Wakefield (chapter 5) note, in many jurisdictions former criminals are no longer eligible for educational or public housing benefits. These benefits often involve the very programs that might allow them to turn from crime and settle into a community.

The policy chapters—and the reforms and changes they offer—illustrate these principles. For instance, Altschuler (chapter 4) emphasizes that the juvenile justice system's movement from rehabilitation to retribution has fostered social exclusion. As a result, youth are denied the services that would most likely help them move from a life of crime toward productive citizenship.

The principles of social inclusion reflect and reveal broader principles about the ties that bind members of a community. They send messages about who counts and whose voice should be heard. The programs and policies discussed here often send the message, often not explicit, that the groups involved do not count. At best, the goal is to *minimize* the burden these groups create for other members of society. This "problem management" perspective pays little mind to whether or not these groups *maximize* their contribution to society.

This narrow vision is unfortunate because the young adult years are a formative time for civic attachment and social incorporation that can have a long-term payoff (or a long-term cost). The 2004 Kids Count Report presented some sobering statistics about the growing numbers of eighteen- to twenty-four-year-olds who are disconnected from society and its institutions. In 2002 one in six in this age group held no degree beyond high school, had no job, and were not enrolled in school. The 3.8 million young people who were in this group represented an increase of 19 percent over the three prior years.

Yet the Kids Count report also points to improvements in several indicators of neonatal and early childhood well-being that suggest that—given political will—policies can be effective in redressing vulnerabilities. We are optimistic that targeted policies can reduce the number of youth adrift and disconnected.

Technical matters, such as age requirements for program participation, and philosophical ones, such as social inclusion, are related in that the latter provides the political motivation to implement and fund the former. Consider the Civilian Conservation Corps (CCC) of the 1930s. Not only was the program designed to benefit unemployed youth by employing them and providing educational benefits, it also was a chance for these youth to contribute both to their families ($25 out of their $30 monthly paycheck was sent home to their family) and to the nation (largely through environmental projects). Rather than a "generation lost," a creative policy of social inclusion raised the literacy and education levels of a generation and incorporated them into the body politic. Millions of CCC enrollees went on to contribute to their country and communities by holding down steady jobs, raising families, enlisting in military service, and becoming what ultimately has been called "America's long civic generation" (Bass forthcoming).

We hope that America will do as well for itself and for its vulnerable youth by taking social inclusion as a fundamental principle of systematic new policies addressing the transition to adulthood. In this way, an investment in the transition to adulthood for these vulnerable youth can be, and must be, an investment in the future of the entire nation.

REFERENCES

Bass, M. forthcoming. The Civilian Conservation Corps. In *Youth Activism: An International Encyclopedia*. Edited by L. Sherrod, C. A. Flanagan, and R. Kassimir. Westport, CT: Greenwood Publishing Company.

Foley, R. 2001. Academic characteristics of incarcerated youth and correctional education programs: A literature review. *Journal of Emotional and Behavioral Disorders* 9: 248–259.

Foster, E. M., and E. J. Gifford. 2005. Developmental and administrative transitions for special populations: Policies, outcomes, and research challenges. Pp. 501–533 in *On the frontier of adulthood: Theory, research, and public policy*. Edited by R. A. Settersten, Jr., F. F. Furstenberg, Jr., and R. G. Rumbaut. Chicago: University of Chicago Press.

Hart, D., and R. Atkins. 2002. Civic development in urban youth. *Applied Developmental Science* 6: 227–236.

Moffitt, T. E., A. Caspi, M. Rutter, and P. A. Silva. 2001. S*ex differences in antisocial behaviour: Conduct disorder, delinquency, and violence in the Dunedin longitudinal study.* Cambridge: Cambridge University Press.

Salzer, M. S., and L. Bickman. 1997. Delivering effective children's services in the community: Reconsidering the benefits of system interventions. *Applied and Preventive Psychology* 6: 1–13.

Sampson, R. J., S. W. Raudenbush, and F. Earls. 1997. Neighborhoods and violent crime: A multilevel study of collective efficacy. *Science* 277: 918–924.

Settersten, R. A., Jr. 2005. Social policy and the transition to adulthood. Pp. 534–560 in *On the frontier of adulthood: Theory, research, and public policy.* Edited by R. A. Settersten, Jr., F. F. Furstenberg, Jr., and R. G. Rumbaut. Chicago: University of Chicago Press.

Settersten, R. A., Jr., F. F. Furstenberg, Jr., and R. G. Rumbaut, eds. 2005. *On the frontier of adulthood: Theory, research, and public policy.* Chicago: University of Chicago Press.

Whitehead, J. T., and S. P. Lab. 1996. *Juvenile justice: An introduction.* 2nd ed. Cincinnati: Anderson Publishing.

Contributors

JOSEPH P. ALLEN
Department of Psychology
University of Virginia

DAVID M. ALTSCHULER
Institute for Policy Studies
Johns Hopkins University

REBECCA L. BILLINGS
Judge Baker Children's Center

ROBERT WM. BLUM
Department of Population and Family Health
    Sciences
Johns Hopkins Bloomberg School of Public
    Health

HE LEN CHUNG
Law and Psychiatry Program
University of Pittsburgh School of Medicine

MARK E. COURTNEY
Chapin Hall Center for Children and School
    of Social Service Administration
University of Chicago

CONSTANCE FLANAGAN
Department of Agricultural and Extension
    Education
Pennsylvania State University

E. MICHAEL FOSTER
School of Public Health
University of North Carolina at
    Chapel Hill

LESLIE GALLAY
Social Science Research Institute
Pennsylvania State University

J. HEIDI GRALINSKI-BAKKER
Harvard Medical School
and
Judge Baker Children's Center

JOHN HAGAN
Department of Sociology
Northwestern University
and
American Bar Foundation

STUART T. HAUSER
Harvard Medical School
and
Judge Baker Children's Center

DARCY HUGHES HEURING
Graduate Program in History
Northwestern University

PHYLLIS LEVINE
Center for Education and Human Services
SRI International

MICHELLE LITTLE
Department of Psychology
Temple University

PHILLIP M. LYONS, JR.
Criminal Justice Center
Sam Houston State University

BILL MCCARTHY
Department of Sociology
University of California, Davis

GARY B. MELTON
Institute on Family and Neighborhood Life
Clemson University

D. WAYNE OSGOOD
Crime, Law and Justice Program
Department of Sociology
Pennsylvania State University

GRETCHEN R. RUTH
Chapin Hall Center for Children
University of Chicago

LAURENCE STEINBERG
Department of Psychology
Temple University

JEREMY TRAVIS
John Jay College of Criminal Justice
City University of New York

CHRISTOPHER UGGEN
Department of Sociology
University of Minnesota

CHRISTY A. VISHER
Justice Policy Center
The Urban Institute

MARY WAGNER
Center for Education and Human Services
SRI International

SARA WAKEFIELD
Department of Sociology
University of Minnesota

MICHAEL S. WALD
Stanford Law School
Stanford University

PATIENCE HAYDOCK WHITE
George Washington University School of
    Medicine and Health Sciences

Index